LONG ISLAND
ISLAND
ALIVE!

Francine Silverman

HUNTER

Hunter Publishing, Inc.
130 Campus Drive
Edison, NJ 08818-7816
☎ 732-225-1900 / 800-255-0343 / Fax 732-417-1744
Web site: www.hunterpublishing.com
E-mail: comments@hunterpublishing.com

IN CANADA
Ulysses Travel Publications
4176 Saint-Denis, Montréal, Québec
Canada H2W 2M5
☎ 514-843-9882 ext. 2232 / fax 514-843-9448

IN THE UK
Windsor Books International
The Boundary, Wheatley Road
Garsington, Oxford OX44 9EJ England
☎ 01865-361122 / Fax 01865-361133

ISBN 1-58843-321-8
© 2003 Hunter Publishing, Inc.

This guide focuses on recreational activities. As all such activities contain elements of risk, the publisher, author, affiliated individuals and companies disclaim any responsibility for any
injury, harm, or illness that may occur to anyone through, or by
use of, the information in this book. Every effort was made to insure the accuracy of information in this book, but the publisher
and author do not assume, and hereby disclaim, any liability for
loss or damage caused by errors, omissions, misleading information or potential travel problems caused by this guide, even if
such errors or omissions result from negligence, accident or any
other cause.

Cover: *Sag Harbor, Long Island* © Superstock
Maps by Toni Wheeler, © 2003 Hunter Publishing, Inc.
Index by Nancy Wolff

4 3 2 1

About the Author

Francine Silverman is a veteran feature writer for newspapers and magazines. She honed her skills as a reporter with Gannett Westchester Newspapers in Yonkers, New York, and as a freelancer. Her travel articles have appeared in *The Inquirer* (Philadelphia), *The Record* (NJ), *New York Post*, *River*, *Camperways*, *Travel Smart* newsletter, *Travel Agent Magazine*, *MotorHome*, and inflights *Kiwi*, *Mabuhay* and *Passport Sabena*. These days her passion is travel writing, and *Catskills Alive!* marked the capstone of her career. That guidebook is going into its second edition and, she is confident, so will *Long Island Alive!*

Bookmark the author's Web site at www.nystatetravel.com. It will save you time – the site has links to many of the sites featured in both guidebooks.

About the Alive Guides

Reliable, detailed and personally researched by knowledgeable authors, the *Alive!* series was founded by Harriet and Arnold Greenberg.

This accomplished travel-writing team established the renowned bookstore, **The Complete Traveller**, at 199 Madison Avenue in New York City.

Dedication

To Ron and Amy and our loving Long Island cousins, Betsy and Michael Gluckman.

To Tony Matti for helping us relive fond memories of Fire Island.

This book is also dedicated to the disproportionate number of Long Islanders who lost loved ones on September 11, 2001.

Acknowledgments

Writing a guidebook requires the cooperation of hundreds of people. I've met so many wonderful folks on Long Island – residents, merchants, proprietors, government employees – that it's impossible to name them all. I'm especially grateful to those who opened their homes and hearts to me.

I'd like to express my deep appreciation to my publisher, Michael Hunter, and editor, Lissa Dailey, for their continued support and guidance.

We Love to Get Mail

This book has been carefully researched to bring you current, accurate information. But no place is unchanging. We welcome your comments for future editions. Please write us at *Alive Guides*, c/o Hunter Publishing, 130 Campus Drive, Edison, NJ 08818, or e-mail your comments to comments@hunterpublishing.com. Due to the volume of mail we receive, we regret that we cannot personally reply to each letter or message, but your comments are greatly appreciated and will be read.

Contents

Suffolk County's North Shore

Suffolk County's South Shore

Fire Island

Suffolk County's North Fork

Maps

Areas Covered in this Book

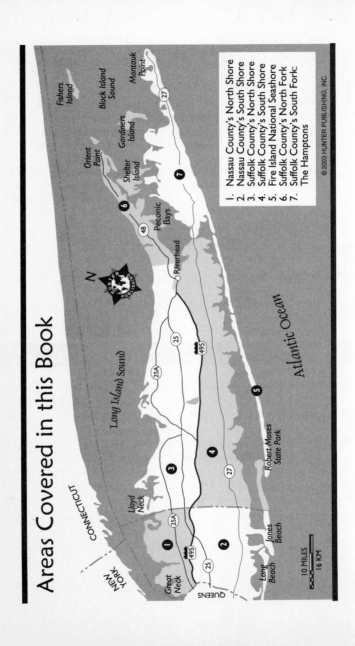

1. Nassau County's North Shore
2. Nassau County's South Shore
3. Suffolk County's North Shore
4. Suffolk County's South Shore
5. Fire Island National Seashore
6. Suffolk County's North Fork
7. Suffolk County's South Fork: The Hamptons

© 2003 HUNTER PUBLISHING, INC.

Introduction

For the purposes of this book, I have used the **Long Island Expressway** (**I-495** or the **LIE**) as the dividing line between the North and South Shores; chapters are arranged geographically from west to east. Fire Island has its own chapter, as do the North and South Forks of the eastern end of Long Island, though they are all part of Suffolk County.

When borders get blurred, the placement of listings can be subjective. The North Shore's famed Gold Coast, for example, runs through Nassau County to Centerport in Suffolk County. In this case, I put the Gold Coast in Nassau County, where most of the sights are located.

Riverhead straddles both the North Shore of Suffolk County and the North Fork. However, since more attractions and wineries are in its eastern section, I placed Riverhead in the *Suffolk County's North Fork* chapter.

History

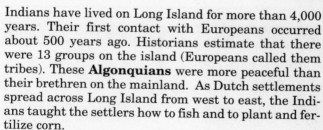

Indians have lived on Long Island for more than 4,000 years. Their first contact with Europeans occurred about 500 years ago. Historians estimate that there were 13 groups on the island (Europeans called them tribes). These **Algonquians** were more peaceful than their brethren on the mainland. As Dutch settlements spread across Long Island from west to east, the Indians taught the settlers how to fish and to plant and fertilize corn.

This peaceful coexistence was short-lived, however. In 1644, dissenters from the Puritan regimes in New England crossed the Long Island Sound and began to settle the eastern end of the Island. The growth of Dutch settlements on the western end led to conflicts between the Dutch and English. In 1650, in an attempt to resolve the tensions, the two groups agreed on a border between their territories that exists today as the line between Nassau and Suffolk counties. In 1664, the British fleet conquered the Dutch, and New Amsterdam became the Colony of New York. All of Long Island was then annexed to the new colony. Brooklyn and Queens remained part of Long Island until 1898, when they became boroughs of New York City.

FOR HISTORY BUFFS

Living history weekends are held regularly at historic sites throughout Long Island. For information, call ☎ 1-877-FUN-ON-LI, ext. 405, or visit these Web sites: www.liheritage-trail.com and www.funonli.com.

Friends for Long Island's Heritage supports a host of museums and historical sites in Nassau and Suffolk counties and maintains offices in both. Membership includes free admission to all museum sites and invitations to special exhibitions. For information, call ☎ 516-571-7600 or ☎ 631-854-4971, or check their Web site, www.fflih.org. The museum shop is online at www.liheritageshop.com.

Derivation of Indian Names

The Algonquian presence on Long Island nearly disappeared by the 1700s. Today, only the Poosepatuck and Shinnecock Indian Reservations remain in Suffolk County. In contrast, the Matinecocks and Montauketts had no land base and thus their descendants are scattered across Long Island.

Historians disagree on the meaning of Indian words. In deference to the experts, one or more meanings are provided where possible. Also, spelling varied in early records, leading to confusion today. Montauk, for example, was spelled 19 different ways, and Moriches, Center Moriches and East Moriches underwent a dozen spellings after the first Europeans arrived.

◆ **Long Island:** When Dutch explorer Adrian Block sailed around the island in 1614 he named it Lange Eylandt and the name stuck. The Indian name for the island was Paumanok, meaning "land of tribute." The English settlers provoked hostilities with the Pequots of Connecticut and for years these Pequots were able to exact tribute from the Montauks and other tribes of eastern Long Island.

◆ **Amagansett:** "Place of good water."

◆ **Aquebogue:** "The place where the flags grow." In this case the cattails of Lily Pond.

◆ **Caumsett:** Matinecock Indian name for the area around present day Caumsett State Park, meaning "place by a sharp rock." The boulder was a hazard to navigation and was removed.

◆ **Cutchogue:** Corchaug means "principal place."

◆ **Hauppauge:** Hap-pogue, or Happauge, means "sweet waters" or "a flooded or overflow water place." The name applies to the springs at the head of the Nissequogue River.

◆ **Manhasset:** Previously called Cow Neck for its fine pasture, Manhasset is a derivation of the Indian term Manhansett, meaning, "island neighborhood." The Manhansett Indians gave Shelter Island its name.

◆ **Massapequa:** "Great water-land" or "land on the great cove." Massapequa is a variation of Massapeague, the home of the Massapeags, located on Fort Neck. It now belongs to the Floyd-Jones estate, in the town of Oyster Bay.

◆ **Merrick:** The name was originally applied to the Hempstead plains, meaning "bare land" or "plains country."

◆ **Montauk:** The Montaukett Indians originally inhabited this "hilly land."

◆ **Moriches:** This neck of land was initially called Merquices, after its Indian owner, Meritche.

- **Napeague:** This isthmus between Amagansett and Montauk comes from "niep," meaning water, and "eague," meaning land. This is appropriate, since half of it is composed of tidal and freshwater marshes.

- **Patchogue:** Pat-chogue, from the Pochough Indians, is defined as "where they gamble and dance."

- **Quogue:** This area was called Quaquanantunk, and later abbreviated Quoque, meaning "the round clam."

- **Rockaway:** The town takes its name from the Rechquaakie Indians, who lived along the Hempstead peninsula.

- **Ronkonkoma:** Raconkumake was a fresh pond in the center of Long Island, where the town is located. The word means "the fence or boundary fishing-place."

- **Sagaponack:** It means "land of the great ground nuts (potatoes)." Sagaponack was known for years as "Sagg." Sag Harbor to the north was known in the early days as "Harbor of Sagg" or "Sagg Harbor." The Indians called Sag Harbor Wigwagonock.

- **Setauket:** From a word that means "land at the mouth of river."

- **Shinnecock:** This means "people of the level land."

- **Syosset:** The word probably comes from the Indian word "suwasset," meaning "place in the pines."

- **Wantagh:** Wan-tagh was an Indian village in Hempstead.

- **Wyandanch:** Wyandance (or Wyandanch) was the sachem (chief) of Paumanack and a friend of the white settlers.

Geology & Geography

Long Island is about 100 miles long, and is the largest island adjoining the continental United States. Its widest point spans about 20 miles. Long Island reached its present geological form about 6,000 to 8,000 years ago.

Introduction

The Glaciers

Before the glaciers, the island was largely under water. By the time the last ice sheet left, the island had an elevated central spine and distinctive north and south forks. The land pushed forward by the glaciers became the **Ronkonkoma Moraine**, a series of low hills (or spine) that runs from Brooklyn to Montauk. Holes formed by the last glacier became the bays and harbors of the North Shore.

Lake Ronkonkoma runs east to west along its center. The hills and rocky cliffs facing Long Island Sound to the north are part of the **Harbor Hills Moraine**. Lake Ronkonkoma, 100 feet deep, was the largest depression and is the largest lake on Long Island.

The place where a glacier stops moving south and begins to melt is called a **terminal moraine**. On Long Island, such action created the South Shore and its 50 miles of ocean beaches. The South Shore of Brookhaven was formed when the water from the melting glacier carried sand and gravel from the moraines, building up a sandy plain. Farther west, land that eroded from the moraines formed a flat plain extending toward the Atlantic Ocean; this is known as the Hempstead Outwash. The action of the ocean on this outwash created a series of barrier islands along the South Shore that serve to protect the inland bays.

☞ DID YOU KNOW?

Long Island's evolution is far from over. The one-foot-per-century rise in sea level and pounding storm waves are gradually shrinking the island. They are also propelling the barrier islands inland: Fire Island is moving toward the South Shore at a rate of about 1.7 feet per year.

Environment

Estuaries

An estuary is defined as an area where saltwater from the ocean meets and mixes with fresh water from rivers and the land. Both the **Long Island Sound** and **Peconic Bay** fall into this category.

The Peconic Bay

The Peconic Bay is home to roughly 145 bird species.

The Peconic Estuary comprises the body of water between the North and South Forks and is one of 28 estuaries in the National Estuary Program, which was established by the Federal Water Quality Act of 1987 to promote wise management of estuaries threatened by pollution, development or overuse. The Peconic system comprises pine barrens, bluffs, dunes, beaches, harbors, creeks, bays, and 3,600 acres of tidal wetlands, as well as a watershed area of roughly 110,000 acres of land within six East End townships.

The Nature Conservancy has designated the Peconic Estuary system one of the Last Great Places in the Western Hemisphere. The Peconic watershed covers a large amount of territory on Eastern Long Island, including five East End towns – Southampton, East Hampton, Shelter Island, Southold, and Riverhead, as well as a bit of Brookhaven. Its primary threat comes from stormwater runoff that carries pollutants to the waterways, and from groundwater containing toxic chemicals that can result in excess organic nitrogen known as "brown tide." Although harmless to humans, a brown bay kills bay scallops and bay-bottom plants that need light.

According to *The Ultimate Guide to the Peconic Estuary*, published by the Peconic Estuary Program Citizens Advisory Committee (PEPCAC), "the Peconic Estuary watershed contains a higher percentage of undisturbed habitats and a greater diversity of natural communities than anywhere else in all New York

State." Marine animals common to the estuary are sea turtles, seals, whales and dolphins; the greatest threat to these animals is strangulation from plastic material carelessly tossed in the water by humans.

★ TIP

The Web site www.savethepeconic-bays.org has a wealth of information on the Peconic Estuary System.

Long Island Sound

Ninety miles long and 21 miles wide at its widest point, Long Island Sound divides the North Shore of Long Island from the south shore of Connecticut. **Save the Sound**, ☎ 516-759-2165, www.savethesound.org, is a Stamford, Connecticut-based organization with an office at Garvies Point Museum in Glen Cove (see page 43), provides educational programs, runs a summer camp, maintains the Long Island Sound Library in Stamford, monitors the water quality and initiates projects to clean up the Sound.

★ TIP

More information on the Sound is available on the Web site of the Long Island Sound Foundation, www.lisfoundation.org.

Wildlife

Deer

Long Island's deer population has continued to rise over the years, largely due to the absence of natural predators like coyotes. For the first time, in 2001, the deer-hunting season was opened a month early, on October 1 (it runs through December 31). The previous year, hunters took 2,278 deer, which helped put a dent in the population. Deer hunting regulations are particularly liberal on Long Island and farmers hold permits to take deer year-round. The US Fish and Wildlife Service has a Deer Management Assistance Program for land owners and managers. For information, ☎ 631-444-0311.

⚡ CAUTION

Many deer are hit by cars at night, and drivers should be alert, especially on less traveled roads.

Piping Plovers

Potential hazards to plovers include beach litter – which attracts predators that prey on plover eggs and chicks – and unleashed dogs.

A small, sand-colored shorebird, the piping plover was common along the Atlantic Coast during much of the 19th century but nearly disappeared by 1900 because of excessive hunting. Following passage of the Migratory Bird Treaty Act in 1918, the numbers recovered, only to decline again after World War II. This has been attributed primarily to increased development and recreational use of beaches.

The piping plover breeds only in North America, and is considered a threatened species. Recent surveys place the population at 875 nesting pairs, 200 of them on Long Island. Most of these birds winter along the coast from North Carolina to Key West, Florida, and are the first of the shorebirds to arrive at the breeding grounds; they are here from early to mid-March and depart about mid-September.

Piping plovers often breed near dunes in areas with little or no beach grass, and line the ground with shells and pebbles. You will notice dunes roped off on beaches along the South Shore of Long Island. This is done to protect existing colonies from disturbance.

Several federal, state and local agencies are working to halt the decline of the plover and the least tern, a New

York State endangered species found on shorelines of bays, the Sound and the ocean.

For more information, or to volunteer as a plover warden, contact **The Nature Conservancy**, Long Island Chapter, 250 Lawrence Hill Road, Cold Spring Harbor, NY 11724, ☎ 631-367-3225; or the **Department of Environmental Conservation**, Bureau of Wildlife, SUNY, Bldg. 40, Room 216, Stony Brook, NY 11790, ☎ 631-444-0310.

Marine Life

Sea turtles and **whales** occasionally wash up on beaches along the South Shore. The **Riverhead Foundation for Marine Research and Preservation** maintains a 24-hour hotline – ☎ 631-369-9829 – and spotters are asked to call even if the animal is dead so it can be tested for disease.

Wildlife Refuges

The **Long Island National Wildlife Refuge Complex**, administered by the US Fish and Wildlife Service, is comprised of eight National Wildlife Refuges (NWRs) and one Wildlife Management Area on Long Island. Their mission is to protect the estuary system, bays and forests for migrating wildlife. Visitors are more welcome in some refuges than others. The complex, headquartered in Shirley (on the South Shore, off LIE Exit 68 or the Southern State Parkway Exit 58), can be reached at ☎ 631-286-0485.

☛ DID YOU KNOW?

Three animals common to New York State but no longer found on Long Island are the **coyote**, **bobcat** and **black bear**.

Climate

Month	Avg Temp (F) Day / Night	Avg Precipitation Rain / Snow
January	38° / 26°	3.69" / 7.8"
February	40° / 27°	4.25" / 9.3"
March	49° / 34°	4.83" / 6.7"
April	61° / 44°	4.28" / .5"
May	72° / 52°	3.83" / 0"
June	80° / 63°	2.7" / 0"
July	85° / 68°	3.49" / 0"
August	84° / 67°	4.54" / 0"
September	76° / 60°	4.03" / 0"
October	66° / 50°	3.61" / 0"
November	54° / 41°	4.63" / .3"
December	42° / 30°	5.00" / 6.7"

Source: Metro Weather Service (Valley Stream)

In summer, the South Shore of Long Island records cooler temperatures than the North Shore due to wind and sea breezes.

Long Island Living

Long Island's two counties, **Nassau** and **Suffolk**, are divided into townships. The island's only two cities are in Nassau County. **Glen Cove**, which at the time had only 27,000 residents, became a city in 1918, and **Long Beach** in 1922. Within each township are countless villages and hamlets.

Facts

* **Largest ethnic group:** Italian Americans (27%)
* **Resident Population:** Nassau County: 1.2 million; Suffolk County: 1.3 million
* **Total population:** 2,698,800. In a recent survey, Long Island was ranked 16th in population among 323 US metropolitan areas.
* **Fastest-growing town:** Brookhaven's population has grown to 430,000, more people than in most of the nation's cities. The town will celebrate its 350th anniversary in 2005.
* **Most populous town:** The only town in New York with more residents than Brookhaven is Hempstead, whose population is about 725,000.
* **Highest point:** Jayne's Hill in Melville. More than 400 feet above sea level, it is located in West Hills County Park at the end of Reservoir Road.

Getting Here & Getting Around

Navigating Long Island

By Car

Long Island is approximately 100 miles long from the Nassau-Queens county line to Montauk Point. Access to the Island is by bridge or tunnel, via Queens and Brooklyn. Bridges are the **Triboro** (from Manhattan or The Bronx), **Whitestone** and **Throgs Neck** (from The Bronx), the **Queensboro**, a/k/a the **59th Street Bridge** (from Manhattan), and the **Verrazano Narrows Bridge** (from Staten Island). Tunnels from Manhattan are the **Midtown Tunnel** and the **Brooklyn-Battery Tunnel**. The major east-west routes on Long Island are the **Long Island Expressway** (tagged the

Use of a hand-held cellular phone while driving is illegal in New York State – the first state to enact such a law.

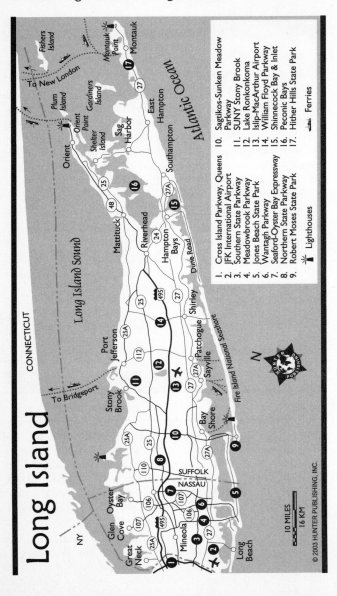

Long Island

CONNECTICUT

Long Island Sound

NY

Atlantic Ocean

Fire Island National Seashore

Great Neck
Glen Cove
Oyster Bay
Mineola
Long Beach
Stony Brook
Port Jefferson
Patchogue
Sayville
Bay Shore
Shirley
Mattituck
Riverhead
Hampton Bays
Southampton
Sag Harbor
Shelter Island
Orient
Orient Point
Plum Island
Gardiners Island
Fishers Island
East Hampton
Montauk
Montauk Point

Dune Road

To New London
To Bridgeport

SUFFOLK
NASSAU

10 MILES
16 KM

N
THE HUNTER PUBLISHING

© 2003 HUNTER PUBLISHING, INC.

1.   Cross Island Parkway, Queens
2.   JFK International Airport
3.   Southern State Parkway
4.   Meadowbrook Parkway
5.   Jones Beach State Park
6.   Wantagh Parkway
7.   Seaford-Oyster Bay Expressway
8.   Northern State Parkway
9.   Robert Moses State Park
10. Sagtikos-Sunken Meadow
     Parkway
11. SUNY Stony Brook
12. Lake Ronkonkoma
13. Islip-MacArthur Airport
14. William Floyd Parkway
15. Shinnecock Bay & Inlet
16. Peconic Bays
17. Hither Hills State Park

Lighthouses

Ferries

"Big LIE" because of frequent traffic tie-ups), **Northern State Parkway**, **Southern State Parkway** and **Sunrise Highway**. North/south routes include the **Cross Island Parkway**, **Meadowbrook State Parkway** and **Wantagh State Parkway**.

For purposes of this book, mileage is calculated from the New York City side of the Throgs Neck Bridge, which I generally take to Long Island. When you see, for example, "66 miles" following an attraction, it represents mileage from the bridge toll plaza to the destination.

> ★ TIP
>
> Alas, the Long Island Expressway only has one rest area on each side so be prepared. Both are between Exits 51 and 52. A Suffolk County visitor information center is located on the eastbound side.

By Train

The Long Island Rail Road (LIRR), the nation's largest commuter railroad, serves 134 stations and operates 741 trains on weekdays. Its primary east-west routes extend from **Penn Station** in Manhattan to Montauk on the South Fork and Greenport on the North Fork, with branch lines to Port Washington, Oyster Bay and Port Jefferson. The LIRR also has special beach packages and escorted sightseeing tours to Long Island attractions. In New York City, call ☎ 718-217-LIRR (5477); in Nassau County, ☎ 516-822-LIRR; in Suffolk County, ☎ 631-231-LIRR; www.mta.info; click on the Long Island Rail Road tab.

By Bus

MTA Long Island Bus links 96 Long Island communities in Nassau County, western Suffolk County, and eastern Queens. MTA also provides Jones Beach summer service; ☎ 516-766-6722.

10 REASONS TO VISIT LONG ISLAND

◆ 23 state parks and more than 50 county parks. Three of the state parks opened in 2001, each with bird-watching, nature trails and picnicking facilities: 153-acre **Nissequogue State Park** in Kings Park; 40-acre **Cold Spring Harbor** on Route 25A; and 98-acre **Shadmore** in Montauk.

◆ Superb restaurants

◆ Scenic waterways

◆ Gilded Age mansions open to visitors

◆ World-class concert halls and arenas

◆ Hundreds of miles of white sandy beaches

◆ More than 100 museums

◆ Some 7,000 extant structures built prior to the 20th century.

◆ Unique architecture

◆ Animal refuges and preserves

By Air

Long Island residents use the two major New York airports, both located in Queens – **Kennedy** (JFK) and **LaGuardia** (LGA). In Suffolk County there are five small public and private airports. **Islip-MacArthur Airport** (www.macarthurairport.com) in Ronkonkoma, the largest in passenger traffic, has six scheduled carriers, 95 daily flights and 1.04 million passengers annually. The others are **Republic Airport** in East Farmingdale, www.republicairport.net; **Brookhaven-Calabro Airport** in Shirley; **Francis S. Gabreski Airport** in Westhampton Beach, www.gabreskiairport.com; and **East Hampton Airport** in East Hampton. Helicopter service and private planes are listed on page 431.

Recreation

Parks, Campsites & Golf Courses

State and county parks generally charge fees – but only from late spring to early fall. Some park regulations state that only residents are welcome or that residents need their leisure passport or green key (see below), but only in season. When the season is over, why not enjoy Long Island's magnificent parks? They're the place to be in the fall when the leaves change or in winter when many parks with trails allow cross-country skiing.

Nassau County parks and golf courses are open only to residents and their guests. Residents must have a **Leisure Passport** to play golf, tennis, ice skate, swim or participate in any other organized sport (hotels often provide their guests with passes). Leisure Passes are issued by the Nassau County Department of Recreation, Parks & Support Services (☎ 516-572-0218, www.nassau.co.us/parks) and must be obtained in person. Passes are $15 and are good for three years. Leisure Passport application centers are open daily, 10am-4pm, at Cantiague Park in Hicksville, Grant Park in Hewlett, Eisenhower Park in East Meadow, Christopher Morley Park in Roslyn-North Hills, North Woodmere Park in North Woodmere, Wantagh Park in Wantagh, and Nassau Beach Park in Lido Beach. Residents who are 60 or older, disabled or veterans are entitled to a lifetime pass as long as they maintain Nassau County residency.

Suffolk County parks are open to all. Residents may purchase a **Green Key Card** ($20 adults/$9 seniors) good for three years, entitling them to a reduced parking fee. Cards can be obtained at any of the county golf courses, campgrounds or the Parks Administration Office in West Sayville, ☎ 631-854-4949. You will need to show proof of residency and a photo ID. None of this applies to "passive" parks, which means no staff or amenities, and thus no fee.

Non-residents using Suffolk County parks and golf courses simply pay a higher entrance fee. However, non-residents must purchase a **Tourist Key** ($35 per year) to make advance reservations for golf or campsites. Golf reservations can be made up to seven days in advance for Green Key cardholders and three days in advance for Tourist Key holders. Green Key Card holders can make camping reservations by calling the Green Key reservation system at ☎ 631-244-PARK (7275). Although reservations are not required, campers are advised to call a minimum of two weeks in advance.

> ★ TIP
>
> If you have further questions about the Green Key or Tourist Key, call the Suffolk County Parks Department at ☎ 631-854-4961, Monday-Friday. For general park information and and upcoming events, call ☎ 631-244-PARK and follow the prompts.

In addition to the county parks, there are four state parks in Nassau and 11 in Suffolk. New York State parks do not require a permit (with the exception of Connetquot River State Park Preserve near Oakdale). Parking fees are charged in season. For more information on state parks in Nassau and Suffolk counties, ☎ 631-669-1000 and ask for "Permits," or see www.nysparks.state.ny.us/. For links to the individual state parks in Suffolk County, visit www.co.suffolk.ny.us/exec/parks.

WHO WAS ROBERT MOSES?

Love him or hate him, Robert Moses – New York City Commissioner of Parks from 1934-1960 – had an enormous impact on New York City and Long Island, especially between 1946 and 1953. Robert Caro, in his 1974 book *The Power Broker*, profiled the life of this influential New Yorker. According to Caro, no public improvement was built by any agency unless Moses approved its design and location. To build highways, this man who rarely drove displaced 250,000 people. Moses' projects on Long Island and in eastern Queens include the Laurelton, Cross Island, Interborough, Northern State, Southern State, Wantagh, Saugauties, Sunken Meadow and Meadowbrook parkways, and Sunken Meadow, Hither Hills, Orient Point, Fire Island, Captree, Bethpage, Belmont Lake, Hempstead Lake, Valley Stream and Hecksher state parks.

Hiking

A wonderful Internet site for hikers is www.hike-li.com. Various year-round hikes are listed by the current month; they are operated by **Greenbelt Trail Conference**, ☎ 631-360-0753; **East Hampton Trails Preservation Society**, ☎ 631-329-4227; and **Southampton Trails Preservation Society**, ☎ 631-537-5202. The site also has links to, among others, the Long Island Sierra Club, Long Island Orienteering Club, Group for the South Fork, Long Island Pine Barrens Preservation Society, and South Fork Natural History Society, ☎ 631-297-7944, www.sofo.org, plus sites for horsemen and bicyclists.

Permits are required to hike, bike, fish, horseback ride or hunt in parklands managed by the New York State Department of Environmental Conservation (DEC). On

Long Island, these include **Rocky Point Natural Resources Management Area** (hiking, biking, horseback riding, seasonal hunting); **David A. Sarnoff Pine Barrens Preserve** (hiking and seasonal hunting); **Otis Pike Preserve** (hiking, biking, horseback riding, fishing, hunting and canoeing); **Barcelona Neck**, East Hampton Cooperative Area (hiking and seasonal hunting); **Westhampton Conservation Area** (hiking, hunting and horseback riding); **Calverton Conservation Area** (biking, hiking and hunting); **Peconic River Conservation Area** (fishing); **Eastport Conservation Area** (hiking only); and **Kings Park Conservation Area** (hiking only). Applications for three-year permits are available from the DEC, Sporting License Office, SUNY Building 40, Stony Brook, New York 11790-2356, ☎ 631-444-0273, www.dec.state.ny. us.

Biking

It is not surprising that bicycle clubs abound on Long Island given its mostly flat terrain. Several communities have local clubs, but visitors are welcome to compete in races (with an entry fee). Most individual annual memberships are $15 and many clubs issue newsletters to members.

The bicycle stores that are listed in this book sell and repair road, mountain and juvenile bikes, although the makes may vary. Most carry accessories as well. However, only a handful rent bikes, and that information is provided as well.

Concerned Long Island Mountain Bicyclists (CLIMB), ☎ 631-271-6527, www.climbonline.org, is a group dedicated to the growth and safe enjoyment of mountain biking. During the biking season, work parties are held on weekends, where volunteers help to maintain trails, signs and markers, evaluate trail conditions, and organize the creation of new trails (anyone can participate). A group ride is held after the work party. The club also organizes bus trips to mountain biking locations, the most popular of them being Lake Minnewaska in New Paltz. Off-island trips are offered to members and non-members alike, but member bikers get first dibs. Most of CLIMB's 600 members are from Nassau and Suffolk counties but some are New York City residents. The experience level of members varies from beginner to super expert, but most are in the intermediate range. Weekend rides are generally appropriate for beginning to intermediate riders.

Fishing

Long Island has some of the best year-round fishing on the East Coast. New York State does not require a license for recreational saltwater fishing (although there are minimum size requirements on some species), whereas a state license is required for freshwater fishing. Non-residents may fish free from any public pier but, like beach-goers, fishermen pay parking fees between Memorial Day and Labor Day at most parks and beaches. Several open boats operate daily (see listings of charter operators under *Boating* in each section of the book) and no reservations are required.

FISHING INFORMATION ON THE WEB

Information on Long Island fishing is available on the Web at **www.lieast.com/fishing.html**, and at **www.noreast.com** (for saltwater fishing). At **www.easternfisherman.com**, you can browse marinas by state or region, read tips and reports from other anglers, check the weather on Long Island, and find restaurants easily accessible from the marinas. The Web site of the New York Marine Trades Association, **www.boatnys.com**, provides information on marine specialists, including marinas, dealers and insurance agencies.

Shop Till You Drop

Living in the nation's fourth wealthiest area, Long Islanders have the disposable income to support 1,196 shopping centers that include nine indoor malls. In addition, chain stores abound in some areas and independently owned boutiques and shops are found in virtually every town (see *Shop Till You Drop* in each chapter for local listings). Some stores are listed at www.shopsofli.com.

After Dark

Long Island is a microcosm of New York City, offering something for everyone. For night owls, the choices range from restaurants and late night bars with live music to celebrated concert halls featuring top names in entertainment. In between are lounges, comedy clubs, nightclubs and special interest establishments.

Check *Newsday* each Friday for an up-to-date listing of performances. The *Stepping Out* page of *This Month on Long Island*, a freebie distributed throughout Long Island, lists clubs and piano bars. Other good Web sites for music lovers are http://nightlife.longisland.com; www.longislandmusicscene.com and www.wantagh.li/bar.htm.

Best Places to Stay

Most of the accommodations featured in this book offer some or all of these amenities: shampoo, conditioner, hair dryer, terry bathrobe, down comforters, and air conditioning. To avoid repetition, only additional or lack of amenities are mentioned.

The following price scales are intended as guidelines to help you choose lodging to fit your vacation budget.

Many lodgings advertise continental breakfast, which used to mean coffee and crumb cake and nothing more. Today, it may include bagels, muffins, French toast,

pancakes, cereal, yogurt, donuts, fruit, hard-boiled eggs
– and crumb cake.

ACCOMMODATIONS PRICE SCALE
Price scale is based on the cost of a double room, two people per room on a weekend, before hotel taxes (11.3% in Nassau; 9.25% in Suffolk)
Inexpensive. . . . . .under $130
Moderate . . . .$130-$200
Expensive. . . . .$201-$300
Deluxe . . . . .more than $300

MOTEL PRICE SCALE
Price scale is based on the cost of a double room, two people per room, in season, and does not include tax.
Inexpensive. . . . . .under $100
Moderate . . . .$100-$150
Expensive. . . . . .over $150

Best Places to Eat

You will notice that some restaurants have **Great Restaurants** (www.greatrestaurantsmag.com) as one of their Web sites. I discovered the site after having dined in about 16 of the restaurants mentioned on it and agreed with every one of their choices. I e-mailed Great Restaurants for the criteria used in their selections and the response was as follows:

- ◆ Recommendations from Richard Scholem (a columnist and restaurant critic for *The New York Times*, Long Island section)
- ◆ A score of 18 and above for food on the *Zagat Survey* (Zagat ratings range from 1 to 30)
- ◆ Recommendations from chefs and owners
- ◆ Recommendations from their readers
- ◆ Their own experiences

This doesn't mean that the other restaurants featured in this book are inferior. Some are too new to be reviewed; others may be terrific, but are just not included yet on the site.

BEFORE YOU GO...

Among the directories of Long Island restaurants and bars on the Web are:

General . . . . www.longisland.com
Long Island Food Net . . . . www.lifn.com
Dining . . . . www.dininglongisland.com; www.restaurantslongisland.com (which has links to movie theaters as well); www.webscope.com/li/restaurants.html
Mad for menus? . . . . www.lifoodmenus.com
Clubs . . . . www.liclubs.com; www.clublongisland.com

DINING PRICE SCALE	
Price scale includes one entrée, with glass of wine and coffee. There is an 8.5% tax on food in both Nassau and Suffolk Counties.	
Inexpensive.	under $25
Moderate	$25-$40
Expensive.	over $40

Information Sources

Tourism

Long Island Convention & Visitors Bureau, 330 Motor Parkway, Suite 203, Hauppauge, NY 11788, ☎ 631-951-3900 or 877-FUN-ON-LI (877-386-6654), www.licvb.com. Living history weekends are held regularly at historic sites throughout Long Island. For information, contact the LICVB or visit www.liheritage-trail.com.

Recommended Reading

The American Institute of Architects, Long Island Chapter, and The Society for the Preservation of Long Island Antiquities. *AIA Architectural Guide to Nassau and Suffolk Counties, Long Island.* Dover Publications, 1992. www.aia.longisland.com.

Beauchamp, William M. *Aboriginal Place Names of New York.* Originally published by New York State Education Dept., 1907; reprinted by Grand River Books, 1971.

Bookbinder, Bernie. *Long Island – People and Places – Past and Present*, A Newsday Book. Harry N. Abrams, 1998.

Caro, Robert A. *The Power Broker-Robert Moses and the Fall of New York*. Vintage Books, 1974.

DeMille, Nelson. *The Gold Coast*, Warner Books, 1990.

Dyson, Verne. *Anecdotes and Events on Long Island*. Ira J. Friedman, 1969.

Epstein, Jason and Barstow, Elizabeth. *East Hampton: A History and Guide*. Random House, 1985.

Furman, Gabriel. *Antiquities of Long Island*. Ira J. Friedman, 1968. First published 1874.

Gianotti, Peter M. *A Guide to Long Island Wine Country*. Newsday, 2001.

Randall, Monica. ***The Mansions of Long Island's Gold Coast***. Rizzoli International Publications, 1979; 1987.

Strong, John A. ***The Algonquian Peoples of Long Island From Earliest Times to 1700***. Empire State Books, 1997.

Tooker, William Wallace. ***The Indian Place-Names on Long Island***. Port Washington, NY: Ira J. Friedman, 1962.

Useful Web Sites

◆ Although individual Web sites are provided with many entries in this book, links to about 25 Long Island attractions can be found at **www.fieldtrip.com/ny/index_ny.htm**.

◆ A wonderful site with links to nearly everything on Long Island is **www.fordyce.org/long_island**. It includes links to *Newsday* restaurant reviews. Another site, with links to accommodations, movie listings and more, is **www.lileisure.com**.

★ TIP

To find information on any town in the United States, go to **www.areaguides.net**. For Long Island listings, click New York. If you have a specific town in mind, simply type in its name; for example, http://merrickny.areaguides.net or http://lynbrookny.areaguides.net.

◆ One of Long Island's foremost search engines is **www.liseek.com**. Other good ones are:

www.longislandbrowser.com
www.digitalcity.com/longisland
www.citidexli.com
www.longislandinfo.com

www.searchli.com
http://longisland.about.com
www.longislandtourism.com

◆ For lighthouse lovers, **www.longislandlighthou-ses.com** has links to all the lighthouses on Long Island.

◆ A complete list of charter boats is at **www.longislandtourism.com/charters.htm**.

◆ Horse lovers will find information at **www.longislandhorse.net/barns.htm**.

◆ Golfers will find courses listed at **www.licvb.com/golf.cfm**; **www.ligolfer.com** has a list of golf courses and practice ranges, profiles of a few courses, articles and tips.

◆ Tennis players will enjoy browsing at **www.longislandtennis.com**.

◆ History buffs will enjoy visiting **www.lihistory.com**.

◆ For an on-line directory of Long Island health clubs, go to **www.wantagh.li/healthclubs.htm**.

For links to every community on Long Island, go to www.licentral .com, click "Long Island Towns" and scroll down.

⭐ TIP

Still have questions about Long Island that this book doesn't address? Mr. Long Island has most of the answers. Check out "Long Island's Most Popular Web Site," **www. LongIsland.com**. Scroll down to the bottom to "Ask Mr. Long Island."

Publications

Newsday is the newspaper of record for all of Long Island and parts of Queens. You can read it on-line at www.newsday.com. The weather for LaGuardia and MacArthur airports is at the upper right-hand corner along with a link to *Newsday's Fun Book*, a compen-

26   Information Sources

dium of information on sites and activities on Long Island and Queens that is mailed to subscribers. The Web site, regularly updated, can be accessed directly at www.newsday.com/funbook.

If you're interested in purchasing more books about Long Island, wish to subscribe to *Newsday,* order the *Fun Book* for $5.95, or buy some memorabilia, log on to www.listore.com.

Long Island Wine Gazette, ☎ 631-725-3899 (editorial/advertising) or 212-769-1143 (Manhattan office) is a free quarterly tabloid distributed on the North Shore, in the Hamptons and at 90 Manhattan locations.

The Wine Press – Your Guide to Long Island Wine Country is a free glossy magazine published quarterly by the Long Island Wine Council and Times/Review Newspapers of Mattituck; ☎ 631-298-3200, www.timesreview.com.

Boaters will enjoy the complimentary publication, ***Long Island Boating World***, found at various marinas; ☎ 631-225-7100, www.liboatingworld.com.

Refer to the *A to Z* section of each chapter of the book for listings of publications and Web sites, plus Chamber of Commerce and local businesses.

Radio Stations

WALK 97.5, ☎ 631-475-5200, www.walkradio.com, features news, music, features, contests.

WBAB 102.3, ☎ 631-587-1023, www.wbab.com, plays rock 'n roll.

WBLI 106.1, www.wbli.com, offers contemporary hit music and news.

WBZO 103.1 FM, ☎ 631-423-6740, www.b103.com, plays oldies.

WKJY-FM – WJOY 98.3, ☎ 631-770-4200, www.kjoy.com, has a morning show featuring music, traffic and weather reports.

Introduction

WLIR 92.7, ☎ 631-955-0927, features hit music and bills itself as "Long Island's party station."

WLNG 92.1 FM, ☎ 631-725-2300, Sag Harbor, plays music and broadcasts high school sports.

WPLT 1610 AM, Greenport; visitor information.

WRCN 94.3 and **103.9**, ☎ 631-451-l039, www.wrcn.com, offers rock 'n roll.

WUSB 90.1FM, ☎ 631-632-6901 (studio); ☎ 631-632-6500 (office); www.wusb.org, is a non-commercial radio station with a varied format of music, news, interviews and commentary.

TV Stations

Channel 12 Cable, News12 Long Island, www.news-12.com.

WLNY-TV, ☎ 631-777-8855, Melville

WLIG-TV, ☎ 631-727-1741, Riverhead

WVVH-TV, ☎ 800-757-WVVH, www.wvvh.com, Hamptons.

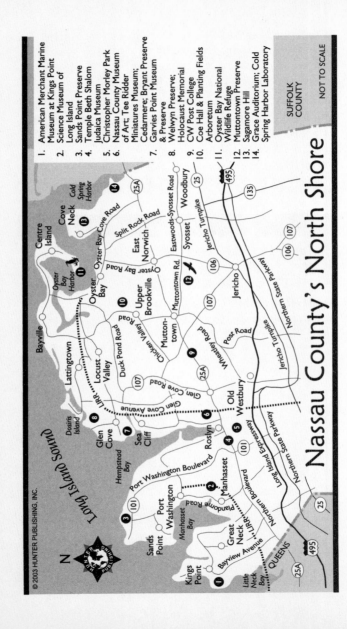

© 2003 HUNTER PUBLISHING, INC.

Long Island Sound

N
HUNTER PUBLISHING

1. American Merchant Marine Museum at Kings Point
2. Science Museum of Long Island
3. Sands Point Preserve
4. Temple Beth Shalom Judaica Museum
5. Christopher Morley Park
6. Nassau County Museum of Art; Tee Ridder Miniatures Museum; Cedarmere; Bryant Preserve
7. Garvies Point Museum & Preserve
8. Welwyn Preserve; Holocaust Memorial
9. CW Post College
10. Coe Hall & Planting Fields Arboretum
11. Oyster Bay National Wildlife Refuge
12. Muttontown Preserve
13. Sagamore Hill
14. Grace Auditorium; Cold Spring Harbor Laboratory

SUFFOLK COUNTY

NOT TO SCALE

Kings Point
Sands Point
Port Washington
Manhasset Bay
Great Neck
Little Neck Bay
Bayview Avenue
QUEENS
495
25A

Hempstead Bay
Dosiris Island
Sea Cliff
Glen Cove
Lattingstown
Bayville
Centre Island
Oyster Bay Harbor
Oyster Bay
Cove Neck
Cold Spring Harbor
25A
Split Rock Road
Oyster Bay-Cove Road
East Norwich
Upper Brookville
Muttontown
Chicken Valley Road
Duck Pond Road
Locust Valley
Glen Cove Avenue
LIRR
107
Glen Cove Road
Old Westbury
25A
Roslyn
101
Port Washington Boulevard
101
Northern Boulevard
LIRR
Plandome Road
Long Island Expressway
Northern State Parkway
Wheatley Road
Muttontown Rd.
Post Road
Jericho Turnpike
Jericho Turnpike
Jericho
Syosset
Woodbury
Eastwoods-Syosset Road
106
106
107
107
107
25
135
495
Northern State Parkway
25

Nassau County's North Shore

Nassau County's North Shore

About 15 miles from midtown Manhattan, Nassau County is comprised of three townships: Oyster Bay, Hempstead and North Hempstead. Hempstead, founded in 1644, was the first and most famous English town in Dutch territory; today it is the nation's largest township, with 725,639 residents. Nassau County has two cities, **Long Beach** on the South Shore and **Glen Cove** on the North; and 64 villages. The county seat is in Mineola.

The North Shore of Nassau County is made up of a series of peninsulas; its many harbors and bays were the result of the last glacier, which dug huge holes in the land as it moved south. Each peninsula is ethnically, economically and religiously diverse, although overwhelmingly white; development on each of the peninsulas is centered around a major town, village or city. First-class stores, hotels and restaurants attract people from all over. This part of Nassau County is less developed than the South Shore, thanks to the barons of industry who bought acres of farmland about a century ago to insure that no roads or buildings would impinge upon their property. Known as the **Gold Coast**, the North Shore is blessed with rolling terrain, woodlands and waterfront on Long Island Sound.

The **Town of North Hempstead** (Hempstead was named after an English village) occupies 58 square miles, and its 212,063 residents live in Great Neck, Locust Valley, Port Washington, Roslyn, Old Bethpage, Oyster Bay, Sea Cliff, or a part of Old Westbury.

Tucked between Little Neck and Manhasset Bays and 11 miles from the Throgs Neck Bridge is **Great Neck**, probably the most cosmopolitan of Long Island's communities. Considered the gateway to the North Shore and its famous Gold Coast, Great Neck has only 37,295

Glen Cove's population is 26,622, far smaller than either the Town of Oyster Bay or the South Shore village of Hempstead, which has almost 50,000 residents.

Nassau County's North Shore

residents on 9.6 square miles, but a whopping 14 houses of worship.

The **Town of Oyster Bay's** 102.5 square miles extend from Long Island Sound to the Atlantic Ocean. Its 292,657 residents are scattered among 18 villages: Bayville, Brookville, Centre Island, Cove Neck, Farmingdale, Lattingtown, Laurel Hollow, Massapequa Park, Matinecock, Mill Neck, Muttontown, Old Brookville, Oyster Bay Cove, Sea Cliff, Brookville and parts of East Hills, Old Westbury and Roslyn Harbor. The town is the site of two of Long Island's primary historic sites: Theodore Roosevelt's home at Sagamore Hill, and Planting Fields Arboretum. Oyster Bay's hilly terrain and heavily wooded regions, especially around Brookville and Muttontown, are a favorite among bikers and hikers. Situated along Oyster Bay Harbor and tagged "the pearl of Long Island," Oyster Bay was once a major port and shipbuilding center and home to many prominent American millionaires such as J.P. Morgan and F.W. Woolworth. Within the city of Oyster Bay is Glen Cove, a city of seven square miles located on Hempstead Harbor.

Getting Here & Getting Around

By Car

The Long Island Expressway (Interstate 495) is Long Island's major east/west roadway, extending from Manhattan to Riverhead. Also running west-to-east are **Route 25A** (Northern Boulevard) and **Route 25** (Jericho Turnpike); these roads intersect with Nassau County's major north/south connectors: the **Cross Island Parkway** at the Queens/Nassau border; **Glen Cove Road**; **Route 107** (Cedar Swamp Road); and **Route 106** (Oyster Bay Road).

Rental Cars

Rates for a mid-sized car run $50 to $55 per day, with additional charges for mileage.

Thrifty Car Rental, 124 Northern Boulevard, Great Neck, ☎ 516-482-0222, www.thrifty.com.

Dollar Rent A Car, 1037 Northern Boulevard, Roslyn, ☎ 516-365-6900, www.dollar.com.

By Taxi

Taxi fares from Kennedy and LaGuardia Airports to most points on Nassau County's North Shore range from $25 to $30.

Friendly's, Great Neck, airport/local and long trips; ☎ 516-466-0066.

Great Neck Taxi, airport/local and long trips; ☎ 516-482-0077, or 516-466-0130.

Gold Coast Taxi, Great Neck, airport and long trips, no local; their rate depends on the number of passengers; ☎ 516-487-2600.

By Limousine

Graywright Limousines, Great Neck, in business since 1988; ☎ 516-482-6283.

M&V Limousines, 180 Jericho Turnpike in Syosset, serves all of Long Island. Another office is in Smithtown. ☎ 800-489-5788, www.mvlimo.com.

By Ferry

Fox Navigation, Garvies Point Road, Glen Cove, carries passengers only, year-round, between Glen Cove and New London CT; ☎ 888-SAILFOX (724-5369), www.foxnavigation.com. The trip takes a little over two hours; fare is $59 to $99 round-trip.

Nassau County's North Shore

Sunup to Sundown

From Mansions to Museums

In the early 1900s, the wealthy were attracted by the natural beauty along the North Shore of Long Island. Farmland was snatched up, and architects and landscape designers were hired to create country estates. During the Jazz Age, more than 500 estates were occupied. According to Nelson DeMille's *The Gold Coast* (1990), European aristocracy built so many manors, châteaux, estates and fiefdoms along this Gold Coast that by 1929 it had "the largest concentration of wealth and power in America, probably the world." Today, many of these mansions are museums.

Skirting the Gold Coast is Route 25A, one of the earliest roadways on Long Island. In 1790, George Washington traveled the trail in his horse-drawn carriage. In honor of this presidential journey, the span from Great Neck to Port Jefferson has become known as the **Long Island Heritage Trail**. The *Heritage Trail Guide*, produced by the North Shore Promotion Alliance, organizes 100 miles of the trail's attractions into one-day itineraries. For a copy of the guide, contact the Ward Melville Heritage Organization at ☎ 631-751-2244, or write to them at PO Box 572, Stony Brook, NY 11790. Their Web site, www.liheritagetrail.com, also has information. A card offering discounts at local attractions, restaurants and lodging is available along the trail at participating venues.

> ★ TIP
>
> If you're car-less, or simply prefer trains, the **Long Island Rail Road** offers escorted sightseeing tours to many Heritage Trail attractions from May through November; ☎ 718-217-LIRR.

AMERICAN MERCHANT MARINE MUSEUM
US Merchant Marine Academy
300 Steamboat Road
Kings Point
☎ 516-773-5515 or 5527
www.usmma.edu/museum/
Suggested donation $2

The United States Merchant Marine Academy
(USMMA) was established in 1942 by the federal government on an estate purchased from auto tycoon Walter P. Chrysler. The Academy educates officers for the
American Merchant Marine and US Naval Reserve. A
brochure outlines a walking tour of seven sites on the
campus, including the maritime library, which is open
to the public Monday through Friday, 8am-4:30pm;
switchboard, ☎ 516-773-5000. Call for a copy of the
Academy's brochure or additional information.

Chrysler's 35-room mansion became the Academy's
administration hall. Another building, which had belonged to William Barstow (a pioneer in the development of electricity a century ago) became a museum.
Barstow's crowning achievement was electrifying the
Brooklyn Bridge. The museum boasts a magnificent
painted ceiling, a Waterford chandelier and smashing
views of Long Island Sound and the Throgs Neck
Bridge.

The museum's theme is "Ships made in America!" and
its goal is to foster greater appreciation for the role of
the merchant marine in American's maritime past.
Along with model ships and nautical artifacts, it hon-
ors 142 cadets and midshipmen who perished in World
War II (Kings Pointers, as graduates of the Academy
are known, were the only federal academy students
sent into war zones). Study the ships carefully – an
open book exam will test your knowledge of merchant
vessels! The museum is open Tuesday through Friday,
10am-3pm; Saturday and Sunday, 1pm-4:30pm.

The Academy campus is open daily and weekends from
9am-5pm; it is closed to visitors during the month of
July and on federal holidays. Take the Throgs Neck

Nassau County's North Shore

As of this writing, the Merchant Marine Museum is not wheelchair-accessible.

Bridge to the Cross Island Parkway South; stay to the right on the Cross Island and take the second exit to Northern Boulevard East. Travel about three miles, then go left onto Great Neck Road. Continue over the railroad bridge and along Bayview Avenue and Kings Point Road (same road – the name changes). Turn left onto Steamboat Road and proceed to the Academy's main gate.

SCIENCE MUSEUM OF LONG ISLAND
1526 North Plandome Road
Plandome
☎ 516-627-9400
http://ourworld.compuserve.com/homepages/SMLI

This is not a traditional museum – there are no exhibits. Headquartered in a Victorian mansion on Leeds Pond Preserve since 1962, it's a hands-on, handicapped-accessible facility for the study of natural sciences, set on 36 wooded acres of freshwater streams and beachfront. Its teachers also bring their science workshops to 387 schools on Long Island, Queens, Manhattan and Westchester.

Looking to occupy your child over the holidays? The museum is open 365 days a year, running after-school programs, Scouting events, birthday parties, weekend family workshops, overseas expeditions for adults, and a summer science day camp. Any child over three may participate, and you don't have to be a Long Island resident or have a child in school to register for a workshop, but pre-registration is required.

The museum is open daily at 9am, including holidays. To get here, take the LIE to Exit 33N. Continue along the service road, and at the second light turn left onto Community Drive. Look for the sign for 25A (Northern Boulevard), and turn right there. At the Amoco station, turn left onto Plandome Road and continue two miles to a stop sign. Turn left onto North Plandome Road and follow it around to Rock Hollow Road, where you'll see signs for the museum.

HEMPSTEAD HOUSE & FALAISE

Sands Point Preserve
95 Middle Neck Road
Port Washington
☎ 516-571-7900
www.longislandtourism.com/castle-gould.htm

Due to the historic nature of the building, Falaise is not wheelchair-accessible.

Sands Point Preserve is home to two castles – Hempstead House and Falaise – and six marked trails. Daniel Guggenheim arrived in Sands Point in 1917 and purchased a 300-acre estate from Howard Gould, son of the notorious stock manipulator Jay Gould. The estate's house, built in the style of Ireland's Kilkenny Castle, was named Hempstead House because it overlooked Hempstead Bay. Boasting the largest collection of Wedgwood in the United States, Hempstead House was once considered among the most opulent homes on the Gold Coast; it is open for self-guided tours Friday-Sunday, May-October. Castle Gould, originally the estate's carriage house, now houses the Visitors Center, museum shop and science exhibits. Traveling interactive exhibits have focused on bats, sharks, cats and dinosaurs.

Falaise, which means "cliff" or "bluff" in French, was a wedding present from Daniel Guggenheim to his son, Captain Harry F. Guggenheim. Built in 1923, the four-story tapestry brick manor is a 16th-century Norman-style with tile roof, set on the bluffs of Long Island Sound. Inside is an art museum. The only way to see it is on a guided tour that goes through 15 of the 26 rooms, up and down tiled stairways. Harry was an avid flyer and a friend of Charles Lindbergh, who often stayed at the mansion for some peace and quiet. We stood in the room where Lindbergh wrote *We,* an account of his epic transatlantic flight in 1927.

Sands Point Preserve hosts the annual Medieval Festival in September.

The younger Guggenheim also raised and raced thoroughbred horses, and we visited his trophy room, which displays awards and paintings. We stood in the dining room, which had been converted to a bedroom for the horse-head scene in the *Godfather* movie. A maid working at Falaise was unaware of the circum-

stances and fainted when she saw the head in the bed.
Or so said our knowledgeable guide.

"Some works of art in this house you'll not see again,"
our docent, Nina, told our tour group. Harry and his
second wife, Caroline Morton, traveled abroad collect-
ing such treasures as 17th-century Italian lava columns, a 27-foot Persian rug depicting the Tree of Life,
Spanish furniture that folds up for easy transport, a
French choir pew, and Medieval grotesque figures over
the doors that were thought to ward off evil spirits.

*Harry
Guggenheim
was heir to a
mining for-
tune and
served as
Ambassador
to Cuba from
1924-1933.
New York
City's
Guggenheim
Museum is
named for his
uncle, Solo-
mon R.
Guggenheim.*

Harry Guggenheim and his third wife, Alicia Patter-
son, founded *Newsday*. Alicia (the daughter of Joe Pat-
terson, founder and editor of the *New York Daily News*)
served as *Newsday's* editor and publisher; the first edition came out on September 3, 1940 at a cost of 3¢. The
paper really took off after World War II with the mass
exodus of New Yorkers to the suburbs, especially Long
Island, which brought new industries to the area.

The glorious view from the terrace at Falaise (and from
Alicia's bright and airy bedroom) of Long Island Sound,
with Westchester County to the left, Glen Cove to the
right and Connecticut straight ahead, is alone worth
the $5 fee.

Both Hempstead House and Falaise were deeded to
Nassau County in 1971. The 216-acre nature preserve
is six miles from the LIE's Exit 36N. Travel north on
Searingtown Road, which becomes Port Washington
Boulevard and then Middle Neck Road. Open May-Oc-
tober, Wednesday-Sunday, noon to 3pm.

NASSAU COUNTY MUSEUM OF ART
One Museum Drive
Roslyn
☎ 516-484-9337/9338
www.nassaumuseum.com
Admission $6 adults; $4 children

*The café at
the Nassau
County Mu-
seum is open
noon to 3pm.*

The NCMA is housed in a three-story Georgian mansion, once owned, in the 19th century, by poet and
preservationist William Cullen Bryant, who later lived

at Cedarmere (see page 39). The estate was purchased in 1919 by Henry Clay Frick (co-founder of US Steel) for his son, Childs, who lived here with his wife, Frances, for almost 50 years. She was an avid horticulturist; her formal gardens have recently been restored to their original design. When Childs died in 1965, Nassau County purchased the home and converted it into a museum.

Today, we can all feel like aristocracy, at least for a few hours, with one turn of the steering wheel. In an instant we go from commercial hubbub to a serene country estate. Here, 36 sculptures – including works by Calder and Rodin – dot the 145-acre landscape.

Although organized like the Metropolitan Museum of Art and visited by more than 200,000 people annually, the NCMA is more manageable in size. Who among us hasn't tired going from exhibit to exhibit? On my visit, the permanent collection was set aside to make room for a comprehensive exhibit on Napoleon; he was a passionate patron of the arts who popularized the Empire style of décor and dress. Along with paintings of Napoleon's historic battles were objects actually used by him or members of his family, most notably his distinctive silk hat and a gilded mahogany desk that belonged to Josephine's son from a former marriage. Previous exhibits concentrated on the American Revolution and the Civil War. These are examples of the museum's emphasis on integrating the arts and history.

The museum is handicapped-accessible, and it is open year-round; call for days and times. To get there, take the LIE to Exit 39N; take Glen Cove Road North and go about two miles to Northern Boulevard (Route 25A); turn left. At the second traffic light, turn right into the museum entrance. After passing the art studio, park in the lot on the left and walk to the main museum. There is a small parking lot just past the museum, but if it's filled you'll have to drive around the grounds again because of the one-way access roads.

Nassau County's North Shore

Henry Clay Frick built a mansion on Fifth Avenue in Manhattan and filled it with priceless paintings and fine furniture. Today, the Frick Collection is open to the public as a museum.

THE TEE RIDDER MINIATURES MUSEUM
15 Museum Drive
Roslyn
☎ 516-484-7841
Admission $6 adults; $4 children

One way to solve a space problem is to design everything in miniature. Then you can display 26 fully decorated rooms from different periods and styles, as the Tee Ridder Miniatures Museum has done so well. Inside the building, donated by Eric Ridder in memory of his wife, are the creations of Madeleine "Tee" Ridder (1926-1991), a Locust Valley resident and patron of the arts who incorporated her interests in sports, gardening, music and design into painstakingly crafted rooms. Her eclectic and impeccable taste is reflected in the fine pieces she purchased abroad. Do you prefer English gardens? French salons? Chinese drawing rooms? Country kitchens? The museum has it all and more. Pre-teens like these dioramas, possibly because of their dollhouse quality. In fact, an unfinished dollhouse that Tee was working on at the time of her death is on display. The museum stages eight special exhibits annually and conducts monthly workshops. The museum is open year-round; call for days and hours. It is handicapped-accessible. The Tee Ridder Museum is located on the grounds of the Nassau County Museum of Art, above; the fee includes same-day admission to both museums.

CEDARMERE
Bryant Avenue
Roslyn
☎ 516-571-8130
Free admission

> *It has always seemed to me Bryant, more than any*
> *other American, had the power to suck in the air of*
> *spring, to put it into his song, to breathe it forth*
> *again... never a wasted word...*
>
> — Walt Whitman

William Cullen Bryant (1794-1878) lived in Roslyn for
35 years. He is more or less forgotten, yet his achieve-
ments are remarkable. Millions who read the *New York
Post* would be astonished to learn that Bryant was editor of its predecessor, the *Evening Post*, for more than
three decades. Students of American literature still
read his best known poem, *Thanatopsis*, published in
about 1815. In the 1830s he was regarded as the leading American poet.

A passionate botanist, Bryant wrote articles for the
Post and lobbied extensively for "extensive pleasure
ground for shade and recreation" in New York City. The
original Bryant property included a farmhouse, a mill
building, and two ponds. Across Old Northern Boulevard lay farmlands and orchards. His estate, overlooking Hempstead Harbor, ultimately grew to 200 acres
and was called Cedarmere for the cedar trees around
the pond. The grounds were designed by Frederick Law
Olmsted, architect of New York's Central Park. Today's
site covers seven acres, and includes the house, pond,
bridge, ice house and tool shed. On Sundays in spring
and summer Cedarmere is the site of concerts, lectures,
old-fashioned games and guided tours of the gardens
and gothic mill.

Cedarmere is open from May through October, Saturday and Sunday, 1-5pm. To get here, take the LIE to
Exit 39N and turn left onto Glen Cove Road. Continue
to the third traffic light past Northern Boulevard.
Make a left under the railroad trestle, then another left

at the stop sign onto Bryant Avenue. Bear left at the traffic light and go another .4 mile to the north parking lot on your right.

TEMPLE BETH SHALOM JUDAICA MUSEUM
401 Roslyn Road
Roslyn Heights
☎ 516-621-2288

The teaching of Judaism is generally done from the pulpit, and Jews have always associated the religion with words. But art also teaches us about Judaism, as this museum so beautifully demonstrates. Fine silver objects as well as calligraphy and carvings speak volumes.

The exhibits are devoted to Jewish holidays and change three times a year. Informative text explains the meaning behind each display. We visited on a Sunday in winter, when the exhibit covered Purim and Passover, and the sweet sound of singing wafted from the Hebrew school.

This exhibit focused on a 50th-anniversary gift to the congregation of a Tree of Life shtender, the simple lectern used for study and prayer. A receptacle for ritual objects of Jewish practice, it has been largely overlooked. The artist saw in the shtender a work of art in itself, embossing a tree of life motif into natural wood.

The synagogue is right off Northern State Parkway West, Exit 29 (Roslyn Road). Admission is free and the museum is handicapped-accessible. Open Monday through Thursday, 9am-5pm; and Friday and Sunday, 9am-1pm (closed Saturday).

SAGAMORE HILL NATIONAL HISTORIC SITE
Sagamore Hill Road
Oyster Bay
☎ 516-922-4447
www.nps.gov/sahi
Admission $5, by tour only

No trip to Long Island is complete without a visit to the beloved home of its most famous figure. The 23-room mansion looks much as it did when Roosevelt lived there with his second wife and six children. Every effort has been made to re-establish its historic appearance; today, Sagamore Hill is painted "TR" blue and gray in keeping with the original colors. Nature can't be controlled, of course. While Roosevelt could see the bay from his window, we cannot. Trees now block the view, "an unwelcome contribution from the birds," our guide lamented. On the other hand, the beautiful copper beech fronting the property was just a seedling in Teddy's time.

Named for a local Indian chief, Sagamore Mohenas, Sagamore was more than a summer White House. It was *the* Roosevelt home, where TR romped with his children and to which he always returned. The day before he died, Roosevelt whispered to his wife, "I wonder if you will ever know how I love Sagamore Hill." When Roosevelt's mother and his first wife, Alice, died within eleven hours of each other – Alice of Bright's disease, an inflammation of the kidneys, two days after giving birth to baby Alice, and his mother of typhoid fever – Roosevelt wrote in his diary, "The light is gone out of my life." Ironically, shortly before dying in his sleep in a sleigh bed next to the nursery, Roosevelt asked someone to "put out the light."

The north room of the three-story Victorian is fixed at 1905, the year it was added to the house. This is the signature room where Teddy's daughter, Ethel, was married, and where he was laid out when he died in 1919. It's the largest room of the house, with a 20-foot ceiling, and it's constructed of American elm and cypress. Roosevelt added this room after his election to a second

Nassau County's North Shore

At least 15 places on Long Island are named for Theodore Roosevelt.

term. It was used for entertaining and is truly a show-place. Animal skins and big-game trophies abound throughout the house, but here elephant tusks are arched over the entranceway and an African cape buf-falo looms above the fireplace. This room is also a re-pository of exotic gifts from emperors and sultans.

The upstairs gun room is where Teddy retreated for privacy in a house full of kids and visits from world leaders. An avid reader and author of 38 histories and biographies, he may have typed his manuscripts on the small typewriter, a gift from Douglas MacArthur when he was chairman of Remington Corporation – it's a real relic! One doubts that he sat in the chair made of steer horns, though.

The mansion has a wheel-chair ramp to the first floor only.

The Theodore Roosevelt Association purchased the man-sion and surrounding 83 acres after Edith died. In 1963, the National Park Service took over. Across the field is the **Old Orchard Museum**, where you can watch a 20-minute video on Teddy Roosevelt. The Geor-gian mansion housing the museum was built on an old apple orchard for Theodore Jr., who lived there until his death of a heart attack during World War II. The house is being renovated and new exhibits are planned.

Before the turnoff for Sagamore Hill, you'll see a gravel parking lot for **Theodore Roosevelt Sanctuary** and **Youngs Memorial Cemetery**. The gravesite, behind a black wrought-iron fence, is on a hill overlooking Oys-ter Bay. Park your car and climb the 26 steps to the resting place of our 26th president and his second wife, Edith Kermit Carow Roosevelt (1861-1948). A burial ground since 1658, the cemetery is named for Thomas Youngs, whose original house served as a home to nine successive generations of the Youngs family. The grounds are open at 9am daily.

The Theodore Roosevelt Sanctuary, 134 Cove Road, ☎ 516-922-3200, cares for injured birds, provides habi-tat advice and educates the public. It runs a spring camp and has nature walks led by its naturalists. The nature center, gift shop and grounds are open daily un-til 4:30pm. The Sanctuary is part of the National Audu-

bon Society and shares its Web site, www.audubon.org/
affiliate/ny/trs.

To reach Sagamore Hill, take the LIE to Exit 41 and
travel north on Route 106. Turn right at the intersec-
tion with Route 25A; at the third light make a left onto
Cove Road. Travel about 1½ miles and follow signs.
Open year-round, 9:30am-4pm; closed Monday and
Tuesday, October-May.

> ★ TIP
>
> More on the former president can be
> found online at www.theodoreroose-
> velt.org, Web site of the Theodore
> Roosevelt Association, a national or-
> ganization headquartered in Oyster
> Bay.

GARVIES POINT MUSEUM AND PRESERVE
Barry Drive
Glen Cove
☎ 516-571-8010
www.fieldtrip.com (click "New York" and then "Environmental Education")
Admission $2 adults; $1 children five-12

The geology and archeology of Long Island are the focus of this museum, a modern single-story building in
the 62-acre Garvies Point Preserve. Originally part of
the Garvie family estate, the preserve is named for Dr.
Thomas Garvie, a prominent physician who emigrated
from Scotland in 1803 and settled in Glen Cove; the site
has five miles of marked trails plus a special trail for
the visually impaired. Ask for a brochure for the self-
guided walks.

A series of dioramas illustrates Indian life on Long Island, and its glacial history is explained. A replica of an
archeological dig of an Indian burial site illustrates the
variety of artifacts found in each layer. There are also
changing exhibits that present various collections of
minerals, fossils, Indian artifacts and local historical

items. Sixteen different school programs are conducted at the museum. If you're lucky, you'll listen in on a lecture on Long Island geology or nature.

☞ DID YOU KNOW?

Glacial erratics are boulders that are foreign or erratic to this area but were deposited here by a glacier. Three glacial erratics are on the property.

Films on nature topics are shown on weekends at 11am, 2pm and 3pm. Year-round workshops for all ages range from fossil identification to nature walks. The museum also conducts sculpture classes in clay, wood, plaster and stone for adults and children over 13. Summer workshops for children ages five-12 focus on Native American culture.

★ KID FRIENDLY

In the room overlooking Hempstead Harbor is a wigwam with openings for grandma to snap pictures through, and a canoe for kids to climb into.

The site is operated by the Nassau County Department of Recreation and Parks. There is a lovely gift shop, and there are picnic tables on the grounds. To get here, take the LIE to Exit 39N. Turn left at the exit and when road becomes Glen Cove Bypass bear left at the fork. Continue past the police station and post office until you face the firehouse. Turn right, and at third light turn left and follow the signs to the museum; it is 23.4 miles from the Throgs Neck Bridge. The museum is partially wheelchair-accessible. Open year-round, Tuesday-Sunday, 10am-4pm.

THE HOLOCAUST MEMORIAL & EDUCATIONAL CENTER OF NASSAU COUNTY

Welwyn Preserve
100 Crescent Beach Road
Glen Cove
☎ 516-571-8040
www.holocaust-nassau.org
Free admission

No matter how many museums are devoted to the Holocaust, there are always more harrowing and heroic stories to tell. Here we read accounts of survivors who faced insurmountable odds, view portraits of children who perished, and read of the persecution against humanity. The exhibits include photographs, sculptures, and paintings that memorialize all Jews and are not specific to Long Island. But it's the art created by local schoolchildren that is especially moving, such as a cardboard train beside clothes of the condemned.

This educational museum presents lectures, offers group tours, and sponsors literary compositions in Long Island schools, all dedicated to honoring the six million who perished and to eliminating prejudice. The museum's reference library stocks thousands of books and is staffed Monday, Wednesday and Friday, 10am-4pm.

The center is located in the magnificent 204-acre Welwyn Preserve, and has several nature trails. The Georgian mansion, completed in 1910, has not been altered, and its wood-paneled walls and shiny wood floors are in stark contrast to the somber theme. It was originally the summer home of Harold Pratt, one of seven children of Charles Pratt, partner in Standard Oil and founder of Pratt Institute. In later years, the building had various tenants, and was vacant and neglected when a group of Holocaust survivors decided to create a memorial center. It opened in 1994, is wheelchair-accessible, and is the property of Nassau County. An award-winning garden once graced the grounds; the center's newest initiative is the replanting of a children's memorial garden.

Welwyn means "happiness" in Welsh.

Nassau County's North Shore

To get here, take the LIE to Exit 39N and follow Glen Cove Road north to where it meets Route 107. Follow 107 north to the end. Turn right at the firehouse onto Brewster Street, then turn left onto Dosoris Lane (fourth traffic light). Turn left at New Woods Road, and make the second right onto Crescent Beach Road, then an immediate right into the Welwyn Preserve.

COE HALL AT PLANTING FIELDS ARBORETUM
Oyster Bay-Glen Cove Road
Oyster Bay
☎ 516-922-9210
www.plantingfields.org
Admission is $5 adults; $3.50 seniors; $1 children six-12; there is also a $5 parking fee at Arboretum gate

Planting Fields, a National Historic Register property, hosts more than 200 diverse events annually.

The only way to see Coe Hall is by taking the guided tour, and it's well worth the fee. The 65-room "country house" was built in the Tudor Revival style, emulating the architectural mode popular during the reign of England's Elizabeth I. Our impeccably informed guide, Gabe, spoke about the architecture and history of the house, the Coe family, and the English monarchy during the Elizabethan period. A 19th-century stained-glass panel of Elizabeth I adorns the vestibule.

Coe Hall, built in 1918-1921, has typical Tudor elements, such as half-timbering, a steeply pitched roof and clustered chimneys. We learned that each block in the Indiana limestone façade was hand-dressed by Scottish stonemasons; that the house has 17 fireplaces; that the interior wood is mainly oak; and that 10-15 domestics worked here.

William Robertson Coe was a British-born insurance broker who rose through the ranks to become chairman of the board of Johnson & Higgins, a large marine insurance firm. His second wife, and the only one of his three spouses to bear him children (she had four), was the daughter of a founder of the Standard Oil Company. Mai Rogers Coe loved European culture, spoke fluent French and shared her husband's passion for horticulture and landscape design. Her fine and eclectic tastes are evident throughout the house, from the elegant drawing rooms to the couple's "informal living quarters" – a hunt room with rams' heads, paintings and tapestry, where musicians entertained from the balcony. The entrance hall, designed like a courtyard and centered by a spectacular 17th-century Dutch chandelier, is a far cry from the buffalo breakfast room with décor bordering on kitsch (its massive mural, painted in 1922, reflects Coe's love of the American West).

The famed Olmsted Brothers, whose firm designed New York's Central Park, helped transform the estate into a horticultural showplace. There are several greenhouses; one, the **Camellia Greenhouse**, has the largest camellia collection under glass in the Northeast. The 150-year-old purple beech visible from Coe Hall's second floor guest rooms is one of two that Mai played beneath as a child in Massachusetts. The species is currently in decline, but was a signature plant during the Gold Coast era and was commonly found on grand estates. The trees have massive roots like elephant legs and broad crowns. It's a miracle that even one of Mai's European beeches survived after being barged across Long Island Sound, pushed by a steamroller, and pulled two miles uphill by a team of horses before being placed into frozen ground at the arboretum.

Near the mansion is **Rhododendron Park**, where a sign indicates that Coe collected and planted rare hybrid plants in the 1920s and '30s. Evergreens and flowering trees shade the plants and many are identified. Coe deeded the estate to the people of the State of New York in 1949 – for $1.

☛ DID YOU KNOW?

There are more than 900 species of rhododendrons!

To reach the arboretum, take the LIE to Exit 41N or the Northern State Parkway to Exit 35N. Proceed north on Route 106 and follow into Oyster Bay. Turn left on

Lexington Avenue (Hess station on corner) and look for a partially obscured sign; turn left at the light onto Mill Hill Road, then turn left onto Oyster Bay-Glen Cove Road; take the next right, which is Planting Fields Road. The entrance is on left; the arboretum is 26.2 miles from the Throgs Neck Bridge. Coe Hall is open for guided tours daily, April through September. The first floor of the house is wheelchair-accessible.

> ★ TIP
>
> Because Planting Fields Arboretum covers 409 acres of trees, shrubs, gardens and greenhouses, it's not easy to find Coe Hall. Request a map at the admission cottage.

BANFI VINTNERS

Nassau County has only one commercial vineyard and it's not open to the public. A 60-room Elizabethan-style manor house on a 127-acre estate on Cedar Swamp Road in Old Brookville is the world headquarters of **Banfi Vintners**, the leading wine importer in the US and a major producer of premium varietals in Montalcino, Tuscany and Piedmont, Italy. Banfi planted grapes in 1982 on 47 acres of the Old Brookville estate; their Old Brookville Chardonnay, vinified at the cellars of Premium Wine Group in Mattituck, is sold throughout the Metropolitan New York area and retails for about $15 a bottle. For more information, call ☎ 516-626-9200, www.banfivintners.com, www.oldbrookvillechardonnay.com.

Historical Societies & Tours

Port Washington

COW NECK PENINSULA HISTORICAL SOCIETY
336 Port Washington Boulevard
Port Washington
☎ 516-365-9074
www.cowneck.org

The society operates two historic house museums that are on the State and National Registers of Historic Places. In 1967, the society purchased the **Sands-Willets House**, which dates from 1735. Now being restored to its original appearance, it was the family home of Revolutionary War hero Colonel John Sands IV and his six brothers, all of whom were active in the War for Independence. Edmund Willets, a prominent merchant and Quaker, purchased the house in the 1840s and expanded it. His son, Thomas Willets, inherited the house in 1882. A Dutch barn on the property, dating from 1690, holds exhibits of antique tools, carriages, and local memorabilia.

The society also runs tours of the **Thomas Dodge House**, c. 1721, located at 58 Harbor Road, Port Washington – a rare example of an early 18th-century farmhouse on its original site. Several generations of the Dodge family occupied the house until 1991.

Tours of both houses are by appointment. Check the society's Web site for a calendar of events.

Nassau County's North Shore

WHAT'S IN A NAME?

Port Washington is named for our first president. Although Washington never slept here, he did visit in 1790. The surrounding area was originally called Cow Neck until 1857, when residents decided it needed a more dignified name and changed it to Port Washington to commemorate the president's visit.

Roslyn

Picturesque Roslyn rests in a valley and resembles the
hill towns on the Hudson River in Westchester County.
The village's duck pond, gristmill and clock tower serve
to enhance the many restaurants, galleries, antiques
shops and boutiques. Lamb & Rich, the NYC firm of architects that designed Sagamore Hill in Oyster Bay,
created the Roslyn clock tower. A gift to Roslyn in 1895
from the family of Ellen E. Ward in her memory, the 44-
foot stone tower is the centerpiece of 37 structures built
between 1690 and 1865.

HISTORIC SITE

Trinity Episcopal Church in Roslyn is on
the National Register of Historic Places. The
church and its original parish house (1906-9)
were designed by noted architect Stanford
White of McKim, Mead &White, with English
medieval-style architectural features, such as
soaring wooden trusses. Its two west transept
windows were made by Tiffany Studios.

The **Roslyn Landmark Society**, ☎ 561-621-3040,
runs tours of the **Van Nostrand-Starkins House**,
221 Main Street, on Saturdays and Sundays, 1-4pm,
from June through October. The house, dating from
about 1680, belonged to a blacksmith and is the oldest
surviving building in Nassau County. Each year, on the
first Saturday in June, a number of Roslyn's privately
owned historic houses are opened by their occupants
for self-directed tours. For a walking tour guide, contact the **Roslyn Village Hall**, ☎ 516-621-1961. To
reach the village of Roslyn, take Northern Boulevard
east. After passing Port Washington Boulevard/Sear-
ingtown Road (before you reach the viaduct), bear right
onto Old Northern Boulevard. Continue downhill and
bear right into the village.

★ FAMOUS FACES

Author Michael Crichton grew up in
Roslyn.

Oyster Bay

The Oyster Bay Historical Society is headquartered in
the c. 1720 **Earle-Wightman House**, 20 Summit
Street, Oyster Bay, ☎ 516-922-5032, www.oysterbay-
history.org, where it maintains a museum and research
library containing 750 volumes, 1,000 manuscripts and
1,000 photographs relating to the military, maritime
and religious history of Oyster Bay. As the 19th century
began, the house belonged to two successive Baptist
ministers, including the Reverend Charles S. Wight-
man. In 1966 the house was donated to the town for the
society's use. The museum's collections reflect the history of Oyster Bay from Colonial times to the present.
The public is invited to visit the museum and library
Tuesday-Friday, 10am-2pm; Saturday, 9am-1pm; and
Sunday, 1-4pm; or at other times (except Monday) by
appointment. Admission is $1.50. The society also pub-
lishes a quarterly magazine, *The Freeholder*, which is
available at many museums and historic sites on Long
Island.

Nassau County's North Shore

Parks & Preserves

CHRISTOPHER MORLEY PARK
Searingtown Road
Roslyn-North Hills
☎ 516-571-8110

This 98-acre county park is designed for the athlete. It
boasts three swimming pools; a playground; handball,
basketball, volleyball and tennis courts; softball fields;
and an ice rink. The fee for two hours of skating is $10
for non-resident adults, $6 for children. The park also
has picnic areas, a boat basin for model boats and a dog
run.

Next to the dog run is Morley's "Knothole," a small rustic cabin built in the mid-1930s, with the Latin inscription written by philosopher Erasmus, *Assiduus sis in Bibliotheca quae tibi paradisi loco est,* which, loosely translated, means, "Working assiduously in the library is paradise." Inside are the poet/author's studio desk, furniture and bookcases. Morley's friend Buckminster Fuller designed the dymaxion (prefabricated) bathroom. The Knothole is open for viewing Sundays only, 1-4:45pm, June-October; admission is free. For more information about the Knothole, ☎ 516-571-8113.

Take the LIE to Exit 36N and go north on Searingtown Road; the park is less than a half-mile past the golf course; open year-round.

CHRISTOPHER DARLINGTON MORLEY

Morley was already an established man of letters when he moved to Roslyn Heights in 1920 at age 30; he lived there until his death in 1957. A Rhodes Scholar, he was a columnist for the *New York Evening Post* and co-founder of the *Saturday Review of Literature*, which he wrote for and edited for 17 years. Morley is probably best remembered for his sensational novel *Kitty Foyle*, which made the bestseller lists in 1939 and 1940 and was the basis of a movie starring Ginger Rogers. A stream-of-consciousness narrative about a working-class girl facing a critical decision, it was shocking for its time and didn't play well in certain parts of Roslyn. Syndicated gossip columnist Liz Smith said the book changed her life, inspiring her to move from Texas to New York many years ago.

MUTTONTOWN PRESERVE

Muttontown Lane
East Norwich
☎ 516-571-8500
www.fieldtrip.com; click New York and look for Environmental Education/Nature Centers

Nassau County's largest preserve covers 550 acres and includes 10 miles of marked nature trails. Twenty miles of bridle paths are open year-round (although there are no horse rentals here, the parking area off Route 106, north of Muttontown Road, is adjacent to the equestrian practice rings and can accommodate horse vans as well as cars). Pick up maps for self-guided trail walks and brochures on local flora and fauna at the practice rings.

A 100-acre parcel within the preserve houses the **Bill Paterson Nature Center** on Muttontown Lane, off Route 25A in East Norwich. Paterson, a native of Baldwin who died about a decade ago, was supervisor of Muttontown Preserve from 1968 to 1992. During that time, he developed hiking trails, prepared nature brochures, began insect and plant collections, recorded the changes in bird populations and taught the skills of birding to others. Frank Hurley, a beekeeper hobbyist, has stepped into his shoes. He'll bring in the beehive for anyone who asks, and walkers are welcome to join him and his volunteers on a trek through the magnificent preserve. "We have a lot of fun here," he said. Monthly walks, held February through October, focus on geology, bird-watching and nature; some are free and others have a $3 fee. Registration is required. The preserve and the center are open 9:30am-4:30pm, but Hurley is there part-time so make sure to call for a schedule of talks and walks.

Health & Beauty

Fitness Centers

All clubs listed are open daily, year-round.

New York Sports of Great Neck has two locations, at 15 Barstow Road, Great Neck, ☎ 516-829-2582, and 54 Ira Road, Syosset, ☎ 516-496-9800. Both have a day fee of $25 and provide childcare at $4 per hour; www.nysc.com.

30 Minute Fitness, 552 Middle Neck Road, Great Neck, ☎ 516-466-8410, offers one-on-one fitness with a personal trainer for a half-hour. Call for fees.

North Shore Fitness Clubs, 38 Great Neck Road, Great Neck, ☎ 516-773-4888. Full-service club is downstairs in Waldbaum's complex. Day fee, $25. Childcare, $3 per hour.

Two facilities are in the same building at 770 Middle Neck Road, Great Neck, but neither provides childcare. **Something Physical** offers classes at $20/single or packages of 10 ($130) or 20 ($240) with optional use of the equipment; ☎ 516-487-0425. **Kings Point Fitness** has exercise machines but no classes; day fee, $20; ☎ 516-773-8778.

Nubest Personal Fitness Gym, 1482 Northern Boulevard, Manhasset, ☎ 516-627-3377, www.nubestpersonalfitness.com. Full-service fitness facility. Day fee, $20. No childcare.

Fitness & Racquetball, 10 Gordon Drive, Syosset, ☎ 516-496-3100, www.sportimetfm.com, has 12 racquetball courts and full-service fitness facility. Day fee for all services, $30.

Dany Holdstein Two Worlds, 340 Wheatley Plaza, Greenvale, ☎ 516-484-6604, is not a health club and has no membership fees or dues. Rather, it is devoted to personal service and offers a wide range of classes for various proficiency levels as well as one-on-one training. No childcare; call for fees.

Island Sports Club, 4 Cedar Swamp Road, opposite the LIRR station in Glen Cove, ☎ 516-759-1700. Complete fitness facility. Day fee, $20. Childcare is free. This company's other facility is Hauppauge Sports Club; see page 208.

YMCA at Glen Cove, 125 Dosoris Lane, Glen Cove, ☎ 516-671-8270 (Ext. 12 for front desk), www.ymca-li.org. Guest fee (with member only) $20. Childcare punch-card is $40 for 20 visits. Six-lane Olympic pool and outdoor pool complex. Open daily; closes at 2pm on Sunday.

Gold's Gym, 235-C Robbins Lane, Syosset, ☎ 516-933-1111, www.goldsgym.com. Day fee, $15. Free childcare. Open Monday-Friday.

Day Spas

Spa Med, 43 Glen Cove Road, Greenvale, ☎ 516-777-2633. Skin and massage therapy by appointment. Open daily.

Spa D'Est, 360 Wheatley Plaza, Greenvale, ☎ 516-484-8228. Full spa and hair salon by appointment. Closed Monday.

Aspen Day Spa, 10 Cedar Swamp Road, Glen Cove, ☎ 516-671-1632. Face and body treatments by appointment. Closed Sunday.

Lorilee's Aromatherapy, 21 West Main Street, Oyster Bay, ☎ 516-922-6362, www.lorilee.com. Face and body treatments by appointment. Closed Sunday.

Spa & Wellness Center, 1035 Oyster Bay Road, East Norwich, ☎ 516-624-7957. Face and body treatments by appointment; yoga and personal training available. Closed Sunday.

Recreation

Boating

Cruises & Boat Rentals

Lady Liberty Cruises, ☎ 516-486-3057, www.lady-libertycruises.com, has four-hour dinner and brunch cruises to the Statue of Liberty. Cruises depart from Manhasset Bay Marina in Port Washington, from May through October. Reservations are required. Dinner cruises are $79 to $89 per person; brunch cruises are $59 for adults and $39 for children; charters are also available.

Sigsbee Sailing Center, 24 Matinecock Avenue, Port Washington, ☎ 516-767-0971, has sunset cruises, Fridays, May-August, and also offers half- and full-day sailboat rentals, May-October.

Haven Marina, 12-20 Matinecock Avenue, Port Washington, ☎ 516-883-0937, rents sailboats and canoes and offers sailing lessons. Open daily, May-October.

Marinas

Brewer Capri Marina, 15 Orchard Beach Boulevard, Manorhaven, ☎ 516-883-7800, www.byy.com, is one of several marinas run by Brewer Yacht Yard. Storage, dockage, fuel, marine store, pool, showers, lounges, laundry. Open year-round. There is also a restaurant, DiMaggio's on the Bay, ☎ 516-944-5300.

> ★ TIP
>
> Tobay Marina, Harry Tappen Marina and Theodore Roosevelt Marina are operated by the Town of Oyster Bay. Visit the town's Web site, www.oysterbaytown.com, click on Town Parks, Beaches & Facilities, then on Launching Ramps, Boat Basins & Marinas.

W and W Marine, 1 Orchard Beach Boulevard, Manorhaven, ☎ 516-944-9200. Storage, dockage, electric, restrooms, boat sales). Open year-round. There is also a restaurant here, the Harbor Inn.

Toms Point Marina, 1 Sagamore Hill Drive, Port Washington, ☎ 516-883-6630. Storage, dockage, electric, showers, laundry. Open year-round.

Harry Tappen Boat Basin, Shore Road, Glenwood Landing, ☎ 516-674-7100. Fuel, pool, outdoor showers, beach, playground, picnic. Open mid-April to Labor Day.

Brewer Yacht Yard, 128 Shore Road, Glen Cove, ☎ 516-671-5563, www.byy.com. Winter storage, fuel, electric, showers, pool. Open daily, year-round.

Jude Thaddeus Glen Cove Marina, 76 Shore Road, Glen Cove, ☎ 516-759-3129. Winter storage, fuel, showers. Open daily, year-round. A restaurant, Steamboat Landing, ☎ 516-759-3921, is open year-round; closed Monday in the off-season.

Oyster Bay Marine Center, 5 Bay Avenue, Oyster Bay, ☎ 516-922-6331, www.obmc.com. Dockage, storage, electric, fuel, snack bar on weekends, marine store. Closed Sunday in winter. The pier is on Oyster Bay Harbor and is a picturesque place for a short stroll. Follow Route 106 (that road becomes South Street) to end and turn left at arrow. Bear right at fork into marina. Open year-round.

Theodore Roosevelt Park, off South Street, Oyster Bay, ☎ 516-624-6202, has a boat basin and marina, beach, picnic area, tennis, restrooms, and a snack bar in summer. Open mid-April to mid-November.

West Marine, 621 Jericho Turnpike, Syosset, ☎ 516-364-4330, or ☎ 800-BOATING, www.westmarine.com, has 240 stores throughout the United States. Carries everything for the boater: fishing supplies, electronics, apparel, footwear, books, videos, charts. Open year-round.

Biking

The Long Island Bicycle Club, founded in 1975, has 305 members. Organized rides are scheduled every Saturday and Sunday, mainly on the North Shore, with riding groups geared for all abilities. Off-Long Island weekends are only open to members, who also engage in LIBC-sponsored social events. Non-members are welcome on a day bike ride but must bring their own helmets. Annual membership is $20. Call Brenda Walker at ☎ 516-285-4406, or Bill Selsky at ☎ 516-379-4484, for more information; www.bicyclelongisland.org/libc.

North Shore Cyclery & Fitness, 3 Northern Boulevard, Great Neck (on the city line between Great Neck and Little Neck), ☎ 516-482-1193, www.northshorecycle.com. The family-owned business also sells fitness equipment. Open daily, year-round. Member of American Bicycle Centers.

Port Washington Cyclery, 999 Port Washington Boulevard, Port Washington, ☎ 516-883-8243, is open daily, year-round. Member of American Bicycle Centers.

Bikeworks, 7 Northern Boulevard, Greenvale, one block west of Glen Cove Road, ☎ 516-484-4422, is open year-round, daily, except Wednesday.

Visentin Bike Pro Shop, 51 Pine Hollow Road and Route 106, Oyster Bay, ☎ 516-922-2150, is celebrating almost 40 years in business. Open daily most of the year; closed Sundays in winter.

The Bicycle Planet, 540 Jericho Turnpike, Syosset, one block west of Route 135, ☎ 516-364-4434, www.thebicycleplanet.com, is open daily, year-round.

Hiking

The mission of the **Nassau Hiking & Outdoor Club** (NHOC), ☎ 516-483-8606, www.nhoc.org, is to enjoy and teach respect for the outdoors. Its more than 300 members hike, bike, ride horseback, camp, and/or picnic together. Hikes are on Long Island, in Westchester, Connecticut and upstate New York. Membership is $15 per year for an individual, $20 for a family; prospective members may participate in one activity with no fee.

Tennis

Port Washington Tennis Academy, 100 Harbor Road in Port Washington, ☎ 516-883-6425, www.pwta.com, has 17 indoor courts and a quarter-mile running track. Junior programs run in two five-month sessions from September-February and February-June, and two five-week sessions in summer. Adult clinics are for a month at a time.

Sportime, ☎ 888-NY-TENNIS, is a chain of multi-sport facilities with all locations providing free childcare. They have two facilities on the North Shore:

Sportime at 1 Landing Road, Roslyn, ☎ 516-484-9222, has tennis only, with 12 indoor Har-Tru courts. Day fee, $56.

Sportime at Jericho Turnpike & Underhill Boulevard, Syosset, ☎ 516-364-2727, has fitness and tennis facilities. There is a $15 day fee for the fitness facility, with up to four visits allowed; a tennis guest is free with a member for the first visit and $15 thereafter.

Woodbury Racquet & Fitness Club, 1 Jericho Turnpike, Woodbury, ☎ 516-367-3100, www.woodburytennis.com. Separate memberships at tennis and fitness facility. Five Har-Tru tennis courts. Day fee, $37-$57 per hour for court. Day fee at fitness club, $10. Childcare is free.

Golf

Christopher Morley Golf Course, Searingtown Road, Roslyn, ☎ 516-571-8120. This nine-hole, par 30 course is a good beginner course. Walking allowed. Soft spikes not required. Open mid-March to late December; closed Monday.

Harbor Links Golf Course, 1 Fairway Drive, Port Washington, ☎ 516-767-4816, has two courses: an 18-hole, par 72 and a nine-hole, par 31. Carts mandatory on weekends and soft spikes required. Pro shop, putting area, lessons, golf school, soccer fields, snack bar. Open March-December.

Glen Cove Golf Course, Lattingtown Road, Glen Cove, ☎ 516-671-0033. Resident and non-resident players must obtain a permit from this 18-hole, par 66/67 semi-private course. Walking is allowed. Lessons, rentals, putting area, pro shop, bar, snack bar and restaurant. Open year-round, but on weekends only January-March. The Soundview Restaurant, ☎ 516-676-9781, is open for lunch and dinner year-round.

Town of Oyster Bay Golf Course, Southwoods Road, Woodbury, ☎ 516-677-5960; pro shop, ☎ 516-364-1180. Created from an old estate, this 121-acre 18-hole, par 70 course and clubhouse are quite hilly and beautiful. Non-residents are welcome but fees are higher and town residents have first priority. The course is open Tuesday through Sunday; lessons are available. There is a snack bar, putting area, rentals and restaurant (Singleton's, ☎ 516-921-5707. Open daily, year-round.

Shop Till You Drop

Great Neck Plaza, ☎ 516-829-1301, www.greatneck-plaza.net, has 250 shops and restaurants along Middle Neck Road. A large indoor parking garage for shoppers offers free parking on weekends after 3pm. There is also outdoor municipal parking with four-hour meters. Great Neck Plaza ends at Kensington Village, where there is a park with a metal giraffe. For a free shopping and dining guide, call or check on-line.

 TIP

The best venues for antiques browsing are Port Washington, Manhasset and Huntington.

★ FAMOUS FACES

Great Neck has every reason to be proud of resident Sarah Hughes, Gold Medalist in figure skating at the 2002 Winter Olympics. A homecoming parade was held in her honor on March 10, 2002 along Middle Neck Road, which was renamed "Sarah Hughes Way" for the day. Around 60,000 fans turned out.

Miracle Mile, on Northern Boulevard in Manhasset, has high-end stores such as Tiffany's and Brooks Brothers. All the stores open daily at 10am.

Book Mark Café, at One East Main Street in Oyster Bay, ☎ 516-922-0036, is a combination bookstore/restaurant (see page 79). The child-friendly bookstore has a room with child-sized upholstered chairs and a toybox. They have both new and used books for adults.

After Dark

Performing Arts

JEANNE RIMSKY THEATER
Landmark on Main Street
232 Main Street
Roslyn
☎ 516-767-1384 (office, Monday-Friday, 9am-5pm)
☎ 516-767-6444 (box office)
www.LandmarkonMainStreet.org

The Landmark building, which is listed on the national, state and local registers of historic sites, houses the Jeanne Rimsky Theater (with 500 newly reupholstered seats); this facility has played host to such musical talents as Marilyn Horne, Lainie Kazan, Richie Havens, Skitch Henderson and Marvin Hamlisch. The season runs from September through June; ticket prices for concerts and recitals are $20-$35.

In 2001, the **Landmark Family Theater** opened with its first season of live theatrical performances. The ticket price for children's theater is $10-$12, except for special events like Broadway Kids when the price is $20. The Landmark is also planning a program of lectures, most of which will be free and open to the public. The building also houses a children's center, teen center, gymnasium and meeting room. All are available for rental.

TILLES CENTER FOR THE PERFORMING ARTS

CW Post Campus of Long Island University
Route 25A
Brookville
☎ 516-299-3100
www.tillescenter.org

The New York Philharmonic and the Alvin Ailey American Dance Theater are among the prominent artistic organizations that have appeared here. Tilles Center Productions, founded in 1981, has also performed at Lincoln Center, Carnegie Hall and Symphony Space, and co-produces New York City's annual *Messiah* performances.

The center's 2,200-seat auditorium and 491-seat recital hall are used for chamber music concerts, cabaret, and children's' theater. These sites also serve as the theatrical home for other Long Island cultural organizations. Recent initiatives have featured an expanded jazz series and folk music festival.

GRACE AUDITORIUM
Cold Spring Harbor Laboratory, Main Campus
One Bungtown Road
Laurel Hollow
☎ 516-367-8455
www.cshl.org/events

Like Brookhaven National Laboratory (see page 276), Cold Spring Harbor Laboratory (on the water across from the village of Cold Spring Harbor) is a world-renowned research institution. Its director, Nobel laureate James Watson, along with Francis Crick, discovered the structure of the DNA molecule. Cold Spring Harbor Laboratory sponsors a Harbor Concert Series from April to October. The Saturday concerts are held in the Grace Auditorium on the laboratory's 107.2-acre campus, and feature classical and jazz soloists; the season subscription price is $40.

James Watson, Cold Spring Harbor Lab's director, was recently knighted by the Queen of England.

BE A FRIEND OF THE ARTS
Friends of the Arts, ☎ 516-922-0061, www.friendsofthearts.com, sponsors the following performing arts programs: the Long Island Summer Festival; Jazz Festival; Beethoven Festival; and Concerts at Coe Hall chamber music series. All are held at Planting Fields Arboretum State Park in Oyster Bay. **Children's Carousel**, a puppet theater, is at the Landmark building (see page 61). Friends of the Arts also sponsors **ArtReach** programs for Long Island students in grades K-12.

LONG ISLAND FILM & TV FOUNDATION
305 North Service Road
Dix Hills
Nassau County, ☎ 516-571-3168
Suffolk County, ☎ 631-421-7006
www.longislandfilm.com

The mission of this organization is to promote Long Island as a choice shooting location for films, commercials, documentaries and TV programs. To further its efforts to assist and honor the independent filmmaker, the Foundation sponsors film expos and awards ceremonies showcasing local talent; expedites the procurement of permits; and serves as a resource arena for Long Island-based screenwriters, directors, actors, technicians, designers and producers. Meetings are open to professional and non-professional film and video personnel and the general public. The organization also publishes the annual 30-page *Nassau County Film & TV Resource Guide*. The Foundation is currently involved in the construction of a motion picture production studio to be known as the Long Island Film & TV Production Studios.

Bars & Clubs

NORTHSHORE CAFE
36 Glen Head Road
Glen Head
☎ 516-676-9839

The Giraffe Room and Fiddleheads, both listed under Best Places to Eat, also feature entertainment.

This upscale restaurant and gathering place is open for lunch and dinner, Tuesday-Saturday, with live music Thursday and Friday. Closed Sunday and Monday. Thursday evenings generally feature cabaret, Fridays usually offer R&B or classic rock. No cover; over-30 crowd.

THE LIVING ROOM
16 Middle Neck Road
Great Neck
☎ 516-504-7566

The Living Room is open daily, for lunch and dinner (bar menu). The lounge is under new management but as it now stands, Thursday and Friday feature a DJ and Saturday jukebox music. Gentlemen pay a $5 cover on Thursday nights. The crowd is 23 and up.

☞ DID YOU KNOW?

The giraffe is the symbol of Great Neck – for obvious reasons.

ECLIPSE
6550 Jericho Turnpike
Commack
☎ 516-858-9200

Open Thursday-Saturday. Thursday there's a $12 cover; Friday $10; and Saturday $15. Age of crowd varies according to entertainment. No food is served.

Festivals & Events

August

Planting Fields Arboretum in Oyster Bay plays host to a **Jazz Festival** the first weekend in August. The event, produced by Friends of the Arts, ☎ 516-922-0061, www.friendsofthearts.com, showcases exciting jazz artists; past performers have included Branford Marsalis, Thelonious Monk and Lou Rawls. Tickets range from $22-$37.

September

Sands Point Preserve (see page 35) hosts the annual **Medieval Festival** over two weekends in September. The festival features exhibits, musical performances, fashion shows, puppet shows, archery and jousting. 95 Middle Neck Road, Sands Point, ☎ 516-571-7900. Call for admission and schedule information.

October

Weekend Oyster Festival, Central Business District, Oyster Bay, ☎ 516-624-8082, www.oysterbay.org, features arts and crafts, historic boat exhibit, oyster eating and shucking contests, 5K run. Held the weekend after Columbus Day.

Best Places to Stay

All the accommodations listed below are open year-round. Hotels that are geared to business travelers usually have copious seating areas in the guest rooms. The Long Island Marriott has tables that double as desks, and the Harrison Conference Center has two telephones per room. More often than not, room amenities include an iron and ironing board and a hair dryer.

ACCOMMODATIONS PRICE SCALE
Price scale is based on the cost of a double room, two people per room, in season, and does not include the 11.3% hotel tax.
Inexpensive . . . . under $130
Moderate . . . . $130-$200
Expensive . . . . $201-$300
Deluxe . . . . more than $300

Great Neck

INN AT GREAT NECK
30 Cuttermill Road
☎ 516-773-2000
www.innatgreatneck.com
Expensive to Deluxe

Inn at Great Neck is a member of Small Luxury Hotels of the World.

Most people don't think of Great Neck, a wealthy community close to the Queens/Nassau border, as a place to visit. Yet this small luxury hotel in the heart of town could easily be a destination in itself. Complete with an excellent restaurant, the **Giraffe Room** (see *Best Pla-*

ces to Eat, page 74), and surrounded by some 300 stores, a movie theater and several eateries, the 85-room hotel is an ideal place to spend a weekend even if you stay put. It has a small exercise room and 35 complimentary videotapes to keep you and/or your kids entertained (the tapes do go fast, however, so plan ahead). The hotel is also an ideal location if you are visiting the Gold Coast mansions.

The hotel's pleasant and efficient staff and Art Deco décor evoke an era when luxury was only enjoyed by a fortunate few. The guest rooms, including two designed for the handicapped, are spacious and comfortable, and the oversized marble bathrooms are especially luxurious. Four of the 15 suites have whirlpool baths that are well worth the extra bucks. Regardless, all rooms feature amenities such as minibars, PC capability, CD stereo, and vanity alcoves. With four meeting and banquet rooms, The Inn at Great Neck can accommodate groups of up to 350 people for business meetings, social functions and private parties.

The hotel is two blocks from the train station. By car, take the LIE to Exit 33N and turn left at the light onto Lakeville Road (which becomes Middle Neck Road). Continue to village of Great Neck. At the intersection with the railroad on the right and Fleet Bank on the left, turn left onto Cuttermill Road. The hotel is the third building on the left; it's only 11 miles from the Triboro Bridge.

THE ANDREW
75 North Station Plaza
Great Neck
☎ 516-482-2900
Moderate

A boutique hotel is characterized as one that offers personalized service, superior location, high-concept design, a spare but glamorous lobby, and a gracious residential quality. It generally has 250 rooms or less.

The Andrew, named for the owner's first grandchild, is Long Island's first boutique hotel and fits the description to a T. The 62-room hotel in the center of Great Neck has replaced the neglected Bayberry-Great Neck after an $8 million renovation, and sleek design and dedication to service are its hallmark.

In the 1980s owner Philip Pilevsky, a Long Islander, opened the original trendy boutique hotel and its successors in Manhattan, the Paramount and the Royalton, with renowned partners Steve Rubell and Ian Schrager. More recently, Pilevsky's Philips Hotel Group opened Bryant Park Hotel overlooking Bryant Park and the New York Public Library, and, due to open in the summer of 2002, the Shore Club, a 320-room resort and spa in Miami's South Beach.

The Andrew combines the best of the big city with the comfort of a small town. The lobby of the four-story hotel is small but elegant. The residential quality is evident once you step across its limestone floors and are greeted with welcoming hellos from the front desk. New York architect Shamir Shah was chosen to design the Andrew because of his "modern design sensibility... unique approach to luxurious minimalism and restrained elegance." The angular furnishings are accented in tones of beige and black, the beds have leather paneled headboards and silk dust ruffles, and the bathroom cabinets are marble-topped. In-room amenities include bathrobes, safe deposit boxes, and a wet bar in the suites; refrigerators are available on request. The TVs come equipped with a DVD/CD player and the hotel's DVD library has 43 selections. A continental breakfast is served in a room that doubles as a catering space for parties of up to 150 people.

Located across from the railroad station, the Andrew is within walking distance of the Great Neck Plaza stores (see page 60). Guests of the hotel are entitled to use the facilities of New York Sports (see page 54), diagonally across the street. The hotel's parking garage is for guests' vehicles.

★ FAMOUS FACES

Great Neck is on a peninsula with nine villages, each with its own government. All were incorporated between 1911 and 1931 and have been home to such celebrities as Groucho Marx, Oscar Hammerstein, Paul Newman, and Alan King. F. Scott Fitzgerald was also a resident and used the peninsula's town of Kings Point as the inspiration for West Egg in his classic novel *The Great Gatsby*.

Glen Cove

HARRISON CONFERENCE CENTER
a/k/a Harrison House
Dosoris Lane
Glen Cove
☎ 516-671-6400
www.harrisonglencove.com
www.harrisonconference.com
Inexpensive to Moderate

Many years ago, our cousins (non-Long Islanders) were married at the Harrison Conference Center – a Georgian mansion once called The Manor and considered by one reviewer to be "one of the 12 best country houses in America." The wedding guests had big, comfortable rooms and food stations steps from the door. I remember thinking this was the most beautiful setting for a wedding I'd ever seen. It's no wonder Harrison hosts weddings every weekend, sometimes morning, noon and night – but never more than one at a time. More recently, a business magazine hailed the Harrison as one of the 10 best conference centers in America.

Fast forward to 2002 and little has changed, except now tourists are encouraged to share in the amenities

The Harrison Center is handicapped-accessible.

once reserved for businessmen and brides. The room rate includes a lavish buffet breakfast and the ever-present fruit, cookies and drinks.

Built in 1910, the Manor was home to John and Ruth Pratt. An executive with the Standard Oil Company, John had four brothers with estates in the area. George's Tudor Gothic Killenworth is now the Russian consulate; Frederic's Poplar Hill is a nursing home; Herbert's The Braes is the Webb Institute of Naval Architecture; and Harold's neo-Georgian mansion is part of the Welwyn Preserve (see Holocaust Museum, page 45). Ruth Baker Pratt was a Republican Congresswoman representing the Silk Stocking District of Manhattan; she lived at the Manor until her death in 1965. Harrison Conference Services acquired the estate in 1967; it's now part of Hilton Hotels Corporation.

Harrison Conference Center is a member of the International Association of Conference Centers.

Secluded on a 55-acre estate, the Harrison melds modern comforts with gracious living. The ambience is designed for privacy. The health club is reserved for guest use, and The Pub (see below) is tucked away on the third floor. With 200 guest rooms, four suites and 27 conference rooms, the property is sprawling, so bring your sneakers. You'll need them.

There's a well-equipped gym, outdoor and indoor solar-ium-style pool and whirlpool, racquetball and tennis courts, Ping-Pong table, sauna, steam and massage rooms, jogging trail, and the original two-lane bowling alley – a real curiosity. **The Pub** has cushy seating, game tables, billiards, a jukebox and large screen TVs. Bring the kids; the food is great and inexpensive. It opens at 1pm on weekends and at 5pm weekdays.

Guests are entitled to complimentary use of the hotel's mountain bikes and special rates at nearby **Glen Cove Golf Course**. Four Sound beaches are in the area, but none within easy walking distance – especially on hot days. The nearest, **Prybil Beach**, is picturesque, with a walking pier jutting out over the water. Hotel guests are provided with beach passes but no parking permits so you might want to hang out at the garden pool.

From the LIE take Exit 39N; proceed north on Glen Cove Road for 6.4 miles. When the firehouse is directly in front, turn right onto Brewster Street and at the fourth traffic light turn left onto Dosoris Lane. The main entrance is one mile on the right – 22 miles from the Throgs Neck Bridge.

> ★ TIP
>
> Before heading out to Glen Cove, you might want to check the Web site of the **Glen Cove Downtown Business Improvement District**, www.glencovedowntown.com, or call them at ☎ 516-759-6970.

Woodbury

THE INN AT FOX HOLLOW
7755 Jericho Turnpike
Woodbury
☎ 800-291-8090
www.theinnatfoxhollow.com
Moderate to Expensive

The Inn at Fox Hollow was only a month old when I stayed here, yet everything was in place – from the beautifully appointed European-style suites to the buffet breakfast. Long Islanders are familiar with Fox Hollow, the magnificent catering hall, but the inn sharing the eight acres opened in February, 2002. The Scotto Brothers, who own several catering establishments on the Island, realized the need for an extended stay hotel to house wedding guests and others. Overnighters are welcome, too. All 145 rooms are suites – with full kitchens, lush velvet fabrics, and spacious marble bathrooms (12 suites are designed to accommodate guests with physical disabilities).

The inn provides services such as complimentary grocery shopping to long-term guests, and features a fully equipped business center, fitness center and outdoor pool. Five meeting rooms are available for small conferences. People familiar with Fox Hollow Caterers have stepped onto the checkerboard marble floor of the inn's elegant lobby and exclaimed, "That's what I expected from the Scotto Brothers." There is a warmth to the inn, emanating from both the lobby fireplace and the social ambience. A light dinner is served until 7pm and a hot or cold breakfast is included in the room rate; coffee is available round the clock.

Motels

MOTEL PRICE SCALE

Price scale is based on the cost of a double room, two people per room, in season, and does not include the 11.3% hotel tax.

Inexpensive.................	under $100
Moderate	$100-$150
Expensive....................	over $150

ROYAL INN MOTOR LODGE
1177 Northern Boulevard, Manhasset
☎ 516-627-5300
78 units. Moderate.

GOLD COAST INN
1053 Northern Boulevard
Roslyn
☎ 516-627-2460
60 units. Inexpensive.

TIDES MOTOR INN
Bayville Road
Locust Valley
☎ 516-671-7070
www.tidesmotorinn.com
64 units. Inexpensive to Moderate.

EDGEWOOD MOTEL
38 Jericho Turnpike
Jericho
☎ 516-333-4440
72 units. Inexpensive.

Some handicapped-accessible rooms.

HOSTWAY MOTOR INN
101 Jericho Turnpike
Jericho
☎ 516-334-8811
74 units. Inexpensive.

MEADOWBROOK MOTOR LODGE
440 Jericho Turnpike
Jericho
☎ 516-681-4200
www.meadowbrookmotorlodge.com
83 units. Inexpensive.

Some handicapped-accessible rooms.

BEST WESTERN WOODBURY INN
7940 Jericho Turnpike
Woodbury
☎ 516-921-6900
85 units. Moderate.

Nassau County's North Shore

Best Places to Eat

DINING PRICE SCALE
Price scale includes one entrée, with glass of wine and coffee. There is an 8.5% tax on food in both Nassau and Suffolk Counties.
Inexpensive . . . . under $25
Moderate . . . . $25-$40
Expensive . . . . over $40

Great Neck

GIRAFFE ROOM
Inn at Great Neck
30 Cuttermill Road
☎ 516-773-2000
www.innatgreatneck.com
www.greatrestaurantsmag.com
Moderate

This cozy room features banquettes in earth tones, which may be in homage to the ever-present giraffe, whose image is even on the waiters' ties. If you like Caesar salad sans anchovies and raw eggs (the latest trend), this may be the best one you'll find. For your entrée, the spicy rack of lamb is highly recommended. Other signature dishes are prime rib, sea bass and salmon. The restaurant and lounge are open until midnight. Live jazz begins at 8:30pm on Thursday, Friday and Saturday. Prix fixe menu is $19.95, Sunday through Friday; and $29.95 on Saturday. Kids' menu available.

TIP

Sample the Giraffe Room's big and briny cold shrimp, either at dinner or at Sunday brunch. Crisp on the outside, this fabulous crustacean has a fresh, meaty texture inside. You'll thank me.

BOCCA DI ROSA
24 Middle Neck Road
☎ 516-487-9169
www.greatrestaurantsmag.com
Moderate

Open three years, this brightly lit and cheerful restaurant with tiled floors serves superb fish and meat. Our party of four could not refrain from the superlatives as we sampled our selections from the large menu and specials. The spaghettini allo scoglio with clams, shrimp, mussels and baby clams in fresh tomato sauce was described as sensational and fresh, the snapper Livornese and veal chop excellent, and the steamed mussels delicious. Our Long Island cousin was so taken with this outrageously good restaurant that he vowed to come back again.

The restaurant is laid out with banquettes along the walls and tables in between. Service is pleasant and efficient. None of us ordered dessert with our cappuccino but we were served a complimentary plate of biscotti.

TIP

Be sure to make dinner reservations for Saturday nights, even in the dead of winter. Despite the slew of restaurants in Great Neck, most are booked because diners come from all over.

Glen Cove

THE COLES HOUSE
149 Glen Street
☎ 516-676-4343
www.greatrestaurantsmag.com
Moderate to Expensive

The name suggests an inn and indeed, the seven intimate dining rooms, some with working fireplaces and original wide floorboards and wooden farmhouse doors (peeling paint and all), give the illusion of a country inn. The building is a National Historic Landmark.

The restaurant, opened in November 1999, is a family operation, headed by long-time Glen Cove resident Rocco Cirigliano. A jovial man, his passion is restoring old houses. Coles House is named for J.H. Coles, a descendant of Robert Coles, a founder of Glen Cove. J.H. built the farmhouse around 1810, but it was abandoned and neglected when Cirigliano began his five-year restoration.

The French room has only two tables for a most romantic evening; another has three. The Yellow Room is the largest, for those who enjoy company while dining. The four-course prix fixe dinner ($29) is highly recommended. If it's available, begin with the flavorful, silky smooth lobster bisque. Among the entrées, the grilled pork loin – succulent as a steak – is perfect with a side of melt-in-your-mouth sweet potatoes, crisp green beans, and cauliflower florets. The dish was presented as pretty as a picture, and it came as no surprise to learn that executive chef David Leicht is a graduate of the Culinary Institute of America (CIA).

Newsday awarded Coles House three stars ("Excellent"); *The New York Times* rated it "Very Good." The review came out two months after the restaurant opened and the food critic admitted that it would have received an even higher rating but for erratic service. I'm happy to report that on our visit the waitstaff was both pleasant and efficient.

The Coles House is open for lunch and dinner year-round; closed Monday. Reservations are recommended. From the LIE take Exit 39N. Turn left onto Glen Cove Road and proceed north for six miles (the road becomes Route 107). When you reach Glen Cove, turn left onto Glen Street at the traffic light; Coles House is on your immediate right. If no parking is available in front, make a right turn onto Butler Street and then an immediate left into the porte-cochere entrance for the restaurant. Coles House is wheelchair-accessible.

PAGE ONE RESTAURANT
90 School Street
☎ 516-676-2800
www.pageonerestaurant.com
www.greatrestaurantsmag.com
Inexpensive to Moderate

The New American menu at Page One has a "Floribbean" flair, fusing Hawaiian, Caribbean and Floridian food and spices. The décor is Spanish-style with stucco walls, arches and soft lighting. Try the Louisiana catfish blackened with black bean sauce or the Australian rack of lamb. If you're a sushi lover, the tuna roll appetizer is highly recommended. Other popular dinners are macadamia coconut-crusted mahi with a mai-tai glaze served in a banana leaf, and pepper-dusted veal tenderloin with braised artichoke hearts and portobello mushrooms. Plantain chips decorate the exquisitely presented plates. Page One has received well-deserved accolades for its eclectic cuisine. Jeanine Di-Menna, the Glen Cove-reared chef and co-owner, is also community minded, serving as president of the Glen Cove Improvement District. She, too, has garnered awards.

Page One can accommodate special dietary needs.

The $19.95 prix fixe menu includes salad or soup and dessert. Coffee is extra. You can access the menu, along with recipes, events, and a bio of DiMenna on the restaurant's Web site. Page One is conveniently located next to the movie theater (bring your ticket stub for a free glass of wine). A sidewalk café is open for warm-weather dining and monthly cooking classes are held. Page One is open daily, year-round, for lunch and dinner. Reservations required on Saturday night.

Oyster Bay

FIDDLEHEADS
62 South Street
☎ 516-922-2999
www.greatrestaurantsmag.com
Moderate

Lemon yellow walls and an open kitchen stimulate your senses the moment you arrive. "This is one of the true fish houses on the North Shore," proclaims a man at the next table. If this is so, three cheers for CIA-trained Michael Ross, chef and owner, for filling the gap with a fine waitstaff and deft hand. Named for edible fiddlehead ferns, Fiddleheads takes good care of your taste buds, and you'll love the generous and attractive offerings. Pan-fried catfish in a spicy stew of green beans, crawfish and sweet potato is a winner. Their chocolate ice cream sandwich with dark chocolate chunk ice cream is a chocoholic's dream dessert.

Fiddleheads features entertainment Tuesday through Thursday at 7pm and a jazz brunch on Sunday.

The New American à la carte menu includes fish, pasta, chicken and steak. The seafood brunch is prix fixe at $15 per person, $7 for children. Open daily for lunch and dinner in summer; closed Monday rest of the year. Reservations recommended on weekends. The restaurant is wheelchair-accessible.

WHAT'S IN A NAME?
Dutch explorer David Pietersen deVries wrote in his journal of June 4, 1639, "At night came to anchor in Oyster Bay... There are fine oysters here, hence our nation (the Netherlands) has given it the name Oyster Bay."

BOOK MARK CAFE
One East Main Street
☎ 516-922-0036
www.greatrestaurantsmag.com
Inexpensive to Moderate

The Book Mark Café has taken the concept of eating in-side a bookstore a step further. The café portion of the bookstore is actually a restaurant, with waitress ser-vice and an extensive wine menu. The walls are filled with books and changing artworks. If the dinners are anything like the lunches, expect to leave here satisfied and stuffed. Lunch selections include burgers, salads and crab cakes. Open year-round, daily for lunch, Wed-nesday-Sunday for dinner. Lunch reservations are ac-cepted and dinner reservations are recommended. Book Mark Café holds frequent book signings, talks, exhibits and children's activities. Call for schedule. The café is handicapped-accessible.

Woodbury

FOX HOLLOW
7725 Jericho Turnpike
☎ 516-921-1415
www.theinnatfoxhollow.com
Moderate

Although this eatery opened in 1964 and boasts many loyal customers, few realize that Fox Hollow Caterers has a restaurant on the second floor – and a wonderful one at that. A pianist begins playing at 7pm every night, adding to the romance. There are two dining rooms; the Rose Hunt Room is separate from the bar while close enough to the music.

The menu runs the gamut, but you can't go wrong with pasta. Try the linguine con vongole, thin pasta flavored with fresh Little Neck clams from local waters and just the right touch of pepperoncini.

According to our waiter, even wedding guests at Fox Hollow are not aware there is a restaurant here – probably because they're sampling the same superb food at the affair. Open weekdays for lunch and dinner, dinner only on Saturday; closed Sunday. Reservations essential on weekends.

Lite Bites

BRUCE'S BAKERY
34 Middle Neck Road
Great Neck
☎ 516-829-CAKE
www.brucesbakery.com

Bruce's newest location is at 1045 First Avenue in Manhattan.

This popular café, retail store and caterer provides complimentary sweet rolls at every meal and a doggie bag with your check. Fresh baked goods are its trademark and Bruce's "celebrity look-a-like" cakes have been renowned since the Westbury Music Fair needed a special cake to commemorate Bob Hope's 80th birthday. The café also participates in community service initiatives and was the 1997 recipient of Great Neck's prestigious Giraffe Award. Open daily for breakfast, lunch and dinner.

BAGEL BOSS
400 Willis Avenue
Roslyn Heights
☎ 516-626-5599 or 888-BOSS-TIME
www.bagelboss.com

Located in a shopping plaza, Bagel Boss serves New York bagels and kosher appetizing and has a friendly staff. Check out its mouth-watering Web site. Open daily, year-round.

OLD FASHIONED BAGEL CAFE
43C Glen Cove Road
Greenvale
☎ 516-621-1520

From the road, the "Hot Bagels" sign is a fooler. This is a full-service deli, serving hot platters, cold cuts, homemade salads, and dieters' delights. It has two rows of booths. The café is in a shopping center just north of Northern Boulevard; open daily, year-round, for breakfast and lunch.

PAGE TWO BAKERY
124 South Street
Oyster Bay
☎ 516-922-7002

The bakery has croissants and muffins for breakfast and panini with turkey or ham and/or soup for lunch. Open Tuesday-Sunday, year-round; take-out is available for breakfast and lunch.

SOUTH STREET CAFE
100 South Street
Oyster Bay
☎ 516-922-1545

Everything here is made fresh daily, from mozzarella and muffins to focaccia bread. Open daily, year-round for breakfast and lunch; eat in or take out a salad, soup or customized sandwich.

North Shore A to Z

Animal Hospitals

Great Neck Animal Hospital, 660 Northern Boulevard, Great Neck, ☎ 516-482-0588. Small animals; boarding and grooming. Open daily.

Syosset Animal Hospital, 700 Jericho Turnpike, Syosset, ☎ 516-921-0700. Small animals; boarding. Closed Sunday.

Oyster Bay Animal Hospital, 64 Pine Hollow Road, Oyster Bay, ☎ 516-624-PETS (7387), www.oysterbay-animalhospital.baweb.com. Small animals; boarding. Office open daily, but only available for appointments Monday, Tuesday, Wednesday, Friday and Saturday.

Brookville Animal Hospital, 691 Glen Cove Road, Glen Head, near North Shore Honda, ☎ 516-674-3322. Small animals and exotics; by appointment; boarding. Open daily.

Animal General, 6320 Northern Boulevard, East Norwich, ☎ 516-624-7500. Small animals and exotics; boarding. Across from Rothmann's Steakhouse. Open daily.

Woodbury Animal Hospital, 141 Woodbury Road, Woodbury, near the post office, ☎ 516-367-7100. Small animals; by appointment. No boarding. Closed Sunday.

Animal Shelters

North Shore Animal League, 25 Davis Avenue, Port Washington (LIE Exit 36, north for four miles and left on Davis Avenue), ☎ 516-883-7575, www.nsal.org. Shelter, adoptions, medical care. Probably the best known of adoption centers (along with Bide-A-Wee), North Shore has placed more than 800,000 lost or abandoned pets since 1944. Open daily, year-round.

Town of North Hempstead Animal Shelter, 75 Marino Avenue, Port Washington, ☎ 516-944-8220, www.northhempstead.com (click "community services"). Stray dogs are held 10 days and then put up for adoption. To facilitate adoptions, a volunteer group, Shelter Connection, helps choose the proper food along with walking and training the dogs while they are being held at the shelter. Open Monday-Saturday.

Town of Oyster Bay Animal Shelter, 150 Miller Place, Syosset, ☎ 516-677-5784, www.town-of-oyster-bay.org/tinfo/animal.htm. Strays are held for seven days and then put up for adoption. Open Monday-Saturday.

Banks

The following banks have multiple branches throughout Nassau County. For specific locations, check the bank's Web site.

Astoria Federal Savings Bank .... www.astoriafederal.com

Bank of New York .... www.bankofnewyork.com

Chase Manhattan Bank .... www.chase.com

Citibank .... www.citibank.com

Dime Savings Bank of NY .... www.dime.com

First National Bank of LI .... www.fnbli.com

Fleet Bank .... www.fleet.com

HSBC .... www.us.hsbc.com

North Fork Bank .... www.northforkbank.com

Roslyn Savings Bank. .... www.roslyn.com

State Bank of LI .... www.statebankofli.com

Houses of Worship

Baptist

Bible Baptist Church, 178 Cold Spring Road, Syosset, ☎ 516-921-8747.

Manhasset Baptist Church, 626 Plandome Road, Manhasset, ☎ 516-627-2270 www.mbcweb.org.

Mt. Olive Baptist Church, 163 South Street, Oyster Bay, ☎ 516-922-5139.

Salem Baptist Church, 21 Burns Avenue, Glen Cove, ☎ 516-676-7843.

Catholic

Church of St. Mary, 110 Bryant Avenue, Roslyn, ☎ 516-621-2222.

Our Lady of Fatima, 6 Cottonwood Road, Port Washington, ☎ 516-767-0781, www.portwashington.org.

St. Patrick's Church, 235 Glen Street, Glen Cove, ☎ 516-676-0276.

St. Hyacinth Roman Catholic Church, 319 Cedar Swamp Road, Glen Head, ☎ 516-676-0361.

St. Boniface Martyr Roman Catholic Church, Carpenter and Glen avenues, Sea Cliff, ☎ 516-676-0676.

St. Dominic Roman Catholic Church, 93 Anstice Street, Oyster Bay, ☎ 516-922-4488.

Episcopal

All Saints Episcopal Church, 855 Middle Neck Road, Great Neck, ☎ 516-482-5392, http://agapenetwork.org/allsaints.

Trinity Episcopal Church, Northern Boulevard, Roslyn, ☎ 516-621-7925.

St. Paul's Episcopal Church, 28 Highland Road, Glen Cove, ☎ 516-676-0015.

Christ Church, 61 East Main, Oyster Bay, ☎ 516-922-6377. Christ Church was attended by Theodore Roosevelt for many years.

St. Bede's Episcopal Church, 220 Berry Hill Road, Syosset, ☎ 516-921-0755.

Jewish – Orthodox

Roslyn Synagogue, 257 Garden Street, Roslyn Heights, ☎ 516-484-0697.

Young Israel of Great Neck, 236 Middle Neck Road, Great Neck, ☎ 516-829-6040.

Jewish – Conservative

Jericho Jewish Center, Broadway & Jericho Road, Jericho, ☎ 516-938-2540.

Lake Success Jewish Center, 354 Lakeville Road, Lake Success, ☎ 516-466-0569.

Midway Jewish Center, 330 South Oyster Bay Road, Syosset, ☎ 516-938-8390.

Oyster Bay Jewish Center, 11 Temple Lane, Oyster Bay, ☎ 516-922-6650.

Temple Israel of Great Neck, 108 Old Mill Road, Great Neck, ☎ 516-482-7800.

Temple Beth Israel, Temple Drive, Port Washington, ☎ 516-767-1708.

Temple Beth Shalom, 401 Roslyn Road, Roslyn Heights, ☎ 516-621-2288 (see page 40).

Jewish – Reform

North Country Reform Temple, corner Crescent Beach and New Woods Roads, Glen Cove, ☎ 516-671-4760, www.ncrt.org.

North Shore Synagogue, 83 Muttontown Road, Syosset, ☎ 516-921-2282, www.northshoresynagogue.org.

Temple Beth El of Great Neck, 5 Old Mill Road, Great Neck, ☎ 516-487-0900.

Temple Judea of Manhasset, 333 Searingtown Road, Manhasset, ☎ 516-621-8049.

Temple Beth Am, 150 Middle Neck Road, Port Washington, ☎ 516-883-3144, www.communitysynagogue.org.

The Port Jewish Center, 20 Manor Haven Boulevard, Port Washington, ☎ 516-621-6800.

Temple Sinai of Roslyn, 425 Roslyn Road, Roslyn Heights, ☎ 516-944-7202, www.templesinairoslyn.com.

Lutheran

Faith Evangelical Lutheran Church, 231 Jackson Avenue, Syosset, ☎ 516-921-3330.

Trinity Lutheran Church, 74 Forest Avenue, Glen Cove, ☎ 516-676-1340.

Nassau County's North Shore

Methodist

*The First
Presbyterian
Church in
Oyster Bay,
built in the
Stick style in
1873, is on
the National
Register of
Historic
Places.*

United Methodist Church, 1515 Middle Neck Road, Port Washington, ☎ 516-883-1430.

United Methodist Of Glen Cove, School and Highland roads, Glen Cove, ☎ 516-671-3013.

Presbyterian

First Presbyterian Church, 60 East Main, Oyster Bay, ☎ 516-922-5477.

Roslyn Presbyterian Church, 140 East Broadway, Roslyn, ☎ 516-621-3139, www.roslynpresbyterian.org.

Information Sources

Chambers of Commerce

Glen Cove Chamber of Commerce, ☎ 516-676-6666, www.glencovechamber.org.

Great Neck Chamber of Commerce, ☎ 516-487-2000, www.greatneckchamber.org.

Locust Valley Chamber of Commerce, ☎ 516-671-2299, http://locustvalleybx.com.

Manhasset Chamber of Commerce, ☎ 516-627-5022, www.manhasset.org.

Oyster Bay Chamber of Commerce, ☎ 516-922-6464, www.oysterbay.org/chamber.html.

Port Washington Chamber of Commerce, ☎ 516-883-6566, www.antonnews.com/portwashingtonnews/portwacofc.

Syosset Chamber of Commerce, ☎ 516-364-6650, www.syossetchamber.com.

Community Web Sites

Great Neck . . . . www.greatneck.com
Manhasset . . . . www.manhasset.org

Port Washington.......... www.portwashington.org
Roslyn .... www.historicRoslyn.org
Glen Cove .... www.glencovechamber.org
Locust Valley .... www.locustvalley.com
Town of Oyster Bay .... www.oysterbaytown.com
Oyster Bay .. www.oysterbay.org, www.oysterbayli.com
Laurel Hollow.............. www.laurelhollow.org

Liquor Stores

Coves Discount Liquors, 242 Glen Cove Avenue, Glen Cove, ☎ 516-671-5573.

Great Neck Wines & Spirits, 13 North Station Plaza, Great Neck, ☎ 516-466-7585.

Post Wine & Spirits, 510 Jericho Turnpike, Syosset, ☎ 516-921-1820.

Medical Facilities

St. Francis Hospital, 100 Port Washington Boulevard, Roslyn, ☎ 516-562-6000, www.stfrancisheartcenter.com.

FAMOUS FACES

Perry Como, who died in 2001, moved to Sands Point in 1946 where he lived with his family for many years. Although he moved to Florida in the 1970s, he returned to Long Island each year to participate in one of his favorite charities, the St. Francis Hospital Celebrity Golf Classic.

Nassau County has 14 hospitals with a total of 4,748 beds.

North Shore University Hospital (NSUH), 300 Community Drive, Manhasset (731 beds), ☎ 516-562-0100.

Nassau County's North Shore

NORTH SHORE UNIVERSITY HOSPITAL

NSUH is the top hospital among the nation's largest metropolitan areas, according to a study conducted by the Washington DC-based Consumers' Checkbook, an independent, non-profit consumer education organization. An article in the May/June 2002 issue of *Modern Maturity* titled *The Top Hospital in America* showed that North Shore ranks first among 50 hospitals (St. Francis Hospital in Roslyn and Cedars-Sinai Medical Center in Los Angeles shared second place) and that North Shore rated top among 10 hospitals in cardiovascular surgeries (followed by St. Francis). Other NSUH locations are in Glen Cove, Syosset, and Plainview. NSUH is one of 18 hospitals in the North Shore Long Island Jewish Health System (www.northshorelij.com).

Movies

Cineplex Odeon (6), 5 School Street & Highland Road, Glen Cove, ☎ 516-671-6668 (recording), 5161-671-6866 (box office).

Clearview Port Washington Cinemas (7), 116 Main Street, Port Washington, ☎ 516-944-6200 (recording), 516-883-6464 (box office).

Clearview Soundview Cinemas (6), 7-9 Soundview Marketplace, Port Washington, ☎ 516-944-3900 (recording), 516-944-3903 (box office).

Clearview Squire Theatre (7), 115 Middle Neck Road, Great Neck, ☎ 516-466-2020 (recording), 516-466-9172 (box office).

Manhasset Triplex, 430 Plandome Road, Manhasset, ☎ 516-627-7887 (recording), 516-365-9188 (box office).

Roslyn Quad, 20 Tower Place, Roslyn, ☎ 516-621-8488 (recording), 516-621-3970 (box office).

Newspapers

The *Great Neck Record, Manhasset Press, Port Washington News, Roslyn News, Glen Cove Record Pilot, Oyster Bay Enterprise Pilot,* and *Syosset-Jericho Tribune* (which serves Syosset, Jericho, Woodbury, Brookville, lower Brookville and Muttontown) are published by **Anton Newspapers**, ☎ 516-747-8282, www.antonnews.com. To read any of them on-line, simply add its name to Anton's Web site; for example, www.antonnews.com/greatneckrecord.

Pharmacies

Beacon Pharmacy, 103 Main Street, Port Washington, ☎ 516-883-1155.

Snouder's Corner Drug Store, 108 South Street, Oyster Bay, ☎ 516-922-4300.

Zip Codes

Brookville, Greenvale..................... 11548
East Norwich 11732
Glen Cove 11542
Glen Head................................. 11545
Great Neck .... 11020 and 11027
Jericho................................... 11753
Kings Point 11024
Locust Valley/Lattingtown................. 11560
Manhasset/Plandome....................... 11030
Manhasset Hills 11040
Mill Neck................................. 11765
Old Westbury 11568
Oyster Bay 11771
Port Washington/Manorhaven/Flower Hill..... 11050
Roslyn/Flower Hill 11576
Roslyn Heights 11577
Sea Cliff................................. 11579
Syosset 11791
Woodbury 11797

Nassau County's South Shore

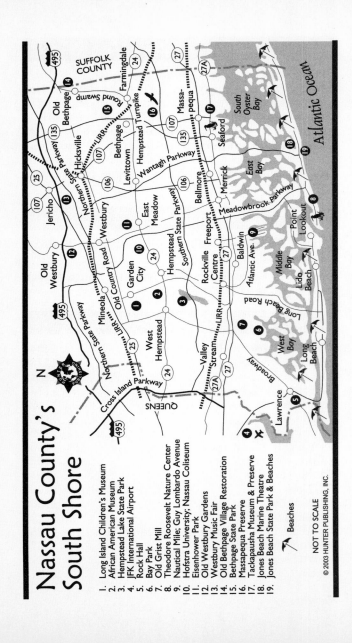

1. Long Island Children's Museum
2. African American Museum
3. Hempstead Lake State Park
4. JFK International Airport
5. Rock Hall
6. Bay Park
7. Old Grist Mill
8. Theodore Roosevelt Nature Center
9. Nautical Mile; Guy Lombardo Avenue
10. Hofstra University; Nassau Coliseum
11. Eisenhower Park
12. Old Westbury Gardens
13. Westbury Music Fair
14. Old Bethpage Village Restoration
15. Bethpage State Park
16. Massapequa Preserve
17. Tackapausha Museum & Preserve
18. Jones Beach Marine Theatre
19. Jones Beach State Park & Beaches

Beaches

NOT TO SCALE

Nassau County's South Shore

Getting Here & Getting Around

By Car

The **Southern State Parkway** runs along the South Shore; other east/west routes for Nassau County include **Hempstead Turnpike** (Route 24) and **Sunrise Highway** (Route 27). All intersect with the major north/south routes: the **Meadowbrook State Parkway**, the **Wantagh State Parkway**, and the **Seaford-Oyster Bay Expressway** (Route 135).

Rental Cars

Daily rates for a mid-sized car range from $50 to $60; some agencies offer free mileage.

All American Vans, 78 Franklin Avenue, Valley Stream, ☎ 516-223-5700. All sizes of luxury vans; unlimited mileage.

Thrifty Car Rental, 327 West Merrick Road, Valley Stream, ☎ 516-561-6766, closed Sunday; 16 Newbridge Road, Hicksville, ☎ 516-931-1515; www.thrifty.com.

Enterprise Rent-A-Car, 184 Merrick Road, Lynbrook, ☎ 800-736-8222, or 516-887-6700.

Budget Rent-A-Car, 130 Franklin Avenue, Garden City, ☎ 516-483-5359; Sears Automotive Center, 195 North Broadway, Hicksville, ☎ 516-932-7368; and 2169 Jericho Turnpike, New Hyde Park, ☎ 516-354-5460; www.budget.com.

By Taxi

Taxi fares between JFK and LaGuardia airports and most towns on the South Shore range from $20 to $35, depending on distance and the number of passengers.

Ollies Taxi and Airport Service, Franklin Square. In Nassau County, ☎ 516-487-3420 or 437-0505; in Queens, ☎ 718-229-5454.

All Island Taxi of Uniondale, ☎ 516-489-3333 or 228-1212. Airports and out of town. "The largest taxi fleet on Long Island."

Valley Stream Taxi & Airport Service, 10 Station Plaza, Valley Stream, ☎ 516-825-6900 (taxi service); ☎ 516-825-6035 (airport service).

Winston Airport Shuttle, ☎ 800-424-7767, www.winstontrans.com. Share-ride van or luxury sedan to JFK, LaGuardia, or Islip-MacArthur; private cars only to Newark or NYC. Pickups from Brooklyn to the tip of Long Island.

By Limousine

All County Limousines, ☎ 516-785-0500, 800-923-LIMO, www.allcountylimo.com. Serves Long Island, Westchester, New York Metropolitan area.

At Your Service Transportation, ☎ 516-255-LIMO or 888-340-LIMO (5466), www.atyourservicelimos.com.

Galaxy Limousines, ☎ 888-616-8900, or pager, 516-925-9950.

Stargate Limousine, 66 West Merrick Road, Valley Stream, ☎ 516-561-5245.

Sunup to Sundown

Museums

AFRICAN AMERICAN MUSEUM
110 North Franklin Street
Hempstead
☎ 516-572-0730
www.rooseveltlongisland.org/museum
Free admission

Open to the public since 1970, this street-level museum memorializes events and celebrities that represent the black experience: busts of black leaders Harriet Tubman, Paul Robeson and George Washington Carver, African sculptures and masks, and paintings of the civil rights movement. Films, lectures, and special and educational programs complement the exhibits.

The museum is open year-round, Thursday through Saturday, 10am-4:45pm; Sunday, 1-4:45pm. To get here, take the Southern State Parkway to Exit 21N (Nassau Road); proceed to Jackson Street. Turn left and continue to the corner of Franklin and Jackson.

LONG ISLAND CHILDREN'S MUSEUM
11 Davis Boulevard, off Charles Lindbergh Boulevard
Mitchel Center, Mitchel Field
Garden City
☎ 516-222-0207
www.licm.org
Admission for adults and children over age one, $8; seniors, $7; members and children under age one, free

If you've ever visited the museum's former home in the old *Newsday* building on Stewart Avenue, you'll be truly amazed at its new digs. While it's always been the ultimate hands-on museum, it's now about eight times the size of the former facility, with a dozen large interactive exhibits compared to five small ones. In the past, many visitors had to be turned away because of inadequate space; the new facility can hold 1,000 visitors at a time. The museum projects an annual audience of 250,000; that's half the number of children under 13 on Long Island.

Some of the most popular exhibits have been expanded. The bubble machines, for instance, limited visitors to creating soap bubbles by operating a pulley. Now kids can create the bubbles and climb inside the machine. Where once the museum had children operate wheelchairs on a bumpy ramp to sensitize them to challenges encountered by the disabled, exhibits now demonstrate how the deaf and blind surmount their obstacles as well. This includes a vibrating bed that acts as an alarm clock, and Braille typewriters. A trip to the beach may never be the same once kids shape a sand dune with wind or form a beach with rolling waves at the new exhibit, Sandy Island.

> ★ TIP
>
> Climbing ramps at the Children's Museum are geared for both able-bodied and handicapped children. The 150-seat theater provides space for wheelchairs; it's equipped with an audio-enhancement system for the hearing impaired, and the stage is accessible by ramp.

Since opening in February 2002 in historic Mitchel Field, at a cost of $17 million, the museum has received local and national coverage. Occupying 40,000 square feet in a renovated hangar, it's one of numerous projects being developed on the former military base. The newest attraction – a **Cradle of Aviation** complex, with 60,000 square feet of exhibit space and an **IMAX Dome Theater** – opened in May 2002 to coincide with the anniversary of Charles Lindbergh's legendary solo flight from nearby Roosevelt Field. Other buildings are planned to house the **Nassau County Firefighter's Museum and Safety Center**, the **Museum of Sci-**

ence and Technology, an **Aerospace Adventure Program**, and a pavilion for the 90-year-old **Nunley's carousel** from the defunct amusement park in Baldwin. Interactive performances and presentations are held every weekend, and special programs for preschoolers are offered on weekdays. A cafeteria with vending machines and a gift shop are on site, and there is ample parking. Open Wednesday-Sunday, year-round.

TACKAPAUSHA MUSEUM & PRESERVE
Washington Avenue
Seaford
☎ 516-571-7443
Admission adults, $2; children, $1

Is your child studying animals in school or is he or she a budding geologist? Are you interested in how Long Island came to be or which species can be found in local marshes? This museum focuses on the living environment of Long Island as well as the wider world. The museum is manageable in size; displays include animal skulls, such as one from an opossum, the only native omnivore on Long Island. Simply written text presents general facts about mammals, reptiles, birds, insects and fish, with special focus on species found on the Island. The Junior Naturalists' corner has interactive computers, puzzles, games and coloring pages that are popular with kids of all ages.

The Tackapausha Museum is handicapped-accessible, but the restrooms are not.

The 84-acre Tackapausha Preserve – Nassau County's first nature preserve – is a wildlife sanctuary devoted to recreation, hiking and education. Ask for a guide at the front desk.

Wildlife and birds are singled out because of their proliferation on Long Island. As the text points out, its marshes are among the most important areas in the entire Northeast for waterfowl. A vital link on the great Atlantic flyway, they attract thousands of migrating birds each spring and fall. Visitors learn which species winter here and that 98% of the brants (wild geese) in

Nassau County's South Shore

New York State are found on Long Island (no surprise to golfers!).

The preserve is 28.1 miles from the Throgs Neck Bridge and accessible from the Southern State Parkway, Exit 28A. Follow Route 135 south to Exit 2. Go east on Route 27, then turn right at the second light onto Washington Avenue (a 7-11 is on the corner). Look for a modern building one block before Merrick Road. The museum is open year-round, Tuesday-Saturday, 10am-4pm; and Sunday, 1-4pm. The preserve is open daily, dawn to sunset.

WHAT'S IN A NAME?

Tackapausha was the sachem (chief) of the Massapequa band and "overlord" of several of the western Long Island bands of Native Americans during the 1600s.

Historic Sites

ROCK HALL MUSEUM
199 Broadway
Lawrence
☎ 516-239-1157
Free admission

Rock Hall Museum is on the National Register of Historic Places.

In the 18th century, the area that is now Lynbrook to Rockaway Point was the province of seven plantation owners – the Davisons, Hewletts, Hickses, Pettits, Motts, Martins and Cornells – who came across the Long Island Sound from Connecticut seeking religious freedom. These seven English immigrants raised cattle and sheep and produced grain for the New York market with the help of slaves. Today we know this region as the Five Towns – Inwood, Woodmere, Cedarhurst, Hewlett and Lawrence – one of the earliest-settled areas on Long Island. Although close to the city, the peninsula was undeveloped and free from smallpox and other diseases that ravaged New York City.

Rock Hall, built in about 1767, was the home of the Martin family until 1823. Josiah Martin, who had come from Antigua in the British West Indies, exported sugar, rum and molasses through agents in New York and London. The farm once had 600 acres (now it has only three) with an unobstructed view of the ocean and several outbuildings, including slave quarters, icehouse and kitchen. Food was stored and prepared in the cold cellar but cooked outside for fear of fire in the wood house. In 1824, the Hewlett family acquired Rock Hall and 125 acres from Martin's heirs. Responding to the rising popularity of Rockaway beaches, they opened Rock Hall to summer guests. In the early 1900s the family gifted Rock Hall to the Town of Hempstead.

Rock Hall is considered one of the last great manor houses extant on Long Island and a foremost example of Colonial Georgian architecture. The three-story house has the gambrel roof and cupolas popular during that period. The formal rooms have high ceilings, closets and fine furnishings and each has a fireplace bordered by Dutch tiles. An exhibit of items found during archeological digs at the homestead, such as pottery shards and beer bottles, is on view as well.

In 1771, Josiah Martin commissioned John Singleton Copley, America's leading portrait painter, to paint a portrait of his favorite grandchild, Mary Elizabeth, to fit in the paneling over the fireplace in the main parlor. It's the only likeness of a Martin in existence.

Video and guided tours are available; visitors may also take a self-guided tour. Two floors and the cellar are open to the public, but there is no wheelchair access.

Rock Hall is easy to reach from the city via the Nassau Expressway (878), which becomes Rockaway Turnpike and goes right into Lawrence. Turn right at the light onto Broadway. Rock Hall is about a mile on the left before the school, 19 miles from the Throgs Neck Bridge. Open year-round, Wednesday-Saturday, 10am-4pm, and Sunday, noon to 4pm.

Nassau County's South Shore

OLD GRIST MILL HISTORICAL MUSEUM
Woods and Atlantic Avenues
East Rockaway
☎ 516-887-6300 (village hall)

The mill, located in a park with a playground and band
shell, was established in 1688. It was used to mill rye,
wheat and corn for peninsula farmers and to saw logs
for shipyards, helping to make East Rockaway an active port. The museum houses several rooms of authentic South Shore antiques; it is handicapped-accessible.
Open weekends, June to Labor Day, 1-5pm. Take the
Southern State to Malverne, Exit 17. Go south on
Ocean Avenue; cross the railroad tracks in East Rockaway and turn right onto Centre Avenue, then left onto
Atlantic Avenue. The grist mill is about two blocks on
the left.

OLD WESTBURY GARDENS
71 Old Westbury Road
Old Westbury
☎ 516-333-0048
www.oldwestburygardens.org
Admission to house and gardens: $10; $8 for seniors; $5
for children over six.

One could easily imagine a coach-and-four pulling up
to the stately three-story brick mansion after clip-
clopping over the long gravely path. Wrong era, though
– Westbury House is less than a century old. Framed by
formal English gardens, it was the home of John
("Jay") Shaffer Phipps (1874-1958), son of steel mag-
nate Henry Phipps, and Margarita ("Dita") C. Grace
Phipps (1876-1957), daughter of one of the founders of
Grace Shipping Lines in South America. Born in Peru,
Dita was a teenager when her family moved to Battle
Abbey in Sussex, England, near the site of the battle of
Hastings, which took place in 1066. They lived there
for 21 years. The romantic tale has it that Dita was re-
luctant to leave England to marry Jay until he prom-
ised her an English-style mansion reminiscent of her
Sussex home.

Westbury House, the Charles II-style mansion completed in 1906 on this 150-acre estate, is a testament to his word. In England, for example, closets were taxed as extra rooms, so Westbury has none; clothes were stored on shelves or in armoires. A pretense of the time is reflected in the library, where books for family reading are on one side and showy gold leaf volumes on the other. The geometric rose garden, designed in the tradition of a 17th-century parterre, is said to be modeled after the one at Battle Abbey.

Family friend and acclaimed English landscape architect George A. Crawley designed the 66-room house and grounds with the Phippses' approval. As you'd expect, the mansion contains many gems, among them paintings by esteemed artists of the time such as Sir Joshua Reynolds, John Singer Sargent, and Thomas Gainsborough; there is also a Chinese Chippendale and lace collection. What evokes the "wow" factor, however, is the enormous bathroom, where the toilet and clawfoot tub are aesthetically camouflaged.

The Phippses had four children and were quite family-oriented. Peggie's playhouse was a thatched tea cottage with fireplace and pantry; her brothers had small log cabins. The area where the Phipps children played is now the Cottage Garden, where visiting children can look through the cottage windows and play inside the log cabins and the sandbox.

The Phippses had several homes, but they returned to Westbury House seasonally for 50 years. As the Latin inscription above the ornate doorway suggests, they warmly welcomed guests: "Peace to those who enter... good health to all who depart."

Peggie, the only surviving member of the Phippses' four children, is now in her nineties. During her mother's illness, she enlisted her brothers' help in insuring the survival of Westbury House, and was instrumental in creating the J.S. Phipps Foundation. Westbury House opened to the public in 1959 and will celebrate its centennial in 2006.

Nassau County's South Shore

Old Westbury Gardens, listed on the National Register of Historic Places, includes the house and gardens on 88 acres, a café and a garden shed, which is open through the July 4th weekend. Each season a special exhibit is featured. But the magnificent gardens are the real draw, attracting visitors from all over the world. With about 20 different gardens to explore, each season provides a different spectacular landscape; it's worth visiting in spring, summer and fall.

The Phippses were ardent dog lovers , and buried their pets in the dog grave-yard amidst the greenery.

Begin your tour at the giant American beech beside the house. The tree was already mature when planted in 1910; its branches now shade the entire west porch. There are five kinds of beeches on the property but, according to Patricia Speciner, director of communications, this one is ailing. "We're trying to save it," she says. "Trees are our best resource."

From there, step down to a pastoral pool with its floating swan ferry. Move on to the Walled Garden, which covers two acres. Initially planned as an Italian garden, the emphasis on statuary has been softened with flowers ablaze in color. The Ghost Walk, well shaded with hemlocks, was inspired by spectral sightings of long-departed monks slain by William the Conqueror's soldiers. At its end are replicas of peacocks that once roamed the gardens, with tails formed of trained yew.

Continue your walk through the Cottage Garden to view the back of the house, which is photographed more often than the front. From here you'll find a former apple orchard where there are benches to contemplate the beauty of it all.

From April 28 through October, Old Westbury Gardens is open daily, except Tuesday, 10am-5pm. In November, it's open Sunday; then sporadically through mid-December. House tours are held every half-hour and garden tours twice daily. If you prefer viewing the house and grounds on your own, pick up one of the pamphlets (available for several different interests) in the box behind the directional signs near the parking lot. The house is handicapped-accessible, but the unpaved pathways to the gardens are not.

In addition to tours, Old Westbury Gardens has a full program of activities throughout the season, including children's theater, woodland walks, talks, tours, workshops, garden programs, festivals and concerts; there is a holiday celebration in December.

Old Westbury Gardens is 16.4 miles from the Throgs Neck Bridge. Exit the LIE at 39S and stay on the service road for 1.2 miles. At the second light, turn right onto Old Westbury Road and continue for a quarter-mile to the entrance on the left.

OLD BETHPAGE VILLAGE RESTORATION
Round Swamp Road
Old Bethpage
☎ 516-572-8400
www.fieldtrip.com/ny
Admission adults, $6; children and handicapped, $4; under five, free

The moment you leave the long tree-lined road and enter the village, you're in a time warp. Everyone is dressed in 19th-century garb and well versed in the traditions of the village. Each of the 60 historic structures has been moved from another place on Long Island, with the exception of one house from the Hudson Valley. Most of the furnishings are not original but are representative of the era.

Unlike the mansions on the North Shore, most of the houses in this area belonged to merchants and farmers. Budget cuts have eliminated demonstrations by actual tailors and blacksmiths, among others, but the costumed staff and volunteers rotate houses and do a splendid job of imparting information to visitors. Some do mini-demonstrations.

The "hatter," for example, doesn't actually make a hat, but quickly demonstrates the tedious process of taking virgin felt and making it into an everyday wool or formal fur hat. "A man did not go out of doors without a hat," he told a group of fourth graders from Great Neck, to emphasize the hatter's importance to the community. Even a half-century after the startup of this shop, he adds, the average workweek was 72 hours. The "hatter" suggests the children visit his simple homestead next door as an eye-opener.

By all means do that. Let your children see the tight space in the stuffy attic where the five sons of Lewis Ritch, a Middle Island hatter, shared two beds. The daughter slept in the kitchen. "It's a difficult concept for kids today," the guide observed. "Not only to share a room but to share a bed." After leaving the hatter's home, walk behind the Kirby House and view the four-seat outhouse.

The Noon Inn in East Meadow was an early B&B. Two male guests (friends or strangers) would occupy the two upstairs beds. The downstairs bar had no set menu but would serve whatever was available. John Layton's house and general store was a fixture in East Norwich. The newest and largest house in the village, c. 1866, it was the local hub where farmers bought everything they couldn't grow – tools, tin-ware, toys, cloth, patent medicines, preserving jars, and a coffee grinder the size of a spinning wheel.

The restoration is located on land owned and farmed by Richard S. Powell during the 1840s and 1850s. Nassau County acquired the 165-acre farm on the Nassau/Suffolk border in 1963 when the farmhouse and carriage shed were the only buildings on site (now those buildings house the farm animals). Put on your walking shoes and expect to spend a fascinating three hours, for less than you'd spend on a movie. About half the houses have ramps for the handicapped. Weekend demonstrations, games, concerts and festivals are held at the Village from March to August. See *Festivals & Events*, page 144.

Take the LIE to Exit 48. Head south on Round Swamp Road. The entrance is about a half-mile on the left. Open Wednesday-Sunday, March through December; closed January and February. There is a cafeteria and a gift shop.

HISTORIC NOTE

In 1936 Grumman Aircraft Engineering Corp. picked Bethpage for the location of its airport and factory. The company ultimately evolved into Long Island's largest employer and transformed Bethpage into a thriving, modern suburb. The lunar module that landed on the moon in 1969 was built in Bethpage. After Grumman was taken over by Northrop in 1994, the site was dismantled.

Historical Societies & Tours

**LONG BEACH HISTORICAL
& PRESERVATION SOCIETY**
226 West Penn Street
Long Beach
☎ 516-432-1192

The society is dedicated to preserving Long Beach's homes, estates and heritage and to educating the public through museum exhibits and monthly lectures (they are currently installing plaques around town to identify places of historic interest). The museum contains exhibits relating to Long Beach history, with artifacts from archeological digs, and is open Tuesday, Wednesday and Thursday by appointment. Public lectures by local speakers are held the third Thursday of every month at 7:30pm (except in February and March), on topics pertaining to Long Beach – the first planned community on Long Island. The society's office is open 9am-noon, Monday to Friday; closed February 1 through April 15.

Nassau County's South Shore

FREEPORT HISTORICAL SOCIETY
350 South Main Street
Freeport
☎ 516-623-9632

Housed in an old bayman's shack, the society's 10-room museum features a 13-star US flag dating from 1777, along with artifacts from Freeport's history and biographical information on vaudevillians who lived in the area. The museum is open 2-5pm on Sundays only, April 28-December 31.

HISTORICAL SOCIETY OF THE BELLMORES
PO Box 912
Bellmore
☎ 516-785-2593

The society has a garage-size museum containing local maps and photographs; it is located on Pettit Avenue across from the railroad station and in front of the fire house. Once used as a freight office by the Long Island Rail Road, it's open year-round by appointment and during Bellmore's street fair in September, at no charge. Also free to the public are monthly lectures, from September to April, on local and national topics of interest to Long Islanders, such as canals of Bellmore, movie palaces and Civil War battles; these are held at the Bellmore Memorial Library on Bellmore Avenue, south of Sunrise Highway, on the second Tuesday of the month.

LEVITTOWN HISTORICAL SOCIETY
Levittown Memorial Educational Center
150 Abbey Lane
Levittown
☎ 516-735-9060
www.levittownhistoricalsociety.org

The society maintains a museum featuring exhibits of the country's first planned suburb. Hours are Wednesday, 2:30-4:30pm; and Friday, 7-9pm. The museum is on the lower level of the Levittown Memorial Educational Center. To get here, take the Southern State to Exit 28N and go north on Wantagh Avenue to Hempstead Turnpike. Go west on the Turnpike about a half-mile to Ranch Lane, and proceed south. At the fourth stop sign, turn right onto Abbey Lane. The museum is located inside Gerald Claps Technical Center.

HISTORICAL SOCIETY OF THE MASSAPEQUAS
Merrick Road, across from Cedar Shore Drive
Mailing address: PO Box 211, Massapequa, NY 11758
☎ 516-799-2023
www.massapequahistory.com

The society hosts two annual antiques shows, in April and November; a Strawberry Social & Craft Fair in June; and a Fall Apple & Harvest Festival in October. They also open the **Old Grace Church** (dating from 1844) on Sundays, from May through September, from 2-4pm; and other times by appointment.

Major Thomas Jones, namesake of Jones Beach, is buried in the cemetery of Massapequa's Old Grace Church.

Family Fun

A wonderful way to combine a learning experience with play is to start your day at the **Theodore Roosevelt Nature Center**, located at the western end of Jones Beach (☎ 516-679-7254, http://nysparks.state.ny.us), where a 1,700-foot boardwalk leads down to the ocean. Opened in May 2000, the center's theme is Long Island's South Shore Estuary Preserve, which extends for 70 miles from West Bay in Nassau County to Shinnecock Bay in Suffolk County. The nature center is named for the president who, as a child, carried frogs in his hat, stored dead mice in the family icebox and used his water pitcher as a home for snakes. A display devoted to Roosevelt documents his amazing accomplishments as president in placing under public protection some 230 million acres of US land for bird sanctuaries, wildlife refuges, forests and parks.

The exhibits cover seashore, salt marsh and dune habitats, and highlight their importance in protecting coastal communities and the wildlife common to these

Nassau County's South Shore

environments. (A stuffed snowy owl has been the main feature since the release of the film *Harry Potter.*) There's also a display on endangered species and tanks with live fish and turtles. Outside is a huge sandbox with the bones of a blue whale and an "explosure" for breeding birds. These cages have tiny openings for piping plovers but keep out larger predators. ("Where do plovers go in winter?" I asked. To Florida, of course!)

Both museum and boardwalk are handicapped-accessible. The center is open weekends, year-round, and sponsors a host of activities for children and adults, including guided seal hikes in mid-winter. During the summer, the center is open Wednesday-Sunday. Admission is free but parking is $5.

To reach the center, take the Southern State to Exit 22 onto Meadowbrook Parkway south, bearing right at the sign for West End beaches. After paying the fee, continue straight and loop around toward the ocean. The building is up ahead.

Sightseeing

Freeport

NAUTICAL MILE
Woodcleft Avenue
Freeport
☎ 516-377-2200 (local chamber of commerce)

Freeport was originally called Raynortown after cowherder Edward Raynor, but during the colonial era sea captains referred to the settlement as a "free port" since goods could be offered without the customs charge that had to be paid in other ports. The "Seaport in Freeport" is part of an ongoing revitalization program. Pedestrian walkways on both sides of the mile-long avenue make for a walker's paradise. Like any seaport, there are restaurants, clam bars, boats for sale, a seaport museum and shops with a nautical theme. There's a wonderful mural on the side of a building in one of the parking lots (although it may be difficult to see when the lot is full of cars) depicting the pier as it might have looked in olden days. Some of the boats pictured are actually in the harbor and a few eateries shown are still operating. Indeed, some of the establishments have been there for decades. Fiore Bros., the wholesale and retail fish market near the far end, has been in business since 1920.

The nautical mile ends in a scenic pier with benches from which to enjoy the view. An old-timer recalled that this spot once had an eatery on pilings where he could get a hamburger and Coke for 15¢. The parking lot across from it was a speakeasy.

Take Sunrise Highway to South Long Beach Road in Freeport. Drive a few blocks to Atlantic Avenue and turn left. Turn right at Guy Lombardo Avenue, and take another right onto Front Street, then turn left onto Woodcleft Avenue. The trip is 26.5 miles from Triboro Bridge. The seaport is open daily, year-round, although in winter the restaurants open only at lunchtime and most of the shops are closed until around Valentine's Day.

☞ DID YOU KNOW?

Bandleader Guy Lombardo moved to the east shore of Woodcleft Canal in 1940 and lived there until his death in the mid-1970s. Known as "Mr. Freeport," he owned the popular East Point Restaurant and several racing boats.

Garden City

Garden City was one of the first planned communities in the country, and the upscale village is a testament to its planner, **Alexander Turney Stewart**. The tree-lined streets, benches, cobblestone sidewalks and brick storefronts can be traced to his initiative. A Scotch-

Nassau County's South Shore

Irish immigrant who opened a small dry-goods store in lower Manhattan, Stewart became one of the richest men in the world. It was said at the time that he owned more real estate in Manhattan than anyone except William Astor.

Toward the end of his life, in 1869, Stewart purchased more than 7,000 acres of the Hempstead Plains at $55 per acre (he subsequently acquired more land, for a total of almost 10,000 acres – extending from Floral Park to Bethpage). This was an astounding price given that it was land eroded from the hills formed by the glacier and for centuries had remained flat and treeless. For a time it was used as pasture for sheep and cattle, but by the 19th century the livestock industry had moved to the western prairies. Undaunted by this neglected wasteland, Stewart created a model village with everything designed on a grand scale. Built in a geometric pattern with wide streets, the entire village was planted with thousands of trees and shrubs. Stewart was also responsible for the railroad that rumbles through town at ground level. The Garden City Hotel is across from the library and railroad station, where a bust of Stewart reminds commuters of the man behind their beautiful village.

In 1872 Stewart had a dozen large, identical houses built, which each cost about $17,000; and set the standard of taste for wealthy families. Six of these original houses remain. The beige Victorian at 32 Cathedral Avenue (corner of Fourth Street) is listed on the Garden City Heritage Tour Map as an excellent example of this style. The other five are on Hilton and Rockaway avenues and Eleventh Street.

The house on Cathedral Avenue is just beyond the magnificent **Cathedral of the Incarnation**, with its pinnacles and flying buttresses; both house and cathedral are within walking distance of the Garden City Hotel (see page 147). After Stewart died, his 71-year-old widow, Cornelia, had this Gothic church built in his memory (along with two cathedral schools and a bishop's residence). A National Historic Landmark, the brownstone Episcopal church is, as *The New York Times* observed, "one of the most remarkable structures on Long Island." Its spire rises some 210 feet and is visible for miles. Turn right when leaving the Garden City Hotel, then turn left at Cathedral Avenue.

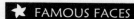

★ FAMOUS FACES

Actress Susan Lucci and author Nelson DeMille live in Garden City.

Health & Beauty

Fitness Centers

All are open daily, year-round, unless otherwise specified.

Valencia Health Club, 1319 Hempstead Turnpike, Elmont, ☎ 516-352-9646. Full-service fitness facility. Day fee, $10. No child care.

Valley Fitness, 132 Rockaway Avenue, Valley Stream, ☎ 516-568-0788. Full-service fitness facility. Day fee, $10. Childcare, $1 per child.

Hollywood Atrium Club, 235 Mill Street, Lawrence, ☎ 516-239-4343. Full-service facility open daily. Free baby-sitting. Day fee with member, $15; without member, $20.

Gennaro Athletic Club, 369 Atlantic Avenue, East Rockaway, across from East Rockaway Village Hall, ☎ 516-599-3060. Fitness facility. No classes or childcare. Day fee, $9.

Island Garden, 45 Cherry Valley Avenue, West Hempstead, ☎ 516-292-4956, www.islandgarden.com, is a 42,000 square-foot multi-purpose complex featuring a full-service fitness center, basketball, softball, baseball and soccer. Day fee for fitness center, $7. Call ahead for other facilities.

Mineola Health Club, 244 Herricks Road, Mineola, ☎ 516-741-5783, www.mineolahealthclub.com. Full-

Nassau County's South Shore

service fitness facility. Day fee, $7. Childcare, $2 per hour, per child.

Sky Athletic Club, 310A Merrick Road, Rockville Centre, ☎ 516-678-9400. Full-service fitness facility with coed and women's-only section, kids fitness program, free nursery. Day fee, $12.

Hollywood Fitness Center, 2995 Long Beach Road, ☎ 516-594-6000. Oceanside. Free supervised nursery. Day fee, $15.

Iron Island Gym, 3465 Lawson Boulevard, Oceanside, ☎ 516-594-9014. Full-service fitness facility. Open daily. Day fee, $10; free childcare.

Nelson's Gym, 3163 Long Beach Road, Oceanside, ☎ 516-763-4444. Small fitness facility (no classes). First-timers free. No childcare. Open daily.

Personal Best, 2166 Merrick Road, Merrick. One-on-one personal training, ☎ 516-223-0404. Day fee, $25/half-hour; $50 per hour. Trial session and packages available. Open Monday-Saturday.

Ultimate Gym, 67 Bloomingdale Road, Hicksville, ☎ 516-937-3740, www.ultimategym.com. Complete fitness facility. Tanning. Day fee, $12. No childcare.

Woman's Domain Health & Fitness Club, 382 Old Country Road, Hicksville (quarter mile east of Wantagh Parkway), ☎ 516-681-5879. Full-service fitness facility exclusively for women. Free childcare. Day fee, $20. Open daily.

Sunrise Health and Racquet Club, 6000 Sunrise Highway, Massapequa (across from Sunrise Mall), ☎ 516-795-5000, www.sunrisehealthclub.com. Full-service fitness facility with seven racquetball courts. Guests must be accompanied by member and pay a $15 fee. Free nursery care.

New York Sports Clubs is a group of full-service fitness facilities with a reciprocal arrangement among members. The Long Beach and East Meadow clubs also have swimming pools. All charge a day fee of $15 with member, $25 without. Of its nine locations on Long Island, five are on the South Shore of Nassau County: 265 East Park Avenue, Long Beach, ☎ 516-432-5849; 2909 Lincoln Avenue, Oceanside, ☎ 516-594-8300; 833 Franklin Avenue, Garden City, ☎ 516-741-1500; 625 Merrick Avenue, East Meadow, ☎ 516-485-5100; and a new club that opened in March of 2002 at 155 Franklin Place, Woodmere, ☎ 516-792-9292, www.nysc.com. All of these have childcare available; fees and times vary by location, so call for details.

Bally Total Fitness is a group of full-service fitness facilities with a reciprocal arrangement for members. Guests get a free one-day pass. There is no fee for childcare; www.ballyfitness.com. Area centers are at 60 Merrick Road, Rockville Centre, ☎ 516-887-7500; 373 Old Country Road, Carle Place, ☎ 516-997-6220; and 2935 Hempstead Turnpike, Levittown, ☎ 516-579-3900.

Lucille Roberts has full-service fitness facilities for women; they are open daily, and offer reciprocal arrangements to some members. Childcare, $1 per hour, per child. Day fee at some clubs, $10. 1000 Sunrise Highway, Massapequa, ☎ 516-541-8840; 298 Sunrise Highway, Rockville Centre, ☎ 516-766-8443; 231 Glen Cove Road, Carle Place, ☎ 516-746-4333; 359 South Oyster Bay Road, Plainview, ☎ 516-681-2464.

Gold's Gym. Each Gold's Gym is owned separately so there is no reciprocal arrangement for members. Visit www.goldsgym for other locations. The following are in Nassau County: 190 Broadway, New Hyde Park, ☎ 516-742-4477; 230 Hempstead Avenue, Lynbrook, ☎ 516-599-8441, day fee $10, no childcare; 190 Broadway, Garden City, ☎ 516-742-4477, day fee, $12, no fee for childcare; 2060 Bellmore Avenue, Bellmore, ☎ 516-221-1800, no fee for the first visit, $12 thereafter, free childcare.

Powerhouse Gym has four locations on the South Shore with reciprocal arrangements. All are primarily training gyms and charge a $10 day fee. 640 Merrick Road, Lynbrook, ☎ 516-593-9100; 1749 Grand Avenue, Baldwin, ☎ 516-546-4444; 635 South Street, Garden

Nassau County's South Shore

City, ☎ 516-745-5709 (Gleason's boxing gym is located in this facility). The facility at 2608 Merrick Road, Bellmore, ☎ 516-826-3000, offers classes, and has childcare available Monday-Saturday.

Sportime has 11 locations on Long Island, four on the South Shore of Nassau County, with a reciprocal arrangement for members. Some specialize in fitness or multi-sport, others in tennis, and some combine both. The toll-free number is ☎ 888-NY-TENNIS. 60 The Plaza, Atlantic Beach, ☎ 516-239-3388, open from May to early October; 175 Merrick Road, Lynbrook, ☎ 516-887-1330, has a full-service fitness and multi-sport facility with six indoor tennis courts (visitors must come with member); 4105 Hempstead Turnpike. Bethpage, ☎ 516-731-4432, is strictly a multi-sport facility offering basketball, roller hockey, soccer, lacrosse and volleyball; and 5600 Old Sunrise Highway, East Massapequa, ☎ 516-799-3550, with five Har-tru tennis courts for members only, and a workout room. Some of these locations offer childcare; call for details.

Day Spas

Ariyana European Spa, 29 Hempstead Avenue, Lynbrook, ☎ 516-561-5866. Body, skin and massage treatments by appointment or walk-in. Closed Monday.

Frasada, 301 Long Beach Road, Oceanside, ☎ 516-766-7076, www.frasada.com. Full-service spa and beauty salon, by appointment. Closed Monday.

Dejavu Spa & Nails, 524 Jericho Turnpike, Mineola, ☎ 516-746-2910. Skin treatments and nail salon, by appointment or walk-in. Closed Sunday.

Rain Day Spa, 8025 Jericho Turnpike, Woodbury, ☎ 516-921-5772, www.raindayspa.com. Full-service spa, by appointment. Closed Monday.

Je T'aime Salon & Day Spa, 974 Atlantic Avenue, Baldwin, ☎ 516-623-2772. Full-service, by appointment only. Closed Sunday and Monday.

Maximus Day Spa, 2075 Merrick Road, Merrick, ☎ 516-623-4300, www.maximusspasalon.com. Full-service hair salon and spa. Walk-ins welcome. Open daily.

Recreation

Boating

Cruises & Charters

These riverboats, fishing charters, and casino cruises leave from Freeport's **Nautical Mile** or **Guy Lombardo Avenue**. The best alternative to calling individual fishermen – who are often out on the seas – is to contact Captain Bob Kaye, Dockmaster, at Freeport Boatman's Association, 540 Guy Lombardo Avenue, ☎ 516-378-4838.

DOLPHIN CHARTERS & CRUISES
540 Guy Lombardo Avenue
☎ 516-379-5450

Dolphin Charters (not to be confused with Dolphin Cruise Lines) runs fishing trips and cruises geared to groups. Captain Tony Greco has been fishing in Freeport since he was eight; he and his son Gary take fishing boats out by day and cruise local waters at night. Operates March 30-November. Charter fees for all-day fishing trips run between $675 and $1,000, depending on the type of fish sought (tuna and shark are the highest) and the number of people going out. Other cruises range from $45 to $100 per person.

MAJESTY CASINO CRUISES
☎ 516-777-LUCK (5825)
☎ 516-223-5402
www.majestycasino.com

Cruises depart twice daily. Day ($20) and night ($25) cruises include lunch or dinner, three drinks and dessert. Reservations essential. Operates year-round.

Nassau County's South Shore

THE *MIDNIGHT GAMBLER II*
☎ 516-377-7400, or 516-777-LUCK (5825)

This gambling cruise operates all year. Your $15 fee includes a free ticket for a hot buffet and coffee, tea or soda. No reservations needed. The cruises are about five hours long, and depart twice daily, at 11:30am and 7:30pm.

NAUTICAL CRUISE LINES
☎ 516-623-5712
www.nauticalcruiselines.com

This company operates a luxury yacht, *Nautical Princess*, and two paddlewheelers. Private parties comprise the bulk of its business. Brunch and dinner cruises ($49 to $65) are offered to the public in season. Sunday seal-watching cruises begin in late January. Operates all year.

CAPTAIN LOU'S FLEET
28 Woodcleft Avenue
☎ 516-766-5716/623-5823.

In business for 20 years, Captain Lou operates all year. He has seven boats, two of them for half- or full-day fishing trips. Call for rates.

CAPTAIN PETE
540 Guy Lombardo Avenue
☎ 516-223-1158

Moonlight cruises on a 105-passenger boat, and 65-foot charter boats that can accommodate 80 people. Operates April-December. Call for prices.

NORTHSTAR II
540 Guy Lombardo Avenue
☎ 516-937-1489

The *Northstar* is a 60-foot fiberglass charter boat available for moonlight cruises for 70 passengers. Reservations required; call for fees. Operates April-November.

SUPER SPRAY II
540 Guy Lombardo Avenue
☎ 516-223-2507

Captain Jim operates this 90-foot fishing boat for half-day and night trips, April-November. Moonlight cruises available; call for information.

Seal Watch

A snout here, a hump there. Passengers aboard the *Lady J V*, a 120-capacity party boat, keep their eyes fixed on the waves. Otherwise, they'd miss the show on Hempstead Bay. Where do the seals come from? As far away as Greenland, says Captain Pat. "This is their Florida." For the past three years, the **Riverhead Foundation for Marine Research and Preservation**, ☎ 631-369-9840 (select "0"), www.riverheadfoundation.org, leads two-hour cruises from the East Marina at Point Lookout. This is a wonderful family adventure, and sightings are almost guaranteed. Although harbor seals may haul out onto land at different times, they tend to stay in one location. Also, studies show that within a season they tend to return to one or two particular haul-out sites with regularity. Kids love spotting the seals, shouting "there's one" to their parents' delight. Seals start coming to Long Island in mid-November and return north in May.

A naturalist from the foundation gives a short presentation; then passengers are on their own. After an hour out in the cold, everyone turns to the snack bar for some nourishment. When the deck is quiet, the show really begins. By now your eyes are trained to spot the black specks on the water and you can watch the show from inside the warm cabin. Although it would be nice to see the seals sunning themselves, there is something special about viewing them frolicking in their natural environment. Bring binoculars if you have them; a few pairs are available on board to borrow.

If you locate a sick, injured or dead seal, whale, dolphin, porpoise or sea turtle, contact the New York State Marine Mammal and Sea Turtle Stranding Program at ☎ 631-369-9829.

Nassau County's South Shore

ABOUT HARBOR SEALS

- Harbor seals are just one type of seal; others are harp, hooded, gray and ringed.

- Adult harbor seals are four to six feet long and weigh between 250 and 300 pounds.

- Their coloring is silver, tan or black with speckling. Their coat often looks dark when wet, but can be very light when dry.

- The harbor seal's scientific name, *Phoca vitulina*, loosely means "sea dog," and indeed their faces do resemble dogs without ears.

- Unlike most pinnipeds (meaning "featherfooted" or "wing-footed"), adult harbor seals rarely interact other than to mate.

- Harbor seals are the least vocal of all pinnipeds, usually snorting or hissing only when they feel threatened.

- Harbor seals live for about 25-30 years. Predators include killer whales, sharks and eagles.

- Harbor seals haul out of the water to rest, sun themselves, give birth and nurse their young. Generally, harbor seals do not touch each other on land, but if touched by another will respond with growling, head-butting or aggressive flipper-waving.

- The US Marine Mammal Protection Act of 1972 made it illegal to hunt or harass any marine animal in US waters.

Another seal watch, a guided walk in Montauk Point State Park, is held on weekends from early December through April. See page 475 for information.

The Riverhead Foundation offers seal observation cruises from January through March. As operator and supporter of the New York State Marine Mammal and Sea Turtle Stranding Program, the Foundation is the only group permitted to rescue and rehabilitate marine life in New York State. The fee of $20 for adults, $15 for children, benefits that program. Last year, the Foundation rescued 188 seals; 72% of them have since been tagged and released. To reach Point Lookout, take the Meadowbrook Parkway south to Exit M10 and follow the Loop Parkway to light; turn left. East Marina is on the left as you approach Point Lookout.

Fishing Clubs

The **Freeport Tuna Club** was formed in 1937; it is the oldest fishing club in New York State, and it has evolved into the largest. Its more than 200 individual members are both boat owners and non-boat owners, experienced and novice anglers, and residents from as far away as Florida. The club fishes mainly on Long Island and, although its true love is tuna, it presents awards for all species that are caught. Seminars, events and fishing contests are held year-round. Call Chris Squeri at ☎ 516-358-7114, www.ftcfishing.com.

The **Long Island Flyrodders**, based in Hicksville, was founded in 1979 and has about 300 members. The club frequently fishes on the Connetquot River, a world-class trout stream located in Oakdale. Non-members are invited to monthly meetings but, because of insurance reasons, only members may participate in the club's monthly trips throughout the US. Call Lee Weil at ☎ 516-997-6743, www.lifr.org.

Marinas

Hunter Pointe Marina, Woodcleft Canal, 417 Woodcleft Avenue, Freeport, ☎ 516-623-3020, www.boatin.com. Annual storage, sales, restrooms, showers. The marina is open April-October; sales office is open year-round, ☎ 516-867-4240 or 800-339-6929.

K&K Outboard, 3875 Long Beach Road, Island Park, ☎ 516-431-1865. Sales, dockage, storage, electric, fuel, restrooms, huge parking lot. Open year-round; closed Monday.

Nassau County's South Shore

Old Harbour Marina, 2479 Adler Court, at Town Dock, Seaford, ☎ 516-785-0358. Bait, tackle, electric. Restaurant/bar. Open April-September.

Kydd's Marine Center, 25 Alhambra Road, Massapequa, ☎ 516-541-7747, www.kyddsmarine.com. Storage, dockage, electric, restrooms, marine store. Open daily, year-round. New showroom at 555 Montauk Highway in Lindenhurst.

Whaleneck Marina, 3000 Whaleneck Drive, Merrick, ☎ 516-378-8025, www.whaleneckmarinaplus.com. Storage, dockage, electric, restrooms, restaurant (Cucina Bay, ☎ 516-378-7495). Open year-round; closed Monday.

Scotty's Marina and Fishing Station, 72 Bayside Drive, Point Lookout, ☎ 516-432-4665, www.scottys-marina.com. Storage, boat rentals, snack bar, bait and tackle, marine store. Open daily, April-November.

Bay Breeze Marina, 3920 Atlantic View Avenue, Seaford, ☎ 516-781-6004. Hauling, storage, dockage, electric, restrooms. Open year-round.

Treasure Island Marina, 2880 Ocean Avenue, Seaford, ☎ 516-221-7156. Storage, dockage, electric, pool, clam & oyster bar, restrooms, showers, hauling. Open daily, year-round.

Kayaking

Empire Kayaks, 4 Empire Boulevard (on Middle Bay), Island Park, ☎ 516-889-8300. Sales, rentals and lessons in kayaking. Open daily, June to Labor Day. Closed Tuesday in winter.

Biking

Sales & Rentals

Bike Junkie, 272 Broadway, Bethpage, ☎ 516-932-7271, specializes in mountain bikes.

Cycle & Fitness, 1966 Wantagh Avenue (on the corner of Sunrise Highway), Wantagh, ☎ 516-781-6100, www.brandcycle.com, www.brandfitness.com, carries all the famous brands of bicycles. The shop has a total fitness department, specializing in treadmills. Open daily, year-round.

Central Bicycle, 126 North Central Avenue, Valley Stream, ☎ 516-825-6091, repairs all makes and models. Sells bikes and lawn equipment. Open daily, year-round, except Sunday in winter.

Valley Stream Bicycle and Fitness Center, 95 East Merrick Road, Valley Stream, ☎ 516-825-8181, www.valleystreambicycle.com and www.valleystreamhockey.com, sells bikes and exercise equipment and has a complete ice-hockey shop. Open daily, year-round.

South Shore Cycle, 4187-A Austin Boulevard, Island Park, ☎ 516-889-8947. Motorcyle shop. Considering rentals. Two miles from Long Beach. Open daily, year-round.

Sunrise Cyclery, 4828 Sunrise Highway, Massapequa Park, ☎ 516-798-5715. Family business since 1955. In April 1999 received the prestigious Velo Business Top 100 award, being named one of the Top 100 Bicycle Stores in North America (voted by the top bicycle and accessory manufacturers). Open daily, year-round.

Long Beach Bicycle Store, 51 Main Street, East Rockaway, ☎ 516-599-0060, sells Mongoose bikes only – mountain, road, juvenile. No rentals. Open daily, year-round.

Lynbrook Bicycles, 224A Merrick Road, Lynbrook, ☎ 516-887-5166. No rentals. Open 5-7pm weekdays, and all day Friday to Sunday.

AMERICAN BICYCLE CENTERS

The following bike shops, members of American Bicycle Centers, are independently operated. All (including their two shops on the North Shore) sell a variety of bikes, such as mountain, road, hybrid and juvenile, and some carry fitness equipment. All sell and repair bikes;

the only one that has rentals is Long Beach Bicycle & Fitness. All are open daily, year-round, unless otherwise indicated.

Bicycle Country, 301 Nassau Boulevard (near Adelphi University), Garden City South, ☎ 516-483-9266.

Long Beach Bicycle & Fitness, 755 East Park Avenue (next to Bagel Club), Long Beach, ☎ 516-432-9632. Rentals. Closed Tuesday and Sunday in winter.

Rockville Centre Bicycles, 17 North Park Avenue (opposite Fantasy Theatre), Rockville Centre, ☎ 516-678-6918. Closed Sunday in winter.

South Shore Bicycle, 1067 Broadway, Woodmere (former site of Woodmere Bicycle), ☎ 516-374-0606. Closed Tuesday in winter.

Danny's, 3259 Hempstead Turnpike, Levittown, ☎ 516-520-0707. Closed Tuesday in the winter.

Williams Cycle, 83 Woodbury Road, Hicksville, ☎ 516-822-6235.

Bicycle Clubs

Massapequa Park Bicycle Club was founded in 1970 and has more than 500 members, including people from New York City and New Jersey. During the summer, the club promotes both road and mountain biking with weekend and weeknight rides, and sponsors the 100-mile **Ancient Mariner Century** along Montauk Highway, claimed to be the easiest century tour in the northeast. It also sponsors tours of 25, 50, 65 and 100 miles around the Hamptons. The club is quite social and takes several trips here and abroad each year. Its annual seven-day trip to Cape Cod is $95 and includes eight meals. Rides are free and open to people of all ages and abilities. Non-members are welcome but most people end up joining. Call John at ☎ 516-798-5583, www.massparkbikeclub.org.

Parks

VALLEY STREAM STATE PARK
Southern State Parkway
Valley Stream
☎ 516-825-4128
$5 per car from May to early October

At 97 acres, this is the smallest of Long Island's state parks but there's ample space for picnicking and ball playing. There are also basketball courts, playgrounds, horseshoe pits, bocce courts, volleyball courts, a picnic store in summer and cross-country skiing in winter. A multi-use path is shared by bicyclists, in-line skaters and runners, and there is a parcourse. Take the Southern State Parkway to Exit 15A and follow the signs.

State parks are open daily, from sunrise to sunset, year-round.

HEMPSTEAD LAKE STATE PARK
Southern State Parkway
Hempstead
☎ 516-766-1029
$5 per car from May to early October

This park was developed around Hempstead Lake, the largest freshwater lake in Nassau County. In 1925, Robert Moses convinced the City of New York to dedicate 2,200 acres of city water for Nassau County's state parks and parkways. Rustic and beautiful, the 775-acre park has something for everyone: bridle paths, playgrounds, picnic areas, ball fields, basketball and tennis courts (clay and all-weather), walking and biking paths, fishing, dog walks, a lovely lake area, and a carousel with wooden horses (with real horsehair tails) built around the turn of the century.

Horses may be rented from a private concessionaire just outside the park, which offers guided trail rides, individual rides and lessons. Tennis time is on a first-come, first-served basis (the all-weather tennis courts are open year-round; the clay courts are open late April through early November, weather permitting). In-line skating and swimming are prohibited. A New York

Nassau County's South Shore

A ride on the carousel at Hempstead Lake State Park is $1 for children over six; the carousel is open Memorial Day weekend through September.

State fishing license, which may be obtained at most bait and tackle shops (not at the park), is required for patrons over 16 years of age. To get here, take the Southern State Parkway to Exit 18; also accessible from Peninsula Boulevard.

★ TIP

According to a birder, the common merganser is a common sight at Hempstead Lake in winter.

BAY PARK
First Avenue
East Rockaway
☎ 516-571-7250

Bay Park is a 96-acre county park, with benches along a bayside channel. The park has picnic areas, a golf course, and a dog run, and is a good place to ride a bike. From the Southern State, take Exit 17S and go three miles south on Ocean Avenue; look for signs.

Swimming

TULLY INDOOR POOL & RECREATION CENTER
1801 Evergreen Avenue
New Hyde Park
☎ 516-327-3140

Open year-round to North Hempstead residents and guests, except a few days a year for maintenance. The recreation center is off Denton Avenue in Michael Tully Park.

AQUATIC CENTER
Eisenhower Park
East Meadow
☎ 516-572-0502 (pool)
☎ 516-572-0348 (park)

This mother of all pools was primarily built with funds
from the New York State Dormitory Authority to host
the swimming events at the Goodwill Games in 1998.
The 10-lane pool is 68 meters long and 25 meters wide,
larger than a basketball court. The pool is open to the
public and is rarely crowded, although the two weight
rooms, Jacuzzi and sauna are off-limits to non-members (members wear identifying bracelets).

A removable bulkhead separates the lap lanes from the
free swim area favored by children. A patio is set up
with tables, where swimmers may eat al fresco (bring
your own food). When the center occasionally closes for
swim meets (up to 35 days a year), the bulkheads are
removed; more often swim teams and school competitive events limit the lanes available for lap swimmers.
Members receive a schedule of these events, but non-
members should call beforehand to assess availability.

The water level can be raised and lowered in the children's portion of the pool to accommodate children and/
or seniors, and competitions that need the full length of
the pool. The water temperature averages 80°. The
facility is handicapped-accessible. Eisenhower Park is
open daily, year-round. Daily pool fees for non-residents are $10 for adults, $6 for children over age three;
for Nassau County residents with a valid leisure passport, admission is $5 for adults and $3 for children over
age three; children under three are admitted free.
Memberships are available for both residents and non-
residents.

LONG BEACH MUNICIPAL POOL
Magnolia Boulevard and West Bay Drive
Long Beach
☎ 516-431-3890
Admission: $5 adults; $2 children

This is an Olympic-size pool and weight room; it's open
to all, and has a hoist and a ramp into pool for handicapped swimmers. Open daily, year-round.

HEMPSTEAD TOWN POOLS
☎ 516-431-3900 (Department of Parks & Recreation)

Generally located in town parks, town pools are restricted to district and non-district residents. Fees are
$1 to $2.50, depending on residence.

Beaches

The South Shore has beautiful ocean beaches and, although many are private or belong to beach clubs, there
are plenty of public beaches. **Long Beach**, **Jones
Beach**, and **Fire Island** are the most popular. In addition, several beaches belonging to the Town of Hempstead are open to non-residents and are popular with
families.

WHAT'S IN A NAME?
Reynolds Channel is the inlet that separates
Long Beach from the mainland. It was named
for William Reynolds, a Brooklyn developer
who acquired the barrier island from the Town
of Hempstead in 1907 in order to build homes,
hotels and a boardwalk. To publicize the project, he had a herd of elephants march in from
his Coney Island Dreamland.

The closest public beaches to New York City are those
on the barrier island known as Long Beach (west of the
City of Long Beach is Atlantic Beach, where the clubs

have summer memberships; to the east only the Malibu is private). The fastest route to Long Beach is to take the Meadowbrook Parkway south from the Northern State or Southern State or the LIE, then get on the Loop Parkway, which ends opposite the entrance to Point Lookout on Lido Boulevard. To reach Long Beach, turn right. These beaches either charge for parking or have an entrance fee (with lower fees, of course, for residents with permits). However, if you have a car full of people and the non-resident parking fee is $15, it's still a bargain. Keep in mind that there are no decent lodgings in the area. If you don't have a friend or relative to put you up, consider Long Beach as a day trip.

Billy Crystal grew up in Long Beach and was voted the wittiest student in his class at Long Beach High School.

WHERE TO EAT IN LONG BEACH

Eateries are not far from the beach. **Gino's Restaurant and Pizzeria**, 16 West Park Avenue (the city of Long Beach's main shopping street), is a local favorite, serving the "best pizza"; ☎ 516-432-8193. **The Bagel Club**, 759 East Park Avenue, is a sizable space with lots of tables and a Quick Draw machine for people who like to gamble while eating; ☎ 516-432-2582.

OCEAN BEACH PARK
No phone

Ocean Beach Park in the City of Long Beach has an extremely wide beach with an equally wide (60-foot) boardwalk for walkers, joggers and bicyclists. At 2.06 miles in length, it's the island's longest continuous boardwalk, made of Douglas fir and yellow pine. There are lifeguards in season, when the access fee is $6. Non-metered parking spaces on the street are fairly plentiful given that you can enter the beach at various points. The sand is soft and the beach crowded on a sunny and warm day, although it never gets as jammed as Jones Beach. Restrooms are under the boardwalk opposite

Nassau County's South Shore

the jetties but there is only one food concession, next to
King David Manor (a senior residence). The railroad
station is in the center of town near the beach. The
beachfront is lined with condos and retirement homes.
In recent years, Long Beach has experienced a renewal
and many historic buildings have been restored to their
former splendor.

TOWN OF HEMPSTEAD BEACHES
☎ 516-431-3900 (Department of Parks & Recreation)

The four Town of Hempstead beaches along Lido Boulevard and to the east of Long Beach are **Lido Beach**,
Sands, **Lido West** and **Point Lookout**. Sands, open
daily, year-round, is known as the "picnic beach" because of all the gazebos with barbeque pits. It is not a
beach club and there are no members. The parking fee
at each is $6 for residents and $15-$17 for non-resi-
dents. All have lifeguards and food stands. Lido Beach
and the Sands have pools and charge a fee to swim.
Some or all of these amenities are included at each of
these beaches: basketball, tennis and handball courts,
baseball field, horseshoes, bocce courts, playground,
picnic area, showers.

★ TIP

All-terrain wheelchairs are available at Nassau Beach Park in Lido
Beach to those with a Nassau County Disabled Leisure Passport. Call
☎ 516-571-7700 one week in advance
to reserve.

NASSAU BEACH PARK
☎ 516-571-7700

East of the Sands is the County of Nassau Beach Park,
with a pool, cabanas for seasonal rental, and campsites. The pool is near the park's administration office,
which has a Leisure Passport Office for Nassau County
residents, as well as restrooms and brochures. (Leisure

Passport Offices, open daily, from 10am-4pm, are located in several parks in the county; for additional information about Leisure Passports, see page 15.)

Town parks are good resting spots, although use is restricted to residents in season. From Broadway in Woodmere, take Woodmere Boulevard .8 mile to the end. **Woodmere Town Dock** is on Brosewere Bay, affording views of the marshy islands common to the south shore. Hungry? Head back to Broadway and turn right, then make another right at East Rockaway Road; it becomes Main Street in East Rockaway. **East Point Fishery**, 1 Main Street, ☎ 516-599-0044, is a fish market/café with an outdoor deck (closed Mondays); and, across the street, is its restaurant (☎ 516-887-3532), open for dinner (closed Tuesdays).

JONES BEACH
☎ 516-785-1600
www.nysparks.com, or www.visitjonesbeach.com

Each summer, Jones Beach State Park, on Ocean Drive in Wantagh, draws six to seven million visitors from all over the world. One might wonder how a 6½-mile beachfront with a two-mile-long boardwalk can accommodate all these people. It's almost like a small city. Consider these startling statistics. Jones Beach has:

- ◆ 2,400 acres
- ◆ 21,000 parking spaces
- ◆ 12,000 lockers
- ◆ A 231-foot water tower holding 315,000 gallons of water exclusively for Jones Beach State Park.
- ◆ 250 lifeguards
- ◆ Two Olympic-size swimming pools
- ◆ 14 cafeterias and refreshment stands

Other amenities include a beautiful pitch & putt golf course in the shadow of the tower; basketball; shuffleboard and paddle tennis courts; playgrounds; a boat basin; and softball fields. When the sun sets, it's time

Nassau County's South Shore

for relaxation at the 14,000-seat Jones Beach Marine Theatre, world-famous for outdoor summer concerts (see *Performing Arts*, page 137). No biking is permitted on the boardwalk between April 1 and October 1. The outdoor pools are open to all between late June and Labor Day. The West Bath House is open daily; the fee is $3 for adults, $1 for children under 12 and seniors. The East Bath House is open weekends and holidays only; the fee is $2 for adults, $1 for children and seniors.

Jones Beach's water tower is patterned after the Campanile in Venice and looks nothing like a water tower.

To reach Field 4, the main parking area for Jones Beach, take the Southern State Parkway to Exit 27S (Wantagh Parkway South). The beach is 31 miles from the Throgs Neck Bridge.

Running

The 400-member **Long Island Road Runners Club**, ☎ 516-569-4959, www.lirrc.org, holds 80 events yearly in Eisenhower Park. Anyone can enter a road race for a $5 fee (register on the day of the race). Race schedules are posted on their Web site (click "LIRRC Links" for other running clubs).

Roller Skating

United Skates of America, 1276 Hicksville Road (Route 107), Seaford, ☎ 516-795-5474, www.usa-skating.com. Roller rink, skating lessons for all ages, video games, café and prizes. Club Matrix, "Long Island's Hottest Teen Club," dances and skates at the rink Friday nights, 8:45-11:30pm; www.clubmatrix-usa.com. The rink is 1.3 miles from Sunrise Highway in a shopping plaza. Open year-round. Admission, $6; skate rental, $2.50. Currently, public skating is Saturday, 12:30-3pm, 3:30-6pm and 6:30-8:30pm; and Sunday, 12:30-3pm and 3:30-6pm. Call for weekday schedule and directions to the rink.

Tennis

Sportime at Bethpage, 101 Norcross Avenue, Bethpage, ☎ 516-933-8500, or 888-NY-TENNIS. Six indoor courts. Free child care. Members-only club; guest with member pays $15 per hour for court.

Golf

Bethpage State Park, 99 Quaker Meetinghouse Road, Farmingdale, ☎ 516-249-0700, or 516-249-0707. The park's infamous black course was the site of the US Open in 2002; it is the first public course to hold that distinction. The park has five 18-hole courses: black, par 71, open from April to mid-November; blue, par 72, open year-round; red, par 70, open from April to December; yellow, par 71 and excellent for beginners, open year-round; and green, par 71, open year-round. Walking is allowed and soft spikes are mandatory. There's a pro shop, restaurant, practice area, putting green, lessons, carts, and club rentals. Call for tee times.

> ★ NOTABLE QUOTE
>
> "I guarantee when they hold the Open there, it [Bethpage] will become world-renowned," predicted *Powers Golf Guide 2000*.

North Woodmere Golf Course, Hungry Harbor Road, North Woodmere, ☎ 516-571-7814, is a nine-hole, par 31 executive course. Walking allowed. Lessons, pro shop, putting green, driving range. Open year-round. Closed Thursday.

Bay Park Golf Course, Ocean Avenue, Lynbrook, ☎ 516-571-7242, is a nine-hole, par 30 course. Walking allowed. Lockers, putting area. Open mid-March to mid-December.

Nassau County's South Shore

Lido Golf Club, 255 Lido Boulevard, Lido Beach, ☎ 516-889-8181, is an 18-hole, par 72 links course. Walking allowed. Locker rooms, rentals, practice area, pro shop, restaurant, snack bar. Open year-round.

Merrick Road Park Golf Course, 2550 Clubhouse Road, Merrick, ☎ 516-868-4650. Nine-hole course is flat but challenging. Walking only. Driving range, putting area, pro shop. Open year-round.

Eisenhower Park, Hempstead Turnpike, East Meadow, ☎ 516-572-0327, has three 18-hole courses, each par 72. Lessons, putting area, pro shop, restaurant, bar, snack bar. Open year-round.

Peninsula Golf Course, 50 Nassau Road, Massapequa, ☎ 516-798-9776, is a nine-hole, par 37 course. Walking allowed. Putting area, pro shop, restaurant, snack bar. Open year-round.

★ TIP

The **New York Golf Center** in the Broadway Mall, Hicksville, is a golfers' heaven. The store has 12,000 square feet of inventory, including golf equipment, clothes and accessories, and is a four-time winner of "America's 100 Best Golf Shops," a competition run annually by *Golf Shop Operations*, a *New York Times / Golf Digest* publication. Open daily, year-round. ☎ 516-933-7533; outside of New York State, ☎ 888-364-5348.

Shop Till You Drop

Malls & Shopping Streets

BAY HARBOUR MALL
Rockaway Turnpike and Peninsula Boulevard
Lawrence
☎ 516-746-1300

Stores and restaurants at Bay Harbour include Boston
Market, Burlington Coat Factory, Marshall's, and Marty's Shoes. The mall is open Monday-Saturday, 9:30am-
9pm; and Sunday, 10am-6pm.

GREEN ACRES MALL
Sunrise Highway
Valley Stream
☎ 516-561-1157
www.licvb.com/shopping.cfm

Green Acres features JCPenney, Macy's, Sears and 200
specialty stores, plus the Green Acres Cinema. The
mall is open Monday-Saturday, 10am-9:30pm; and
Sunday, 11am-6pm; it is just past the Queens/Nassau
border.

FRANKLIN AVENUE
Garden City

This is not a mall, but a neighborhood. The lovely
Franklin Avenue shopping district in Garden City –
long compared to New York City's Fifth Avenue – has
undergone a $4 million beautification project, attracting new restaurants and upscale stores and boutiques.
Of late the street has evolved into the "Wall Street of
Long Island" for its 14 bank branches, 10 brokerage
houses and many insurance companies. One of the
unique stores here is **Mineola Flag Co.**, 679 Franklin
Avenue at the corner of Seventh Street, ☎ 516-294-
3311, specializing in flags of all nations, decorative
flags, and flag pins, decals, and badges (closed Sun-

day). Another is **Once Upon A Dish**, 659 Franklin Avenue, ☎ 516-742-6030, where you paint your own pottery. You choose the piece, already cleaned and fired. No experience is necessary, and instruction is provided if you wish. They are open from 10am, Monday-Saturday, year-round; the fee is $8 per hour; $6 for children under 12, in addition to the cost of the piece. Well-known stores such as **Lord & Taylor**, ☎ 516-742-7000, and **Saks Fifth Avenue**, ☎ 516-248-9000, are also on Franklin Avenue.

ROOSEVELT FIELD
Old Country Road
Garden City
☎ 516-742-8000
www.shopsimon.com

Roosevelt Field is the nation's fifth-largest mall with 2.3 million square feet of space. It has 260 stores, including Macy's, JCPenney, Sears, Nordstrom and Bloomingdale's. Open Monday-Saturday, 10am-9:30pm; Sunday 11am-7pm. Take Exit M2 off Meadowbrook Parkway.

☞ DID YOU KNOW?

Charles Lindbergh took off from Roosevelt Field in 1927 on his first solo flight across the Atlantic. In 1955, Roosevelt Field airport became Roosevelt Field Shopping Center.

THE MALL AT THE SOURCE
Old Country Road
Westbury
☎ 516-228-0303
www.shopsimon.com

This 733,000-square-foot retail center and entertainment complex houses more than 60 stores, anchored by Fortunoff. The mall is open Monday-Saturday, 10am-

9:30pm; and Sunday, 11am-6pm. It is easily accessible from Meadowbrook Parkway, Exits M2E or M3E.

BROADWAY MALL
Route 106/107
Hicksville
☎ 516-822-6336
www.licvb.com/shopping.cfm

Broadway Mall has 130 stores anchored by Macy's, JCPenney, and IKEA. It is also home to the 12-screen Broadway Multiplex Cinemas. Open Monday-Saturday, 10am-9:30pm; and Sunday, 11am-6pm. The mall, located at Hicksville/Newsbridge Roads, a half-mile south of Northern State Parkway Exit 35S, has three restaurants and a food court with 12 outlets.

TRI COUNTY FLEA MARKET
3041 Hempstead Turnpike (Route 24)
Levittown
☎ 516-579-4500
www.licvb.com/shopping.cfm

Billed as "America's largest jewelry exchange," the complex features 100 jewelers, plus a furniture department, apparel, beauty salon and food court. Take Wantagh Parkway, Exit W3; go a half-mile east. Hours are Thursday and Friday, noon-9pm; Saturday and Sunday, 10am-6pm.

SUNRISE MALL
Sunrise Highway (Route 27)
Massapequa
☎ 516-795-3225
www.sunrisemall.com

Macy's, JCPenney, Sears and Eddie Bauer are among the 160 shops here. The mall is a quarter-mile west of Route 100, and is open Monday-Saturday, 10am-9:30pm; and Sunday, 11am-6pm.

★ FAMOUS FACES

Jerry Seinfeld grew up in Massapequa and graduated from Massapequa High School in 1972. He once
joked that Massapequa is an old Indian name meaning "by the mall."

Specialty Shops

OAKTREE BOOKSTORES
Oaktree has three branches in Nassau County, at 672
Dogwood Avenue, Franklin Square, ☎ 516-564-4369;
674 Sunrise Highway, Baldwin, ☎ 516-771-7796; and
80 Merrick Avenue, Merrick, ☎ 516-377-3226. The
stores are small, but offer a 30% discount for all hardcover books on *The New York Times* Best Seller Lists,
and 20% for softcover ones.

MUTTS & BUTTS
2076 Merrick Road
Merrick
☎ 516-379-6391
www.muttsandbutts.com

Attention, pet lovers! Mutts & Butts is a city block long.
"Long Island's department store for pets" sells every
small animal except dogs and cats, but carries everything for you and your pet – be it dog, cat, reptile, or
bird. There's a fish room and a bird room; books on caring for pets ranging from lizards to hedgehogs; pet food;
and gift items, such as cards and key chains embossed
with your favorite animal. Look for the store across
from the Dairy Barn.

POINT ARTWORKS
9 Lido Boulevard
Point Lookout
☎ 516-432-7852

The store carries a large selection of nautical gifts, along with stuffed animals, picture frames, notepaper and wrapping paper; it also has a year-round Christmas shop.

RIBBONESQUE
50 Lido Boulevard
Point Lookout
☎ 516-432-8936
www.ribbonesque.com

This new boutique features "handmade treasures" for home, house and garden. Linda Rudell fashions unique items with or from ribbons, steering away from country or surfside themes. Small gifts are her specialty and she takes special orders. Open Monday-Saturday, from 11am; and Sunday, by appointment.

Point Lookout is a tiny hamlet of some 800 year-round residents that swells to 4,000 in summer.

After Dark

Performing Arts

ROCKVILLE CENTRE GUILD FOR THE ARTS
PO Box 950
Rockville Centre
☎ 516-764-1558

Now into its 21st season, the Guild is a volunteer organization dedicated to showcasing professional and local talent. The Guild offers a wide variety of year-round activities in the performing and visual arts, all in Rockville Centre. Community productions of plays, concerts and dance ($12-$19) and children's theater ($8-$10) are presented either at South Side Middle School (Hillside and Park Avenue), or at the Hayes Theater at Molloy

Nassau County's South Shore

College (1000 Hempstead Avenue, Rockville Centre). It also sponsors a poetry group.

LONG ISLAND FILM & TV FOUNDATION
305 North Service Road
Dix Hills
Nassau County, ☎ 516-571-3168
Suffolk County, ☎ 631-421-7006
www.longislandfilm.com

The mission of this organization is to promote Long Island as a choice shooting location for films, commercials, documentaries and TV programs. See page 202 for additional information.

MALVERNE CINEMA & ART CENTER
350 Hempstead Avenue
Malverne
☎ 516-599-9336

Every other month from December to June, in conjunction with their first-run art films, the center features guest speakers such as directors and make-up artists; often the speakers are directly connected with the concurrent movie. The center also produces a film festival and holds special events, such as an Al Jolson retrospective.

ADAMS PLAYHOUSE
Hofstra University
Hempstead Turnpike
Hempstead
☎ 516-463-6644

Members of various university departments, as well as visiting professionals, perform here year-round. One of the university's acting companies, Hofstra USA Productions, was formed in 1966 and set the tone for a new acting tradition on campus, specializing in rarely seen plays performed by campus and community talent. Tickets are $8-$10 for student-produced plays and $22-$25 for professional productions.

FANTASY PLAYHOUSE
317 Merrick Road
Lynbrook
☎ 516-599-1982

The playhouse incorporates both a main stage and a theater for children's productions. The company operates year-round, performs extra shows during holidays and school breaks, and is available to travel to almost any location.

JONES BEACH MARINE THEATRE
Ocean Drive
Wantagh
☎ 516-221-1000, or 785-1600 (box office)
www.livetonight.com

A summer venue known for presenting a variety of performers, the outdoor theater has featured entertainers such as James Taylor, Rod Stewart and Men at Work.

BROADHOLLOW THEATRE COMPANY
Box office and information, ☎ 631-581-2700
www.broadhollow.org

The BroadHollow Theatre Company has three locations on Long Island: the BroadHollow Theatre, 200 Stewart Avenue, Bethpage; Center Stage at Molloy College, 1000 Hempstead Avenue, Rockville Centre; and BayWay Arts Center, 265 East Main Street, East Islip. This non-Equity theater performs musicals, dramas and comedies year-round. During the school year the company offers educational repertory to local schools, and Saturday children's theater at its BayWay Arts Center in East Islip and Broadhollow Theater in Bethpage; tickets are $16-$20, and $8 for children's theater. The company also holds acting classes and runs a summer acting camp.

Nassau County's South Shore

LANTERN THEATRE
Brookside School
Meadowbrook Road
North Merrick
☎ 516-221-4485
http://lanterntheatre.hypermart.net

This is Long Island's oldest theater, founded 48 years ago. The non-equity actors perform three (non-musical) plays a year and usually one classic every other year. Most of the productions come straight from Broadway or off-Broadway to be performed for the first time on Long Island. Tickets are $10; $9 for seniors and students. Their season runs from October to May. The theater is just south of Exit 23S off the Southern State Parkway.

NASSAU VETERANS MEMORIAL COLISEUM
1255 Hempstead Turnpike
Uniondale
☎ 516-794-9300
www.NassauColiseum.com

For an up-to-date schedule of events at Nassau Coliseum, Westbury Music Fair or Jones Beach Marine Theatre, log on to www.liveto-night.com.

Long Island's major arena – with 18,000 seats and a 60,000-square-foot exhibition hall – was opened in 1972 at a cost of $32 million. The Coliseum is home to the New York Islanders hockey team, the New York Saints indoor lacrosse team, and New York Dragons football; the facility also hosts two to five major concerts each summer, along with business conventions, trade shows, fairs and circus events. Superstars Elton John and Billy Joel were among the scheduled entertainers in 2002. See their Web site for directions.

WESTBURY MUSIC FAIR
960 Brush Hollow Road
Westbury
Ticket sales ☎ 631-888-9000
Information ☎ 516-334-0800
www.musicfair.com

The fair opened in 1956 in a tent. Within a decade it was replaced with a year-round fully enclosed theater. Tony Bennett (who returned in 2002) and Lena Horne performed there in the 1970s; Patti LaBelle, The Monkees and Johnny Mathis were among the performers in 2000; and Willie Nelson, Judy Collins and Harry Belafonte in 2001. That same year, *The Wizard of Oz* and *Catskills on Broadway* were presented. More recently, performers included Julio Iglesias, Betty Buckley and Howie Mandel. According to its Web site, the 3,000-seat Westbury Music Fair is one of the top five theaters nationwide, hosting about 150 shows a year. Something is happening here year-round, excluding January. Call or check their Web site for directions.

LECTURE SERIES

Adelphi University in Garden City holds a series of lectures during the academic year that are open to the public, most of them free. The Spring 2001 lineup listed political commentator David Gergen and bestselling authors Anna Quindlen, Jonathan Kozol and Alice Hoffman. For details, ☎ 516-877-4555, http://events.adelphi.edu/calendar/events.

CULTURAL ARTS PLAYHOUSE
714 Old Bethpage Road
Old Bethpage
☎ 516-694-3330

CAP is a musical theater and acting academy for children in grades K-12. Ticket prices for shows such as *Jack & The Beanstalk* and *Alice in Wonderland* are $8. In addition to the children's productions, which are

Nassau County's South Shore

held September-June, CAP's main stage presents a year-round schedule of Broadway dramas and musicals performed by professional actors; tickets for professional productions are $18; $16 for seniors and students. Call for directions.

Bars & Clubs

THE MERRY PEDLAR
339 Jericho Turnpike
Floral Park
☎ 516-488-8780

Dancing to live music from the 1930s to the 1960s, Thursday-Saturday; draws a mature crowd. Closed Monday.

BRADSTREET'S
161 Union Avenue
Lynbrook
☎ 516-887-2400

Entertainment on weekends: dinner shows, DJs, bands. No cover. Crowd is over 30. Open daily.

BACK STREET BLUES
60B North Park Avenue
Rockville Centre
☎ 516-766-MOJO (6656)
www.backstreetblues.net

Thursday night is blues jam – open for all to participate; jam bands perform Friday; Saturday afternoons are shows for all ages over 14. Saturday nights feature blues and Sunday is reggae. The club's kitchen is open every night, though the full menu is not always available.

CALICO JACK'S
3297 Long Beach Road
Oceanside
☎ 516-766-9822

Open mike on Tuesdays (draws the 21-45 age group) and acoustic bands on Wednesdays. Different bands featured Friday and Saturday nights attract varied ages. Open daily, for lunch and dinner (bar menu). Older crowd during day. No cover weekdays; $5 cover on weekends.

ELEANOR RIGBY'S
133 Mineola Boulevard
Mineola
☎ 516-739-6622
www.mineola1.com/eleanorrigbys

This sports bar and restaurant, open daily for lunch and dinner, features live music every Saturday night.

LA CISTERNA
109 Mineola Boulevard
Mineola
☎ 516-248-2112

La Cisterna features opera with dinner, performed by a professional artist, on the last Wednesday of each month.

THE CARLTUN
Eisenhower Park
East Meadow
☎ 516-542-0700, Ext. 1
www.thecarltun.com

Live jazz Friday and Saturday evening. No cover charge.

Nassau County's South Shore

THE CREASE
16 Merrick Avenue
Merrick
☎ 516-378-3626

Live bands Friday and Saturday beginning between 9
and 10pm. Mixed crowd depending on entertainment.

BUNNERY INN
3120 Hempstead Turnpike
Levittown
☎ 516-735-9431

Karaoke on Tuesday, Friday and Saturday. Open mike
Thursday. Cover $5, with free drink on Friday and Sat-
urday. Open daily.

Comedy

BROKERAGE COMEDY CLUB
2797 Bellmore Avenue, at Merrick Road
Bellmore
☎ 516-785-8655

Comedy nights, Thursday-Sunday. No credit cards, two-
drink minimum and cover charge. Mixed crowd. Club
has been in existence for 21 years.

GOVERNOR'S COMEDY CABARET
& RESTAURANT
90 Division Avenue
Levittown
☎ 516-731-3358

Eddie Murphy and Rosie O'Donnell have performed at both Governor's and Brokerage comedy clubs.

Dinner packages available. Cover and two-drink minimum. Among the comedians who have played at "one of
the top clubs in the country" are Jerry Seinfeld, Rosie
O'Donnell and Eddie Murphy. Open Thursday-Sunday.
Governor's has another location in Medford; see *Suffolk County*, page 296.

Dance Clubs

OZ NIGHTCLUB
Cherry Valley Shopping Center
514 Hempstead Turnpike
West Hempstead
☎ 516-481-8915

Open Friday (rap and reggae) and Saturday (disco). DJ both nights. Dress code: jacket required, no jeans or sneakers. Cover charge: Friday, $15; Saturday, $15 for men and $10 for ladies. Mixed crowd, over 23.

JAM ROC
45 Main Street
Hempstead
☎ 516-292-9200

Three floors feature dancing, reggae, R&B and hip-hop music Thursday-Saturday. $10 or more cover charge. Crowd is over 21.

WINNER'S CIRCLE
39 Post Avenue
Westbury
☎ 516-997-4050

Dance lessons, party mix. Open Thursday-Sunday; cover charge. Crowd is over 25.

Dinner Theater

ESCAPES SUPPER CLUB
6 Merrick Mall
Merrick
☎ 516-378-3770

Male revue for women opened in 1977. Cover charge, but dinner packages available. Doors open at 7pm, Friday and Saturday show begins at 9pm. Reservations required.

Nassau County's South Shore

Festivals & Events

February

Held over two weekends, the **Long Island Boat Show** at Nassau Coliseum includes educational displays and hundreds of exhibitors representing all aspects of boating, including pleasure, water skiing, diving and fishing. For more information, ☎ 516-691-7050 or check the sponsor's Web site, at www.nymta.com (New York Marine Trades Association).

April

The Historical Society of the Massapequas sponsors two annual **Antiques Shows**, one in April and one in November, usually at the beginning of the month. Both are held at the Berner Middle School, Carman's Mill Road in Massapequa. Admission is $4. Call the society at ☎ 516-799-2023 for more information.

May

Hofstra University in Hempstead holds its **Dutch Festival** on the South Campus. The festival, which is among the university's most popular events, features 100,000 tulips in bloom, a Volks parade with Dutch costumes, dancers, food, crafts, and puppet and magic shows. Admission is free; festival hours are 10am-5pm, rain or shine. Call or check the Web site for directions and other details; ☎ 516-463-6582, www.hofstra.edu.

The **Spring Festival** at the Old Bethpage Fairgrounds is a 19th-century experience, with horticultural exhibitions, sheep shearing, brass band concerts, old-time baseball games, 18th-century military drills and 19th-century contradancing. The festival is held Memorial Day Weekend, 10am-5pm; ☎ 516-572-8400.

June

The **British Country Fair** celebrates the heritage of Old Westbury Gardens with music and dancing, such as English Morris, Irish Step, Scottish Highland and maypole. There are also crafts, games, a marionette theater, petting zoo, pony carriage rides, demonstrations of sheep-shearing and exhibits of birds of prey. The fair is held noon-5pm at the Gardens, but selected vendors are on site from 10am. Free with admission to the gardens. 71 Old Westbury Road, Old Westbury, ☎ 516-333-0048, www.oldwestburygardens.org.

The **Shark Tournament** takes place at Guy Lombardo Marina in Freeport with about 300 participating boats. Visitors may attend the weigh-in, where excess shark steaks are available for sale. The bulk of the catch is donated to local food programs. The event is held from 6am-6pm and sponsored by the Hudson Anglers of Freeport, ☎ 516-867-9608, www.fhanglers.com. For information about other events in Freeport, call Freeport Village Hall at ☎ 516-378-7323.

The three-day **Strawberry Festival** on Newbridge Road in North Bellmore, ☎ 516-679-1875, is Nassau County's largest fruit festival, attracting about 50,000 strawberry fans. The event features games, rides and strawberry treats.

A **Strawberry Social & Crafts Fair**, generally held the Saturday of Father's Day weekend, features crafts, strawberry shortcake, face painting, entertainment, fresh produce, and a strawberry coloring contest. The fair is at Old Grace Church on Merrick Road and Cedar Shore Drive, Massapequa. Free admission. For more information, contact the Historical Society of the Massapequas at ☎ 516-799-2023.

October

The **Long Island Fair** kicks off on Columbus Day weekend and runs for six days. The Old Bethpage Village fairgrounds replicates the original Mineola Fair site established in 1866 by the Queens County Agricultural Society. The fair is a 19th-century agricultural exhibition complete with traditional games, entertainment, displays and elephant and pony rides. Old Bethpage Village Restoration, Old Bethpage, ☎ 516-572-8400. Admission is $10 for adults; $5 for seniors and children.

An **Apple & Harvest Festival**, usually held in mid-October, features baked apples and apple pies, face painting, entertainment, fresh produce and a pumpkin coloring contest. The fair is at Old Grace Church on Merrick Road and Cedar Shore Drive, Massapequa. Free admission. For more information, contact the Historical Society of the Massapequas at ☎ 516-799-2023.

November

The Historical Society of the Massapequas second **Antiques Show** of the year; Berner Middle School, Carman's Mill Road, Massapequa. Admission is $4. Call the society at ☎ 516-799-2023 for more information.

Best Places to Stay

All accommodations are open year-round.

ACCOMMODATIONS PRICE SCALE
Price scale is based on the cost of a double room, two people per room on a weekend, and does not include the 11.3% hotel tax.
Inexpensive.................under $130
Moderate ....$130-$200
Expensive...................$201-$300
Deluxe ....more than $300

Garden City

GARDEN CITY HOTEL
45 Seventh Street
Garden City
☎ 516-747-3000, or 800-547-0400
www.gch.com
Deluxe

"They always treat you like family," commented a regular guest at the Garden City Hotel. We were in the elevator, which transports you from the gleaming marble lobby with its exquisite antique furnishings to a parlor with more of same – all before reaching your spacious and well-appointed room.

Inquire about money-saving weekend packages at the Garden City Hotel.

The guest was right on the mark. At first blush, this family-owned hotel seems imposing – a massive building capped with a cupola. Completed in 1983, it's the fourth version of the hotel; the original was built in 1874 for wealthy guests from New York, Long Island and Boston. After being gutted by fire, it was rebuilt in 1901. William Vanderbilt, an avid race car driver, was a frequent guest (his 48-mile motor parkway designed for racing and pleasure driving was the model for parkways, interstates and speedways in the US, Germany and Italy). And, in 1927, Charles Lindbergh and his flight team stayed at the hotel before his record-setting flight to Paris.

The Garden City Hotel is a member of Preferred Hotels & Resorts Worldwide.

Today, whatever your station, the friendly and courteous staff treats you like royalty. The 280-room hotel has 32 suites and 10 handicapped-accessible rooms. Rounding out the amenities are a gift shop, beauty parlor, 15- by 30-foot pool and exercise equipment, restaurant (see **Polo Grill**, page 154), nightclub (complimentary admission for hotel guests), fully equipped business center and conference/ballroom.

To reach the hotel, take the Northern State Parkway to the Meadowbrook Parkway South, and get off at Exit M3W (Stewart Avenue west). Proceed to the corner, and at the traffic light make a right onto Stewart Ave-

Nassau County's South Shore

nue. Continue about 2½ miles to the end and make a left onto Hilton Avenue. At the first light, turn onto Seventh Street. The hotel entrance is on your right, 30 miles from the Throgs Neck Bridge.

Uniondale

LONG ISLAND MARRIOTT HOTEL & CONFERENCE CENTER
101 James Doolittle Boulevard
Uniondale
☎ 516-794-3800
www.longislandmarriott.com
Moderate to Expensive

Need directions to Long Island destinations? The concierge at the Long Island Marriott has a file box of printed instructions to get you where you want to go.

Visitors attending events at the adjacent Nassau Coliseum or Eisenhower Park will find this hotel the most convenient place to stay. It's also well designed for both business travelers or families – the comfortable guest rooms have ample seating, multi-purpose tables and computer hook-ups. There are 615 guest rooms and nine suites, with two handicapped-accessible rooms on each floor. Like the airy lobby, the solarium-style pool, flanked by fitness machines, is under a skylight. Other amenities include a whirlpool, sauna, hair salon, and racquetball courts. The health club has outside memberships so it's not unusual to find people pumping iron here.

The hotel's two moderately priced restaurants have a very different ambience. **Allie's American Grill**, open for breakfast, lunch and dinner, serves sandwiches, salads, burgers, and light and full entrées in a serene setting (breakfast is livelier). **Champions Sports Bar**, open for lunch and dinner, also has a full menu but allows smoking at the bar. The restaurant is in the back but there's no guarantee against secondhand smoke. This doesn't seem to deter sports fans; we were there in January when the Jets were playing Oakland in the playoffs and Champions was packed.

The Long Island Marriott is located near the Meadowbrook Parkway. For precise directions from your home, call the hotel or click "driving instructions" on its Web site. You can park your car yourself or pay a fee for valet parking. The hotel is virtually inaccessible without a car, but those arriving by train can take a taxi from the Westbury station two miles away.

Motels

MOTEL PRICE SCALE

Price scale is based on the cost of a double room, two people per room, in season, and does not include the 11.3% hotel tax.

Inexpensive . . . . under $100
Moderate . . . . $100-$150
Expensive . . . . over $150

FIVE TOWNS MOTOR INN
655 Rockaway Turnpike
Lawrence
☎ 516-371-2600
110 units. Moderate.

LONG BEACH MOTOR INN
3915 Austin Boulevard
Island Park
☎ 516-431-5900
67 units. Inexpensive.

CAPRI MOTOR INN
434 Hempstead Turnpike
West Hempstead
☎ 516-485-7300
86 units. Moderate.

One handicapped-accessible room.

Nassau County's South Shore

QUALITY HOTEL
80 Clinton Street
Hempstead
☎ 516-486-4100
182 units. Inexpensive to Expensive.

Handicapped-accessible rooms.

CAPRI LYNBROOK MOTOR INN
5 Freer Street
Lynbrook
☎ 800-656-0002, or 516-599-8800
62 units. Moderate.

Handicapped-accessible rooms. The Capri is one block south of Sunrise Highway directly behind Harrow's Department Store.

DIPLOMAT MOTOR INN
1000 Sunrise Highway
Rockville Centre
☎ 516-678-1100, 800-228-5521
www.dmimotel.com
99 units. Inexpensive.

HOLIDAY INN
6173 Sunrise Highway
Rockville Centre
☎ 516-678-1300
www.holiday-com/rockvilleny
100 units. Expensive.

Pet-friendly; welcomes all size pets.

FREEPORT MOTOR INN & BOATEL
445 South Main Street
Freeport
☎ 516-623-9100
60 units. Inexpensive.

YANKEE CLIPPER MOTEL
295 South Main Street
Freeport
☎ 516-379-2005
36 units. Moderate.

BUDGET INN
400 Carman Mill Road
Massapequa
☎ 516-795-4800
30 units. Inexpensive.

BEST WESTERN BAR HARBOUR
5080 Sunrise Highway
Massapequa Park
☎ 516-541-2000, 800-528-1234
www.bestwestern.com
51 units. Moderate.

Open year-round.

GATEWAY INN
Sunrise Highway
Merrick
☎ 516-378-7100
60 units. Inexpensive.

WESTBURY HOLIDAY INN
369 Old Country Road
Carle Place
☎ 516-997-5000
152 units. Expensive.

Handicapped-accessible rooms.

Nassau County's South Shore

PINES MOTOR LODGE
101 Taylor Avenue
Westbury
☎ 516-832-8330, 877-PINES NOW
www.pinesmotorlodge.com
60 units. Inexpensive.

They have another location on Suffolk County's South
Shore, in North Lindenhurst; ☎ 631-957-3330.

HOLIDAY INN
369 Old Country Road
Westbury
☎ 516-997-5000
www.holiday-inn.com/westburyny
152 units. Expensive.

Ten handicapped-accessible rooms.

COLISEUM MOTOR INN
1650 Hempstead Turnpike
East Meadow
☎ 800-540-5050, 516-794-2100
110 units. Moderate.

DAYS INN
828 South Oyster Bay Road
Hicksville
☎ 516-433-1900, 800-DAYSINN (329-7466)
www.daysinn.com
70 units. Moderate.

Handicapped-accessible rooms. Open year-round.

ECONO LODGE
429 Duffy Avenue
Hicksville
☎ 516-433-3900
www.econolodge-hicksville.com
82 units. Inexpensive.

Handicapped-accessible rooms. Open year-round.

HOLIDAY INN AT PLAINVIEW
215 Sunnyside Boulevard
Plainview
☎ 516-349-7400
www.holiday-inn.com/plainviewny
125 units. Moderate.

Handicapped-accessible rooms.

RESIDENCE INN BY MARRIOTT
9 Gerhard Road
Plainview
☎ 516-433-6200
www.residenceinn.com
170 units. Expensive.

Pet-friendly; accepts all pets under 25 pounds.

RODEWAY INN
333 South Service Road
Plainview
☎ 516-694-6500
www.rodewayinn.com
84 units. Inexpensive to Moderate.

Handicapped-accessible rooms.

Best Places to Eat

DINING PRICE SCALE
Price scale includes one entrée, with glass of wine and coffee. There is an 8.5% tax on food in both Nassau and Suffolk Counties.
Inexpensive . . . . under $25
Moderate . . . . $25-$40
Expensive . . . . over $40

Mineola

JANI
121 Mineola Boulevard at 1st Street
Mineola
☎ 516-294-5625
Inexpensive to Moderate

A Chinese/Japanese restaurant with several Long Island locations, Jani serves artfully prepared and delicious dishes. With a mirrored ceiling, large windows and an open kitchen, the Mineola restaurant is bright and cheerful. One wall houses the chef's collection of teapots from around the world. The cuisine has been described as "gourmet" by one source and "routine" by another. It's both – standard fare with flair.

Jani's other locations are 294 Sunrise Highway, Rockville Centre, ☎ 516-766-2554; 260 North Broadway, Hicksville, ☎ 516-433-0622; 947 Hempstead Turnpike, Franklin Square, ☎ 516-358-1603; and 350 Route 110, Huntington Station, ☎ 631-421-5264. All serve lunch and dinner, year-round.

Garden City

POLO GRILL
Garden City Hotel
45 Seventh Avenue
Garden City
☎ 516-747-3000
Moderate to Expensive

Sunday brunch at the Garden City Hotel is $49.

Zagat reports that the Polo Grill is a "class act all the way," and "not your average hotel restaurant." Well said! Blending the dark wood of a polo club with high-tech lights on a mirrored ceiling and antique Queen Anne chairs, this restaurant warrants splurging for a special occasion.

Victor, the charming manager, makes you feel like a VIP. The knowledgeable waiters present a tray of freshly baked breads. The sun-dried tomato bread and onion rolls will melt in your mouth, but beware of stuffing yourself, because the New American cuisine is superb and the desserts are to die for. Chef Steven DeBruyn is a winner. Trained at Koksyde, considered the best hotel school in his native Belgium, he was named best junior cook of Belgium in 1986. After working in top restaurants in Belgium and Paris, DeBruyn came to the hotel in 1994 and now supervises all meals.

Don't miss the tender, pan-roasted venison with Port wine poached figs, sautéed mustard greens and spiced butternut squash purée. Bring your significant other, swoon to the live piano music, and savor the moment. Open daily for breakfast, lunch and dinner. Reservations are essential (Saturdays are busiest).

Freeport

42 WOODCLEFT
42 Woodcleft Avenue
Freeport
☎ 516-868-3332
Inexpensive to Moderate

Opened Mother's Day 2000, this restaurant, along with the Nautilus Restaurant next door, is located at the landward end of Freeport's Nautical Mile.

> ★ TIP
>
> 42 Woodcleft is among the quieter restaurants on Freeport's Nautical Mile. The action takes place at Otto's, a seaport institution; Hudson & McCoy; and other restaurants closer to the ocean. Younger people, louder music and gridlock were observed one late spring evening; summer must be a real scene.

Nassau County's South Shore

The design of 42 Woodcleft is wonderful and wheel-chair-accessible. The bar is in a separate room with a door to keep the noise and smoke away from diners. A low ceiling and pillars between tables, hung with photos of old Freeport, act as buffers.

Service is superb and the menu features traditional waterfront fare. Dishes are beautifully presented and amply laden, but save room for dessert. The chocolate chip layer cake is moist and rich with just the right amount of sweetness.

To reach Woodcleft Avenue, follow directions to Nautical Mile (page 106). Parking is available across the street. Open daily, for lunch and dinner, year-round; reservations recommended.

★ TIP

Find more information about Free-port's restaurants at www.freeport-dining.com.

Wantagh

BOARDWALK RESTAURANT
Jones Beach State Park
Wantagh
☎ 516-785-2840
Inexpensive to Moderate

The problem with this super-casual restaurant is that a conglomerate owns it. No restaurateur worth his salt would book a wedding with 200 guests and keep 70 other tables dissatisfied. When we were there, it was early September and several waiters had returned to school. Hungry customers were not being served. Granted, this was the last supper of the season, and John Mellencamp was performing at Jones Beach Marine Theatre. The Boardwalk Restaurant has a captive audience. We watched the walkers on the boardwalk from our table by the window. We saw the sun set and our view vanish before the waitress showed. She looked so harried we didn't have the heart to complain. The food, however, is fine. The menu offers light fare, reasonably priced entrées and daily specials. My crab cake sandwich with sweet potato fries was most welcome! On a recent visit, a sign indicated that the restaurant is about to undergo a $1.1 million renovation and is scheduled to close between October 2002 and March 2003. But will service improve? Open daily for lunch, dinner and Sunday brunch during beach season.

★ TIP

Parking is free in the Boardwalk Restaurant's parking lot if you plan to eat there within three hours. A $20 refundable deposit secures your reservation.

Farmingdale

A.W. STEVENS
99 Quaker Meeting House Road
Bethpage State Park
Farmingdale
☎ 516-501-9700, Ext. 38
www.awstevens.com
Moderate

Even non-golfers will feel comfortable in this windowed restaurant. Opened in the spring of 2000, it has the ambience you'd expect – clubby with dark woods and fabrics. Except for the views, it feels far removed from the links. If golf interests you, watch the action from the patio. Lunch salads, hot entrées and sandwiches are quite reasonable, with no dish exceeding $7.95. Dinner is à la carte; fish and steak entrées average $22.95, and salads $5.

To reach the restaurant, take the Southern State Parkway to Exit 31N onto Bethpage State Parkway. Continue to the traffic circle. Make the first right out of the circle (do not exit circle at Central Avenue) and stay left to the clubhouse entrance. Open year-round; for lunch (daily), and dinner (Thursday through Sunday); reservations preferred.

Lite Bites

BAGELMAN
84 Merrick Avenue
Merrick
☎ 516-223-7031

Bagelman is a good place to go before heading to Jones Beach. Eat in or take out. Open daily, for breakfast and lunch.

SEAFORD HOT BAGELS
3970 Merrick Road
Seaford
☎ 516-679-1944

This is a large popular bagelry with lots of booths. Open daily, year-round.

BISTRO TO GO
662 Franklin Avenue
Garden City
☎ 516-747-3696

This deli/café has fresh and creative sandwiches and salads (closed Sunday).

Bistro to Go, Bagelman, Upper Crust and Riesterer's are within walking distance of the Garden City Hotel.

BAGELMAN
664 Franklin Avenue
Garden City
☎ 516-746-2881

A bagel store and deli, Bagelman is open daily for breakfast and lunch. Eat in or take out.

UPPER CRUST CAFE
931 Franklin Avenue, Garden City
☎ 516-248-5677

Stop in for freshly made pizza, pasta, salads, soups, sandwiches and yogurt. Sit in or take-out. Open Monday-Saturday.

RIESTERER'S CAFE OF GARDEN CITY
96-98 Seventh Street, Garden City
☎ 516-294-3560

Riesterer's is a card store with a bakery and coffee shop in back; open daily at 7am.

South Shore A to Z

Animal Hospitals

Animal Hospital of Elmont, 782 Elmont Road, (between Linden Boulevard and Dutch Broadway), Elmont, ☎ 516-285-4848. Small animals; by appointment; boarding. Closed Sunday.

Elmont is known as "The Home of Belmont Race-track."

Aaronson Animal Hospital, 320 Peninsula Boulevard (near Rockaway Turnpike), Cedarhurst, ☎ 516-295-4500. Small animals; boarding; walk-ins welcome. Open daily.

Wolfe Animal Hospital, 560 Peninsula Boulevard (between Rockaway Turnpike and Mill Road), Cedarhurst, ☎ 516-295-1416. Primarily dogs and cats; boarding; appointments and walk-ins welcome. Open daily.

Hewlett Animal Hospital, 1225 Broadway (near Mill Road), Hewlett, ☎ 516-295-4447. All animals; deluxe suites with TVs and VCRs (can you believe it?). Open daily.

Crawford Animal Hospital, 690 Merrick Road (at borderline of Lynbrook and Valley Stream), Lynbrook, ☎ 516-599-0256. Small animals and exotics; boarding; walk-ins welcome during prescribed hours. Open daily.

Hilton Animal Hospital, 120 Merrick Road, Lynbrook, ☎ 516-887-2914. All animals; boarding. Open daily.

A&A Veterinary Hospital, 414 Franklin Avenue (next to Garden World), Franklin Square, ☎ 516-763-2246, www.aavets.com. All size animals; boarding. Open daily.

Sunrise Animal Hospital, 74 North Long Beach Road, Rockville Centre, ☎ 516-766-4350. Primarily dogs and cats; boarding. Open daily (not affiliated with hospital of same name in West Islip).

Animal Medical Hospital, 779 Peninsula Boulevard (right off Southern State Parkway, Exit 19), Hempstead, ☎ 516-483-7007, www.drwylerpetdoc.com. All size animals, including exotics; boarding. Closed Sunday.

Baldwin Harbor Animal Hospital, 2933 Milburn Avenue, Baldwin, ☎ 516-379-5010. Dogs and cats only; boarding. Closed Sunday.

South Shore Animal Hospital, 3296 Merrick Road, (near Cedar Creek Park), Wantagh, ☎ 516-826-3400. Small animals; boarding. Open Sunday, 10-11am for emergencies.

Wantagh Animal Hospital, 1416 Wantagh Avenue, Wantagh, ☎ 516-221-2020. Small animals; boarding; walk-ins welcome Monday-Saturday; evenings by appointment. Closed Sunday.

Animal Shelters

In 2003 Bide-A-Wee will celebrate a "century of caring."

Bide-A-Wee Home, 3300 Beltagh Avenue, Wantagh, ☎ 516-785-4687 (clinic), ☎ 516-785-4079 (shelter), www.bideawee.org. Open daily, 10am-5pm, for adoptions. Dogs and cats are accepted by appointment only. The full-service vet clinic, open by appointment only, is closed Wednesday and Sundays. A pet memorial park is on the grounds as well.

Town of Hempstead Animal Shelter, 3320 Beltagh Avenue, Wantagh, ☎ 516-785-5220, www.townofhempstead.org/home/current/petmonth.htm. The shelter holds strays for six days and then offers them for adoption. Closed Sunday but open for adoptions.

Banks

The following banks have multiple branches throughout Nassau County. For specific locations, check the bank's Web site.

Astoria Federal Savings Bank . . . . www.astoriafederal.com

Bank of New York . . . . www.bankofnewyork.com

Chase Manhattan Bank . . . . www.chase.com

Citibank . . . . www.citibank.com

Dime Savings Bank of NY . . . . www.dime.com

First National Bank of LI . . . . www.fnbli.com

Fleet Bank . . . . www.fleet.com

HSBC . . . . www.us.hsbc.com

North Fork Bank . . . . www.northforkbank.com

Roslyn Savings Bank . . . . www.roslyn.com

State Bank of LI . . . . www.statebankofli.com

HISTORIC SITE

The Roslyn Bank building in Roslyn is a Georgian Revival structure dating from 1931; it is on the National Register of Historic Places.

Houses of Worship

Baptist

St. John's Baptist Church, 4 Henry Street, Inwood, ☎ 516-239-1413.

First Baptist Church of Lawrence, 252 Lawrence Avenue, Lawrence, ☎ 516-239-2233.

Valley Stream Baptist Church, 1865 Central Avenue, Valley Stream, ☎ 516-285-7565.

New Hyde Park Baptist Church, 635 New Hyde Park Road, New Hyde Park, ☎ 516-352-9672.

Lynbrook Baptist Church, 225 Earle Avenue, Lynbrook, ☎ 516-599-9402, www.lynbrookbaptist.org.

Shiloh Baptist Church, 96 North Central Avenue, Rockville Centre, ☎ 516-764-8311.

First Baptist Church in the Garden, corner Stewart Avenue and Clinton Road, Garden City, ☎ 516-746-0358.

Union Baptist Church, 24 Hastings Place, Hempstead, ☎ 516-483-3088.

Calvary Baptist Church, 132 Frederick Avenue, Roosevelt, ☎ 516-623-3037.

Freewill Baptist Church of Freeport, 443 North Main Street, Freeport, ☎ 516-378-9708.

Wantagh Baptist Church, Wantagh Avenue and Twin Lane, Wantagh, ☎ 516-785-3996.

Plainedge Baptist Church, 96 Stewart Avenue, Bethpage, ☎ 516-731-6736, www.plainedgebaptist.com.

Catholic

Cathedral of St. Agnes, Rockville Centre, 29 Quealy Place, ☎ 516-766-0205. St. Agnes is the diocesan seat for Long Island.

Holy Name of Mary, 55 East Jamaica Avenue, Valley Stream, ☎ 516-825-1450.

Holy Spirit, 500 Jericho Turnpike, New Hyde Park, ☎ 516-354-0359.

St. Christopher's Roman Catholic Church, 11 Gale Avenue, Baldwin, ☎ 516-223-0723.

St. Hedwig, 1 Depan Avenue, Floral Park, ☎ 516-354-0042.

St. Ignatius Martyr Church, 721 West Broadway, Long Beach, ☎ 516-432-0045.

St. Joseph's Catholic Church, 1346 Broadway, Hewlett, ☎ 516-374-0290.

St. Raphael's Roman Catholic Church, 600 Newbridge Road, East Meadow, ☎ 516-785-0236.

DIOCESAN INFORMATION

The Diocese of Rockville Centre on Long Island ministers to nearly 1.5 million Catholics in 134 parishes in Nassau and Suffolk counties. To find a parish that interests you, log on to www.churchandcommunity.com, a beautiful Web site with color photographs of churches and cathedrals, and links to several Long Island associations and businesses.

Episcopal

All Saints Episcopal Church, 2375 Harrison Avenue, Baldwin, ☎ 516-223-3731.

Christ Episcopal Church, 51 Blade Avenue, Lynbrook, ☎ 516-599-4109.

Grace Episcopal Church, 23 Cedar Shore Drive (at Merrick Road intersection), Massapequa, ☎ 516-798-1122.

Holy Trinity Episcopal Church, 54 Brooklyn Avenue and 7th Street, Valley Stream, ☎ 516-825-2903.

St. Andrews Episcopal Church, 50 Anchor Avenue, Oceanside, ☎ 516-536-7677.

St. George's Episcopal Church, 319 Front Street, Hempstead, ☎ 516-483-2771.

HISTORIC SITES

St. George's (c. 1823), and its rectory at 217 Peninsula Boulevard (c. 1793), were both designed in the Federal style and are on the National Register of Historic Places.

Nassau County's South Shore

St. James of Jerusalem Episcopal Church, 220 West Penn Street, Long Beach, ☎ 516-432-1080.

St. Phillips & St. James Episcopal Church, 432 Lakeville Road, New Hyde Park, ☎ 516-354-0458.

Trinity St. John's Church, 1142 Broadway, Hewlett, ☎ 516-374-1415.

Jewish – Orthodox

Congregation Beth Sholom, 390 Broadway, Lawrence, ☎ 516-569-3600.

Congregation Shaarei Zedek, 16 New South Road, Hicksville, ☎ 516-938-0420.

Congregation Toras Chaim, 1170 William Street, Hewlett, ☎ 516-374-7363.

Lido Beach Synagogue, 1 Fairway Road at Lido Boulevard, Lido Beach, ☎ 516-889-9650, www.lido-shul.org.

Young Israel of Lawrence-Cedarhurst, 8 Spruce Street, Cedarhurst, ☎ 516-569-3324, www.yilc.org.

Young Israel of Long Beach, 120 Long Beach Boulevard, Long Beach, ☎ 516-431-2404, www.yilb.com.

Young Israel of Merrick, 107 South Hewlett Avenue, Merrick, ☎ 516-378-2573.

Young Israel of Oceanside, 150 Waukena Avenue, Oceanside, ☎ 516-764-1099.

Young Israel of Plainview, 132 Southern Parkway, Plainview, ☎ 516-433-4811.

Young Israel of West Hempstead, 630 Hempstead Avenue, West Hempstead, ☎ 516-481-7429, www.yi-wh.org.

Young Israel of Woodmere, 859 Peninsula Boulevard, Woodmere, ☎ 516-295-0150.

Young Israel of North Woodmere, 634 Hungry Harbor Road, Valley Stream, ☎ 516-791-5099.

Jewish – Conservative

Baldwin Jewish Center, 885 East Seaman Avenue, Baldwin, ☎ 516-223-5599.

Bellmore Jewish Center, 2550 South Centre Avenue, Bellmore, ☎ 516-781-3072.

Beth Shalom-Oceanside Jewish Center, 2860 Brower Avenue, Oceanside, ☎ 516-536-6112, www.oceansidejc.org.

Congregation Beth David, 188 Vincent Avenue, Lynbrook, ☎ 516-599-9464.

Congregation Beth El, 99 Jerusalem Avenue, Massapequa, ☎ 516-541-0740.

Congregation Beth Sholom, 700 East Park Avenue, Long Beach, ☎ 516-432-7464, www.bethsholomlb.org.

Congregation B'nai Israel, 91 North Bayview Avenue, Freeport, ☎ 516-623-4200.

Congregation Sons of Israel, 111 Irving Place, Woodmere, ☎ 516-374-0655.

Israel Community Center of Levittown, 3235 Hempstead Turnpike, Levittown, ☎ 516-731-2580.

Hewlett-East Rockaway Jewish Center, 295 Main Street, East Rockaway, ☎ 516-599-2634.

Malverne Jewish Center, 1 Norwood Avenue, Malverne, ☎ 516-593-6364.

Manetto Hill Jewish Center, 244 Manetto Hill Road, Plainview, ☎ 516-935-5454.

Merrick Jewish Center, 225 Fox Boulevard, Merrick, ☎ 516-379-8650.

New Hyde Park Jewish Community Center, 100 Lakeville Road, New Hyde Park, ☎ 516-354-7583.

Temple Beth El, 46 Locust Avenue, Cedarhurst, ☎ 516-569-2700.

Temple B'nai Sholom, 100 Hempstead Avenue, Rockville Centre, ☎ 516-764-4628.

Temple Hillel Southside Jewish Center, 1000 Rosedale Road, Valley Stream, ☎ 516-791-6344, or 516-374-0655.

Temple Israel of South Merrick, 2655 Clubhouse Road, Merrick, ☎ 516-378-1963.

Wantagh Jewish Center, 3710 Woodbine Avenue, Wantagh, ☎ 516-785-2445.

Jewish – Reform

Central Synagogue of Nassau County, 430 DeMott Avenue, Rockville Centre, ☎ 516-766-4300.

Community Reform Temple, 712 The Plain Road, Westbury, ☎ 516-333-1839, http://shalomcrt.org.

East Bay Reform Temple, 2569 Merrick Road, Bellmore, ☎ 516-781-5599.

Garden City Jewish Center, 168 Nassau Boulevard, Garden City, ☎ 516-248-9180.

Suburban Temple, 2900 Jerusalem Avenue, Wantagh, ☎ 516-221-2370.

Temple Avodah, 3050 Oceanside Road, Oceanside, ☎ 516-766-6809.

Temple Beth Am, 2377 Merrick Avenue, Merrick, ☎ 516-378-3477.

Temple Beth Elohim, 926 Round Swamp Road, Old Bethpage, ☎ 516-694-4544, www.mytemple.org.

Temple Chaverim, 1050 Washington Avenue, Plainview, ☎ 516-367-6100, www.temple-chaverim.org.

Temple Emanuel, 3315 Hillside Avenue, New Hyde Park, ☎ 516-746-1120.

Temple Emanuel of Long Beach, 455 Neptune Boulevard, Long Beach, ☎ 516-431-4060.

Temple Emanu-el of Lynbrook, Ross Plaza, Lynbrook, ☎ 516-593-4004, www.emanuel-li.org.

Temple Judea of Massapequa, 98 Jerusalem Avenue, Massapequa, ☎ 516-798-5444.

Temple Sinai of Long Island, 131 Washington Avenue, Lawrence, ☎ 516-569-0267.

Lutheran

Ascension Lutheran Church, 145 Franklin Avenue, Franklin Square, ☎ 516-352-1263.

Bethlehem Lutheran Church, 1375 Grand Avenue, Baldwin, ☎ 516-223-3400.

Christ Lutheran Church, 300 Hillside Drive South, New Hyde Park, ☎ 516-746-4889.

Christ Lutheran Church, 3384 Island Road, Wantagh, ☎ 516-221-3286.

Holy Trinity Lutheran Church, 240 Lincoln Avenue, Rockville Centre, ☎ 516-766-2815.

Lutheran Church of Our Saviour, 888 Rockaway Avenue, Valley Stream, ☎ 516-825-5453.

St. John's Lutheran Church, 13 Blade Avenue, Lynbrook, ☎ 516-599-0778.

St. John's Lutheran Church, 1 Van Roo Avenue, Merrick, ☎ 516-379-3858.

St. Paul's Lutheran Church, 449 Stewart Avenue, Bethpage, ☎ 516-931-8262.

St. John's Lutheran Church By the Sea, East Olive & Riverside Boulevard, Long Beach, ☎ 516-432-7771.

Methodist

Community United Methodist Church, 100 Park Boulevard, Massapequa, ☎ 516-541-7008.

First Church Baldwin United Methodist, 881 Merrick Road, Baldwin, ☎ 516-223-1168.

Grace United Methodist Church, 21 South Franklin Avenue, Valley Stream, ☎ 516-825-1182.

St. James United Methodist Church, St. James Place, Lynbrook, ☎ 516-599-5148.

United Methodist Church of East Meadow, 470 East Meadow Avenue, East Meadow, ☎ 516-794-5855.

United Methodist Church of Merrick, 1425 Merrick Avenue, Merrick, ☎ 516-379-6058.

Woodmere-Lawrence Methodist Church, 1023 Broadway, Woodmere, ☎ 516-374-1865.

Presbyterian

Community Presbyterian Church, 12 Nottingham Road, Malverne, ☎ 516-599-3220.

First Presbyterian Church, 717 St. Luke's Place, Baldwin, ☎ 516-223-2112.

First Presbyterian Church, S Ocean Avenue, corner Smith, Freeport, ☎ 516-379-1114.

First Presbyterian Church, Main Street, Mineola, ☎ 516-746-7419.

First Presbyterian Church of New Hyde Park, 16 South 9th Street, New Hyde Park, ☎ 516-354-5013.

Memorial Presbyterian Church, 189 Babylon Turnpike, Roosevelt, ☎ 516-623-9561.

Presbyterian Church in Elmont, 525 Elmont Road, Elmont, ☎ 516-354-7447.

Presbyterian Church of Merrick, 2101 William Place, Merrick, ☎ 516-378-7761.

Valley Stream Presbyterian Church, 130 South Central Avenue, Valley Stream, ☎ 516-561-0616, http://vspc.cjb.net.

Information Sources

Chambers of Commerce

Baldwin Chamber of Commerce, ☎ 516-223-8080, www.baldwin.org.

Bethpage Chamber of Commerce, www.bethpage-chamber.com.

Chamber of Commerce of the Bellmores, ☎ 516-679-1875, www.bellmorechamber.com.

East Meadow Chamber of Commerce, ☎ 516-483-7103, www.emchamber.com.

Farmingdale Chamber of Commerce, ☎ 516-733-4079, www.farmingdalenychamber.com.

Freeport Chamber of Commerce, ☎ 516-233-8840, www.freeportchamber.com.

Garden City Chamber of Commerce, ☎ 516-746-7724.

Greater New Hyde Park Chamber of Commerce, ☎ 516-437-2021, www.nhpchamber.com.

Hempstead Chamber of Commerce, ☎ 516-483-2000, www.antonnews.com/communities.

Hicksville Chamber of Commerce, ☎ 516-931-7170, www.hicksvillechamber.com.

Long Beach Chamber of Commerce, 516-432-6000, www.antonnews.com/communities.

Lynbrook Chamber of Commerce, ☎ 516-593-3436, www.lynbrookusa.com.

Merrick Chamber of Commerce, ☎ 516-771-1171, http://merrickchamber.com.

Oceanside Chamber of Commerce, ☎ 516-763-9177.

Plainview-Old Bethpage Chamber of Commerce, www.plainview-oldbethpage.com.

Rockville Centre Chamber of Commerce, ☎ 516-766-0666, www.antonnews.com/communities.

Wantagh Chamber of Commerce, ☎ 516-679-0100, www.wantaghmall.org.

Westbury Chamber of Commerce, ☎ 516-997-3966.

Community Web Sites

Valley Stream . . . . www.valley-stream.com
Floral Park . . . . www.fpvillage.org
Hempstead . . . . www.townofhempstead.org

Hewlett. . . . . www.licentral.com/hewlett/htm/community.html

Long Beach . . . . www.thecitybythesea.com

Rockville Centre . . . . . . www.ci.rockville-centre.ny.us, www.antonnews.com/communities/rockvillecentre

Garden City. . . . . www.gardencityny.net

Freeport . . . . www.freeportny.com

Lynbrook . . . . www.lynbrookvillage.com

Merrick . . . . www.merrickny.com

North Hempstead. . . . . www.northhempstead.com

Hempstead . . . . www.townofhempstead.org

Wantagh. . . . . www.wantaghlife.com

Bethpage . . . . www.bethpagecommunity.com

Farmingdale . . . . www.fdale.com

Village of Farmingdale . . www.farmingdalevillage.org

Liquor Stores

Ace Liquors, 1811 Merrick Avenue, Merrick, ☎ 516-379-3090.

Atlantic Bayview Wines & Liquors, 380 Atlantic Avenue, Freeport, ☎ 516-378-9421.

Bellmore Liquors, 1849 Bellmore Avenue, Bellmore, ☎ 516-221-8622.

Bethpage Wine & Liquors Store, 574 Stewart Avenue, Bethpage, ☎ 516-931-0680.

Broadway Liquor & Wine, 125 Broadway, Lynbrook, ☎ 516-596-2512.

Cedarhurst Liquors, 216 Rockaway Turnpike, Cedarhurst, ☎ 516-239-0318.

Cost-Plus Wine & Liquor, 40 Central Court, Valley Stream, ☎ 516-568-2676.

Godly's Wine & Liquors, 1 Legion Place, East Rockaway, ☎ 516-599-6224.

Lance Wine & Liquors, 658 Rockaway Turnpike, Lawrence, ☎ 516-371-2522.

Lisbon Wines & Liquors, 142 Jericho Turnpike B, Mineola, ☎ 516-739-2620.

Oceanside Liquors, 2929 Long Beach Road, Oceanside, ☎ 516-766-5789.

Pop's Wine & Spirits, 256 Long Beach Road, Island Park, ☎ 516-431-0025.

Medical Facilities

Franklin Hospital Medical Center, 900 Franklin Avenue, Valley Stream, ☎ 516-256-6000, www.fhmc.org. is a member of the North Shore Long Island Jewish Health System.

Island Medical Center, 800 Front Street, Hempstead, ☎ 516-560-1200.

Long Island Jewish Medical Center, 270-05 76th Avenue, New Hyde Park. An 829-bed teaching hospital on the border of Queens and Nassau counties, serving the Greater New York area, Queens and Long Island, ☎ 516-470-7000, www.lij.edu.

Long Beach Medical Center, 455 East Bay Drive, Long Beach, includes a 203-bed community teaching hospital and a 200-bed sub-acute and skilled nursing facility, ☎ 516-897-1000, www.lbmc.org.

Massapequa General Hospital, 750 Hicksville Road, Seaford, ☎ 516-520-6000.

Mercy Medical Center, 1000 North Village Avenue, Rockville Centre, ☎ 516-255-0111.

Memorial Sloan-Kettering, 1000 North Village Avenue, Rockville Centre. Medical oncology, ☎ 516-256-3651; radiation oncology, ☎ 516-256-3600; www.mskcc.org.

Mid-Island Hospital, 4295 Hempstead Turnpike, Bethpage, ☎ 516-579-6000.

South Nassau Community Hospital, 2445 Oceanside Road, Oceanside, ☎ 516-763-2030.

Nassau County has 14 hospitals with a total of 4,748 beds.

Nassau County's South Shore

Nassau County Medical Center, 2201 Hempstead Turnpike, East Meadow, ☎ 516-572-0123.

North Shore University Hospital, 888 Old Country Road, Plainview, ☎ 516-719-3000, www.northshore-lij.com, is an acute-care community hospital with 239 beds; this hospital is a part of the 18-hospital North Shore Long Island Jewish Health System.

Winthrop University Hospital, 259 First Street, Mineola, ☎ 800-443-2788, or 516-663-0333, www.winthrop.org, is a 591-bed teaching hospital.

Movies

Bellmore Movies, 222 Pettit Avenue, Bellmore, ☎ 516-783-7200.

Bellmore Playhouse (5), 525 Bedford Avenue, north of Sunrise Highway, Bellmore Village, ☎ 516-783-5440 (recording), 516-783-9669 (office).

Broadway Multiplex (12), 955 Broadway Mall, Hicksville, ☎ 516-935-5599 (recording), 516-935-1313 (office).

Cineplex Odeon Twins, 340 Sunrise Highway, Rockville Centre, ☎ 516-678-3121 (recording), 516-678-3122 (office).

Clearview's Franklin Square Cinemas (6), 989 Hempstead Turnpike, Franklin Square, ☎ 516-775-3257 (recording), 516-775-0063 (office).

Clearview Herricks Cinemas (4), 3324 Hillside Avenue, New Hyde Park, ☎ 516-747-0555 (recording), 516-747-1789 (office).

Grand Avenue Cinemas (5), 1849 Grand Avenue, Baldwin, ☎ 516-223-2323 (recording), 516-223-2415 (office).

Green Acres Cinemas (6), 610 West Sunrise Highway, Valley Stream, ☎ 516-561-2100 (recording), 516-561-2105 (office).

Loews Cinema (8), Roosevelt Field Shopping Center, Old Country Road, Garden City, ☎ 516-741-4009 (recording), 516-741-4008 (office).

Loews Cineplex Fantasy (5), 18 North Park Avenue, Rockville Centre, ☎ 516-764-8000 (recording), 516-764-8240 (office).

Loews Raceway Theaters (10), 1025 Corporate Drive, Westbury, ☎ 516-745-6633 (recording), 516-745-6937 (office).

Malverne Cinema (5), 350 Hempstead Avenue, Malverne, ☎ 516-599-6966 (recording), 516-599-9336 (office). Independent and art films.

Mid-Island Theatre (3), 4045 Hempstead Turnpike, Bethpage, ☎ 516-796-7500 (recording), 516-796-7677 (office).

Oceanside Twin, 2743 Long Beach Road, Oceanside (across from Ocean Star Diner), ☎ 516-536-7565 (recording), 516-766-9509 (office).

Seaford Cinema (6), 3951 Merrick Road, Seaford, ☎ 516-409-8703.

Sunrise Multiplex, 750 West Sunrise Highway, Valley Stream, ☎ 516-825-5700.

UA Lynbrook Theater (6), 321 Merrick Road, Lynbrook, ☎ 516-593-1033, www.uatc.com.

UA Meadowbrook (6), 2549 Hempstead Turnpike, East Meadow (quarter mile west of Wantagh Parkway), ☎ 516-735-7552 (recording), 516-731-2423 (office), www.uatc.com.

Newspapers

New Hyde Park Illustrated (serving New Hyde Park, Albertson, Garden City Park and the Willistons); *Floral Park Dispatch*; *Mineola American*; *Garden City Life*; *Westbury Times* (serving Westbury, Carle Place, Salisbury, New Cassel, Old Westbury, Wheatly and the Brookvilles); *Hicksville Illustrated News*; *Levittown Tribune*; *Massapequa Observer*; *Plainview-Old Beth-*

Nassau County's South Shore

page Herald, *Three Village Times* (covering Elmont, Franklin Square, North Valley Stream, Floral Park and West Hempstead) and *Farmingdale Observer* are published by **Anton Newspapers**, ☎ 516-747-8282, www.antonnews.com. To read any of them on-line, simply add its name to Anton's Web site; for example, www.antonnews.com/farmingdaleobserver; for New Hyde Park add "IllustratedNews," and for Hicksville, "HicksvilleIllustratedNews."

The *West Hempstead Beacon*, *Hempstead Beacon*, *Uniondale Beacon*, *East Meadow Beacon* and *Merrick Beacon* are published by **Beacon Newspapers of Nassau County**, ☎ 516-481-5400.

The *Wantagh-Seaford Citizen*, ☎ 516-826-0812; *Bellmore Life* ☎ 516-378-5320; and the *Freeport-Baldwin Leader*, ☎ 516-378-3133, 516-378-5320, are published by **L&M Publications**.

The *New Hyde Park Herald Courier*, *Williston Times*, *Garden City News* (www.gcnews.com), *Jericho News Journal*, *Mid-Island Times* and *Bethpage Newsgram* are published by **Litmore Publishing Corp.**, ☎ 516-746-0240.

Massapequa Post, ☎ 516-798-5100, www.massapequapost.com, is a family-owned newspaper covering East Massapequa, Massapequa, Massapequa Park, Plainedge, and South Farmingdale.

The *Long Beach Herald*; *Nassau Herald* (serving Cedarhurst, Woodmere, Lawrence, Rockville Centre and Inwood); *Valley Stream Herald*; *Oceanside/Island Park Herald;*, *Franklin Square/Elmont/West Hempstead Herald; Bellmore Herald*; *Village Herald* (serving Lynbrook, East Rockaway, Malverne); *Merrick Herald*; *Baldwin Herald* and *East Meadow Herald* are Herald Community Newspapers published by **Richner Communications**, ☎ 516-569-4000, www.liherald.com. To read any of these papers on-line, go to www.liherald.com and click the paper of your choice. Richner also publishes two smaller papers that are not available on-line: *Long Island Graphic* and *Rockaway Journal*.

The *Baldwin Citizen* (☎ 516-599-5400); and the *Malverne Times* (☎ 516-739-6400), are published by **Nassau Community Newspapers**.

The *Floral Park Bulletin* and *The Gateway* are published by **Nassau Border Papers**, ☎ 516-775-7700.

South Shore Tribune, ☎ 516-431-5628, publishes the *Five Towns Tribune*; *Oceanside / Rockville Centre / East Rockaway Tribune*; *Long Beach Tribune*; *Island Park Tribune*; *Merrick / Bellmore / Central Nassau Tribune*; and *Hicksville / Levittown Tribune*.

Pharmacies

Five Towns Pharmacy & Surgical, 1919 Broadway, Woodmere, ☎ 516-374-2930.

Franwin Pharmacy, 127 Mineola Boulevard, at 1st Street, Mineola, ☎ 516-746-4720.

Ormondy Pharmacy, 781 North Merrick Road, Valley Stream, ☎ 516-285-6147.

Sea Breeze Pharmacy, 2697 Merrick Road, Bellmore, ☎ 516-785-4774.

Zip Codes

Albertson	11507
Alden Manor/Elmont	11003
Alden Terrace	11580
Baldwin	11510
Bellerose/Floral Park	11001
Bellmore	11710
Bethpage	11714
Carle Place	11514
Cedarhurst	11516
East Meadow	11554
East Rockaway	11518
Farmingdale	11735
Franklin Square	11010
Freeport	11520
Garden City	11530

Nassau County's South Shore

Garden City Park 11040
Hempstead 11550
Hewlett 11557
Hicksville 11801
Inwood. 11096
Island Park 11558
Lawrence 11559
Levittown/Plainedge 11756
Long Beach 11561
Lynbrook. 11563
Malverne. 11565
Massapequa 11758
Massapequa Park. 11762
Merrick 11566
Mineola 11501
New Hyde Park. 11040
North Woodmere 11581
Oceanside 11572
Old Bethpage 11804
Plainview 11803
Point Lookout 11569
Rockville Centre 11570
Roosevelt. 11575
Roosevelt Field 11530
Seaford 11783
Uniondale 11553
Valley Stream North 11580
Valley Stream South. 11581
Wantagh 11793
Westbury/New Cassel 11590
West Hempstead/Lakeview 11552
Williston Park/East Williston 11596
Woodmere. 11598

Suffolk County's North Shore

Suffolk County has 100,000 more residents than Nassau County, but is far larger in area – including a large portion of the body of the Island as well as the North and South Forks, Shelter Island and Fire Island – so it is much less densely populated. The county's major towns are Oyster Bay, Huntington, Brookhaven, Smithtown, Islip, Babylon, and Riverhead (the county seat). Brookhaven is geographically the largest town in New York State, covering 368 square miles, but has only 430,000 residents. Compare that to Hempstead's 725,639 residents living within 142.6 square miles.

Getting Here & Getting Around

By Car

The North Shore's major eastbound routes through Suffolk County are the Long Island Expressway, the Northern State Parkway, Jericho Turnpike (Route 25) and Routes 25A and 347. Major north-south roadways are the Sagtikos/Sunken Meadow Parkway, Nicolls Road (Route 97), Route 83, Route 112, and the William Floyd Parkway (Route 46). Many of these roads and parkways change their names as they go from west to east, or from north to south; for example, 25A is known as Northern Boulevard, North Hempstead Turnpike, Main Street (in Huntington), Fort Salonga Road, North Country Road, and Sound Avenue as it makes its way from western Nassau County to the eastern end of Suffolk.

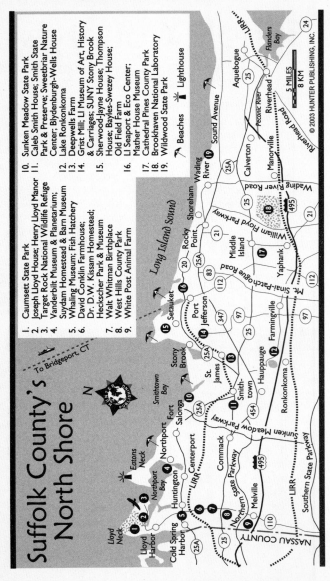

Suffolk County's North Shore

1. Caumsett State Park
2. Joseph Lloyd House; Henry Lloyd Manor
3. Target Rock National Wildlife Refuge
4. Vanderbilt Museum & Planetarium; Suydam Homestead & Barn Museum
5. Whaling Museum; Fish Hatchery
6. David Conklin Farmhouse; Dr. D.W. Kissam Homestead; Heckscher Park & Museum
7. Walt Whitman Birthplace
8. West Hills County Park
9. White Post Animal Farm
10. Sunken Meadow State Park
11. Caleb Smith House; Smith State Park & Preserve; Sweetbriar Nature Center; Blydenburgh-Wells House
12. Lake Ronkonkoma
13. Deepwells Farm
14. Grist Mill; LI Museum of Art, History & Carriages; SUNY Stony Brook
15. Sherwood-Jayne House; Thompson House; Bayles-Swezey House; Old Field Farm
16. LI Seaport & Eco Center; Mather House Museum
17. Cathedral Pines County Park
18. Brookhaven National Laboratory
19. Wildwood State Park

▶ Beaches   ✦ Lighthouse

© 2003 HUNTER PUBLISHING, INC.

Rental Cars

Rates for a mid-sized car range from around $25 up to $75, some with unlimited free mileage. All operate year-round unless otherwise specified.

Budget Rent-A-Car, www.budget.com; 233-A East Jericho Turnpike, Huntington Station, ☎ 631-425-1007; 330 East Jericho Turnpike, Smithtown, ☎ 631-265-3333; 5316 Nesconset Highway, Port Jefferson Station, ☎ 631-928-9200.

Dollar Rent A Car, 598 Broad Hollow Road, Huntington Hilton Hotel, Melville, ☎ 631-845-1221; Islip-MacArthur Airport, 4175 Veterans Memorial Highway, Ronkonkoma, ☎ 631-588-1700.

By Taxi

Lindy's is a local taxi service based in Smithtown with pickups in Smithtown and Commack, ☎ 631-265-2500; and in Setauket with pickups in Setauket, Stony Brook and Port Jefferson, ☎ 631-473-0707.

McRide's offers taxi and van service in East Northport, ☎ 631-261-0235; and Rocky Point (main office), ☎ 631-744-0005. They also have local, airport and service to NYC. Accepts all major credit cards.

By Limousine

M&V Limousines, 10 East Main Street, Smithtown, ☎ 631-360-8175, or 800-498-5788, www.mvlimo.com, serves all of Long Island.

Long Island Limousine, Hauppauge, ☎ 631-234-8400, www.longislandlimousine.com. This service will pick you up at train, bus or motel/hotel depot for half or one-third the price of other limo services.

Friends Limousine Service, Yaphank, ☎ 800-660-9668.

By Bus

Greyhound Bus Lines. . . . . ☎ 800-231-2222
Suffolk County Transit Bus . . . . . . ☎ 631-852-5200

By Ferry

Bridgeport & Port Jefferson Ferry Company, 102 West Broadway, Port Jefferson, ☎ 631-473-0286, www.bpjferry.com, carries passengers and cars year-round between Port Jefferson and Bridgeport, Connecticut. The ride is about 1¼ hours each way. Port Jefferson Harbor is at the north end of Route 112.

Sunup to Sundown

Museums

The only question with wealth is what you do with it.

– John D. Rockefeller Jr.

COLD SPRING HARBOR WHALING MUSEUM
Main Street
Cold Spring Harbor
☎ 631-367-3418
www.cshwhalingmuseum.org
Admission for adults, $3; seniors, $2; children, $1.50; under age five, free.

On the lawn of the museum is a 700-pound cannon that once boomed out signals to tall ships. This gave the villagers time to hurry down to the docks to wave and shout their greetings.

One of Cold Spring Harbor's 19th-century housewives, Helen Rogers, began recording the town's social and maritime history when she was 15. One of her poems about a whaling vessel appears below.

Whaling museums cannot replicate the emotions villagers like Helen Rogers experienced, but instead rely on artifacts and videos to convey the adventure and solitude of a whaler. This museum depicts the dangers of a voyage in a 19th-century whaleboat that resembles a canoe, and displays a mammoth killer whale skull found on the beach at Orient Point. Its scrimshaw collection shows the artistic ability of the sailors that they developed during down-time aboard ship. Two elaborate watchtowers represent whalers' more ambitious scrimshaw projects. A special exhibit on ships in bottles also portrays examples of mastery and infinite patience. Open 11am-5pm daily, from Memorial Day to Labor Day; in off-season, open Tuesday-Sunday. The museum, which is handicapped-accessible, first opened its doors in 1942.

THE ANCIENT WRECK
by Helen Rogers

They say that a handsomer, swifter craft never sailed on the ocean track,

As to sunny climes she hasted oft and came as safely back.

And I well remember each happy face of her bold and youthful crew;

Here was strength and beauty and active grace and hearts so gallant and true.

And I tell you the tale, my listening friend, how that vessel became a wreck

And the gallant forms of those fearless men never again walked a deck.

THE LONG ISLAND MUSEUM OF AMERICAN ART, HISTORY & CARRIAGES

1200 Route 25A
Stony Brook
☎ 631-751-0066
www.longislandmuseum.org
Admission $4 for adults; $3 for seniors over 60; $2 for children ages six-17 and current college students.

This museum began in 1939 as the Suffolk Museum. From the 1950s to the 1980s, several historic buildings were moved to the property and the art, history and carriage museums were opened. The grounds of the privately funded museum now straddle Route 25A; the nine-acre site is beautifully maintained and is wheelchair-accessible. The main entrance and visitors center house changing exhibitions, a decoy museum and miniature rooms. You'll hear the quacking even before reaching the eye-catching diorama of Elfie's Hole, which depicts a small cove on the eastern edge of Shinnecock Bay. As the sign indicates, this marsh was an important hunting ground because of the diversity of waterfowl, and is one of the few places on the South Shore left untouched by residential development.

Famous Long Island carvers created many of the decoys on display. There is also a reconstruction of a bayman's workshop. The miniature rooms illustrate periods of interior architecture and decorative arts from the 16th century through the 1930s.

Watch for traffic before crossing the road to the Dorothy and Ward Melville Carriage House. A ramp leads to 10 galleries with carriages on three levels, ranging from absolutely fabulous European chariots to ordinary buggies. It was Melville's decision to include vehicles of the middle class for fear they would otherwise be lost to history.

There are children's vehicles that were pulled by goats, dogs or ponies; a re-creation of "Stony Brook Station," when a one-way ticket to Stony Brook was $1.60; and, of course, fire engines. The most elaborate, "Parade Hose Carriage," is decorated with etched glass mirrors and topped by statuettes of classical figures. Fire companies used the carriage during civic celebrations to show off their equipment.

> ★ TIP
>
> For those interested in researching any aspect of horse-drawn transportation, the museum's Carriage Reference Library is open to the public by appointment. Holdings include more than 1,200 titles, 1,500 volumes, and 450 trade catalogues of carriages. For information, contact Merri Ferrell, curator, at ☎ 631-751-0066, Ext.222.

Also on the property is a 19th-century one-room schoolhouse, along with a blacksmith shop and the Smith-Rudyard Burial Ground. Long before the museum moved in, the site was part of the John Smith family homestead. Most of the white marble gravestones date back to before the Civil War and one is marked 1796.

Ward Melville collected the works of William Sidney Mount (1807-1868), a Stony Brook artist who became America's first famous "genre" painter. Mount painted scenes from ordinary life, and his *Dance of the Haymakers* (1845) is considered one of the greatest masterpieces of the 19th century. Mount lived in Stony Brook and neighboring Setauket throughout his life. As the most well-known in a family with six artistic siblings, William was acclaimed by a New York critic as "one of the most gifted artists that ever lived."

The Art Museum features changing exhibitions of American art and is also the repository of the works of the Mount family. Call for hours and directions.

Historic Sites

Starting from fish-shape Paumanok, where I was born...
— *Leaves of Grass*, Walt Whitman (1819-1892)

WALT WHITMAN BIRTHPLACE
246 Old Walt Whitman Road
Huntington Station
☎ 631-427-5240
Admission for adults, $3; seniors, $2; children seven-12, $1; six and under free.

Long Island has embraced Walt Whitman, preserving his childhood home and naming streets and businesses after him. The poet's father was an unhappy farmer and skilled carpenter who built the house where his four children were born, in the West Hills section of Huntington. When Walt Jr. was five his family moved to Brooklyn, but he often returned to Long Island to visit friends and rekindle memories; he returned at age 17 to teach school and start the *Long Islander* newspaper, which is published to this day. Many Long Island recollections are contained in *Specimen Days and Collect*, published in 1882.

The Whitman family was prominent on Long Island dating back to the early 17th century. "Whitmanland" covered over 500 acres in what is now West Hills and South Huntington. Several residences there belonged to family members, and 75 gravestones in the area attest to their presence. (Turn left from the Walt Whitman birthplace and make a quick right onto West Hills Road. At Chichester Road turn left and you'll see signs for several historic sites.)

The property was in private hands until 1951 when the Walt Whitman Birthplace Association acquired the house and grounds. In 1957, it became New York's 22nd state historic site. The Federal-style home is sparsely furnished, and has high ceilings, large windows and the original wide floorboards. Whitman's mother was Dutch and his father English; the house is a mixture of styles – Dutch doors and English bone china, for example. The second-floor garret is the most rustic room, with a trundle bed and exposed beams and nails.

Start your tour with a video in the Interpretive Center, dedicated on May 31, 1997. Walt Whitman was the most widely photographed author of the 19th century and hundreds of photos of him taken between the early 1840s and 1891 are displayed. The room also contains the original school desk from one of his classrooms, a copy of *Leaves of Grass* – a compilation of more than 380 Whitman poems – and a replica of a printing press used to publish the *Long Islander*. An attractive circular exhibit chronicling Whitman's life was designed by Ralph Appelbaum, designer of the Holocaust Museum exhibition in Washington. If you're interested, ask to hear the tape of Walt Whitman reading from one of his poems. Both the Interpretive Center and the first floor of the house are handicapped-accessible. The site sponsors monthly poetry readings and a poet-in-residence program.

☞ DID YOU KNOW?

Billy Collins, the Interpretive Center's 2001 Poet-in-Residence, became Poet Laureate of the United States.

To reach the Whitman birthplace, take the LIE to 49N and travel north on Route 110 for 1.8 miles. Before the Exxon station, turn left onto Old Walt Whitman Road. The site comes up shortly on the right. To learn more about the site, visit www.nysparks.com or www.liglobal.com/walt. The property is open daily, 11am-4pm, from Memorial Day to Labor Day; the rest of the year it is open Wednesday-Friday, 1pm-4pm; and Saturday and Sunday, 11am-4pm.

VANDERBILT MUSEUM & PLANETARIUM
180 Little Neck Road
Centerport
☎ 631-854-5555 (information); 854-5579 (receptionist);
or 854-5550 (membership and special events)
www.vanderbiltmuseum.org
Admission is $5-$10; rates vary for tours of grounds,
the mansion, or planetarium shows. Discounts for children and seniors.

The Vanderbilt Museum hosts concerts, plays, living history presentations and other special events throughout the year.

Ever wonder what it's like to live like a Vanderbilt?
Take a tour of William K. Vanderbilt II's palatial 24-
room summer home and you'll find out. The entrance to
Eagle's Nest is adorned with two large stone eagles
that once stood atop the old Grand Central Terminal (it
happens that the architect was a cousin of Vanderbilt's
and a member of a prominent firm that helped build
Grand Central). The tour starts in the central courtyard of the Spanish Revival mansion, but if you have
time step inside Memorial Hall for a taste of what's to
come.

Great-grandson of "Commodore" Cornelius Vanderbilt
(founder of the New York Central Railroad and Staten
Island Ferry), "Willie K" (1878-1944) was born into a
life of privilege and had a passion for sailing and racing
cars. After separating from his first wife, he built a
modest seven-room "bachelor pad" on Northport Harbor where he could easily sail to Newport, Rhode Island
to visit his parents. He began to expand the mansion
after his second marriage in 1927 to divorcee Mrs.
Barclay H. Warburton. The luxurious furnishings in
the house include a hand-carved Florida cypress ceiling in the dining room. Food was prepared downstairs
and sent up in a dumbwaiter. Need something? A floor
pad at the edge of the 11-foot Florentine table sum-
moned the servants, as did a button in the bathtub.

Before he was 40, Vanderbilt devoted much of his time
to car racing. At first, he had no place to race his
Mercedes sports car so he built a 45-mile racetrack. His
Vanderbilt Cup, with a purse of $20,000, brought inter-
national attention to Long Island. That ended with the

deaths of spectators. He later helped create the 50-mile-long Vanderbilt Motor Parkway extending from Queens to Lake Ronkonkoma. A toll road, it was the world's first roadway expressly for automobiles. Vanderbilt ultimately gave the roadway to the state in lieu of back taxes.

When his father died and left Willie K an even richer man, he turned to marine-life explorations aboard the *Alva*, his 265-foot yacht, which he named for his mother. His only son, William K. Vanderbilt III, had the same adventurous spirit, but was killed in an automobile accident at age 26. Memorial Hall, built in his memory, houses the son's collection of African artifacts and big game trophies.

The Marine Museum, which Vanderbilt opened to the public in 1922, is not part of the basic tour but is worth a side trip. Vanderbilt is credited with discovering 67 types of marine life, and the museum displays his vast collection of shells and preserved birds, butterflies and bugs from the world over. The main floor houses artifacts and marine specimens that Willie K collected on two world cruises aboard the *Alva*. (During World War II, Vanderbilt donated the *Alva* to the Navy; it was sunk and never recovered.) The second floor, originally called the Hall of Fishes, holds a collection of smaller specimens that should interest any fisherman. Also worth a visit is the planetarium, reputed to be among the largest and best equipped in the nation; it is wheelchair accessible.

To reach the Vanderbilt Museum from Huntington Village, go east on Route 25A and continue into Centerport. At the fork, be sure to follow Little Neck Road (going north). The museum is on a point overlooking Northport Bay; it comes up shortly on the right. The hilly terrain, cobblestone walkways and narrow stairways are not handicapped accessible. However, the Web site gives viewers a superb virtual tour.

Newsday recently asked historians about their favorite Long Islanders. One wrote that William K. Vanderbilt II's "interest in transportation, technology and global studies left us a tremendous legacy. He's always been a hero of mine."

CALEB SMITH HOUSE
Route 25A
Smithtown
☎ 631-265-6768
Admission by donation

In 1819, Caleb Smith II built this white shingled Federal-style farmhouse in Commack. One of several buildings maintained by the Smithtown Historical Society, it serves as the society's headquarters and is the only one of their properties that is open regularly. The house was scheduled for demolition in 1955 when one of Smith's descendants donated money to have it moved from Commack to its present location, which, when George Washington visited in 1790, was occupied by the Blydenburgh Tavern run by the Widow Blydenburgh. The house is filled with 17th- and 18th-century furniture, paintings and documents. Washington wrote in his diary at the tavern desk, which is now part of the collection. Some pieces are original to the house, like the Bull Rider's Chair with a hard-backed, hardwood seat that looks mighty uncomfortable. The house is right off Route 25 next to the Smithtown library; it is open Monday-Saturday, year-round.

WHAT'S IN A NAME?

Smithtown was named for Richard "Bull" Smith, a headstrong Englishman who rode a bull because he disliked horses. The imposing statue of his bull, Whisper, on Route 25 (Jericho Turnpike) is most visible driving west. Caleb Smith II, a wealthy fourth-generation descendant, may have inherited his ancestor's bullheadedness. During the Revolutionary War, he was whipped and shot at by the Redcoats for refusing to take an oath of allegiance to King George III.

BLYDENBURGH-WELD HOUSE
Blydenburgh County Park
Smithtown
☎ 631-360-0753 (Greenbelt Trail Conference office)
☎ 631-854-4949 (Suffolk County Parks & Recreation)

The Blydenburgh-Weld House (1821), which serves as headquarters for the Greenbelt Trail Conference (see page 17), is on a sweeping lawn leading down to a pond. Free guided tours of the grounds are held every Saturday at 1pm, including the house, gristmill, carriage house, and miller's house. The organization also runs about 150 hikes a year all over Long Island.

The Blydenburghs were descendants of the famous Smith family, for whom Smithtown is named. They inherited the land in 1798 and subsequently built a farmhouse and mill, which today are part of the Blydenburgh Park National Register Historic District. In 1938, the property was sold to David and Molly Weld, of whom Governor William Weld of Massachusetts is a descendant. In fact, it was his parents' 600-acre farm in Smithtown that was taken through eminent domain for parkland, and which later became Blydenburgh Park. The property's Stump Pond was so named because the pond wasn't big enough to generate water for the grist and woolen mills so trees were cut down and only the stumps were left. Two mills burned down, and today only the gristmill remains.

The 588-acre park has bridle paths, campsites, freshwater fishing, bike hostel areas, hiking trails, picnic areas and rowboat rentals. To reach the main entrance, take Northern State Parkway east to the end, then Veteran's Memorial Highway to the park, just before the County Center.

To reach the Blydenburgh-Weld House, take the LIE to Exit 53, then go north on the Sunken Meadow Parkway. Take the exit for Smithtown onto Jericho Turnpike and go east, past the bull statue, to Brookside (at light). Turn right onto New Mill Road. Follow 1.8 miles to the park entrance.

SUFFOLK COUNTY'S NORTH SHORE HISTORIC CHURCHES

- ◆ **Commack Methodist Church** and cemetery, both completed in 1789.

- ◆ **First Presbyterian Church**, Smithtown, was built between 1823 and 1825.

Caroline Church of Brookhaven (in Setauket) is the oldest Episcopal church on Long Island; it was founded in 1729.

- ◆ **St. James Episcopal Church**, rectory and cemetery, which are part of the St. James Historic District. Founded in 1853, the Gothic Revival church gave its name to the village. Its architect, Richard Upjohn, designed Trinity Church in Manhattan. Stanford White, whose country home "Box Hill" was nearby, was a parishioner and designed three of the church's stained-glass windows. He is buried in the cemetery

- ◆ **Setauket Presbyterian Church**, built in the Federal style in 1812, has a burial ground with graves dating back to 1660, when the church was established. Genre artist William Sidney Mount, (see page 183) is buried there.

STONY BROOK GRIST MILL
Harbor Road off Main Street
Stony Brook
☎ 631-751-2244
www.wardmelvilleheritage.org
Admission $3

Only the first floor of the Stony Brook gristmill is handicapped-accessible.

Adam Smith, son of the legendary founder of Smithtown, Richard (Bull) Smith, built the original mill in 1699. After it was destroyed, the present structure was erected in 1751 and the year 2001 marked its 250th anniversary. There were once more than 200 gristmills on Long Island. Of the few mills left, this is the most completely equipped and is listed on the National Register of Historic Places. Moreover, the mill is in full operation during touring hours. A "miller" in overalls greets visitors and explains the multi-step process of grinding wheat or corn to flour on the noisy 1855 machinery. Watching the silky wheat pouring through the hopper, a visitor observed, "You have to have a healthy respect for the engineering." The miller replied that "it may look like Rube Goldberg, [but] it runs just as it did then." The second floor features an old country store. The mill pond across the way is filled with ducks and geese. A new boardwalk around the pond is well shaded; it leads to hiking trails. During April and May and from early September through mid-December, the mill is open Saturday and Sunday, noon-4:30pm. From June through August, it's open Wednesday-Sunday, noon-4:30pm. Educational tours are given from March through December, by appointment only, for groups of eight or more.

☞ DID YOU KNOW?

A Revolutionary War-era fort located between Huntington and Smithtown gave its name to the village of Fort Salonga.

Historical Societies & Tours

SOCIETY FOR THE PRESERVATION OF LONG ISLAND ANTIQUITIES (SPLIA)
161 Main Street
Cold Spring Harbor
☎ 631-692-4664
www.splia.org

The SPLIA is headquartered in Cold Spring Harbor, where it maintains a selection of SPLIA publications and other related materials, brochures and books concerning Long Island. The SPLIA Gallery at the corner of Main Street and Shore Road houses a changing year-round exhibit and gift shop; it is open 11am-5pm, Tuesday-Sunday, May-October; Friday-Sunday, November-

December; and Saturday and Sunday, January-April.
Admission is free. The society maintains the following
four historic house museums; there is a small admission fee at each.

Sherwood-Jayne House, 55 Old Post Road, East
Setauket. This is an 18th-century Colonial farmstead
featuring a barn, corn crib, ice house and sheep. The
house is decorated with hand-painted floral frescos by
an unknown Colonial artisan. Open by appointment,
summer, spring and fall.

The Custom House, Main and Garden Streets, Sag
Harbor. In 1789, Sag Harbor became the nation's first
port of entry and The Custom House is the 18th-cen-
tury home of the port's first US Customs Master, Henry
Packer Dering. Daily activities of the Dering family are
portrayed in the room settings of a formal dinner,
office, children's room, kitchen, pantry and laundry.
Open 10am-5pm, Saturday and Sunday, from Memorial Day through June; daily, July and August; and Saturday and Sunday, from Labor Day to Columbus Day.

Thompson House, 91 North Country Road, Setauket.
The Thompson House has one of the finest collections
of early Long Island furniture, dating to 1750, plus a
Colonial herb garden. Built in 1700, this house is an
unusually large saltbox structure. Hours are 1-5pm,
Saturday and Sunday, Memorial Day-Columbus Day;
and Friday-Sunday, July and August.

Joseph Lloyd Manor House, Lloyd Lane and Lloyd
Harbor Road, Lloyd Harbor. The Lloyd house was occupied by the British when its owner, Joseph Lloyd,
joined other Patriots in Connecticut. Among new im-
provements in the house are a handicapped-accessible
bathroom and docents' kitchen. The manor house is situated in a spectacular setting overlooking Lloyd Harbor and is open for tours on weekends, Memorial Day-
Columbus Day.

HENRY LLOYD MANOR
Caumsett State Park
41 Lloyd Harbor Road
Lloyd Harbor
☎ 631-549-6987

The **Lloyd Harbor Historical Society** maintains the 1711 Henry Lloyd Manor, which is open for tours by appointment year-round. Henry Lloyd was descended from James Lloyd (1653-1693), the first Lord of the Manor of Queens Village (now Lloyd Neck).

HUNTINGTON HISTORICAL SOCIETY
209 Main Street
Huntington
☎ 631-427-7045
www.huntingtonhistoricalsociety.org

The society conducts tours of two historic house museums in Huntington Village. The society also holds events relating to the area's history in spring, summer and fall and sponsors lectures once a month in the spring and fall. The office is open weekdays, 9am-4:30pm.

Huntington Township is celebrating its 350th anniversary in 2003.

David Conklin Farmhouse, c. 1750, on High Street and New York Avenue (Route 110), is the oldest house in Huntington and reflects life and décor in the Colonial, Federal and Victorian periods. Open Tuesday-Friday and Sunday, 1-4pm, year-round.

Dr. Daniel W. Kissam House, c. 1795, 434 Park Avenue, one block south of Route 25A, was the home of Dr. Daniel Whitehead Kissam, who practiced medicine in Huntington until his death in 1839. The site features Egyptian Revival woodwork and houses a consignment shop of antiques and collectibles. A historic barn is on the property. Visits can be arranged on Sundays, from June through August, 1-4pm; advance notice is required.

**GREENLAWN-CENTERPORT
HISTORICAL ASSOCIATION**
31 Broadway
Greenlawn (in Harborfield Public Library)
☎ 631-754-1180
http://gcha.suffolk.lib.ny.us

The Association runs tours of the **Suydam Homestead and Barn Museum**, 1 Fort Salonga Road, Centerport, on Sundays, 1-4pm, May-October. The Suydam
farmhouse is the earliest surviving structure in this
waterfront hamlet and has been associated with the
family since the late 18th century.

**NORTHPORT HISTORICAL SOCIETY
AND MUSEUM**
215 Main Street
Northport
☎ 631-757-9859
www.northporthistorical.org

The museum was opened in 1974 in a building originally funded by Andrew Carnegie in 1914 as the Village Library. It has a permanent shipbuilding exhibit
and memorabilia reflecting life in the Northport area
through all periods of its history, as well as several
changing exhibits each year. Open Tuesday-Sunday, 1-
4:30pm, year-round. No handicapped access.

**LAKE RONKONKOMA HISTORICAL SOCIETY
MUSEUM**
328 Hawkins Avenue
☎ 631-467-3152

The **Lake Ronkonkoma Historical Society** maintains this museum containing local artifacts, Indian
arrowheads and other weapons and memorabilia about
Maude Adams, a famous actress who lived in the area.
Open 10am-noon, Saturdays and by appointment,
year-round.

BAYLES-SWEZEY HOUSE

93 North County Road
Setauket
☎ 631-751-3730
http://members.aol.com/TVHS1

The **Three Village Historical Society** makes its home at this historic two-story farmhouse. It is open daily, 9am-4pm, and tours are by appointment.

The society conducts a variety of programs at other historic sites. Free public programs on topics of historic interest are held the first Monday evening of each month at the **Setauket Neighborhood House**, built in the early 1700s as a hotel. The society conducts weekend tours of the Setauket historic district, a "Spirits of the Three Village Cemetery Tour," one evening each October; and a Candlelight House Tour, on the first weekend in December. The society also sponsors exhibits, walking tours, family programs, and festivals.

MATHER HOUSE MUSEUM

115 Prospect Street
Port Jefferson
☎ 631-473-2665
www.portjeffhistorical.org
Admission: adults, $2; children under 12 free

The **Port Jefferson Historical Society** opens the Mather House from Memorial Day to Labor Day. In June, hours are Saturday and Sunday, 1-4pm; in July and August, hours are Tuesday, Wednesday, Saturday and Sunday, 1-4pm. In addition to the 19th-century home of shipbuilder John Mather are a marine barn, tool shed, a replica country store, butcher and barber shops.

Walking Tours

Stony Brook

Tours of the historic district of Stony Brook Village are sponsored by the Ward Melville Heritage Organization, ☎ 631-751-2244, www.wardmelvilleheritage.org (see page 238). Free guided walks of Main Street are held Wednesdays, 2:50pm, June-September.

Port Jefferson

You've heard of the Seven Hills of Rome, but how about the Seven Hills of Port Jefferson that created tremendous floods? Shoppers had to don hip boots if they wanted to browse the business district shops at high tide. In the mid-1800s, America's third president helped fund a project to dredge the harbor channel to prevent the daily floods and the village was renamed Port Jefferson in his honor.

The Port Jefferson Historical Society has a printed walking tour guide of the hilly historic district on East Main Street. Since the historical society was not yet open for the season when I visited, I picked one up at the Greater Port Jefferson Chamber's office in the **John Roe House** at 118 West Broadway (open Monday-Friday), a saltbox built in 1682 and moved several times. It was relocated to its present spot on the dock in 1982. Roe, a shoemaker from Queens, was the first resident of Drowned Meadow, the original name of the area.

Port Jefferson Harbor, already a picturesque spot, is expanding. A five-acre upgrade of the waterfront is planned, to include a 600-foot-long promenade. The first phase has been completed and it's a lovely grassy area with picnic tables and a play area with marine animal sculptures. To learn more about it, visit www.portjeff.com/park. Most of the historic houses are now occupied by stores or private citizens. An antiques store is located in an old gin mill; a two-story white brick house, c. 1836, belonged to an early shipbuilder, later served as funeral home and now houses an attorney's office. The steeple of the **Baptist Church** on East Main and Prospect Streets is on high ground and was a landmark for captains looking for the **Customs House** in front of the church when Port Jefferson was a Port of Entry (from 1852 to the late 1880s). Another site on the tour is the Thomas Jefferson statue in front of Harbor View Mall at the corner of Main Street and Broadway. There are 31 sites, and the walking tour is a good way to become familiar with Port Jefferson as well as get some exercise.

SHIPBUILDING

Port Jefferson was the leading shipbuilding center in Suffolk County from 1797 (when the community was called Drowned Meadow) to 1902. Even today, practically every Saturday morning, small boats are being built or repaired at the shipyard building on the dock for those interested in watching or volunteering to help on the project.

The two leading shipbuilders here were the Bayles and Mather families. During the golden years between 1836 and 1885, three generations of these families built more than 800 boats. During 1874 alone, four massive three-masted schooners were completed by the James M. Bayles & Son yard. The name Bayles is still prominent along the waterfront – you'll see Bayles Dock, Bayles Chandlery, and the Bayles Shipyard Site.

Yaphank

Yaphank was settled in 1726, and its Historic District (Yaphank Avenue and Main Street) is located just north of the LIE at Exit 67. Buildings worth seeing include the **Hawkins-Jacobsen House** (c. 1850), with unique decorative woodwork; and **St. Andrews Epis-**

copal **Church** (1853), a cream-colored Gothic Revival
with roof crenelations that is a New York State landmark. The **Yaphank Historical Society**, ☎ 631-924-
3401, conducts summer tours on Sundays, 1-4pm.

Parks & Preserves

CALEB SMITH STATE PARK PRESERVE
(formerly Nissequogue River State Park
Jericho Turnpike (Route 25)
Smithtown
☎ 631-265-1054
Parking fee of $5 is charged Tuesday-Sunday, from
April to Labor Day; and weekends only the rest of the
year.

This 543-acre park has trails for hiking and cross-country skiing, and a pond for fishing. Junior anglers (16
and under) accompanied by an adult are invited to fish
on Willow Pond from April 1-October 31 (catch and release only). Hikers should pick up a self-guided trail
map in the park's nature museum. The half-mile loop
was constructed by Eagle Scouts and is clearly delin-
eated and numbered at intervals. The Greenbelt Trail
also runs through the park.

One of the museum's displays, Insects of the World,
features butterflies that are especially colorful, especially those from New Guinea and Peru. The building
also houses several tanks with fish and live crayfish,
frogs and turtles. The interactive exhibits test your
knowledge of birds and wild flowers.

The park and nature museum are open year-round;
Tuesday-Sunday, from April through September; and
Wednesday-Sunday, from October through March.

LAKE RONKONKOMA
Lake Shore Road
☎ 631-854-9699

Ronkonkoma Beach Park at the western end of Long
Island's largest lake is operated by the Town of Islip. In

season (when a lifeguard is on duty on the sandy beach) it's open to town residents only, but the park is open to anyone once the season is over. It has ball fields, basketball and tennis courts, and a playground. Go enjoy the hilly landscape and shade trees. Bring a sandwich and sit at one of the picnic tables overlooking the lake. To get here, take the LIE to Exit 59 and go north on Ocean Avenue (which later becomes Rosedale Avenue); look for the beach on your right.

For a view of the lake at its northern end, continue north on Ocean Avenue and turn right on Smithtown Boulevard. When the road forks, bear right onto Lake Shore Road to Lake Ronkonkoma County Park. Here the beach is longer and narrower than at the Beach Park; it is not as pretty, and no swimming is allowed. It does have a more modern playground, though, along with basketball and handball courts, a ball field and fishing pier (open April-November). A parking fee is charged on weekends and holidays, from Memorial Day through Labor Day; it is $2 for Suffolk County residents and $8 for non-residents.

☞ DID YOU KNOW?

Lake Ronkonkoma, the largest lake on Long Island, is located in New York State's largest town, Brookhaven. Among the many aboriginal beliefs regarding this lake is that the depth is unfathomable and that the fish were placed there by the Great Spirit. These superior beings were not to be eaten.

Wildlife Refuges

TARGET ROCK NATIONAL WILDLIFE REFUGE
Lloyd Harbor Road
Lloyd Neck
☎ 631-286-0485

Target Rock, an 80-acre refuge on the Lloyd Neck peninsula, consists of mature upland forest and a half-mile of rocky beach. A variety of songbirds and mammals are observed here, and in the colder months diving ducks are most common. Harbor seals are occasionally observed. A portion of the beach is closed April-August to provide undisturbed nesting and feeding habitat for piping plovers, other shorebirds, and swallows. The large rock was reportedly named during the Revolutionary War when the British Royal Navy used it regularly for target practice. A nature trail is on the property and nature study, photography, walking and fishing are encouraged. There are parking and entrance fees. The information kiosk is open Monday-Friday, year-round. From LIE Exit 49N, go north on Route 110 to Huntington. Turn left on Route 25A (Main Street), then make a right onto West Neck Road, which becomes Lloyd Harbor Road; continue straight until you reach the entrance on the right.

SWEETBRIAR NATURE CENTER
62 Eckernkamp Drive
Smithtown
☎ 631-979-6344
www.sweetbriarnc.org
Admission to butterfly vivarium: adults, $2; children under 12, $1. Admission to nature center is free.
This 53-acre nature preserve on the Nissequogue River has two main objectives: to educate children about the natural environment and to help rehabilitate injured or sick wildlife. The center accomplishes its mission through lectures, classes, demonstrations, programs, special exhibits and a host of feathered and furry resident "ambassadors." Farm animals, foxes, waterfowl,

and bald eagles were on hand during a recent visit. Large birds of prey are kept in the Flight Conditioning Aviary until they are nearly ready for release into the wild.

The main attraction, though, is the screened Vivarium housing 20 species of farm-bred butterflies. Paying customers may also get to witness the metamorphosis from pupa to winged adult. On a hot day, the shady trail leading to the river is a welcome relief. You can pick it up to the right of the red barn. Turn left at trail marker #2 and you'll notice that several trees are identified.

From Route 25, turn left on Brookside and make another left on Landing Avenue. Go past a vest pocket park where you'll see lots of kids playing, and pass the first sign for the center. Make a left on Eckernkamp Drive and look for sign on left. The preserve is open daily, year-round; the vivarium is open seasonally.

Points of Interest

SUFFOLK COUNTY VIETNAM VETERANS MEMORIAL
Bald Hill Scenic Overlook
Route 83
Farmingville

Any major project requires the financial and emotional support of thousands. This striking memorial took 5½ years to complete. In 1986, the Suffolk County Vietnam Veterans Memorial Commission (☎ 631-331-2616) was formed, and two noted Vietnam veterans were appointed co-chairmen. A design competition was held for the memorial and the commission received 1,300 entries. The four-sided tapered spire designed by Vietnam veteran Bob Fox of Massachusetts was chosen. Its marble façade is made from Georgia White Cherokee, the same marble used for the Capitol and Lincoln Memorial in Washington DC. The memorial was dedicated on Veteran's Day, November 11, 1991.

The 100-foot-tall red, white and blue monolith looming over the landscape is Long Island's highest attraction.

The $1.5 million needed to complete the project was largely funded by local banks, businesses, hotels, radio stations, and townships. Every town in Suffolk County helped, and $100,000 was raised through community initiatives: schoolchildren sold cupcakes; senior citizens sponsored dances; and local businesses sold raffle tickets.

LONG ISLAND FILM & TV FOUNDATION
305 North Service Road
Dix Hills
☎ 631-421-0855
www.longislandfilm.com

The mission of this organization is to promote Long Island as a choice shooting location for films, commercials, documentaries and TV programs. To further its efforts to assist and honor the independent filmmaker, the Foundation sponsors film expos and awards ceremonies showcasing local talent; expedites the procurement of permits; and serves as a resource arena for Long Island-based screenwriters, directors, actors, technicians, designers and producers. Meetings are open to professional and non-professional film and video personnel and the general public. The Foundation is currently involved in the construction of a motion picture production studio to be known as the Long Island Film & TV Production Studios.

Family Fun

COLD SPRING HARBOR FISH HATCHERY & AQUARIUM
Route 25A
Cold Spring Harbor
☎ 516-692-6768
www.cshfha.org
Admission: adults, $3.50; seniors and children, $1.75; under five, free.

This hatchery has been around for 120 years. Twenty years ago, it turned from a state hatchery to a private fish farm, providing brown, brook and rainbow trout to gun and golf clubs and private lakes. In 1994 it was listed on both the State and National Register of Historic Places.

The attractions here include six outdoor rearing pools – where kids can feed the fish – and a hatch house where they can observe newly hatched trout. The aquarium's large assortment of freshwater turtles, fish and amphibians of New York State include a 60-pound snapping turtle named Tiny. The red brick building across from the entrance houses a variety of bass. The hatchery is located off Route 25A (the entrance is right before its sign). It is open 10am-5pm daily, year-round.

The Cold Spring Harbor Fish Hatchery hosts special events throughout the year.

⭐ TIP

The hatchery shares a parking lot with St. John's Church. Be sure to climb the church steps for a beautiful view of the pond.

WHITE POST ANIMAL FARM
250 Old Country Road
Melville
☎ 631-351-9373
www.whitepostfarms.com

Here, kids can ride a pony, bottle-feed baby goats, hand-feed baby deer, alpacas and sheep, or romp in the Little Blue Playhouse. The animal farm has some 300 animals and birds solely for children to enjoy. It's off LIE Exit 49N, a quarter-mile east of Route 110; the farm is open daily, mid-April through October.

SPORTS PLUS
Smith Haven Mall
110 New Moriches Road
Lake Grove
☎ 631-737-2100
www.sports-plus.com

Opposite Macy's in the Smith Haven Mall, Sports Plus is a young person's paradise. Included in the 55,000-square-feet of Las Vegas-like attractions are video games, rides, an iWerks Motion Theatre, a toddler's section, regulation-size ice rink, 48-lane bowling alley, climbing wall, and two restaurants – **Tokens Family Restaurant**, and **Reunions**, a bar/restaurant. Unlike Jillian's (see page 275), this amusement spot is geared to young kids. A special section for the very young includes a mini-sized merry-go-round, Skee-Ball lanes, and age-appropriate video games. Except for the rides, it's pay-as-you-go.

FUN4ALL
200 Wilson Street
Port Jefferson Station
☎ 631-331-9000
www.fun4all-ny.com
Admission $7.99 for ages two-12 for unlimited play;
half price for one-year-olds; free for adults

This is another kid's dream – for children ages two-12.
Like a giant playground, Fun4All is full of youngsters
having fun and making lots of noise. Among the attractions in the half-acre indoor park are slides, towers,
game room and snack bar. Open daily, 10am-8pm.

Music, Theater & Art

Art flourishes where there is a sense of adventure.
– Alfred North Whitehead (English philosopher
and mathematician)

ART LEAGUE OF LONG ISLAND
330 Cuba Hill Road
Huntington
☎ 631-368-0018
www.artleagueli.org

Long Island's leading art school serves more than 155
Long Island towns with classes, exhibitions, events,
and workshops. One of the oldest and largest visual
arts organizations on the Island, it operates a year-
round school of art, publishes an arts newsletter, and
organizes tours, exhibitions and annual events such as
Art in the Park in June and a holiday fine arts and
crafts show in December. A 21-page brochure describes
classes and workshops for adults, teens, children and
families in all media. One Saturday morning program
for families involves drawing Phoebe, a live cockatoo.
Membership and classes, held Monday through Saturday, are open to all.

LONG ISLAND TRADITIONAL MUSIC ASSOCIATION
PO Box 991
Smithtown, 11787
☎ 631-427-7542
www.litma.org

The renovated Brush Barn is the scene of special weekend events year-round.

This 400-member association is in its 23rd year of supporting traditional music, dance and song on Long Island. Members sponsor and participate in 150 events a year, primarily in Smithtown Historical Society's **Brush Barn** (211 Middle Country Road, Smithtown, ☎ 631-424-8682, behind the Epenetus Smith Tavern). The group also performs at various historical society functions, tailoring its music to the event's theme. Traditional music includes Celtic, bluegrass and Cajun. Dance styles include New England barn dancing (contradancing); this is a popular event as dance is participatory – anyone can join in the fun!

The association's other venues are Wading River Congregational Church, North Wading River Road in Wading River; American Legion Hall, 115 Southern Parkway, Plainview; and the Community Center on 27A in Water Mill – the first building on the right after you pass the windmill. The association holds a festival in August.

DEEPWELLS FARM
Moriches Road, across from St. James General Store
St. James
☎ 631-862-6080 (County Cooperative Extension)
☎ 516-571-7600 (Friends for LI Heritage)
www.fflih.org/events/deepwell.htm

William J. Gaynor, mayor of New York City in the early 1900s, used this Greek Revival mansion as his summer home. He named it Deepwells after the two brick-lined wells behind the house. Built in 1845 as a working farm, the property was in deplorable condition when the county purchased it in 1989; photographs on the second floor help visitors appreciate why restoration took seven years. Tours of the house are free and are held Sundays, noon-3pm, from March through December. The house is wheelchair-accessible.

After Gaynor died in 1913, his wife, Augusta, 14 years his junior, blossomed into an opera singer. Her life as a performer is presented in an ongoing series, "Biographies on Stage", which portrays a singing Mrs. Gaynor and her housekeeper greeting prominent figures of the time. Mae West was the guest during my visit to Deepwells; dressed to the nines in a gown with black feathers and flirting with the two men in the audience, Mae West was a laugh a minute. She startled Mrs. Gaynor and offended the maid with her bawdy humor, but not audiences – the show was extended due to popular demand. As "Mae" described her success, "Not bad for a kid from Brooklyn. Shows are produced by St. George Productions, ☎ 631-654-1888, www.salstgeorge.com, which specializes in original historical shows around Long Island.

The shows are followed by lunch with finger sandwiches, fruit, pastries and tea. These six- to eight-week productions, held year-round, are an extremely palatable way to experience history. The fee is $30 for show and lunch. During the Christmas season, Deepwells becomes a holiday showcase with performances, workshops, music and demonstrations.

WILLIAM GAYNOR

Although he was warned by a fortuneteller to stay away from water, William Gaynor died on a ship run by the same company that owned the ill-fated *Titanic*. His body was brought back on the *Lusitania*, just two years before a German submarine sank that ocean liner.

Health & Beauty

Fitness Centers

All facilities are open daily unless otherwise specified.

Eastern Athletic Clubs has reciprocal arrangements among all its Long Island Clubs. Childcare is free, and day fee for non-members is $15. Clubs are at 854 East Jericho Turnpike, Huntington Station (a/k/a the Dix Hills Club), ☎ 631-271-6616; and Pinelawn & Ruland Road, Melville, ☎ 631-420-1310.

Lucille Roberts, ☎ 800-USA-LUCILLE, www.lucille-roberts.com, is a health club for women that only offers reciprocal privileges for gold card members who pay an additional $3 to join. Childcare is complimentary at these two, but parents are asked to tip the sitter. A non-member accompanied by a member has one free tryout; then it's $10 per day. Club locations are at 6155 Jericho Turnpike, Commack, ☎ 631-462-1222; and 2304 Nesconset Highway, Stony Brook, ☎ 631-689-8911.

New York Sports Club, www.nysc.com, is a full-service fitness facility with a reciprocal arrangement among members; day fees, childcare fees and hours vary. Its locations are at 16 New Street, Huntington, ☎ 631-424-7100; and 6136 Jericho Turnpike, Commack, ☎ 631-462-6400 (this facility has a swimming pool).

Hauppauge Sports Club, 100 Parkway Drive South, Hauppauge, ☎ 631-543-6398, is a complete fitness facility; open daily. Day fee, $10. Childcare, $4 per child. They have another location in Glen Cove called Island Sports Club; see page 54.

Bally Total Fitness, 22 Middle Country Road, Lake Grove, ☎ 631-471-6000, or 800-695-8111, www.ballyfitness.com, is a full-service fitness facility. The chain of health clubs provides a reciprocal arrangement for members. Guests with or without member get a free one-day pass. No fee for child care.

Smithtown YMCA, Edgewood Avenue, Smithtown, ☎ 631-265-6344. Limited facility; closed on weekends. Future plans include an indoor pool and health spa.

Gold's Gym, www.goldsgym.com, is a full-service health facility. Day fees and childcare fees vary. Locations are at 100 Landing Avenue, Smithtown, ☎ 631-863-1616; 700-1 Union Parkway, Ronkonkoma, ☎ 631-737-4653; 200 Wilson Street, Port Jefferson Station, ☎ 631-331-6100; and 1 Larkfield Road, East Northport, ☎ 631-757-3377.

World Gym, 607 Middle Country Road, Coram, ☎ 631-732-5500. Full-service fitness facility and basketball court. Day fee, $10; racquetball day fee, $15. Childcare, $1 per hour, per child.

Day Spas

Spa **Adriana**, 266 Main Street, Huntington, ☎ 631-351-1555. Full-service spa and hair salon. Open daily. www.spaadriana.com.

Steven Thomas Day Spa, 231 Jericho Turnpike (a half-mile east of Route 110), Huntington Station, ☎ 631-673-2994. Full-service spa and hair salon. Appointments recommended. Closed Monday.

Bocu Salon & Day Spa, Peppertree Commons (corner of Commack Road and Jericho Turnpike), Commack, ☎ 631-499-1300, www.bocusalonandspa.com. Full-service spa and hair salon. Appointments essential. Open daily.

Face Spa, 1145 Route 112, Port Jefferson Station, ☎ 631-473-8474. Face and body treatments by appointment only. Closed Sunday and Monday.

The Spa at St. Tropez, 905 Route 112, Port Jefferson Station, ☎ 631-473-4090, www.spatropez.com. Appointments preferred but walk-ins welcomed. Closed Monday.

Phases Skin Care Center and Day Spa has two locations: 180 East Main Street, Suite 226, Smithtown, ☎ 631-361-7650; and 97-F Main Street, Village Center,

Stony Brook, ☎ 631-751-1511, www.phasesskincare. com. Face and body treatments for men, women and teens by appointment. Full and half-day packages. Open year-round.

Therapeutically Yours Massage Therapy & Day Spa, 531 Route 111, Hauppauge, ☎ 631-361-8959. Full-service salon. Appointments preferred. Open daily.

Atlantis Health Network, 45 North Country Road, Shoreham, ☎ 631-929-8292. Complete day spa for men and women by appointment. Open Monday-Saturday.

Recreation

Boating

Cruises

EASTERN STAR CRUISES
PO Box 880
East Northport
☎ 800-445-5942
www.easternstarcruises.com

Private charters are available aboard the Eastern Star.

Imagine your room in an inn floating away! Billing itself as "the world's first and only Cruising Country Inn," this luxurious 85-foot yacht can accommodate 10 guests; the six staterooms come equipped with full-size beds and designer comforters for a dreamy night's rest.

The *Eastern Star* sails year-round; from May through October the yacht makes pick-ups for day and overnight charters at various locations on Long Island and throughout the tri-state area. Fall foliage cruises depart from Chelsea Piers in lower Manhattan and other docking locations. Two- to five-night cruise destinations are southern New England and the British Virgin Islands. Charter rates range from $5,000 to $15,000 depending on the number of guests and crew, the length of the trip, the menu and the port of entry.

PORT JEFFERSON FERRY
102 West Broadway
Port Jefferson
☎ 631-473-0286
www.bpjferry.com

The ferry operates 365 days a year between Port Jefferson and Bridgeport, Connecticut. During July and August, it runs moonlight cruises on Wednesdays. Regular rates for a car and driver are around $40; each additional person is around $10; call for reservations.

MARTHA JEFFERSON
Port Jefferson Harbor
☎ 631-331-3333
www.MarthaJefferson.com

For a leisurely cruise on the bay, step aboard this Mississippi River paddle cruiser. Named after Thomas Jefferson's wife, the *Martha* offers daily sightseeing tours and Wednesday and weekend dinner cruises along the North Shore. All dinner cruises (catered by its own restaurant, the **Dockside**) include a buffet, music and dancing; on Friday nights there's a female impersonator to entertain you. Dinner cruises run $39.99 per person. This 85-foot cruiser (capacity 149) is also available for private charter. Cruises operate mid-May through October.

In addition to the Dockside Restaurant, the company operates Port Jefferson Frigate, an ice cream / candy store on Main Street; ☎ 631-474-8888.

DISCOVERY WETLANDS CRUISE
Stony Brook
☎ 631-751-2244
www.wardmelvilleheritage.org
Admission: adults, $15; children under 12, $9

When I signed up for this cruise, I had no idea what it would entail – would we be measuring the consistency of the water or studying the creatures therein as my husband and I had on a boat ride in Mystic, Connecticut? It was only after a group of us, many with cameras and binoculars, boarded the pontoon boat and were handed a sheet asking us to check off the birds we "discovered" on the cruise did I realize this was a birding expedition. We weren't required to do anything but sit back and enjoy the soft breeze as the boat moved gently along (the dock was a lot rockier than the boat).

Our guide was a local high school senior who easily identified each bird and was knowledgeable about the marine environment. She explained that as we moved away from the harbor the water became brackish – a mixture of freshwater and saltwater – creating a "nursery" for wildlife. We first passed Young's Island (a bird sanctuary), and then a house with a "pirate" on the upper porch. We also passed several historic buildings, familiar to some local residents on the excursion.

Of the 15 birds pictured on our sheets, we spotted eight: a great egret; great blue herons that were taller than the high grass; common terns identified by their bright orange bill; piping plovers; belted kingfishers; double-crested cormorants; and, naturally, herring gulls and Canada geese. We also saw many snowy egrets.

The 35-passenger *Discovery* departs from Boatworks, on Shore Road off Main Street in Stony Brook, and cruises the surrounding wetlands for 1½ hours. Reservations are suggested but not necessary. Reserve online or call for the seasonal schedule (departure times vary, according to the tides). *Discovery* sails daily, May-October.

LONG ISLAND SEAPORT & ECO CENTER
101 East Broadway
Port Jefferson
☎ 631-474-4725
www.lisec.org

LISEC is a non-profit organization dedicated to promoting an awareness and appreciation of the North Shore maritime history and its marine environment. In the summer of 2002, in partnership with the Marine Science Research Center at Stony Brook, the center initiated four-hour educational excursions on the research vessel *Sea Wolf*. Participants did water samplings and trawled for fish and plankton. The center plans to continue this program each summer, depending upon interest. The fee is $25-$30. LISEC also sponsors two- to five-hour sails on tall ships, leaving from Port Jefferson's Danfords Dock on specified Saturdays and Sundays between the end of May and November.

Canoeing & Kayaking

Bob's Canoe Rentals, Kings Park, ☎ 631-269-9761, rents canoes and kayaks.

Nissequogue River Canoe & Kayak Rentals, 112 Whittier Drive, Kings Park, ☎ 631-269-2774, or ☎ 631-979-8244, www.canoerentalslongisland.com, has canoe and kayak rentals, and runs guided tours on the Nissequogue River in Smithtown. Open daily, April-November.

Glacier Bay Sports sells and rents kayaks and gives instruction. They have two locations: 81 Fort Salonga Road, Northport, ☎ 631-262-9116; and 2979 Montauk Highway, Brookhaven, ☎ 631-286-0567. Open daily, year-round.

Setauket Harbor, 30 Shore Road, East Setauket, ☎ 631-751-2706, sells and rents canoes and kayaks. Also carries clothing and accessories. Open year-round. Call for winter schedule.

Marinas

H&M Powles Marina, 74 Harbor Road, Cold Spring Harbor, ☎ 631-367-7670. Storage, bait and tackle, fuel, snack bar, electric, marine store. Open from April to mid-November.

Knutson West Marine, 41 East Shore Road, Huntington, ☎ 631-549-7842, www.knutsonwestmarine.com. This marina offers dockage, storage, electric, marine store, showers, laundry, restrooms. Open daily, year-round.

West Marine, 90 West Jericho Turnpike, Huntington Station, ☎ 631-673-3910, or 800-BOATING (262-8464), www.westmarine.com. West Marine has 240 stores throughout the United States. In Suffolk County, their locations are 5000 Nesconset Highway, Port Jefferson (☎ 631-331-9280), and West Islip, Riverhead, Babylon and Patchogue. Everything for the boater: fishing supplies, electronics, apparel, footwear, books, videos, charts. Open year-round.

Seymour's Boat Yard, 63 Bayview Avenue, Northport Harbor, ☎ 631-261-6574. Marine store, dockage, storage, electric, fuel, restrooms. Serving Northport's nautical needs since 1923. Open daily, mid-April to October.

Stony Brook Boat Works, Shore Road, Stony Brook, ☎ 631-751-1230. Dockage, hauling, electric, bait and tackle, marine store. Canoe rentals. Open March to late-December.

Caraftis Fishing Station, 232 Barnum Avenue, Port Jefferson, ☎ 631-473-2288. Bait and tackle, marine supplies. Rents skiffs and dories for half and full days. Open mid-April to mid-November.

J&J Marine Service, 345 Hallock Avenue (25A), Port Jefferson Station, ☎ 631-928-2220. Hauling, storage, retail store. Open Tuesday-Sunday in summer; Tuesday-Saturday in winter.

Ralph's Fishing Station and Marina, 250 Harbor Beach Road (on Cedar Beach), Mt. Sinai, ☎ 631-473-6655. Day rentals of skiffs, runabouts, and kayaks. Dockage, storage, sales, fuel, bait and tackle, beach, electric, and snack bar serving breakfast, lunch, and dinner outdoors. Open year-round.

Biking

Sales & Rentals

Cycle Plus of Huntington, 414 New York Avenue, Huntington, ☎ 631-271-4242. Open year-round. Closed Wednesday.

Frenchie's Cycle World, 165 Walt Whitman Road, Huntington Station (Route 110, across from Walt Whitman Mall), ☎ 631-673-6002. Frenchie's has more than 3,000 bicycles in stock. Open daily, year-round.

Bike Depot, 82 Larkfield Road (one block north of Pulaski Road), East Northport, ☎ 631-754-2151. The Bike Depot is next to the firehouse (their other location is in East Islip). Open daily, year-round.

The Cycle Company, 564 West Jericho Turnpike, Smithtown, ☎ 631-979-7078. This shop also repairs lawn equipment. Open year-round, closed Sunday in winter.

The following members of **American Bicycle & Fitness Centers** sell bikes and fitness equipment and are open daily, year-round.

Adams Schwinn Cyclery, 270 Larkfield Road, East Northport, ☎ 631-261-2881.

Commack Bicycle, 194 Commack Road (across from Chase Bank), Commack, ☎ 631-462-2453.

Smithtown Bicycle, 11 West Main Street, Smithtown, ☎ 631-265-5900.

Campus Bicycle & Fitness, 1077 Route 25A, Stony Brook (opposite the train station), ☎ 631-689-1200. Open daily in season. Limited hours in winter.

Cycle World Plus Bicycles, 1070 Middle Country Road (opposite Home Depot), Selden, ☎ 631-736-7755, www.cycleworldplus.com. Mountain bike specialists.

Rocky Point Cycle, 664 Route 25A (1/8 mile east of Broadway), Rocky Point, ☎ 631-744-5372, www.rockypointcycles.com. Sales and repairs of all bikes; clothing. Occasionally rents bikes. Open daily, year-round.

Bike Discounters has several locations: 427 Route 25A, Rocky Point, ☎ 631-209-0825, or 800-640-2453; 580 Medford Avenue, Patchogue, ☎ 631-289-2009; 2503 Middle Country Road, Centereach, ☎ 631-471-3230; 287 Portion Road, Ronkonkoma, ☎ 631-737-9282; and 159 Route 25A, Mt. Sinai, ☎ 631-331-3235.

Bicycle Clubs

The Bellport-based **East End Cycling Team** has about 60 members who focus on bicycle racing, both on- and off-road. Members meet regularly in the warm weather for training rides on Tuesday and Thursday evenings and year-round on Sundays. Most members live in Suffolk County so that's where they ride. The speed tends to be faster than a "touring" pace.

Races, on the other hand, are open to everyone. In the summer, there are a series of races for three different levels on Friday nights at the Riverhead campus of Suffolk Community College. Races are also held all over the northeast, especially in New York City, under the auspices of the US Cycling Federation/USA Cycling. Contact Chris at the Kreb Cycle Shop in Bellport by phone at ☎ 516-286-1829, by e-mail at krebcycle@earthlink.net, or visit their Web site at http://home.earthlink.net/~martypower/eecthome.html.

Suffolk Bicycle Riders Association was organized in 1977 and is Long Island's largest cycling club, with some 700 members. The rides are free and range from 10 to 100 miles, although the most popular tend to be between 25 and 50 milers. Most rides are east of Route 112 where there is less traffic. All ages and abilities are welcome but the club hopes that people who ride with them regularly will consider joining. E-mail Bill Pope at wpope@optonline.net or call him at ☎ 631-439-9115 (daytime) or ☎ 631-475-4531 (evenings before 8:45pm), www.bicyclelongisland.org/sbra.

WHEELCHAIR ATHLETES

The 30-member **Long Island Wheelchair Athletic Club** (☎ 718-529-7364, www.liw-ac.org) was formed 15 years ago to provide competitive athletics for the physically challenged. The basketball season is October to February and the home courts are in Northport, NY and Clark, NJ.

The program has expanded to include other sports, including track & field, road racing, tennis, swimming, skiing, and sledge hockey (players utilize sledges instead of wheelchairs to play hockey). The racing team participates in marathons year-round. Any disabled person can participate in the adult basketball team, junior basketball team or racing team.

Surfing & Skating

Surf-Snow-Skate, 1675B East Jericho Turnpike, Huntington, ☎ 631-462-WAVE, www.xtremesurfandsport.com. All your boarding needs – for surf, snow, skating and skimming – plus clothing and accessories. Snowboards and surfboards are available for rent. Open daily, year-round.

Plaza Surf & Sports, 89 Route 25A, Rocky Point, ☎ 631-744-5555. This shop sells a full line of sporting goods and apparel. Open daily, year-round.

Beaches & Pools

Town of Brookhaven Beaches

Residents with parking stickers have free use of the beaches. Non-residents pay a fee. All beaches and pools, as well as Lake Ronkonkoma, are open Memorial Day or mid- to late June and close September 3rd.

The beaches on Long Island Sound are **Cedar Beach**, Harbor Beach Road, Mt. Sinai, ☎ 631-451-6100 (☎ 631-473-6926 in season), lifeguards; **Stony Brook**, Sand Street, Stony Brook, ☎ 631-451-6100 (☎ 631-751-3840-seasonal), lifeguards; **West Meadow**, West Meadow Road, Stony Brook, ☎ 631-451-6100 (☎ 631-751-3193-seasonal), lifeguards; and **Shoreham**, North Country Road, Shoreham.

Town of Brookhaven Pools

The town pools on Hawkins Road, Centereach (☎ 631-698-8663) and Buckley Road, Holtsville (☎ 631-475-4507) are open daily, from July Fourth to Labor Day. Admission is $7 for non-residents. For further information, contact the Brookhaven Tourism Commission at ☎ 631-451-9074, or the Suffolk County Department of Parks and Recreation at ☎ 631-451-6100.

Town of Smithtown

Smithtown has four town beaches on the sound (**Short Beach**, **Long Beach**, **Schubert's Beach** and **Callahan's Beach**), which are basically for residents. Non-residents pay $15. For more information, call the Department of Parks, Buildings and Grounds at ☎ 631-269-1122.

Skydiving

Skydive Long Island, 4062 Grumman Boulevard, ☎ 631-208-3900, www.skydivelongisland.com, is Long Island's only student jump center. Skydivers must be at least 18 years old with maximum weight of 225 pounds. Located at Calverton Airport; open April-November.

Horseback Riding

Sweet Hills Riding Center, Sweet Hollow Road, Huntington, ☎ 631-351-9696. Indoor and lighted outdoor arena; lessons in English and western styles; pony rides; boarding, sales, leasing; 1,200 acres of trails in West Hills County Park. Half-hour lesson, $30. Open daily, year-round.

Thomas School of Horsemanship, 250 Round Swamp Road, Melville, ☎ 631-692-6840, www.tsh-camp.com. The school has 100 horses in summer, 50 in winter; this is a 33-acre facility featuring an indoor arena, seven lighted rings, a hunt course, a summer camp, and private (long-term) lessons in English, hunt, and equitation. Open year-round. Closed Monday. Family owned and operated business celebrated its 50th anniversary in 2002.

White Post Farm: see *Family Fun*, page 204.

Smoke Run Farm, Hollow Road, Stony Brook, ☎ 631-751-2803. Sales, boarding, summer day camp. Outdoor arena. Lessons in English style. 45-minute lesson, $45-50. Open year-round; closed Sunday.

Olde Towne Equestrian Center, 471 Boyle Road, Selden, ☎ 631-473-2075. 35 horses, lighted ring, grass hunt course, private and group lessons in English style, hunt, jumper and equitation. Open daily, year-round.

Good Shepherd Farm, 52 German Boulevard, Yaphank, ☎ 631-924-4670. Outdoor facility. Lessons in English style. Half-hour lesson, $35. Open daily, year-round.

Horse owners may bring their own horses to trail ride or use the indoor practice arena at **West Hills County Park**, in Huntington; a permit is required. Park office, ☎ 631-854-4423; park stable, ☎ 631-351-9168.

Horse owners with permits may also use the equestrian facilities at the following parks: **Blydenburgh County Park**, Smithtown, ☎ 631-854-3713l; **Cathedral Pines County Park**, Middle Island, ☎ 631-852-5500; and **Old Field Farm**, Setauket, ☎ 631-724-8415.

TIP

All permits are available at the **Suffolk County Parks Administration Office** in West Sayville, open Monday-Friday, ☎ 631-854-4949.

Tennis

Sportime, 275 Indian Head Road, Kings Park, ☎ 631-269-6300, or 888-NY-TENNIS, www.sportimetfm.com. Sportime has 11 clay and hard tennis courts, and an outdoor pool. Free for first-time guests with member, thereafter $15 for three times only (plus court fee). Free childcare.

World Gym Racquet & Sports Arena, Nesconset Highway and Mark Tree Road, East Setauket, ☎ 631-751-6100. Multi-sport facility with five indoor Har-Tru courts, 12 outdoor clay courts, outdoor pool and newly built indoor pool. Day fee, $10 for fitness center and pool. Court fee, $46 per hour. Babysitting, $4 per hour, per child. Open daily. World Gym also has a location at 607 Middle Country Road, Coram, ☎ 631-732-5500.

Stony Brook Racquet & Health Club, Route 25A & South Jersey Avenue, East Setauket, ☎ 631-751-6767. Five Har-Tru indoor courts and one outdoors. Court fee, $48 per hour during prime time (Monday-Friday, 8am-noon and 4-10pm) or $40 off peak. Has a small fitness club.

Golf

These public and semi-private courses are open year-round, unless otherwise noted.

Crab Meadow Golf Club, 220 Waterside Avenue, Northport, ☎ 631-757-8800. Play at this 18-hole, par 72 town course is restricted to Huntington Town residents and their guests. Soft spikes are mandatory, but walking is allowed. Practice green, driving range and restaurant. Situated on Long Island Sound, the course is challenging in spots. Closed in January.

Dix Hills Country Club, 507 Half Hollow Road, Dix Hills, ☎ 631-271-4788. Nine-hole, par 35, walking-only course. Lessons, rentals, putting area, limited pro shop, snack bar.

Dix Hills Park Golf Course, Vanderbilt Motor Parkway, Dix Hills, ☎ 631-499-8005. Nine-hole, par 31/32. Lessons, rentals, putting area, driving range, pro shop, snack bar. Carts are available, and walking is permitted. The course is closed during Christmas season.

Hollow Hills Country Club, 49 Ryder Avenue, Dix Hills, ☎ 631-242-0010. Nine-hole, par 35. Lessons, rentals, putting area, limited pro shop, bar. Carts available; walking is permitted.

Smithtown Landing Country Club, 495 Landing Avenue, Smithtown, ☎ 631-979-6534. 18-hole, par 72, short and hilly course. Walking allowed and soft spikes required. Also has a nine-hole, par 3 course. Lessons, putting area, pro shop, bar, snack bar. These two municipal courses are only open to residents of the Town of Smithtown and their guests. Open year-round. Closed Mondays in summer.

Hamlet Windwatch Golf Club, 1715 Vanderbilt Motor Parkway, Hauppauge, ☎ 631-232-9850. This semi-private 18-hole course is considered one of the best on Long Island. It has a luxurious new clubhouse, newly renovated restaurant, pro shop and putting green. Soft spikes, but not carts, are mandatory. The wind on Windwatch – one of the highest spots on Long Island – adds to the challenge. Call for tee times a week in advance.

Stonebridge Country Club, Veteran's Memorial Highway, Hauppauge, ☎ 631-724-7500. Carts and soft spikes mandatory at all times. Semi-private 18-hole, par 70 course is open to the public Monday through Thursday. The newly designed course replicates some of the famous links in England and Scotland. Pro shop, snack bar/restaurant.

The Ponds, 100 New Moriches Road, Lake Grove, ☎ 631-737-4649. This is an 18-hole, par 60 executive course with a heated driving range and a snack bar. The course is designed for kids, seniors and any middle level player, regardless of residency. Carts are available but walking is allowed; soft spikes required. The Golf Center, the Ponds' large clubhouse building, is located in the same shopping center as Sports Plus (see page 204).

Heatherwood Golf Club, 303 Arrowhead Lane, Nesconset Highway, Centereach, ☎ 631-473-9000. A smaller-than-full-size, but still challenging 18-hole, par 60 course, Heatherwood has a clubhouse, pro shop, and restaurant. First-come, first served.

Middle Island Country Club, 275 Yaphank Road, Middle Island, ☎ 631-924-3000, www.middleisland-cc.com. Three nine-hole courses, each par 36. Metal spikes allowed. Carts required on weekends. Putting area, pro shop, restaurant, snack bar, driving range. *Golf Digest* awarded three stars for the 1999/2000/2001 seasons. Non-members must call for tee times two days in advance.

Spring Lake Golf Club, 30 East Bartlett Road, Middle Island, ☎ 631-924-5115. This 27-hole, par 36/72 course, has good elevation changes. Soft spikes are not required and carts are mandatory only on weekends in season. Putting green, pro shop, driving ranges, snack bar, restaurant. Open year-round.

Rolling Oaks County Club, 181 Route 25A, Rocky Point, ☎ 631-744-3200. 18-hole, par 65. Walking allowed; soft spikes only. Putting area, pro shop, adjoining restaurant (**J&R Steakhouse**, ☎ 631-744-2101). Both golf course and restaurant open daily, year-round.

Rock Hill Golf & Country Club, 105 Clancy Road, Manorville, ☎ 631-878-2250. 18-hole, par 71. Soft spikes are required. Carts mandatory on weekends. The course is harder than it appears. Driving range, pro shop, putting area, restaurant. Call one week ahead for tee times.

Swan Lake Golf Club, 388 River Road, Manorville, ☎ 631-369-1818. Swan Lake is a public, 18-hole, par 72 course with flat, wide open fairways and the largest greens on Long Island. Carts are mandatory on weekends and soft spikes are required. Pro shop, putting area, restaurant. Call two weeks in advance for tee times.

Pine Hills Country Club, 162 Wading River Road, Manorville, ☎ 631-878-4343. 18-hole, par 73. Soft spikes and carts are mandatory. Long and challenging course. Pro shop, lessons, putting area, driving range, restaurant. Call for tee times up to 14 days in advance.

Miniature Golf

Village Green Miniature Golf, 974 Portion Road, Ronkonkoma, ☎ 631-732-8681. This facility has three 18-hole mini courses of varying difficulty. Open daily, April-October.

Castle Miniature Golf and Amusement, 1878 Middle County Road, Centereach, ☎ 631-471-1267. 18-hole mini golf, go-carts and game room. Open daily when temperature is 40° or higher.

Island Green Golf Center, 495 Middle County Road, Selden, ☎ 631-732-4442. 18-hole mini golf, driving range (heated in winter), golf instruction and putting green. Open daily, year-round.

Shop Till You Drop

Malls

WALT WHITMAN MALL
Walt Whitman Road and Route 110
(near Jericho Turnpike)
Huntington Station
☎ 631-271-1741
www.walt-whitman-mall.com

Got a foot fetish? Walt Whitman Mall has a slew of shoe stores.

Walt Whitman Mall has 100 stores; Macy's, Lord & Taylor, Saks Fifth Avenue, Bloomingdale's, California Pizza Kitchen, and Legal Sea Foods are here, as is a movie theater, the Loews Cineplex Whitman. Barnes & Noble, Today's Man, Bed Bath & Beyond and four fast-food places are in an adjacent shopping complex. The mall is open Monday through Saturday, 10am-9:30pm; Sunday, 11am-7pm.

THE BIG H MALL
Farther north on Route 110, but before you reach Huntington Village, is the Big H Mall. Home Depot is joined by Kmart, Old Navy, and Marshalls.

HUNTINGTON SQUARE MALL
Jericho Turnpike
East Northport
☎ 631-499-5537

Anchored by Sears, this is one of the few retail centers in the region with exclusively middle-market stores, such as Lerner's and Radio Shack.

SMITH HAVEN MALL
Routes 25 & 347
Lake Grove
☎ 631-724-1433

Macy's, JCPenney and Sears anchor Smith Haven Mall, which has 150 stores, four restaurants and a food court with 10 outlets, plus a movie theater, the four-screen Cineplex Odeon. Hours are Monday-Saturday, 10am-9:30pm; Sunday, 11am-6pm.

Shopping Streets

COLD SPRING HARBOR
Main Street
☎ 631-692-8065
www.mainstreet-csh.org

Call for a free brochure of the 40 merchants, galleries, museums and exhibit spaces on this historic Main Street.

HUNTINGTON VILLAGE
Huntington Village, often called The Little Apple, is a microcosm of Manhattan, chock-a-block with stores of every stripe, not to mention the traffic. The difference is in the cleanliness and care of the historic buildings housing the stores. It was no surprise to read that, in 1999, the Suffolk County Legislature began its Downtown Revitalization Program, awarding more than $1.5 million to 50 downtown projects. Civic organizations created projects appropriate to the needs of their downtown business area. The funds were awarded to Huntington Village, Huntington Station, Melville, Northport, East Northport, Cold Spring Harbor, Centerport and Greenlawn. The following are some of the highlights of a trip to Huntington.

♦ **Book Revue**, 313 New York Avenue, Huntington, ☎ 631-271-1442, 800-552-9440, www.bookrevue.com. The size of some Barnes & Noble locations, Book Revue is the largest privately owned bookstore on Long Island and possibly the East Coast. It also has a café, sponsors events, and discounts new and used books. Used books are bought as well. Open daily, year-round.

♦ **Georgie's Woof 'n Poof**, 225 East Main Street (Route 25), Huntington, ☎ 631-385-WOOF (9663). Need a gift for your pooch? East of Huntington Village is this "dog boutique" and grooming facility. Located in a strip mall called North Country Village, the store carries the usual items, such as leashes and doggie toys, plus painted coffee cups and charm bracelets for you. Open daily, year-round.

STONY BROOK VILLAGE

Stony Brook residents have good reason to be proud. Theirs is a picture-perfect village with pristine brick-and-shingle shops and slate sidewalks. Parking is plentiful (and parking restrictions are posted). The village center, hilly in spots, is divided into three sections, all within walking distance. Main Street runs around the complex and the Village Green is across the way. As a university town, Stony Brook is active year-round, and at Christmas time Santa and all the trimmings probably resemble a vintage postcard.

> *Your husband just called, and he said: "You can buy anything you want!"*
> — Note on door of Long Island Museum gift- and bookshop in Stony Brook

♦ **Talbots** and **Godiva Chocolatier** are among a host of well-known retailers on Main Street. Most stores are open daily, year-round.

♦ **The Writing Place**, 97D Main Street, ☎ 631-751-6953, specializes in invitations, personalized stationery and calligraphy. The store also carries fine writing papers, including William Arthur, and the "hot" line of Vera Bradley totes and luggage.

♦ At **Stony Brook Gift Shop**, 135 Main Street, ☎ 631-751-3248, the quality stationery is Crane's – for all occasions. The line of handcrafted greeting cards, however, draws customers all the way from Queens. Other items include Stony Brook souvenirs, collectibles, gift wrap, painted birdhouses and a large year-round selection of Christmas ornaments.

♦ **Cottontails**, 113 Main Street, is a large store specializing in educational toys for children up to age nine and clothing for those under six.

For directions to Stony Brook Village, see Three Village Inn, page 236.

Specialty Shops

FLORIE'S FINALES
71 East Main Street
Smithtown
☎ 631-361-6510, or 888-FLORIES (356-7437)
www.floriesfinales.com

While in Smithtown, be sure to visit Florie's Finales for a different kind of gift. Florie is personal and passionate about her products; she creates beautiful gift baskets for every occasion, and sells fresh-baked pastries, party and corporate favors, chocolate- and caramel-dipped apples and fancy foods from other companies. Stop in for a cup of coffee, or call – she ships nationwide. The baked goods contain only natural ingredients and can be prepared according to low-fat, no-sugar, kosher or non-kosher recipes. Closed Sunday, except for the six weeks from end of November through December.

Florie's Finales is small, but there's a 4,500-square-foot warehouse next door.

ST. JAMES GENERAL STORE
516 Moriches Road
St. James
☎ 631-862-8333

Does the past intrigue you? Tired of mass-produced merchandise? This store is a National Landmark, in operation since 1857; it has never been modernized and remains the typical general store carrying a little bit of everything. In fact, there are so many wonderful gift items that return trips are common. As a mother remarked to her little girl, "Mommy used to come here when she was younger than you." Indeed, kids do love the old-fashioned candy sticks, "patriotic" colored jelly beans, molasses pops, malted milk balls and other goodies – not to mention the toy department in back. Along with stuffed animals are wood puzzles (remember those?) and Victorian collectible dolls. Items on the top shelves are vintage and not for sale, but there's plenty to purchase – "over 4,000 unique items in stock," its ads proclaim. The second floor contains books on local interest, cookbooks and children's books. From Route 25 in Smithtown, take Route 25A east to Moriches Road and turn left. The store is on the right at the intersection of Moriches and Harbor Hill roads, across from Deepwells Farm. Open daily, year-round, except Mondays in mid-winter.

For antiques, look to Northport, St. James and Port Jefferson.

☛ DID YOU KNOW?

The town of St. James was named in honor of the local Episcopal Church.

THE GOOD TIMES BOOKSHOP
150 East Main Street
Port Jefferson
☎ 631-928-2664

Housed in a 19th-century Italianate brick building in the town's historic section, this bookstore carries scholarly, scarce and out-of-print books. All the books are secondhand except for books about Long Island by local authors. Good Times buys books from individuals and it is always on the lookout for scholarly non-fiction books in areas such as history, art and music (but no textbooks). Open Tuesday-Saturday, 11am-6pm; and occasionally on Sunday, 1-5pm.

I like to see a man proud of the place in which he lives.

– Abraham Lincoln (on a plaque in Port Jefferson)

CRAFTIN BUDDIES COUNTRY GIFT SHOP
214 Main Street
Port Jefferson
☎ 631-331-7706

Owner Lauren Noon creates much of the one-of-a-kind hand-painted furniture sold here. She also does custom work. The store carries myriad country gifts, including personalized birdhouses for your favorite chiropractor, cop or tennis bum. After a decade at this location, Noon has opened another store at 136 Middle Country Road in Middle Island. Open daily, year-round.

After Dark

Theater

THEATRE THREE
Athena Hall
412 Main Street
Port Jefferson
☎ 631-928-9100 (box office, open Tuesday through Saturday, 11am-5pm)
☎ 631-928-9202 (business office, Tuesday through Friday, 10am-4pm)

Operating year-round, this 32-year-old theater group performs musicals and dramas for adults ($14-$20) and one-hour original musical productions of famous fairy tales for children ($6-$12). The 40-minute touring productions are geared to grades K-12.

Cafés & Bars

CLASSY COFFEE
20 Clinton Avenue
Huntington
☎ 631-421-5745

This café is open 8am-midnight every day, serving sandwiches, desserts and snacks. There's entertainment nightly, and astrology readings from 3 to 7pm on Thursday. $1 cover. Open auditions are held Monday through Friday for those who wish to perform at Classy Coffee.

NAPPER TANDY'S
Route 25A, Northport
☎ 631-757-4141
15 East Main Street, Smithtown
☎ 631-360-0606

Napper Tandy's is open daily for lunch and dinner; they have a DJ on Thursday and Friday and live bands Wednesday and Saturday. Draws business people during the day and a young crowd at night. They also have a location in Massapequa.

BRUNO'S RESTAURANT
451 Hawkins Avenue
Lake Ronkonkoma
☎ 631-588-9843

Open daily for lunch and dinner. Weekends in winter feature folk singer or music for dancing.

CAFE FIGARO
Wal-Mart/Centereach Mall
Middle Country Road
Centereach
☎ 631-585-2057

Open daily. Piano music Friday (Italian) and Saturday. No cover. Mixed crowd.

DUGOUT SPORTS BAR
639 Commack Road
Commack
☎ 631-499-5554

The Dugout attracts people of all tastes depending on the night's theme (such as karaoke or ladies nights). Thursday and Friday evenings feature a DJ, and Saturday they have live music. During Sunday football broadcasts a free buffet is served at halftime.

BRENNAN'S
546 Route 111
Hauppauge
☎ 631-979-7855

Open daily for full dinner; lunch served on Friday. DJ on Friday and Saturday evenings. Cover $5-$8.

Clubs & Music

CHESTERFIELD'S
330 New York Avenue
Huntington
☎ 631-425-1457

Blues lounge and cigar bar features jazz and blues. Cover. Open Thursday-Sunday.

PAULA JEAN'S SUPPER CLUB
130 Old Town Road
East Setauket
☎ 631-751-9685

Mostly blues and jazz. Proper casual attire. Open Wednesday-Sunday, cover charge Friday and Saturday. The crowd is over 30.

PORT JAZZ
201 Main Street
Port Jefferson
☎ 631-476-7600
www.portjazz.com

Live music begins at 10:30pm, with a different band each night. Thursdays feature jazz and the other nights reggae, R&B and other music. Cover $10. No food served except for a complimentary buffet on summer Sundays. Gentlemen over 25 and ladies over 23 only. Located above Starbucks Coffee. Open Wednesday-Sunday, 8pm until 7am.

FOLK MUSIC SOCIETY OF HUNTINGTON
PO Box 290
Huntington Station
☎ 631-425-2925 (First Saturdays)
☎ 631-661-1278 (Hard Luck Café)
www.exxtra.com/fmsh/FMSH.htm

Founded in 1968, this professional group has grown from seven to more than 200 members. Its First Saturday Concert Series presents regional, national and international folk artists. The music is a variety of folk forms: traditional, contemporary, bluegrass/blues and ethnic. Concerts begin at 8:30pm and are preceded by an open mike at 7:30pm. Parties follow the concert. Admission is $15; seniors $14.

On the third Saturday of most months, local artists perform in the Hard Luck Café Series. Admission is $8; seniors $7. All tickets for both series are only sold at the door, and both are held at the Congregational Church of Huntington (wheelchair accessible), 30 Washington Drive, Centerport, off Route 25A.

Festivals & Events

June

The **Huntington Summer Arts Festival** is produced by the Huntington Arts Council, ☎ 631-271-8423, www.huntingtonarts.org, and takes place each year from mid-June through mid-August on the Chapin Rainbow Stage in Heckscher Park. This performing arts festival offers music and events for all ages; local, regional and national groups participate, and admission is free. Check the Arts Council Web site for a calendar of events beginning in May for the current year.

Thursday is family night in Stony Brook. **Horse-drawn carriage rides** around the village leave every half-hour on Thursdays, 6-8pm. This is one of many family fun events in Stony Brook; for information, ☎ 631-751-2244, www.stonybrookvillage.com.

October

Huntington is home to the **Long Island Fall Festival**, a three-day event that draws 250,000 visitors to Heckscher Park on Main Street in Huntington. The event features four stations of entertainment, a world-class carnival, arts and crafts vendors, food courts, wine-tasting, farmers' market, sailboat regatta, and activities for young children. ☎ 631-423-6100.

December

The **Charles Dickens Festival** features your favorite Dickens characters strolling through the streets of Port Jefferson, along with tolling of the bells, sea chanteys, production of *The Nutcracker*, carriage rides, candlelight tours of sea captains' homes, and wine and fruit right out of the pages of a Dickens novel. A small red trolley transports visitors to and from train station and ferry dock. ☎ 631-473-4724, www.portjeff.com.

Best Places to Stay

The following price scale is intended as a guideline to help you choose lodging to fit your vacation budget.

ACCOMMODATIONS PRICE SCALE
Price scale is based on the cost of a double room, two people per room on a weekend, and does not include the 9.25% hotel tax.
Inexpensive . . . . under $130
Moderate . . . . $130-$200
Expensive . . . . $201-$300
Deluxe . . . . more than $300

Huntington Station

HUNTINGTON COUNTRY INN
270 West Jericho Turnpike
Huntington Station
☎ 631-421-3900, or 800-739-5777
www.huntingtoncountryinn.com
Moderate to Expensive

Small pets are welcome at Huntington Country Inn.

A country inn on Jericho Turnpike, across from King Kullen (open 24 hours) with traffic whizzing by? Okay, it's a stretch. Once a Howard Johnson's, the Huntington Country Inn looks like a motel on the outside, but the new owners have created a countrified ambiance within. Moreover, the 62 guest rooms could win the award for amenities: Jacuzzi tub, makeup mirror, refrigerator/microwave, fax machine, and even a TV in the bathroom in the pricier rooms. Inquire about promotional rates.

The inn has an outdoor pool and a small fitness facility, and offers a continental breakfast. It's conveniently located, with a Loehmann's across the street, and several shopping malls, Walt Whitman's birthplace and Huntington Village a few miles north.

To reach the inn from the LIE, take Exit 49N and follow Route 110 north for 3.3 miles, turning left onto Jericho Turnpike. The building is partially brick with green shutters and is less than a mile along on the left.

Hauppauge

RESIDENCE INN BY MARRIOTT
850 Veteran's Memorial Highway
Hauppauge
☎ 631-724-4188, or 800-331-3131
www.residenceinn.com/ispri
Moderate to Expensive

Pets are welcome at the Residence Inn, but the price is steep: $100 plus $10 per day.

This new hotel was built for the 21st century. Although designed for extended stays, it attracts both overnight guests and families with its spacious suites and amenities – a sunny indoor pool area with a pressed concrete tile floor, a small gym, free grocery shopping service, 24-hour coffee, complimentary snacks in guest rooms and a gathering in the lobby from Monday to Thursday, 5-7pm, with sandwiches to hold you over until dinner. The staff was chosen with care; they have ready smiles and offer assistance when needed.

Opened in May 2002, Residence Inn is flanked by corporate parks but is less than two miles from Sweetwaters (see *Best Places to Eat*, page 245) and 20 miles from Fire Island. The 100 guest rooms (studios and one- or two-bedroom suites) all have sofa beds and fully equipped kitchens with microwave and dishwasher. Breakfast is complimentary, and everyone enjoys using the waffle maker. The hotel is fully equipped for business travelers or social events, but can accommodate only small parties. The one meeting room can hold up to 40 people.

The Residence Inn is two miles from LIE, Exit 57. After exiting, stay on service road until light. Turn left onto Wheeler Road (Route 111). Follow until Route 454 (Veteran's Memorial Highway) and turn right. The Inn is about a quarter-mile on the right.

WYNDHAM WIND WATCH HOTEL
1717 Motor Parkway
Hauppauge
☎ 631-232-9800
360 units. Moderate.

Pet-friendly; pets under 30 pounds, $50 charge. Handicapped-accessible rooms.

COURTYARD BY MARRIOTT
MacArthur Airport
5000 Express Drive South
Ronkonkoma
☎ 631-588-3972, or 800-321-2211
www.courtyard.com/ispcy
Moderate to Expensive

Long Island's newest hotel opened in May, 2002. It has 154 rooms, a restaurant, lounge, indoor pool, fitness center.

Stony Brook

HOLIDAY INN EXPRESS
3131 Nesconset Highway (Route 347)
Stony Brook
☎ 631-471-8000
www.holiday-stonybrook.com
Moderate (inquire about special discounts)

Children stay free at Holiday Inn Express.

This may be what's called a "limited service hotel," (no bar or restaurant), but don't let that fool you. It's first-class; the furniture is polished and unmarred, the rooms are large and comfortable, complete with an up-holstered adjustable chair. Ask for a wake-up call and the phone rings exactly on the dot. It may not be un-usual but it's still service!

A lovely place for a family, the 143-room hotel sports a well-equipped fitness center overlooking a 40x20-foot heated pool (no lifeguard). On the manicured lawns are a playground, picnic tables, volleyball net, and gazebo with a swing for two or three in a serene setting. From the hotel, Stony Brook Village is about a 15-minute ride and Port Jefferson about 10 minutes.

To reach Stony Brook Village from the hotel (6.3 miles), turn right (north) onto Nicolls Road (Route 97) and travel 3.2 miles until the end (the turnoff for Nicolls Road is about a half-block left of the Holiday Inn Express). You'll pass several entrances to SUNY-Stony Brook. Turn left onto 25A and in about a mile and a half the road splits. Bear right onto Main Street and continue about a quarter-mile to the Village Center.

THREE VILLAGE INN
150 Main Street
Stony Brook
☎ 631-751-0555
www.threevillageinn.com
Moderate to Expensive

The inn was built in 1751 and is the only place to stay in Stony Brook Village. Across the village green from the stores, it's not only convenient but, like everything in the village, oozes with charm. It has three large dining rooms with servers dressed in period clothing. The photo gallery of political and theatrical dignitaries who have visited the inn is quite impressive.

The guest rooms are spacious and all have TV and telephone. Seven are in the original section of the inn with its low, beamed ceilings and Colonial furnishings. Six cottages have private entrances. All 26 rooms are decorated differently and some have a fireplace and/or Jacuzzi. The entrance to the inn has a ramp but the rooms are not designed for the handicapped. To reach the village – and the inn – take LIE to Exit 56. Follow Route 111 north to 25A East at Smithtown. Bear left onto Main Street. Proceed a half-mile to the inn. Open year-round.

The Three Village Inn has music every Friday and Saturday night year-round at the piano bar.

Don't miss the imposing figure of Hercules in a pavilion across the road from the Three Village Inn. The figure-head from the USS *Ohio* (1820) has a peacefully sleeping lion wrapped around his body, as if to say that Hercules is fiercer than the beast. Out front is the anchor from that ship. Behind Hercules is the whaleboat *Polaris* from the Charles Hall Expedition to the Arctic in 1870.

WARD MELVILLE

Every village on Long Island, it seems, has a hero. In Stony Brook the honor goes to philanthropist Ward Melville, a 20th-century shoe tycoon (he founded the Thom McAn chain) who turned a down-at-the-heels fishing village into a "living Williamsburg." Melville donated 480 acres of land for use as a state university (it is now part of the 1,100-acre campus of the State University of New York (SUNY) at Stony Brook). He also funded the Museums at Stony Brook (now called the Long Island Museum of American Art, History & Carriages), built Stony Brook's crescent-shaped business district in 1941, and saved 80 acres of wetland from development.

It was Mrs. Melville who coined the term "Three Village" to denote Stony Brook and neighboring Old Field and Setauket.

Ward Melville also founded, and deeded all his property to, the Ward Melville Heritage Organization in 1939. The organization continues to manage his contributions to the community, many of which are named for him. They also sponsor tours of the historic district of Stony Brook Village and conduct free guided walks of Main Street from June-September; for information, ☎ 631-751-2244, or www.wardmelville-heritage.org. See *Walking Tours*, page 196.

Adjacent to the Three Village Inn is the Three Village Garden Club Exchange, at 275 Christian Avenue, ☎ 631-751-0560. For $50 a year, people from all over bring old jewelry, glassware, china, linens, children's toys, musical instruments – you name it – to sell on consignment. The merchandise fills two floors; prices range from $1.85 (for a greeting card) to $235 (for a used golf set and leather bag) and up (for large pieces of furniture). The exchange is housed in what used to be the Stone Jug, an early 1800s storage building. It was later a popular saloon where local artist William Sidney Mount liked to dance, drink and play music.

Note the huge elm trees on the front lawn. The garden club works hard to prevent Dutch elm disease from decimating them as occurred in 1930 when the fungus entered the country in a shipment of wood from France and killed over 95% of the nation's elm trees. The club welcomes financial support.

Farmingville

HAMPTON INN BROOKHAVEN
2000 North Ocean Avenue
Farmingville
☎ 631-732-7300, or 800-HAMPTON
www.longislandhotelsllc.com
Moderate

Long Island Hotels LLC has done a fabulous job with this Hampton Inn, which opened February 26, 2002. All 161 rooms have microwave and refrigerator, the carpeted fitness room is spacious and well equipped, guests get a generous complimentary breakfast, the tiled swimming pool area has many windows and a skylight, and meeting rooms can accommodate up to 150. Moreover, it's the first hotel on Long Island to go completely wireless.

Kids stay free in your room at Hampton Inn.

The gym is also open to outside memberships, which means the equipment must be constantly maintained. A member of Long Island Hotels LLC swore this will never be a problem; she said this limited-service facility has a full-service mentality and that the company's tagline is "excellence in hospitality." With a Holiday Inn Express in Hauppauge and a Hampton Inn & Suites in Central Islip (with three franchised restaurants) both slated to open the second quarter of 2003, the company has ample opportunity to live up to its promises. So far, it rates an "A." The Hampton Inn Brookhaven is just off the LIE at Exit 63.

Motels

MOTEL PRICE SCALE

Price scale is based on the cost of a double room, two people per room, in season, and does not include the 9.25% hotel tax.

Inexpensive . . . . under $100
Moderate . . . . $100-$150
Expensive . . . . over $150

WHITMAN MOTOR LODGE
295 East Jericho Turnpike
Huntington Station
☎ 631-271-2800
www.whitmanmotorlodge.com
44 units. Inexpensive to Moderate.

Pet-friendly; any size pet welcome.

ABBEY MOTOR INN
317 West Jericho Turnpike
Huntington Station
☎ 631-423-0800
30 units. Inexpensive.

ONESTI MOTEL
665 West Jericho Turnpike
Huntington Station
☎ 631-549-5511
17 rooms. Inexpensive.

COMMACK MOTOR INN
2231 Jericho Turnpike
Commack
☎ 631-499-9060
83 units. Inexpensive.

COURTESY INN
1126 Jericho Turnpike
Commack
☎ 631-864-3500
35 rooms. Inexpensive.

HAMPTON INN COMMACK
680 Commack Road
Commack
☎ 631-462-5700
144 units. Moderate to Expensive.

Handicapped-accessible rooms.

HOWARD JOHNSON LODGE
450 Moreland Road
Commack
☎ 631-864-8820, or 800-446-4656
111 units. Moderate.

Handicapped-accessible rooms.

OLYMPIC MOTOR LODGE
650 Vanderbilt Motor Parkway
Hauppauge
☎ 631-231-5050
41 units. Inexpensive.

HOLIDAY INN EXPRESS
2050 Express Drive South
Hauppauge
☎ 631-348-1400
www.hiexpress.com
133 units. Moderate.

Handicapped-accessible rooms.

ECONO LODGE
755 Route 347
Smithtown Bypass
Smithtown
☎ 631-724-9000, or 800-55-ECONO (reservations)
39 units. Inexpensive.

TOWNE HOUSE MOTOR INN
880 Jericho Turnpike
Smithtown
☎ 631-543-4040
38 units. Inexpensive.

ECONO LODGE
3055 Veterans Memorial Highway
at LI MacArthur Airport
Ronkonkoma
☎ 631-588-6800, or 800-55-ECONO (reservations)
59 units. Inexpensive.

Handicapped-accessible rooms.

HOLIDAY INN
3845 Veterans Memorial Highway
at MacArthur Airport
Ronkonkoma
☎ 631-585-9500
www.holiday-inn.com/ronkonkomany
289 units. Expensive.

Handicapped-accessible rooms.

DANFORD'S INN
25 East Broadway
Port Jefferson
☎ 631-928-5200
www.danfords.com
85 units. Expensive.

Handicapped-accessible rooms.

HERITAGE INN AT PORT JEFFERSON HARBOR
201 West Broadway
Port Jefferson
☎ 631-473-2499
46 units. Inexpensive.

All units are on the ground level.

TERRYVILLE MOTOR LODGE
1371 Route 112
Port Jefferson Station
☎ 631-928-5900
50 units. Inexpensive.

Best Places to Eat

No man is lonely while eating spaghetti; it requires so much attention.

— Christopher Morley

DINING PRICE SCALE
Price scale includes one entrée, with glass of wine and coffee. There is an 8.5% tax on food in both Nassau and Suffolk Counties.
Inexpensive....................under $25
Moderate ....$25-$40
Expensive.....................over $40

Huntington Station

MATTEO'S
300 West Jericho Turnpike
Huntington Station
☎ 631-421-6001
www.matteosrestaurant.com
www.greatrestaurantsmag.com
Moderate

What can you say about a family that owns four popular restaurants on Long Island and one in Boca Raton, Florida? More power to them! The restaurant appears to have the formula to keep the crowds coming: It's run like a tight ship, serving good food at reasonable prices and giving diners the choice of half or full portions (family style for two). This works well whether you're a couple or big party.

Matteo's does not take reservations, but the Huntington location has two dining rooms and will take reservations for a party of five or more. Start with a chopped antipasto salad while you're still hungry. You won't be when you leave.

Matteo's other Long Island locations are in Hewlett at 1455 Broadway, ☎ 516-374-0627; Roslyn Heights at 88 Mineola Avenue, ☎ 516-484-0555; and Bellmore at 416 Bedford Avenue, ☎ 516-409-1779. To reach the Huntington restaurant, follow directions to Huntington Country Inn on page 234; Matteo's is next door.

Hauppauge

SWEETWATERS BAR & BISTRO
470 Wheeler Road (Rte 111)
.3 mile north of LIE Exit 56 on left
Hauppauge
☎ 631-348-0808
www.sweetwaters.net
Reservations suggested
Moderate

Be prepared for the bracing noise level as you crisscross the bar to the more tranquil dining rooms. One room doubles as a dining and party room; outside are umbrella tables facing the street. On the night we visited there was no affair, so both rooms were filled with diners. The party room resembles a stage set, with faux plants draped around poles under a black tent ceiling. The young waitresses in black leotards are conscientious and sweet, although the name Sweetwaters is derived from the Indian translation for Hauppauge.

Sweetwaters features live music on Saturday nights.

Seafood, steak, pasta and fondues for two are the staples, along with specials and a less expensive selection "For the Lighter Appetite" at $12-$18. Entrées come with a salad of baby greens and a basket of soft salted pretzels and rolls. The American menu is inventive and the food fresh and cooked with care. Blackened shrimp in spinach lasagna is hot, savory and satisfying. Executive chef Vincent Policano came from Northport Grill in Northport and clearly knows his stuff. Host Jimmy

Gerrain was named Restaurateur of the Year in 2001 by the Long Island Restaurant & Catering Association.

Critics agree that Sweetwaters is hip, casual, warm and welcoming. Joan Reminick of *Newsday* wrote, "We left wanting to return." So will you. Sweetwaters is open for lunch and dinner, Monday-Saturday, and for dinner on Sunday.

Smithtown

CASA RUSTICA
175 West Main Street
Smithtown
☎ 631-265-9265
www.greatrestaurantsmag.com
Moderate to Expensive

Rust-color stucco walls give the downstairs dining room a cave-like appearance and cave dwellers dine there with gusto and gabbiness. Smithtown may seem serene but not inside Casa Rustica. Although every table wasn't filled on this Wednesday night in July, the boisterous family atmosphere made it seem that way. "You'd think this was a Saturday night," a man was overheard to observe. "I figured we'd be the only people here."

According to the waiter at this popular Italian restaurant, the restaurant is packed on weekends. Why not? Service is so smooth that dishes seem to appear by magic. What's more, the food is superb. Opened in 1985, Casa Rustica has received four stars from *Newsday* and in the words of the *Zagat* survey, it serves "consistently delicious cuisine backed up by attentive service." The menu is à la carte but entrées come with vegetables and potato. Open year-round for lunch (Monday-Friday) and dinner (daily); reservations are essential on weekends. The restaurant is wheelchair-accessible, but call ahead.

Stony Brook

PENTIMENTO
93 Main Street
Stony Brook
☎ 631-689-7755
www.pentimentorestaurant.com
Moderate

Dining al fresco here on an August evening, I soon realized that Thursday is Family Night in Stony Brook Village. On the lawn across the way, an animal handler from *Animal Adventures* was introducing various reptiles to hordes of happy children while teaching them about each one's habitat and temperament. Every 12 minutes or so, horses pulling a carriage went clip-clopping by (see *Festivals & Events,* page 232, for information on the carriage rides). Birds were chirping and a basket of homemade herbed focaccia was placed before me. I knew nothing could interrupt my euphoria and I was right. Service was stellar and my pappardelle was nicely flavored with rock shrimp, fresh basil and a trace of red sauce in the Northern Italian tradition. Pasta dishes are less than $20; fish, steak and duck are more. Portions are large – you won't leave hungry. Open year-round for lunch and dinner; closed Monday. Reservations requested.

Lite Bites

NORTHPORT-EAST NORTHPORT PUBLIC LIBRARY
185 Larkfield Road
☎ 631-261-2313
151 Laurel Avenue
☎ 631-261-6930

Both library branches have a library-run café, with hours that follow the general library hours: Monday-Friday, 9am-9pm; Saturday, 9am-5pm; Sundays during the school year, 1-5pm. Closed in summer.

MAMA SBARRO'S PIZZERIA
592 Veteran's Memorial Highway
Hauppauge
☎ 631-360-4343

The Long-Island-based Sbarro organization has 12 locations in Nassau and Suffolk featuring this expanded
version of its original concept. Divided into restaurant
and pizzeria, the huge Hauppauge establishment resembles a New York deli with its wall of caricatures
and photographs of bygone celebrities. The recipes are
Mama Sbarro's and, the menu assures you, the ingredients fresh. "Mama wouldn't have it any other way."
Mama Sbarro's is in the Sears Hardware plaza (at the
intersection of Route 111). Open daily for lunch and
dinner.

ROBINSON'S TEA ROOM
97 Main Street
Stony Brook
☎ 631-751-1232

This is a delightful place for breakfast (French toast
but no bacon or eggs), lunch (sandwiches, wraps, salads), afternoon tea in the "finest British Tradition,"
dessert (freshly baked scones) or a light, early dinner.
The restaurant uses only purified water in its teas and
coffees. There is a wide assortment of fine teas to
choose from. Open daily, year-round.

BROOK HOUSE RESTAURANT
& ICE CREAM PARLOR
123 Main Street
Stony Brook
☎ 631-751-4617

Brook House is open for breakfast, lunch and dinner
and is especially popular with families. Owned by two
women, it's open daily, year-round.

GOURMET GODDESS
111 Main Street
Cold Spring Harbor
☎ 631-692-9646

Cold Spring Harbor resembles a New England whaling town, or "a Norman Rockwell painting of Long Island," as a saleswoman at Gourmet Goddess likes to describe it. Be sure to have lunch at this double-storefront gift store/café with a Parisian awning that dominates the "downtown" commercial district. The friendly proprietors make their own chocolate and baked goods, and prepare different menus daily. When the weather is warm, you can enjoy your gourmet sandwich or salad al fresco.

North Shore A to Z

Animal Hospitals

Cold Spring Hills Animal Hospital, 448 West Jericho Turnpike (near La Palma Restaurant), Huntington, ☎ 631-692-6458. Dogs and cats only. Boarding. Closed Sunday.

Dix Hills Animal Hospital, 1166 East Jericho Turnpike, Huntington, ☎ 631-271-8383. Dogs and cats only. Boarding. Closed Sunday.

West Hills Animal Hospital, 800 West Jericho Turnpike, Huntington, ☎ 631-351-6116. All small animals treated. Avian and exotic medicine. Luxurious boarding. Open 24 hours daily, year-round.

Fort Hill Animal Hospital, 146 East Main Street, Huntington, ☎ 631-427-1655, www.fhah.verizonsupersite.com. Dogs and cats only. Boarding. Open Sunday for emergencies only.

Huntington Animal Hospital, 113 Walt Whitman Road, Huntington Station, ☎ 631-423-7020. Small animals by appointment only. Boarding. Closed Sunday.

North Shore Veterinary Hospital, 835 Fort Salonga Road, Northport, ☎ 631-757-0522. Primarily dogs and cats. Boarding at nearby North Shore Animal Center. Closed Sunday.

Animal Emergency Service, 6230 Jericho Turnpike #C (in shopping center), Commack, ☎ 631-462-6044. Primarily dogs and cats. Open nights, weekends and holidays. They have another facility in Selden.

Nesconset Animal Hospital, 189 Terry Road, near the intersection with Route 347, Smithtown, ☎ 631-361-6061. Cats and dogs only. No boarding. Closed Sunday.

Smithtown Animal Hospital, 891 West Jericho Turnpike, Smithtown, ☎ 631-543-0333. Dogs, cats and reptiles. Boarding. Closed Sunday.

Hauppauge Animal Hospital, 521 Townline Road (near Route 111), Hauppauge, ☎ 631-265-5551. All animals except exotics. Three nights' complimentary boarding. Open Sunday, 9-11am, for emergencies only.

Hawkins Avenue Hospital for Animals, 354 Hawkins Avenue (just off LIE Exit 60), Ronkonkoma, ☎ 631-981-8111. Small animals. Boarding. Closed Sunday.

Animal Medical Hospital of Centereach, 2425 Middle Country Road, Centereach, ☎ 631-585-5353. All animals except fish. Boarding. Closed Sunday.

Centereach Animal Hospital, 1847 Middle County Road (next to Chevrolet dealership), Centereach, ☎ 631-588-1730. Primarily dogs and cats. Boarding. Closed Sunday.

Three Village Veterinary Hospital, 1342 Stony Brook Road, Stony Brook, ☎ 631-689-8877. Small animals. Boarding. Closed Sunday.

Corner Animal Hospital, 24 Woods Corner Road (at the intersection of Route 25A and Nicolls Road), Setauket, ☎ 631-941-3500. Small animals and exotic pets. Boarding. Closed Sunday.

Jefferson Animal Hospital, 606 Patchogue Road, Port Jefferson Station, ☎ 631-473-0415. All animals. Boarding. Closed Sunday.

Roosevelt Animal Hospital, 7 Roosevelt Avenue, Port Jefferson Station, ☎ 631-476-0400. Small animals. Open daily. Sunday, 8-11am.

Farmingville Animal Hospital, 840 Horse Block Road. Farmingville, ☎ 631-698-8000. Small animals. Open Sunday morning for emergencies.

Animal Emergency Service, 280-L Middle Country Road (in a shopping center at the corner of North Ocean Avenue, next to Café Stefano), Selden, ☎ 631-698-2225, www.animalemergencysvce.com. Open daily, 24 hours. Primarily dogs and cats.

Rocky Point Animal Hospital, 526 Route 25A (near Enterprise Rent-A-Car), Rocky Point, ☎ 631-744-8882. Small animals. Boarding. Closed Sunday.

Ridge Veterinary Hospital, 1800 Middle Country Road, Ridge, ☎ 631-345-3366. All animals, from horses and pigs to dogs and cats. Closed Thursday and Sunday.

Animal Shelters

Save-A-Pet Animal Rescue, 608 Route 112, Port Jefferson Station, ☎ 631-473-6333, has strays and privately donated pets looking for homes. Open daily, year-round.

League for Animal Protection of Huntington-Grateful Paw Cat Shelter, 104 Deposit Road, East Northport, ☎ 631-757-4517, www.gratefulpaw.petfinder.org, is a volunteer organization founded in 1973 They maintain a no-kill cat shelter, sponsor a foster dog and cat adoption program and provide humane education at local schools. The animals are from the Huntington pound, located behind the League's facility, where League staff medicates and trains the animals for adoption. Closed Monday.

Little Shelter Dog & Cat Adoption Center, 33 Warner Road, Huntington, ☎ 631-754-8200, www.little-shelter.com, takes abused and abandoned animals from the streets. Their six buildings on a six-acre site include a medical facility; open daily, year-round. Little Shelter also helps with burial arrangements in its Sheltervale Pet Cemetery, and has a 110-acre animal sanctuary upstate for animals that are not adopted, ☎ 631-368-8770.

The STAR Foundation rescues and rehabilitates injured squirrels, rabbits, birds, deer and other wildlife.

STAR (Save the Animals Rescue) Foundation, PO Box 949, Port Jefferson Station, ☎ 631-736-8207, operates a Lost & Found pet hotline, ☎ 800-564-5704, staffed by volunteers who take calls 24 hours a day, every day. With a PetLine membership, your pet receives an ID tag with the 800 number engraved on it, and the animal's description and background information are added to the database. The one time charge ($29) is for lifetime membership. Unregistered animals that cannot be traced are put up for adoption.

In general, town animal shelters hold strays for one week. If the animal is not claimed by then, it is put up for adoption.

Town of Huntington, 106 Deposit Road, East Northport, ☎ 631-286-9270. Open daily.

Town of Smithtown, 410 East Main Street, Smithtown, ☎ 631-360-7575. Open Monday-Saturday.

Town of Brookhaven, 300 Horseblock Road, Yaphank, ☎ 631-286-4940. Open Monday-Saturday.

Banks

The following banks have multiple branches throughout Suffolk County. For specific locations, check the bank's Web site.

Astoria Federal Savings Bank . . . . www.astoriafederal.com

Bank of New York . . . . www.bankofnewyork.com

Bank of Smithtown . . . . www.bankofsmithtown.com

Chase Manhattan Bank . . . . www.chase.com

Citibank . . . . www.citibank.com

Dime Savings Bank of NY . . . . www.dime.com

First National Bank of LI . . . . www.fnbli.com

Fleet Bank . . . . www.fleet.com

North Fork Bank . . . . www.northforkbank.com

Roslyn Savings Bank . . . . www.roslyn.com

State Bank of LI . . . . www.statebankofli.com

Suffolk County National Bank . . . . . www.scnb.com

Houses of Worship

Baptist

North Shore Baptist Church, 25 West Main Street, Kings Park, ☎ 631-269-1050.

Calvary Baptist Church, 324 Jayne Boulevard, Port Jefferson Station, ☎ 631-473-3339.

Catholic

St. Philip Neri, 344 Main Street, Northport, ☎ 631-261-7753.

St. Joseph's, 59 Church Street, Kings Park, ☎ 631-269-6635.

St. Patrick's, 280 East Main Street, Smithtown, ☎ 631-265-2271.

Holy Cross Church, 95 Nicolls Road, Nesconset, ☎ 631-265-2200.

St. Philip & St. James, 454 North Country Road (25A), St. James, ☎ 631-584-5454.

Episcopal

All Souls, Main Street, 10 Mill Pond Road (next to village center), Stony Brook, ☎ 631-751-0034, www.allsouls.com.

All Souls Episcopal Church, c. 1899, was designed by Stanford White.

Trinity Episcopal Church, 130 Main Street, Northport, ☎ 631-261-7670.

St. James, 490 North Country Road, St. James, ☎ 631-584-5560.

Caroline Church of Brookhaven, Village Green, Setauket, ☎ 631-941-4245.

St. Andrew's, East Main Street, Yaphank, ☎ 631-924-5083, www.yaphank.org. St. Andrew's, built c. 1853, is in Yaphank's historic district.

Jewish – Orthodox

Young Israel of Huntington, 598 Park Avenue, Huntington, ☎ 631-385-7276, www.ou.org/network/new/ny-yihunt.htm.

Congregational Lubavitch of Commack, 65 Valleywood Road, Commack, ☎ 631-543-8395.

Stony Brook Hebrew Congregation, Room 249, Student Union Building, SUNY Stony Brook, ☎ 631-751-3971, www.stonybrookhc.com.

Coram Jewish Center (Temple Beth Sholom), 981 Old Town Road, Coram, ☎ 631-698-3939.

Jewish – Conservative

Huntington Jewish Center, 510 Park Avenue, Huntington, ☎ 631-427-1089, www.huntingtonjewishcenter.com.

South Huntington Jewish Center, 2600 New York Avenue, Melville, ☎ 631-421-3224.

Dix Hills Jewish Center, 555 Vanderbilt Motor Parkway, Dix Hills, ☎ 631-499-6644, www.dhjc.org.

East Northport Jewish Center, 328 Elwood Road, East Northport, ☎ 631-368-6474.

Commack Jewish Center, 83 Shirley Court, Commack, ☎ 631-543-3311, www.commackjc.org.

Kings Park Jewish Center, Route 25A, Kings Park, ☎ 631-269-1133.

Temple Beth Sholom, 433 Edgewood Avenue, Smithtown, ☎ 631-724-0424.

Temple Beth Chai of Hauppauge, 870 Townline Road, Hauppauge, ☎ 631-724-5807.

North Shore Jewish Center, 385 Old Town Road, Port Jefferson Station, ☎ 631-928-3737, www.north-shorejewishcenter.org.

Jewish – Reform

Temple Beth David, 100 Hauppauge Road, Commack, ☎ 631-499-0915, www.tbdcommack.org.

Temple Isaiah, 1404 Stony Brook Road, Stony Brook, ☎ 631-751-8518.

Lutheran

St. Paul's Lutheran Church, 120 Vernon Valley Road, East Northport, ☎ 631-754-4422.

Abiding Presence Lutheran Church, Route 25A and Sunken Meadow Road, Fort Salonga, ☎ 631-269-6454.

St. James Lutheran Church, Woodlawn Avenue and Second Avenue, St. James, ☎ 631-584-5212.

Methodist

Dix Hills Methodist Church, 6 Folger Lane, Dix Hills, ☎ 631-271-2290.

Smithtown United Methodist Church, 230 Middle Country Road, Smithtown, ☎ 631-265-6945.

United Methodist Community Church, 216 Christian Avenue, Stony Brook, ☎ 631-751-0574.

Setauket United Methodist Church, 160 Main Street, East Setauket, ☎ 631-941-4167.

United Methodist Church, 792 Hawkins Avenue, Lake Grove, ☎ 631-588-5856.

Christ Church United Methodist, 545 Old Town Road, Port Jefferson Station, ☎ 631-473-4734.

Presbyterian

Bethany Presbyterian Church, 425 Maplewood Road, Huntington Station, ☎ 631-423-6359.

Central Presbyterian Church, 240 Main Street, Huntington Village, ☎ 631-421-3663.

First Presbyterian Church, Main and Church Streets, Northport, ☎ 631-261-6434.

First Presbyterian Church, 175 East Main Street, Smithtown, ☎ 631-265-5151.

Setauket Presbyterian Church, 5 Caroline Avenue, Setauket, ☎ 631-941-4271, www.setauket.presbychurch. org.

Yaphank Presbyterian Church is known as "a Friendly Historical Church."

Yaphank Presbyterian Church, 65 Main Street, Yaphank, ☎ 631-924-3723.

Information Sources

Chambers of Commerce

Cold Spring Harbor Merchants Association, ☎ 631-692-6093, www.cshl.org/cshm.

Huntington Township Chamber of Commerce, ☎ 631-423-6100, www.huntingtonchamber.com (members are listed at www.htccmem.com).

East Northport Chamber of Commerce, ☎ 631-261-3573, www.eastnorthport.com.

Northport Chamber of Commerce, ☎ 631-754-3905, www.northportny.com.

Kings Park Chamber of Commerce, ☎ 631-269-7678, www.kingsparkli.com/chamber.htm.

Smithtown Chamber of Commerce, ☎ 631-979-8069, www.smithtownchamber.org.

Greater Ronkonkoma Chamber of Commerce, ☎ 631-232-3925.

St. James Chamber of Commerce, ☎ 631-584-8510, http://stjamesny.org.

Town of Brookhaven Chamber of Commerce, ☎ 631-451-6668, www.brookhaven.org.

Brookhaven Chambers of Commerce Coalition, represents the chambers of all the municipalities within the Town of Brookhaven, ☎ 631-474-5019.

Three Village Chamber of Commerce, ☎ 631-689-8838 or 631-751-1942, www.threevillagechamber.com.

Selden Chamber of Commerce, ☎ 631-696-7251.

Greater Port Jefferson Chamber of Commerce, ☎ 631-473-1414, www.portjeffchamber.com.

CDM Chamber of Commerce (Council of Dedicated Merchants in Mt. Sinai, Miller Place, Rocky Point and Sound Beach), ☎ 631-821-1313, www.cdmlongisland.com.

Farmingville/Holtsville Chamber of Commerce, ☎ 631-472-1569.

Longwood Chamber of Commerce, Middle Island, ☎ 631-736-0880.

Community Web Sites

Huntington . . . . www.huntington-ny.com
Northport. . . . . www.northportny.com
East Northport . . . . www.eastnorthport.com
Kings Park . . . . www.kingsparkli.com
Smithtown . . . . www.smithnetny.com
Stony Brook . . . . www.stonybrookvillage.com
Three Village . . . . www.stnybrk.com
Port Jefferson . . . . www.portjeff.com
Mt. Sinai . . . . www.mtsinaicivic.org
Yaphank . . . . www.yaphank.org

Liquor Stores

Grapevines 'n Baskets, 322 New York Avenue, Huntington, ☎ 631-385-8463, www.palmervineyards.com/

grapevines.htm, is the retail outlet of Palmer Vineyards on the North Fork.

Bottle Bargains, 1019 Fort Salonga Road, Northport,
☎ 631-757-2187.

Medical Facilities

*Suffolk
County has 12
hospitals with
3,568 beds.*

Huntington Hospital, 270 Park Avenue, Huntington, ☎ 631-351-2000, www.hunthosp.org, www.north-
shorelij.com.

John T. Mather Memorial Hospital, 75 North
Country Road, Port Jefferson, ☎ 631-473-1550,
www.matherhospital.org, has branches all over Suffolk
County.

Veterans Administration Medical Center, 79 Mid-
dleville Road, Northport, ☎ 631-261-4400.

St. John's Episcopal Hospital, Route 25A, Smithtown, ☎ 631-862-3000.

St. Catherine of Siena Hospital, 50 Route 25A,
Smithtown, ☎ 631-862-3000, is a 366- bed hospital that
has been serving northern Suffolk County for 34 years.

Memorial Sloan-Kettering Cancer Center, 800
Veterans Memorial Highway, Hauppauge, ☎ 631-863-
5100, www.mskcc.org.

University Hospital & Medical Center, Nicolls Road,
Stony Brook, ☎ 631-689-8333, www.uhmc.sunysb.edu.
SUNY Stony Brook's 504-bed critical care hospital has
been ranked among the 15 best teaching hospitals in
the nation.

St. Charles Hospital & Rehabilitation Center, 200
Belle Terre Road, Port Jefferson, ☎ 631-474-6000.

Movies

Cinema Arts Centre, 423 Park Avenue, Huntington,
☎ 631-423-7611, www.cinemaartscentre.org, shows a
wide range of films, American and foreign, new and old,
traditional and offbeat, 365 days a year, on three

screens. The ongoing "Anything but Silent" series of silent classics has live piano accompaniment. The center's **Sky Room** lounge features live music every weekend ($10) and is also the site of puppet shows ($7). The **Cinema Community Café**, sponsored by Newsday, is open daily, serving soups, sandwiches, vegetarian dishes and coffee.

Loews Cineplex (1), Route 110 next to Walt Whitman Mall, Huntington, ☎ 631-423-1300 (recording), 631-423-1313 (box office).

Loews Shore 8, 37 Wall Street, one block north of Route 25A, Huntington, ☎ 631-425-7680 (recording), 631-425-7682 (box office).

Elwood Cinemas (2), 1950 Jericho Turnpike, East Northport, ☎ 631-499-7800.

Northport Theatre (1), 250 Main Street, Northport, ☎ 631-261-8600.

Commack Multiplex (15), 100 Service Road, Commack, ☎ 631-462-6953 (recording), 631-462-6952 (box office).

Regal Cinemas (9), 565 Portion Road, Ronkonkoma, ☎ 631-580-9714 (recording), 631-580-9707 (box office).

Loews Cineplex (4), Smith Haven Mall, Lake Grove, ☎ 631-724-9550 (recording), 631-724-9551 (box office).

Loews's Stony Brook Theatre (15), 2194C Nesconset Highway, Stony Brook, ☎ 631-941-0124 (recording), 631-941-0156 (box office).

United Artist Theatres (13), Sunrise Highway, Patchogue, ☎ 631-363-2100 (recording), 631-363-2238 (box office).

PJ Cinemas (7), 1068 Route 112, Port Jefferson Station, ☎ 631-928-3456 (recording), 631-928-3597 (box office).

Movieland Cinema (7), Route 112 and Pine Road, Coram, ☎ 631-696-4200 (recording), 631-696-4282 (box office).

United Artists (12), Routes 112 and 25, Coram, ☎ 631-736-6200 (recording), 631-736-6623 (box office).

Newspapers

Ronkonkoma Review and *Smithtown Messenger*, published by ESP Publications, Smithtown, ☎ 631-265-3500.

Long Islander Newspapers was founded by Walt Whitman and his picture is in the paper's logo.

The Long-Islander, Northport Journal, Record (covering Huntington Township), and *Half Hollow Hills Newspaper*, published by Long Islander Newspapers, ☎ 631-425-7680, www.longislandernews.com.

Smithtown News, Huntington News, Mid-Island News, Northport Observer, Commack News, and *Smithtown News* published by The North Shore News Group, ☎ 631-265-2100, 261-6124 or 261-2100.

Suffolk Life is published by Suffolk Life Newspapers for a group of communities in northern Suffolk County (Huntington, Huntington Station, Dix Hills/Melville, Northport, Central Islip/Hauppauge, Commack/Kings Park, Smithtown, Ronkonkoma, St. James/Nesconset, Stony Brook/Setauket, Centereach/Lake Grove, Selden/Farmingville, Port Jefferson, Coram/Middle Island, and Rocky Point); they are based in Riverhead, ☎ 631-369-0800, www.suffolklife.com.

The Village Times Herald, serving Stony Brook, Old Field, Strong's Neck, Poquott, and the Setaukets (☎ 631-751-1550, www.threevillages.com); *Port Times Record*, serving Port Jefferson, Belle Terre, Port Jefferson Station and Mt. Sinai; *Village Beacon Record*, serving Miller Place, Sound Beach, Rocky Point and Wading River, and *Times of Smithtown*, covering St. James and Nesconset, are published by The Times Beacon Record Newspapers, Setauket, ☎ 631-751-7744, www.tbrnewspapers.com.

Pharmacies

North Shore Pharmacy, 25 Southdown Road, Huntington, ☎ 631-427-6262.

Northport Pharmacy, 824 Fort Salonga, Road, Northport, ☎ 631-757-1010.

Medicine Shoppe Pharmacy, 394 Lakefield Road, East Northport, ☎ 631-368-9492; 2308 North Ocean Avenue, Farmingville, ☎ 631-732-0633; and 249 Middle Country Road, Selden, ☎ 631-732-7373.

Slater's Pharmacy, 407 Hawkins Avenue, Ronkonkoma, ☎ 631-588-1590.

Village Chemists of Centereach, 2677 Middle Country Road, Centereach, ☎ 631-585-8380.

Setauket Pharmacy, 1368 Route 25A (Three Village Shopping Center), Setauket, ☎ 631-689-3535.

Seaport Pharmacy & General Store, 120 Main Street, Port Jefferson, ☎ 631-473-1144. www.seaport-chemists.com. Seaport Pharmacy has a health and wellness center and a board certified nutritionist available for counseling.

Zip Codes

Calverton 11933
Centerport 11721
Centereach 11720
Cold Spring Harbor 11724
Commack 11725
Coram 11727
East Northport/Elwood 11731
Farmingville 11738
Greenlawn 11740
Hauppauge 11788
Huntington/Halesite/Lloyd Harbor 11743
Huntington Station/Dix Hills 11746
Kings Park/San Remo 11754
Lake Grove 11755
Manorville 11949

Suffolk County's South Shore

Getting Here & Getting Around

By Car

The **Long Island Expressway**, the **Southern State Parkway** and the **Sunrise Highway/Sunrise Expressway** are the major west-to-east routes between Nassau and Suffolk counties. Major north-south highways in Suffolk County are the **Sagtikos/Sunken Meadow Parkway**; **Nicolls Road** (Route 97); **Route 83**; and the **William Floyd Parkway** (Route 46).

Rental Cars

Rates for a mid-sized car run around $45 per day.

Budget Rent-A-Car, 200 Main Street, Islip, ☎ 631-581-9713; 1831 Route 112, Medford (franchise), ☎ 631-654-1700; www.budget.com.

A-Car Auto Rental, Montauk Highway, Blue Point, ☎ 877-296-CARS (2277). Serves customers from New York City to Hamptons.

By Taxi

Tommy's Taxi, 88 Park Avenue, Bay Shore, ☎ 631-665-4800. Daily service to and from New York, airports, and Fire Island ferries. Serving the community for 88 years.

McRide's taxi and van service. Shirley and Mastic, ☎ 631-281-8581; Patchogue, ☎ 631-475-6213. Local, airport and service to NYC. Accepts all major credit cards.

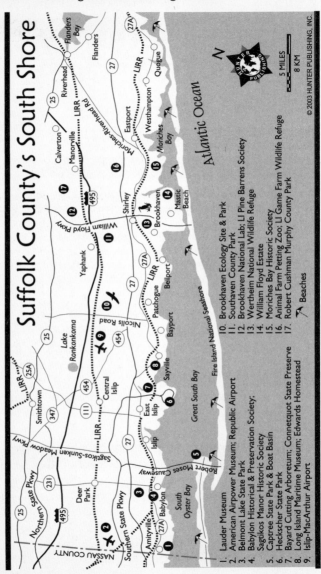

Suffolk County's South Shore

1. Lauder Museum
2. American Airpower Museum; Republic Airport
3. Belmont Lake State Park
4. Babylon Historical & Preservation Society;
   Sagtikos Manor Historic Society
5. Captree State Park & Boat Basin
6. Heckscher State Park
7. Bayard Cutting Arboretum; Connetquot State Preserve
8. Long Island Maritime Museum; Edwards Homestead
9. Islip-MacArthur Airport
10. Brookhaven Ecology Site & Park
11. Southaven County Park
12. Brookhaven National Lab; LI Pine Barrens Society
13. Wertheim National Wildlife Refuge
14. William Floyd Estate
15. Moriches Bay Historic Society
16. Animal Farm Petting Zoo; LI Game Farm Wildlife Refuge
17. Robert Cushman Murphy County Park

© 2003 HUNTER PUBLISHING, INC.

By Limousine

Pickups throughout Long Island for destinations near and far.

Vets Limousine, Patchogue, ☎ 631-447-7112 or 7114. www.vetslimo.baweb.com.

Pristine Limousine, Bellport, ☎ 631-776-7777, or 800-836-8360.

Sunup to Sundown

Museums & Historical Societies

AMERICAN AIRPOWER MUSEUM
Airport Plaza Shopping Center
Farmingdale
☎ 631-293-6398
www.americanairpowermuseum.com
Admission $9

The museum is housed in a former hangar of the Republic Aviation Company, which produced more than 9,000 P47 Thunderbolt fighters during World War II. Other war planes are also on display, along with vintage flying gear, maps and equipment. Check the Web site for scheduled events. Open Thursday-Sunday, 10:30am-4pm, year-round.

LONG ISLAND MARITIME MUSEUM
86 West Avenue
West Sayville
☎ 631-854-4974/631-HISTORY
www.limaritime.org
Donations appreciated

The 16-acre museum tells the maritime history of Sayville and its neighboring South Shore communities over the last 300 years. There are five historic buildings on the property; begin in the main building, formerly the carriage house of an estate.

Suffolk County's South Shore

Established in 1966, the museum houses some 10,000 objects, including 74 boats. On display are ship models, trophies, memorials, and artifacts found in Long Island waters – a pistol found in a sand dune, an ancient clay urn recovered 18 miles off Amagansett at a depth of 26 fathoms. The facility also has a library. A recent revolving exhibit displayed diving gear through the ages.

A time line beginning in 1657 illustrates the staggering number of shipwrecks and vessels in distress along the South Shore from Rockaway Point to Montauk Point. Also exhibited is a metal lifeboat from the 1800s. As clunky as it looks, it gave a drier ride than those used today!

The museum pays tribute to the Dutch immigrants who started the oyster industry in the late 1800s. The warm, brackish waters of the Great South Bay were a favorable environment for the growth of oysters, and most local roads were paved with oyster shells. Blue point oysters, named for a nearby town, became famous. The industry flourished until the Hurricane of 1938 changed the ecology of the bay.

Oysters were replaced by clams, which thrived in the saltier bay. "God took away the oyster but gave us the clam," baymen were known to say. The clam industry has also declined due to the changes in the water, over-harvesting and other factors. Tourism and recreation replaced harvesting. The railroad came to Sayville in 1868 and, in the succeeding five decades, 30 hotels were built in the area. Victorian homes lined the streets; among the grandest was Meadow Edge, owned by Commodore Bourne, president of the Singer Sewing Machine company. He gave his daughter, Florence, about 300 acres of his property as a wedding present. That land covered much of present-day West Sayville and Oakdale. The acreage now belongs to the Suffolk County Golf Course, adjacent to the Maritime Museum. After Florence and husband Anson Hard divorced, Mrs. Hard and her children moved into the Carriage House (now the museum) to cut costs. They left Meadow Edge in the 1950s and donated the estate to Suffolk County with the provision that it not be developed for private commercial use. The outer buildings include an oyster house and bayman's cottage. The museum is open Friday-Sunday, 11am-4:30pm, Memorial Day-October. The grounds are open on weekends during the months when the building is closed. The property includes outbuildings, the family cemetery, and three walking trails, which can be used for cross-country skiing.

SUFFOLK COUNTY'S SOUTH SHORE HISTORIC CHURCHES

- **St. John's Episcopal Church** and cemetery, Oakdale, built 1767.

- **St. Paul's Episcopal Church**, Patchogue, a Stick Style church built in 1883 with parish and rectory added two years later.

- **United Methodist Church**, Patchogue, a Romanesque Revival built in 1889.

WILLIAM FLOYD ESTATE

20 Washington Avenue
Mastic
☎ 631-399-2030
www.nps.gov

William Floyd was a signer of the Declaration of Independence. Eight generations of the Floyd family lived in this house from 1724 to 1975. After Floyd returned from military service during the Revolutionary War, he enlarged the house to accommodate visits from national leaders such as Thomas Jefferson and James Madison. Guided tours of the two-story mansion and self-guided tours of the gardens, outbuildings and cemetery on the 613-acre estate are free. Note the linden tree just west of the house and the beech tree at the west end of the garden; they are among the largest trees on Long Island, reportedly planted by Catherine Floyd (1804-1854). Open Friday-Sunday, from Memorial Day through October; admission is free. The first tour begins at 11am, the last tour at 4:30pm.

THE LAUDER MUSEUM
170 Broadway
Amityville
☎ 631-598-1486
www.amityville.com

The museum, focusing on Amityville and nearby communities, is sponsored by the Amityville Historical Society, which acquired it as a gift from the Franklin National Bank in 1971 through the efforts of William T. Lauder. A retired attorney, Amityville historian and former supervisor of the Town of Babylon, Lauder is director of the museum named for him. Open Sunday, Tuesday and Friday, 2-4pm. Tours may be arranged by appointment. There is no fee.

VILLAGE OF BABYLON HISTORICAL & PRESERVATION SOCIETY
117 West Main Street
Babylon
☎ 631-669-1756

The society maintains a collection of artifacts and pictures relating to Babylon history. Open year-round; April-December, Wednesday and Saturday, 2-4pm; and January-March, Saturday only, 2-4pm.

SAGTIKOS MANOR HISTORICAL SOCIETY
179 Anchorage Drive
West Islip
☎ 631-661-8348

A late New York State historian called Sagtikos Manor "one of the most distinguished historic houses in the United States." The landmark property was built in three architecturally distinct sections, the oldest portion between 1692-97 by Stephanus Van Cortlandt (whose family also built Van Cortlandt Manor on the Hudson River). Costumed docents from the society recreate three centuries of Sagtikos Manor history, Wednesday, Thursday and Sunday, 1-4pm, in July and August; and Sunday only, 1-4pm, in June.

Be certain to call Sagtikos Manor before you visit, as Suffolk County is in the process of buying the property; at this writing the manor is closed to visitors, and days and hours may change.

EDWARDS HOMESTEAD
Corner of Edwards Street and Collins Avenue
Sayville
☎ 631-563-0186

The Sayville Historical Society maintains the homestead, a restored 1785 home with period furnishings, as well as a barn/carriage house and exhibit building, both of which have changing exhibits relating to Sayville history. Open 2-4pm on the first and third Sundays of the month, from October through June, or by appointment.

MORICHES BAY HISTORICAL SOCIETY
Chet Swezey Road
Center Moriches
☎ 631-878-1776

The society is headquartered in the former Havens House on Montauk Highway and Chet Swezey Road. Now a museum, it contains records and pictures of a bygone era in the bay community. Open Saturdays, 10am-5pm, year-round.

Suffolk County's South Shore

HECKSCHER STATE PARK
East Islip
☎ 631-581-2100
www.park-net.com
Parking fee of $7 is charged daily, from April to Labor Day, and weekends only through October.

This 1,657-acre park boasts an Olympic-size outdoor pool with a 75x44-foot diving extension, and a kiddie pool. The pools are open Wednesday-Sunday and the fee is $3 plus $1 for a locker key. Other park amenities are a food concession, bike and bridle paths, campgrounds, bay beaches, cricket, baseball, soccer, and model airplane fields, boat basin, basketball courts, picnic and play areas and fishing in Great South Bay. Open year-round, 8am to sunset. To get here, take Southern State Parkway east to Heckscher State Parkway, and go south to the end. The park is closed Mondays.

★ TIP

Many lifeguards return to school at the end of August and the swimming area is shortened.

BAYARD CUTTING ARBORETUM
Route 27A
☎ 631-581-1002
Oakdale
www.bcarboretum.com
$5 parking fee charged April-Labor Day, and on weekends, Labor Day-October

Summer concerts are held at the Arboretum on Sundays at 11am.

In 1884, William Bayard Cutting purchased the estate of George Lorillard, the tobacco king, to build a country house. The Tudor-style mansion, completed in 1886, is one of the few 19th-century homes left intact on the South Shore. Cutting decorated Westbrook, as it was called, with old English wood paneling and magnificent hand-carved woodwork. Its 22 fireplaces were more decorative than functional since the house was largely occupied in the summer.

In 1952, Mrs. William Bayard Cutting and her daughter, Mrs. Olivia James, donated this "oasis of beauty" to the Long Island State Park and Recreation Commission in memory of Mr. Cutting. A photograph shows Mrs. Cutting handing over the keys to Robert Moses, then president of the Commission. Mrs. Cutting moved most of the furnishings to her new country home, but the stained-glass windows and dark wooden adornments are worth seeing. On the second floor is a mounted bird collection; some of the specimens date back to the late 1800s.

The Arboretum's walkways, public buildings and comfort stations are wheelchair-accessible.

WILLIAM BAYARD CUTTING
(1850-1912)

Cutting's great-grandfather came to America after attending Cambridge University. His eldest son, William, was born in Hempstead, and was among the earliest graduates of Columbia College and Law School, becoming a lawyer at 19. In 1800 he married Gertrude Livingston; Gertrude's sister married Robert Fulton, the steamship inventor, and the brothers-in-law helped establish a regular ferry service between Brooklyn and Manhattan.

William Bayard Cutting – lawyer, philanthropist and political reformer – was involved in land and waterfront development and made possible the growth of the South Brooklyn waterfront. He also helped improve living conditions among New York City's poor by providing model tenements with affordable rents. In 1896, he became a director of the newly organized New York Botanical Garden.

Suffolk County's South Shore

The renowned landscape architects of Frederick Law Olmsted designed the Arboretum; it is set on 697 idyllic acres across the Connetquot River from the Vanderbilt estate and Heckscher State Park. Labels identify the trees (all purchased from Long Island nurseries) and the pathways are wide. Mr. Cutting's informal conifer collection may be the most extensive on Long Island and several trees are the largest of their species in the region (the tall Eastern White Pine en route to the carriage house is probably one of them). The Arboretum is open Tuesday-Sunday, year-round, from 10am until sunset. To reach it, take the Southern State east to the Heckscher State Parkway south. Continue to Exit 45E and take Montauk Highway (Route 27A) to the Arboretum entrance.

Wildlife Refuges

TOWN OF BROOKHAVEN ECOLOGY SITE & PARK
249 Buckley Road
Holtsville
☎ 631-758-9664
Admission free

Bring your camera to the Brookhaven Ecology Site.

What a wonderful way to teach your kids about conservation, animal rehabilitation, and animals native to Long Island while they feed the goats and watch the antics of black bears, birds, bobcats and other wildlife and farm animals. Appealing to all ages, the site is free, save for the 25¢ handful of goat feed.

Opened in 1979, the Ecology Site was built over an 80-acre landfill that was closed in 1974. Buffy, an elderly buffalo, was six months old when she became one of its first residents. Today, the refuge is home to about 100 animals, half of them wild but physically injured or socially handicapped. A typical example of such a handicap is when a wild animal is raised as a pet and becomes unmanageable. Declawed and accustomed to people, it cannot be returned to the wild. Wild animals come through the ASPCA or veterinarians throughout the United States. A closed farm in Smithtown donated many of the farm animals.

Other features include a tropical greenhouse, honeybee hive, reptile and amphibian display, and exhibits on recycling (note the recycled plastic bench). Located in a park, the ecology site is adjacent to a 1.2-mile multi-use path shared by joggers, skaters and bicyclists, an 18-station parcourse, three swimming pools (see page 286), playground and picnic areas.

The 100-acre site is fully handicapped-accessible. Tours are offered to some 15,000 schoolchildren and campers annually, and to private groups of 10 or more. The site is 51.1 miles from the Throgs Neck Bridge. Take LIE to Exit 63S and follow North Ocean Avenue going south. At the fourth traffic light, turn right onto Woodside Avenue and then take another right onto Buckley Road. The park is open daily, year-round, 9am-4pm.

WERTHEIM NATIONAL WILDLIFE REFUGE
Montauk Highway
Shirley
☎ 631-286-0485

The 2,400-acre Wertheim Refuge, open to the public at no charge, protects the Carmans River (a state designated Wild and Scenic River) for such migrating wildlife as black ducks, mallards, wood ducks and gadwalls. Two loops of trails wind through the forest and along the river. The one-mile Indian Landing Trail is accessible only from the river – canoe and kayak rentals are available nearby. Fishing is allowed from boats only.

I followed the White Oak Nature Trail, an easy walk along a dirt path. It was the first of February, foggy and drizzly but unseasonably mild. The 1½- to three-mile loop is numbered at intervals to coincide with the trail guide I picked up – one of many wonderful brochures produced by the US Fish and Wildlife Service. The text tells you what to expect at each station – hardwoods, pitch pine, vernal pond or wildlife. Sure enough, before even reaching Station 2 – which leads to an observation blind to spot wildlife – several white-tailed deer appeared, one staring at me with great interest. No other grazers common to the area were visible – cottontail rabbits, meadow voles, wild turkey, turtles. Another walker pointed out all the foxholes, surmising that the nocturnal foxes were digging for voles. A regular on the trail, he marveled that it's little used considering that it's free.

From Montauk Highway, turn south onto Smith Road and travel .3 mile to the entrance on the right. The refuge office is open daily, year-round, from 8am-4:30pm.

Family Fun

Children are our most valuable natural resource.
                                        – Herbert Hoover

Route 110 in Farmingdale, between the LIE and the Southern State Parkway, is a commercial strip with several amusements for children. To get here, take the LIE to Exit 49S (32.5 miles from the Throgs Neck Bridge); from the Southern State, take Exit 32N; or from the Northern State Parkway, Exit 40S. All lead to Route 110.

ADVENTURELAND
2245 Route 110
☎ 631-694-6868
www.AdventurelandFamilyFun.com

Adventureland has been coming to Long Island every summer for 40 years. It has the usual rides and attractions – Ferris wheel, roller coaster, carousel, train ride, arcade – and much more. The newest ride, an adventure slide, is designed to cool you off, although the rule states "no swimsuits."

Children must be at least 54" tall for the kiddie rides. If you don't know your child's height, measuring posts are scattered around, probably because the "pay-one-price" admission policy is also based on size. A person under 48" tall pays $14.95, while those over 48" tall pay

$19.95. A single-ride ticket is 75¢. Open from the end of March through the last weekend in October.

JILLIAN'S
261 Airport Plaza Boulevard off Route 110
Farmingdale
☎ 631-249-0708
www.jillians.com

Jillian's is located in the same shopping center as Borders Books and the American Airpower Museum.

This is an entertainment megaplex with 34 locations throughout the United States and Canada. The Louisville, Kentucky-based operation opened in Boston in 1988 and in Farmingdale in March 2000. Some reviewers describe Jillian's as an adult recreation complex and this is certainly true at the bars and billiard tables. But in the arcade are far more kids than grownups.

Imagine a gambling casino with flashing neon lights and a deafening noise level. Instead of adults, children are sitting at card-playing machines holding authentic casino cups. Okay, so there's no payoff. How about the kid on his Harley Davidson or in his racing car on the Daytona Speedway? True, these are "virtual" rides, but is this wholesome entertainment?

The 20,000-square-foot arcade and bar also has virtual bowling, plus older forms of entertainment like Skee-Ball and table hockey – and an ATM machine. The quieter areas include six pool tables, shuffleboard, giant screen TVs, dance club, theater, party and banquet rooms, three bars, a restaurant and a café. As if this isn't enough, a sign outside says the complex is expanding.

Children under 18 unaccompanied by an adult are required to make a minimum games purchase of $5 to enter. Jillian's opens daily at 11am, year-round.

Suffolk County's South Shore

THE FAMILY GOLF CENTER
Henry Street
Commack
☎ 631-499-7007

This facility near the Commack Multiplex Cinema has 114 stalls, 45 of which are heated, a pro shop, game room and miniature golf facility.

BROOKHAVEN NATIONAL LABORATORY
William Floyd Parkway (CR 46)
Upton
☎ 631-344-2345
www.bnl.gov

During inclement weather, Brookhaven can draw more than 1,000 people. If you hate crowds, wait for a sunny day!

One of nine national laboratories funded by the US Department of Energy, Brookhaven is a multi-purpose research laboratory that has produced four Nobel-Prize-winning discoveries in physics. Established in 1947, the facility is located on a 5,300-site occupying 5% of the Island's pine barrens. It's among the region's largest employers with nearly 3,000 scientists, technicians, engineers and support staff.

The public is invited to visit during Summer Sunday Tours in July and August. Each Sunday has a different theme. For example, visitors to the medical department learn about its clinical research on addiction, osteoporosis, obesity and aging. A visitor to the National Weather Service witnesses a live launch of a weather balloon. A regular feature is the Whiz Bang Science Show. Admission is free and no reservations are needed – arrive anytime between 10am and 3pm.

The facility is handicapped-accessible and attracts all ages and backgrounds. As one staffer put it, "You don't have to be mad for science."

To reach the lab, take LIE Exit 68 and go north on William Floyd Parkway (Route 46) for 1½ miles to the second traffic light. The lab's gate is on the right.

WHAT'S IN A NAME?

Brookhaven Lab was built on the grounds of a former US Army camp called Camp Upton, then a forest in Yaphank. Its most famous graduate was Sgt. Irving Berlin, who wrote the musical *Yip, Yip Yaphank* during World War I.

☞ DID YOU KNOW?

Calverton National Cemetery is the largest of the country's 130 national cemeteries. Long Island's other national cemetery is in Farmingdale next to Pinelawn Cemetery. Cemeteries of Suffolk County maintains a Web site at www.interment.net/us/ny/suffolk.htm.

ANIMAL FARM PETTING ZOO
Wading River Road
Manorville
☎ 631-878-1785
www.AFPZ.org
Admission for adults, $12; children ages two to 16 and seniors, $7

The zoo has farm animals and their babies to pet and feed, along with puppet, animal and reptile shows, playground and picnic areas. Larger animals include camels, llamas, and kangaroos. Pony and turtle train rides are included in the admission; safari rides are extra. Take Exit 69 from the LIE, then south on Wading River Road. Open 10am-5pm daily and until 6pm weekends, April-October.

Suffolk County's South Shore

LONG ISLAND GAME FARM WILDLIFE PARK
Chapman Boulevard
Manorville
☎ 631-878-6644
www.ligfwildlife.com
Admission for adults, $12.95; children two-11, $10.95;
seniors, $7.95

Located in a 300-acre pine forest, this 22-acre game
farm is in its 33rd season. Its menagerie of 75 different
species of exotic and domestic animals includes three
petting areas and a variety of large animals such as a
giraffe, ostrich and camels. Amusement rides include a
carousel and spinning swings. Admission covers everything except pony rides ($3). Take the LIE to Exit 70,
then go south on Chapman Boulevard. The park opens
for the season in mid-April and is open weekends only,
10am-5pm, in spring and fall, and daily, 10am-6pm, in
summer (Memorial Day-Labor Day). The park closes
for the winter in mid-October.

Health & Beauty

Fitness Centers

All are open daily, year-round, unless otherwise specified.

Bally Total Fitness is a full-service fitness facility.
The chain of health clubs provides a reciprocal arrangement for members. Guests with or without member get free one-day pass. No fee for child care. There
are locations at 1147 Sunrise Highway, Copiague,
☎ 631-842-7000; and 1175 Sunrise Highway, Bay
Shore, ☎ 631-666-5533; www.ballyfitness.com.

Gold's Gym, 41 Mercedes Way, Heartland Business
Park, Deer Park, ☎ 631-586-GOLD (4653). Day fee,
$15. Free childcare.

Great South Bay YMCA, 200 West Main Street, Bay
Shore, ☎ 631-665-4255, www.ymcali.org. Guest must

be accompanied by member and show ID. Day fee, $12. Childcare, $2 per hour, per child.

Lucille Roberts is a full-service fitness center for women. Reciprocal privileges are offered to gold card members who pay an additional $3 to join. Two club locations offer childcare (fees and availability vary); 4601 Sunrise Highway, Bohemia, ☎ 631-567-6665, offers unlimited guest passes at gym's discretion; 349 William Floyd Parkway, Shirley, ☎ 631-399-9464, allows guests (with or without member) a free one-day pass; second visit, $10. For other Long Island locations, call or visit their Web site, www.lucilleroberts.com.

Eastern Athletic, Nicolls Road and Montauk Highway, Blue Point, ☎ 631-363-2882. Day fee, $15. Free childcare. Reciprocal arrangement among Eastern Athletic clubs on Long Island.

Weight Room Plus, Monarch Center, 225 North Montauk Highway, Center Moriches, ☎ 631-878-0005. Full fitness facility. Day fee with member, $7; without, $10. Childcare, $1.50 for 90 minutes.

Day Spas

Hands on Health Massage & Day Spa, 225 Howells Road, Bay Shore, ☎ 631-665-0082. Full-service spa. Appointments are recommended but walk-ins are welcome. Open daily.

Faces, Nails & More Day Spa, 56 Second Avenue, Brentwood, ☎ 631-435-0707, www.facesnailsandmoredayspa.com. Full-service spa and hair salon. Appointments recommended but walk-ins are welcome. Closed Sunday and Monday.

The Spa at Bellport, 117 South Country Road, Bellport, ☎ 631-286-5300. Full-service spa. Open Sunday by appointment; closed Monday. 10% discount off three services.

Suffolk County's South Shore

Recreation

Boating

Cruises & Charters

MOONCHASER
Captree State Park
West Islip
☎ 631-661-5061

The *Moonchaser*, a private charter boat with a fully equipped bar, leaves from Captree State Park for day and night cruises on the Great South Bay. A popular evening excursion is to Flynn's on Fire Island for dinner. Cruises operate from Memorial Day to Labor Day; for details see page 332.

The Captree Boatmen's Association, ☎ 631-669-6464, maintains a comprehensive Web site, www.captree-fleet.com, with all the information one could possibly want about the *Moonchaser* and the fishing boats at Captree State Park, "Home of the Family Fishing Fleet."

SOUTH BAY CRUISES
PO Box 98
Brightwaters
☎ 631-321-9005
www.laurenkristy.com

The *Lauren Kristy* is a 65-foot turn-of-the-century riverboat with two enclosed decks that can accommodate 150 guests. You can arrange for a fully catered private cruise, go on a four-hour luncheon excursion to the Fire Island Lighthouse or spend three hours on a dinner cruise on the quiet waters of the Great South Bay. The boat sails from the Bay Shore Marina at the end of South Clinton Avenue. Cruises are run from April through mid-November, and the cost ranges from $36.50 to $60 per person.

Walt Whitman Birthplace, Huntington Station.
(Photo by Robert Lipper)

Blue Pool, Coe Hall at Planting Fields Arboretum, Oyster Bay

Above: *Spring Scenes, Planting Fields Arboretum.*
Below: *Coe Hall.*
(Both photos by Vincent Simeone)

Above: *Fire Island Lighthouse.*
Below: *Old Hook Mill, East Hampton.*
(Both photos by Robert Lipper)

Above: *Stony Brook Grist Mill.*
(Photo courtesy of the Ward Melville Heritage Organization)

Below: *Farm Stand on Long Island.*
(Photo by Robert Lipper)

Above: *Red Barn Bed & Breakfast, Jamesport.*
(Photo courtesy of the Red Barn)

Below: *Lobby of Inn at Fox Hollow, Woodbury.*
(Photo courtesy of the Inn at Fox Hollow)

Above: *Old Westbury Gardens, central path in Walled Garden.*
(Photo provided by author)

Below: *Montauk Lighthouse.*
(Photo © Dick Lewis, courtesy of Montauk Lighthouse Museum)

Marinas & Boat Rentals

Amity Harbor Marine, 30 Merrick Road, Amityville, ☎ 631-842-1280. Dockage, storage, hauling electric, small marine store, showroom. Open year-round. Closed Monday.

Dinghy Shop, 334 South Bayview Avenue, Amityville, ☎ 631-264-0005, www.dinghyshop.com. Complete source for the sailor and kayaker. Motorboat, sailboat and kayak rentals, repairs, tours, lessons. The shop also runs lots of events and will e-mail you with updates if you so desire. Located at South Bay Sailing Center overlooking Great South Bay. Open Monday-Saturday in summer; Tuesday-Saturday in winter.

Island Wide Marine Service, 259 South Bayview Avenue, Amityville (near Security Dodge), ☎ 631-264-1912. Storage and hauling. Open daily, year-round.

Babylon Fishing Station, 23 Post Place at Town Dock, Babylon, ☎ 631-669-4503. Bait and tackle, fuel. Open daily, mid-March through mid-December.

Rainbow Marine, 185 Sumpwams Avenue, Babylon, ☎ 631-661-1218. Storage, dockage, hauling, electric, small ship store. Open daily, year-round.

Captree State Park, West Islip, ☎ 631-669-6464, www.captreefleet.com. Boat basin marina. Bait and tackle, snack bar, fishing pier, playground, restaurant (Captree Cove). Captree Boatman's Association has a 30-boat fleet and offers year-round fishing. Half and full day and night trips, individual "open boat" trips, and charters. Open daily, March-December.

West Marine, www.westmarine.com, has 240 stores throughout the United States. The West Islip location is at 147 Sunrise Highway, ☎ 631-669-8585, 800-BOA-TING (262-8464). Other Suffolk County branches are located in Port Jefferson; Riverhead; Huntington Station; 124 East Main Street, Babylon, ☎ 631-422-3300; and 405 West Sunrise Highway, Patchogue, ☎ 631-289-5533. Everything for the boater: fishing supplies, electronics, apparel, footwear, books, videos, charts. Open year-round.

Burnett's Marina, 16 Bayview Avenue, Bay Shore (opposite Bay Shore Marina), ☎ 631-665-9050. Winter storage, dockage, bait and tackle, electric, restrooms, showers. Open daily March-December.

Oakdale Yacht Marina, 520 Shore Drive, Oakdale (on the Connequot River), ☎ 631-589-1087. Heated swimming pool, fuel, bait and tackle, hauling, showers, restrooms, snack bar. Open daily. Closed mid-December through mid-January.

Greene's Creek Marina, 83 Atlantic Avenue, West Sayville, ☎ 631-589-5408. Marine store, storage, dockage, bait and tackle, electric, hauling, restrooms. Open March-November.

Beaver Dam Marina, 320 South Country Road, Bellport, ☎ 888-610-BOAT or 631-286-7816, www.boatrenting.com. Transient dockage, storage, bait and tackle, electric, restrooms, showers, marine store. Located on Bellport Bay, walking distance from Bellport Playhouse. Open daily, year-round.

> ★ TIP
>
> Beaver Dam Marina offers hourly, half-day, weekly and seasonal rentals of boats ranging from canoes to high-powered 28-foot cabin cruisers.

Island View Marina, 61 Price Street on Patchogue River, Patchogue, ☎ 631-447-1234. Storage, fuel, electric, hauling, snack bar, shower, restrooms. Open April-October. **Steve's Marine**, ☎ 631-475-6155, is located here as well. Sales. Open Monday-Saturday.

Leeward Cove Marinas, 327 River Avenue, Patchogue, ☎ 631-654-3106. Dockage, storage, electric, hauling, restrooms, showers. Open year-round; closed Sunday. There's also the Dublin Deck Restaurant (open May-September).

Patchogue Shores Marina, 28 Cornell Road, East Patchogue, ☎ 631-475-0790. Winter storage, dockage, fuel, restrooms. Open year-round.

Center Yacht Club, 222 Old Neck Road, Center Moriches, ☎ 631-874-2200. Dockage, storage, fuel, marine store, electric, restroom, showers. Open year-round.

Hart's Cove Marina, a/k/a Abbott's Hart's Cove Marina, 29 Maple Avenue, East Moriches, ☎ 631-878-3700. Family owned business offers fuel, electric, bait and tackle, dockage, storage, sales, restrooms, showers. Open March-November.

Silly Lily Fishing Station/Marina, 99 Adelaide Avenue, East Moriches, ☎ 631-878-0247, www.sillylily.com. Motor boat, sailboat and kayak rentals. Sailing lessons. Dockage, storage, bait and tackle, electric, repairs, fuel, restrooms, mechanic on duty. Open daily, March-November.

Windswept Marina, 215 Atlantic Avenue, East Moriches, ☎ 631-878-2100. Marine store, storage, dockage, fuel, bait and tackle, restrooms, snack bar, showers, hauling, electric, picnic. Open daily, year-round. There's a restaurant, Atlantic Seafood, open daily in season; call for winter hours, ☎ 631-878-0700.

White Water Marine Service, 300 Pine Neck Avenue, (on Swan River), East Moriches, ☎ 631-475-5000. Sales, storage, dockage, hauling, fuel. Open year-round; closed Sunday.

Biking

Al's Cycle Center, 256 Broadway, Amityville, ☎ 631-789-2270. Open daily, year-round.

Deer Park Bicycles, 1921A Deer Park Avenue, Deer Park, ☎ 631-586-5010. Open year-round. Days and hours fluctuate.

Bike Depot, West Main Street, East Islip (across from St. Mary's Church), ☎ 631-581-5557. Open daily, year-round. (They have another location in East Northport).

Suffolk County's South Shore

Byron Lake, 4551 North Sunrise Highway, Bohemia, ☎ 631-589-3912, www.byronlake.com. "The county's largest Schwinn dealer" carries all types of bikes. Open daily, year-round.

Long Island Bicycles, 318 Main Street, Patchogue (one-quarter mile east of Route 112), ☎ 631-758-2926. Open daily, year-round.

Shirley/Mastic Bicycles, 895 Montauk Highway, Shirley, ☎ 631-399-7390, www.cycleworldplus.com. This store is an extension of Cycle World Plus in Selden and shares the same Web site. Mountain bike specialist. Open daily, year-round.

Mastic Bicycles, 895 Montauk Highway, Mastic, ☎ 631-399-7390.

Inlet Surf & Bike Shop, 327 Main Street, Center Moriches, ☎ 631-878-6142. Inlet rents bikes in the summer. In winter, the store becomes a snowboard shop that sells skis and other snow equipment and runs tours. Open daily, year-round.

Hiking

LONG ISLAND GREENBELT TRAIL
23 Deer Path Road
Blydenburgh County Park
Smithtown
☎ 631-360-0753, or 631-854-4949 (Suffolk County Parks & Recreation)

This volunteer organization has some 3,000 members. The 34-mile trail through Nassau and Suffolk counties opened in 1978; in 1982 it was designated as a National Recreation Trail by the Department of the Interior. The Greenbelt Trail passes through four state parks and other county and town holdings, roughly following the courses of the Connetquot and Nissequogue rivers. It begins at Heckscher State Park, the southernmost exit on the Southern State Parkway, and ends at Sunken Meadow Park, the northernmost exit of the Sagtikos Parkway. Follow the white blazes. The trail is not contiguous and can be done in increments. Some suggested day hikes are Sunken Meadow to St. Johnland Road – 2½ miles – or, for more rugged types, Heckscher to Hidden Pond – 14 miles. The trail is free and open to the public. However, during the summer months, some parks along the route may require tolls or resident passes for parking. See page 189 in the *Suffolk County's North Shore* chapter for more about Blydenburgh County Park.

LONG ISLAND PINE BARRENS SOCIETY
PO Box 429
Manorville
☎ 631-369-3300
www.pinebarrens.org

New Jersey may have the largest concentration of Pine Barrens in the Northeast, but the 55,000 acres of pitch pine and scrub oak in Eastern Long Island cannot be ignored. Reaching from Brookhaven to Southampton, it nurtures thousands of plant and animal species.

Founded in 1977, the society is dedicated to preserving this natural treasure through sound land use. As the source of the greatest quantity of pure drinking water on Long Island, the Pine Barrens must be protected. Some 12,000 years ago the last glacier deposited the porous sandy soil that acts as a water filter. Although it was bad news to the region's first farmers who found the "barren" land unsuitable for agriculture, this diverse ecosystem supports "plants that don't exist in other places," according to Richard Amper, the society's executive director. It's also home to birds and butterflies and the endangered tiger salamander, buck moth, spotted turtle and northern harrier hawk.

The Pine Barrens serve as a catch basin for rainwater, which can then be drawn from underground reservoirs, known as aquifers. The purity of the water has become threatened by over-development and contaminants. In 1988, Suffolk County approved the Suffolk County Drinking Water protection program, which includes the acquisition of watershed lands to be financed by a

Suffolk County's South Shore

small sales tax levy. The Long Island Pine Barrens Protection Act was passed in 1993, creating the third largest forest preserve in New York State.

According to Amper, the people of Suffolk County put up over $300,000 to preserve open space in the area. On Earth Day Weekend in 2001, environmentalists from across the Island carried the message that development-at-any-price is the number one threat to their environment, economy and quality of life.

★ ACCESSIBILITY NOTE

A new nature trail in the Pine Barrens has opened for people with disabilities. Three-quarters of a mile long, it's located behind the Pine Barrens Trails Information Center in Manorville, ☎ 631-854-4949.

ROBERT CUSHMAN MURPHY COUNTY PARK
Off River Road at Swan Pond
Manorville
☎ 631-854-4949

This county park covers 2,200 acres, part of the Peconic River watershed, and is a good spot for bird-watching. Fishing (license needed) is available on Swan Pond, which has a boat ramp (free) for canoes and electric-powered boats. Parking is near the boat ramp off River Road.

Swimming

Town of Brookhaven pools are open daily, July 4th-Labor Day. Admission is $7 for non-residents. One facility, in **Holtsville,** has an Olympic-size pool, a diving pool and a kiddie pool (Holtsville Ecology Site, Buckley Road; ☎ 631-475-4507). Another pool is in **Centereach** on Hawkins Road (☎ 631-698-8663). For further information, contact the **Brookhaven Tourism Commission** at ☎ 631-451-9074, or the **Suffolk County**

Deptartment of Parks and Recreation at ☎ 631-451-6100.

YMCA East, 300 Mastic Beach Road, Mastic Beach, ☎ 631-281-1710, www.ymcali.org. Day fee, $6.25. Closed Sunday.

Beaches

Great South Bay Beaches

The following are Brookhaven Town beaches. Residents with parking stickers have free use of the town bay beaches. Non-residents pay a fee. The bay beaches are:

Corey . . . . Corey Avenue, Blue Point
Sandspit. . . . . Brightwood Street, Patchogue
Shirley . . . . Westminster and Grandview, Shirley

Ocean Beaches

The Town of Islip controls the western communities on Fire Island and the Town of Brookhaven the eastern ones. **Great Gun** (opposite Center Moriches) and **Davis Park** (opposite Patchogue) are ocean beaches on Fire Island under the jurisdiction of Brookhaven.

YMCA East, 300 Mastic Beach Road, Mastic Beach, ☎ 631-281-1710, www.ymcali.org. Day fee, $6.25. Closed Sunday.

Bellport Beach

The Village of Bellport is located halfway between New York City and Montauk Point, and is just 2.2 miles across the Great South Bay from Fire Island. The one-square-mile village of 3,000 residents has its own marina, a ferry named *Whalehouse Point*, and a parcel of Fire Island called Ho-Hum Beach, where there's a screened-in gazebo, concession stand and cold-water showers. Non-residents who rent houses in Bellport or stay in one of its guest accommodations may join the fun. To reserve the 45-passenger ferry for a "very affordable" private charter, ☎ 631-286-0327; to check the summer ferry schedule contact the dock master, ☎ 631-286-6093.

☞ DID YOU KNOW?

The seaside village of Bellport is known as the "Unhamptons Hampton."

Horseback Riding

All facilities listed are open daily, year-round.

Babylon Riding Center, 1500 Peconic Avenue, North Babylon, ☎ 631-587-7778, www.babylonridingcenter. com. 35 horses. Private and group lessons in English and western styles; sales, leasing, boarding; large indoor arenas; five miles of trails in Belmont Lake State Park. Half-hour private lesson, $35. Take Exit 37 from the Southern State Parkway; take Belmont Avenue for about a mile, then turn left on Peconic Avenue.

Knoll Farm Riding School, 849 Suffolk Avenue, Brentwood, ☎ 631-435-1880, www.knollfarm.com. 25 horses; indoor arena and four outdoor arenas; boarding; private and group lessons in dressage. Half-hour lesson, $45. Across from Brentwood Railroad station.

Parkview Riding School, 989 Connetquot Avenue, Central Islip (between Sunrise and Veterans Highways), ☎ 631-581-9477. Tack shop; indoor arena; boarding, sales, leasing; private and group lessons in English and western styles. Half-hour lesson, $30.

Whispering Pines Farm, 204 Buffalo Avenue, Medford, ☎ 631-475-2090. 20 horses. Private and group lessons in English style. Half-hour lessons available. Boarding. Open daily, year-round, weather permitting. Across from Medford high school.

Long Island Equestrian Center (a/k/a Southaven Stables, Inc.), Southhaven County Park, Yaphank,

☎ 631-345-2449. Indoor and outdoor arenas; trail rides; pony rides; boarding; leasing; private and group lessons in English and western styles; shows. Half-hour lesson $25. Sunrise Highway Exit 57N.

Riders may use the equestrian facilities at the following places. Permits are required, and are available at the Suffolk County Parks & Recreation administration office in West Sayville, Monday-Friday; ☎ 631-854-4949.

◆ **Southaven County Park**, Yaphank; park office, ☎ 631-854-1414; stable, ☎ 631-345-2449.

◆ **Smith Point County Park**, Shirley; park office, ☎ 631-852-1316.

◆ **Bohemia Equestrian Center**, Bohemia; Suffolk Couty Parks administration office, ☎ 631-854-4949.

Golf

Irritated by Muhammad Ali's perpetual boasts of "I am the greatest," a colleague asked the boxer what he was like at golf. "I'm the best," replied Ali. "I just haven't played yet."

Brentwood Country Club, 100 Pennsylvania Avenue, Brentwood, ☎ 631-436-6060. 18-hole, par 72. Easy course; fairly level with no obstacles. Walking allowed. Soft spikes required. Call early in week for weekend tee times. Pro shop, putting area, rentals, restaurant, bar, snack bar. Open March 15-December 15.

Gull Haven Golf Club, Gullhaven Drive, Central Islip, ☎ 631-436-6059. This regulation length nine-hole course, par 35, has a clubhouse, pro shop, putting green, and snack bar. Soft spikes, but not carts, are mandatory. No reservations for tee times – first come, first served. Good beginner course. Open year-round.

Mill Pond Golf Course, 300 Mill Road, Medford, ☎ 631-732-8206, has three nine-hole courses, par 70-71. Carts mandatory on weekends and in season. Soft spikes required. Call a week in advance for tee times.

Locker rooms, rentals, putting area, pro shop, restaurant, bar, snack bar, lessons. Open year-round.

Bellport County Club, 20 South Country Road, Bellport, ☎ 631-286-7206. 18-hole, par 71 links-style course is flat and open. Private club open to Bellport residents only; closed from the end of December through February. Their restaurant, the Irish Coffee Pub, ☎ 631-286-4227, is open to the general public; closed from January through Valentine's Day.

The Links, 353 William Floyd Parkway, Shirley, ☎ 631-395-7272, www.linksatshirley.com. The Links, which opened in June 2000, has two 18-hole courses; one is a par 3 short course (lit for night play), and the other a par 72 championship course. Walking is allowed weekdays and weekends after 1pm, and soft spikes are required. Pro shop, lessons, driving range, restaurant. Call for reservations up to a week in advance. Open year-round.

West Sayville Golf Course, West Sayville Country Club, Montauk Highway, West Sayville, ☎ 631-567-1704. Recent renovations to this 18-hole, par 72 course include alternate tee markers for golfers wishing to play a slightly shorter course and three large target greens on the practice range.

The **Suffolk County Department of Parks, Recreation and Conservation** operates the following three fairways. All have undergone recent renovations and offer affordable prices (see *Parks, Campsites & Golf Courses* under *Recreation* in the *Introduction* for entrance requirements). All have putting greens, pro shop, driving range and restaurant and offer instruction. All require soft spikes. Same day reservations and walk-ons are accepted. The courses are open year-round, daily in season, unless otherwise noted

◆   **Bergen Point Golf Course**, Bergen Point Country Club, Bergen Avenue, West Babylon, ☎ 631-661-8282, www.licvb.com/golf.cfm. This 18-hole, par 71 course had a facelift in 2000, which included a man-made pond by the ninth hole. The championship links-style layout tests the ability of all skill levels. Walking allowed. Call up to one week in advance for tee times. Closed January and February.

♦ **Timber Point Golf Course**, Timber Point Country Club, Great River Road, Great River, ☎ 631-581-2401, www.licvb.com/golf.cfm. At this writing, Suffolk County is in the midst of a multi-million-dollar renovation of this 27-hole course overlooking Great South Bay. The upgrade is expected to take two years, but during that time 18 of the 27 holes will always be available for play.

♦ **Holbrook Country Club**, 700 Patchogue Road, Holbrook, ☎ 631-467-3417. 18-hole, par 71. Walking allowed. Open March 15-December 15.

Shop Till You Drop

Malls

WESTFIELD SHOPPINGTOWN SOUTH SHORE
1701 Sunrise Highway
Bay Shore
☎ 631-665-8600

Macy's, JCPenney, Sears and Lord & Taylor are among 130 stores at Westfield Shoppingtown. Open Monday-Saturday, 10am-9:30pm; and Sunday, 11am-5pm.

PRIME OUTLETS AT BELLPORT
10 Farber Drive (Exit 56 Sunrise Highway)
Bellport
☎ 631-286-3872, or 877-GO-OUTLETS
www.primeoutlets.com

Prime Outlets has 70 designer and brand name outlet stores, including Bass, Dress Barn, Van Heusen, Reebok, The Gap and London Fog. Open daily.

Specialty Stores

OAKTREE BOOKSTORES
1495 Montauk Highway
Mastic
☎ 631-399-1012

Oaktree stores give 30% off all hardcover books on *The New York Times* Best Seller Lists and 20% off paperbacks. The chain has two other branches in Suffolk County, in Selden and Hampton Bays.

After Dark

Performing Arts

ARENA PLAYERS
296 Route 109
East Farmingdale
☎ 516-293-0674
www.arenaplayers.org

Arena Main Stage subscribers are entitled to a two-for-one discount on tickets to Children's Theatre productions.

This non-Equity theater has two stages – Main Stage and Second Stage – on which it presents musicals, comedies and drama year-round. Tickets for regular productions are $14-$20; tickets for Children's Theatre productions (on the Main Stage) are $8. The repertory company is now in its 52nd year.

BROADHOLLOW THEATRE COMPANY
265 East Main Street
East Islip
☎ 631-581-2700
www.broadhollow.org

This non-Equity theater performs musicals, dramas and comedies year-round at three Long Island locations. During the school year, it offers educational repertory to local schools; Saturday children's theater at its BayWay Arts Center in East Islip and Broadhollow Theater in Bethpage; and acting classes. The company also runs a summer acting camp. Tickets are $16-$20, and $8 for children's theater (Broadhollow's other locations are in Bethpage and Rockville Centre).

CREATIVE MINISTRIES PERFORMING ARTS CENTER
931 Montauk Highway
Oakdale
☎ 631-218-2810 (box office)
☎ 631-218-2812 (administration)

Creative Ministries is a Christian-based theatrical organization. Volunteers, some of whom are professional actors, perform Broadway musicals, comedies and drama as well as children's theater year-round. Musicals range from *Fiddler on the Roof* to *The Wizard of Oz*. The group performs monthly on its main stage and also tours throughout Long Island, Brooklyn and Queens. Tickets range from $12-$17; children's theater tickets are $8. The center also runs children's workshops in dance, acting and voice and a summer theater program for students in grades preK-12. Have a talented child or want to act yourself? Inquire about the next casting call.

BALLET LONG ISLAND
390 Central Avenue
Bohemia
☎ 631-567-4403

Established in 1985, this female-run company presents classical works, original and modern pieces year-round, all choreographed by Artistic Director Debra Punzi. The company of 15 to 22 men and women average 130 performances per year at colleges, theaters and festivals. Three times a year the company performs at its resident theater, Islip Town Hall West, 401 Main Street, Islip. Ticket prices range from $10-$16.

Ballet Long Island made its New York City debut in 1995 at the Merce Cunningham studio. *Dance Magazine* has written that the company's ballet steps and

pointe work are "delivered with an attractive joie de vi-
vre "

AIRPORT PLAYHOUSE
218 Knickerbocker Avenue
Bohemia
☎ 631-589-7588
www.airportplayhouse.com

This non-Equity, semi-professional group has been performing for 23 years. There are 10 shows a year – musicals, comedies, and mysteries – plus a year-round
children's theater. Tickets are $16-$18; $7 for chil-
dren's theater productions.

PATCHOGUE THEATRE FOR
THE PERFORMING ARTS
71 East Main Street
☎ 631-207-1300
www.patchoguetheatre.com

The 1,225-seat Patchogue Theatre is on busy Main
Street, across from the library. In 1998 the theater
launched its first live show in 70 years. Since then, it
has hosted philharmonic concerts, dance competitions,
musicians Art Garfunkel and Chuck Mangione, and comedian Sandra Bernhard. Now managed by the village, the theater operates year-round.

☞ DID YOU KNOW?

The Patchogue Theatre was originally a vaudeville house; it then
served as a movie theater. Until recently it was managed by Gateway
Performing Arts, the company that
operates the Gateway Playhouse;
they renovated the theater to resemble the original 1925 design.

GATEWAY PLAYHOUSE
215 South Country Road
Bellport
☎ 631-286-1133 (box office); 631-286-0555 (business office); 888-4TIXNOW (recording)
www.gatewayplayhouse.com

The Gateway Playhouse, a regional Equity theater, has been family owned for 51 years and is Long Island's only professional musical theater. Heralded as one of the nation's leading summer stock theaters, it was built around a barn, which is now used by its acting school. Gateway performs six major musicals every summer; tickets range from $28 to $33.

In contrast to the Patchogue Theatre, the Gateway is a smaller venue in a more bucolic setting. In 1950, it was converted into a theater-in-the-round. The owner operated the theater with a charter from the UN and it was named by Eleanor Roosevelt, who called the Gateway "the official national theater of the United Nations." Gene Hackman, Ken Howard and Robert Duvall performed there during the fifties.

BROOKHAVEN YOUTH ORCHESTRA
Bellport Outlet II
Bellport
☎ 631-776-2084

Since 1995, BYO has been providing accessible and affordable arts education to children and families in Suffolk County. Under the leadership of the founder, Phil Gelfer, students of all levels have an opportunity to learn and perform in bands and orchestras. BYO has performed at Staller Center Recital Hall and other Long Island venues. In January 2001 the BYO Philharmonic appeared in a sold-out performance at Carnegie Hall at the invitation of Skitch Henderson & The New York Pops. In addition to nine performing groups, there are classes in acting, art and writing.

★ FAMOUS FACES

Isabella Rossellini, a Bellport resident for the last 15 years, is an honorary board member of the Bellport Film Society, which recently established an alternative cinema at the community center.

Bars & Clubs

DA FUNKY PHISH
1668 Union Boulevard
Bay Shore
☎ 631-665-9851
www.dafunkyphish.com

Live music Tuesday-Saturday. Crowd ranges from 21 up, depending on band. Cover charge.

GOVERNOR'S COMEDY CABARET & RESTAURANT
2320 Route 112
Medford
☎ 631-207-9212

Open Friday-Sunday. Cover and two-drink minimum. Dinner packages available. Another location is at 90 Division Avenue, Levittown.

PETER'S RESTAURANT AND PIANO LOUNGE
132 West Main Street
Babylon
☎ 631-422-9233

Open daily for lunch and dinner. Piano and vocalist Wednesday-Saturday.

BRICKHOUSE BREWERY
67 West Main Street
Patchogue
☎ 631-447-2337

Open daily for lunch and dinner. Entertainment Tuesday (guitar), Wednesday (open mike) and live bands (on weekends). Cover $5, Thursday-Saturday. Crowd ranges from late 20s through 40s.

Festivals & Events

March

The Town of Brookhaven Highway Department holds its **Landscape and Garden Show** at the Ecology Site & Park, 249 Buckley Road, Holtsville, ☎ 631-758-9664. Many different styles of backyard landscapes are on display with ponds, waterfalls, trees, shrubs, gazebos and hot tubs. Garden accessories are for sale and free workshops available. The fund-raiser benefits the animals at the Ecology Site. Call for hours.

June

Patchogue's annual **Harbor Festival and Blessing of the Fleet** is held at Shorefront Park in Patchogue, ☎ 631-475-0121, www.pagelinx.com/patchoguecoc. The Sunday event includes a children's treasure hunt (pre-registration recommended), performances, folk music, a pirate crew, local vendors, and blessing of the fleet.

Throughout the summer, an ongoing concert series is presented at **Brookhaven Amphitheater and Cultural Park**, Bicycle Path off North Ocean Avenue, Farmingville, ☎ 631-732-4011. Selections include classical, big bands, Latin, oldies. Call for directions or event schedule.

Suffolk County's South Shore

August

The weekend **Seafood Festival** at the Long Island Maritime Museum in West Sayville, ☎ 631-HISTORY (447-8679), www.limaritime.org, features demonstrations, treasure hunts, entertainment, food, exhibits and vendors.

Best Places to Stay

Motels

MOTEL PRICE SCALE
Price scale is based on the cost of a double room, two people per room, in season, and does not include the 9.25% hotel tax.
Inexpensive . . . . under $100
Moderate . . . . $100-$150
Expensive . . . . over $150

BROADWAY MOTOR INN
727 Broadhollow Road
Farmingdale
☎ 888-966-1122, or 631-249-2810
www.broadwaymotorinn.com
59 units. Inexpensive.

Handicapped-accessible.

SAYONARA MOTEL
831 Broadway
Amityville
☎ 631-789-0400
34 units. Inexpensive.

RAINBOW MOTEL
10 34 Street
Copiague
☎ 631-842-4700
40 units. Inexpensive.

MARINA MOTEL
134 East Montauk Highway
Lindenhurst
☎ 631-957-6300
40 units. Inexpensive.

PINES MOTOR LODGE
636 Route 109
North Lindenhurst
☎ 631-957-3330, 877-PINESMO (746-3766)
www.pinesmotorlodge.com
21 units. Inexpensive.

Pines Motor Lodge also has a property at Old Country
Road and Merrick Avenue in Westbury.

SUNRISE INN
570 Sunrise Highway
West Babylon
☎ 631-669-6106
21 units. Inexpensive.

DEER PARK MOTOR INN
354 Commack Road (near Bayshore Road and Grand
Union Boulevard)
Deer Park
☎ 631-667-8300
50 units. Inexpensive.

Suffolk County's South Shore

BAY SHORE INN
300 Bay Shore Road
Bay Shore
☎ 631-666-7275
71 units. Inexpensive.

Handicapped-accessible rooms.

SUMMIT MOTOR INN
501 East Main Street
Bay Shore
☎ 631-666-6000
42 units. Inexpensive.

HAMPTON INN
1600 Veteran's Memorial Parkway
Islandia
☎ 631-234-0400, or 800-HAMPTON (426-7866)
www.hamptoninn.com
121 units. Moderate.

Handicapped-accessible rooms.

TRIANGLE INN MOTEL
1630 Lakeland Avenue
Bohemia
☎ 631-981-6200
54 rooms. Inexpensive.

LANDS END MOTEL & MARINA
70 Browns River Road
Sayville
☎ 631-589-2040
16 units. Inexpensive to Moderate.

SAYVILLE MOTEL
5494 Sunrise Highway (between Lincoln Avenue and Broadway)
Sayville
☎ 631-589-7000
31 units. Inexpensive.

MACARTHUR RED CARPET INN
4444 Veterans Memorial Highway
Holbrook
☎ 631-588-7700
50 units. Inexpensive.

★ TIP

Call **Hospitality International**,
☎ 800-251-1962, for reservations at
MacArthur Red Carpet Inn or any
of their other properties.

MIDWAY MOTEL
544 Medford Avenue
Patchogue
☎ 631-289-5800
29 units. Inexpensive.

SHORE MOTOR INN
576 West Sunrise Highway
Patchogue
☎ 631-363-2500
26 units. Rates on request.

COMFORT INN
2695 Route 112
Medford
☎ 631-654-3000
76 units. Moderate to Expensive.

SHIRLEY MOTEL
681 Montauk Highway
Shirley
☎ 631-281-9418
26 units. Inexpensive.

Suffolk County's South Shore

SMITH POINT MOTEL
165 William Floyd Parkway
Shirley
☎ 631-281-8887
21 units. Inexpensive.

Best Places to Eat

DINING PRICE SCALE	
Price scale includes one entrée, with glass of wine and coffee. There is an 8.5% tax on food in both Nassau and Suffolk Counties.	
Inexpensive . . . . under $25	
Moderate . . . . $25-$40	
Expensive . . . . over $40	

Sayville

THE SAYVILLE INN
199 Middle Road
Sayville
☎ 631-567-0033
www.sayville.com/sayinn.html
www.greatrestaurantsmag.com
Moderate

The Sayville Inn accepts only American Express.

A cozy country inn and bar, The Sayville Inn has wood-paneled walls, festive decorations and lovely live music (piano, Sunday-Thursday, and guitar, Friday and Saturday, all 6-10pm). The dining room has a romantic, almost Adirondack, feel to it. Co-owner Pamela Raymond was once in show business and her flair for design is evident all about. She likes to change the décor frequently, however, so regulars are constantly surprised.

The Sayville Inn was established in 1888 and "the third century of continuous service" is reflected in its superb service and cuisine. Chef William Bergin recommends his specials, and you won't go wrong in following his advice. Entrées come with salad and are reasonably priced, but you can also have an $8 burger.

The party room was the tavern and retains the original tin ceiling, wooden icebox and bar where Theodore Roosevelt enjoyed his Scotch and milk.

The restaurant is handicapped-accessible and easy to reach from Main Street. Take Foster Avenue (at the light by the Amoco station) for one block and turn left. Restaurant is on the left. Open daily for dinner, year-round.

FRIENDLIEST TOWN

Sayville is the gateway to the Fire Island communities of Cherry Grove, Fire Island Pines, and Sailors Haven/Sunken Forest. For the most part, summer tourists grab a cab from the railroad right to the ferry and overlook the village. Yet, it doesn't seem to have suffered. The village is pretty and unpretentious, busy and friendly. The old and new – such as a Starbucks adjacent to an antiques shop – blend beautifully. Several years ago, Sayville was voted the friendliest town on Long Island in a *Newsday* survey, which comes as no surprise.

Patchogue

BRICKHOUSE BREWERY & RESTAURANT
67 West Main Street
Patchogue
☎ 631-447-BEER (2337)
www.brickhousebrewery.com
Inexpensive

Once a general store owned by an abolitionist, the BrickHouse site was a stop on the underground rail-

See **After Dark** *for the entertainment schedule at BrickHouse.*

Suffolk County's South Shore

road. The brewery and restaurant opened in 1996 as part of the Main Street revitalization. If you look in the window here, all you'll see are colossal vats. Above the machinery hangs a tongue-in-cheek sign reading "Save the Ales."

The restaurant is upstairs; the bar downstairs. The menu is extensive and is good value for your money. Stop at the bar and ask to sample the six featured ales. Their BrickHouse Boys Red, brewed with seven different American malted barleys, was voted "L.I. #1" by *Newsday*; judge for yourself. Open daily, for lunch, dinner and late night hours, year-round. Reservations are not necessary, but during the week BrickHouse is booked with private parties and on weekends one room is usually unavailable. One room holds up to 40 people and the other up to 85.

Mastic

VIOLET COVE
2 Violet Road
Mastic Beach
☎ 631-395-8866
Inexpensive to Moderate

Boats are available for rental at Violet Cove marina.

This brand new restaurant is in a 57-slip marina on Moriches Bay facing Smith Point Park, on the eastern end of Fire Island. The 1938 building was completely renovated and now has two lovely dining rooms for smokers and non-smokers. The menu is the same for both meals except for daily specials. Bring your appetite – the food is fresh and tasty.

According to proprietor Joseph Marcario, this is the only restaurant on the bay between Babylon and Shinnecock. He plans to add a tiki bar, playground and a parking lot in the back to replace the existing one that interferes with the captivating view. Marcario has also scheduled music for Sundays and outside dancing in the summer.

Violet Cove is at the end of Violet Road. Take the William Floyd Parkway to Neighborhood Road; turn right at the Sunoco station onto Cranberry Drive, and turn right again onto Violet Road one block before the bay. Open daily for lunch and dinner, year-round.

IF IT LOOKS LIKE A DUCK

Ducks have been part of life on Long Island for more than 130 years. According to legend, in 1870 a Long Island sailor traveled to China and returned with nine of the snowy white, orange-beaked Pekin ducks. Soon, duck farms sprang up all over Suffolk County, especially around Moriches Bay. At one time there were 130 duck farms on Long Island, producing from 60% to 80% of the nation's ducks. Today, there are only four duck farms left; they provide about 15% of the US supply.

East Moriches

WHITE TRUFFLE INN
578 Montauk Highway East
East Moriches
☎ 631-874-0757
Reservations essential
Moderate to Expensive

This historic restaurant with turquoise shutters successfully combines an Old World ambience with a thoroughly modern menu. Built in the 1850s by a doctor who owned the entire block, the building was his office. The current dining room served as his surgery wing and the third floor housed his staff. Today, the dining room is decorated with tapestries, gilded light fixtures and mirrors, and windows framed by swag chiffon curtains with bishop sleeves. Rooms upstairs are reserved for parties.

Suffolk County's South Shore

White Truffle Inn is a lovely place for lunch, when you can enjoy the garden view and a bountiful salad or crab cake sandwich. Daily specials supplement the limited but excellence cuisine prepared by the owners: Wally, master chef from Argentina, and his Uruguayan wife, Naomi, a pastry chef. (The couple met in New Jersey!) Open Wednesday-Sunday, for lunch and dinner.

Lite Bites

BEST BAGELS IN TOWN
153 Main Street
Mastic Beach
☎ 631-589-5796

Best Bagels has tables and is open daily, year-round.

PAGES
468 Neighborhood Road
Mastic Beach
☎ 631-399-0066

This is an adorable café, bookstore, antiques and gift shop in an old building that has been charmingly modernized. Opened in December 2001, the café serves coffee and desserts, soup in the winter and sandwiches in the summer. There is comfortable seating indoors and out, and they provide games and Internet access. The café holds special events, such as a chess night every Tuesday, and hosts live music performances. From William Floyd Parkway, follow the Mastic Beach Business District sign onto Neighborhood Road. Open daily from 8am to 11pm; open until midnight on Friday and Saturday.

South Shore A to Z

Animal Adoption & Rescue

Town of Babylon Animal Shelter, 51 Lamar Street, West Babylon, ☎ 631-643-9270, www.babylonli.com/btanimal.html. Strays are held one week before being put up for adoption. Open Monday-Saturday.

Brookhaven Animal Shelter, 300 Horseblock Road, Brookhaven, ☎ 631-286-4940, picks up strays. Those not claimed within a week are available for adoption. Open Monday-Saturday.

Suffolk County SPCA, ☎ 631-382-SPCA. Takes calls from the public about abused animals, 24 hours a day.

Animal Hospitals

Basic Pet Care Animal Hospital, 1676 Route 110 (south of SUNY Farmingdale and north of Conklin Street), Farmingdale, ☎ 631-694-0330, www.vet-mall.com. Small animals. Boarding. Closed Sunday.

Farmingdale Animal Hospital, 35 Hempstead Turnpike, Farmingdale, ☎ 631-249-0144. Primarily dogs and cats. Boarding. Open daily by appointment only.

Babylon Animal Hospital, 350 East Montauk Highway, Lindenhurst, ☎ 631-226-2288. Dogs, cats, birds, ferrets, reptiles and larger animals. Closed Sunday.

Southgate Animal Hospital, 1015 Montauk Highway, Copiague, ☎ 631-789-1234. Dogs and cats. Boarding. Closed Sunday.

Deer Hills Animal Hospital, 708 Long Island Avenue, Deer Park, ☎ 631-667-9796, provides grooming, but no veterinary services.

Sunrise Animal Hospital, 521 Sunrise Highway, West Islip, ☎ 631-661-5380. Small animals, but no birds or reptiles. Boarding. Next to Pontiac dealership.

Suffolk County's South Shore

(Not affiliated with hospital of same name in Rockville Centre.) Closed Sunday.

East Islip Animal Hospital, 84 East Main Street, East Islip, ☎ 631-277-2266. Small animals. Boarding. A quarter-mile east of Carlton Avenue on the south side of the street. Closed Sunday.

Oakdale Veterinary Hospital, 1191 Montauk Highway, Oakdale, ☎ 631-567-3050. All animals. Boarding. Closed Sunday. Next to West Sayville fire house and a quarter-mile east of Oakdale/Bohemia Road.

Sachem and Park Hills Animal Hospitals treat dogs, cats, birds and exotic pets, including reptiles, ferrets and rabbits. These hospitals also provide veterinary care for the Holtsville Ecology Park Zoo.

Sachem Animal Hospital, 227 Union Avenue, Holbrook, ☎ 631-467-2121, http://members.aol.com/SachemAH. Open Sunday.

Park Hills Animal Hospital, 2064 Deer Park Avenue, Deer Park, ☎ 631-667-2220, http://members.aol.com/ParkHAH. Closed Sunday.

Blue Point-Bayport Animal Hospital, 765 Montauk Highway, Bayport, ☎ 631-472-1101. Dogs and cats. No boarding. Across from a Carvel. Closed Sunday.

Bellport Animal Hospital, 1631 Montauk Highway, Bellport, ☎ 631-286-9660. Small animals, including exotics, by appointment only. Boarding. Home visits available. Near Bellport Outlet Center. Open Sundays for emergencies 10am-noon.

Floyd Harbor Animal Hospital, 158 Margin Drive West, Shirley, ☎ 631-281-1888. Small animals. Boarding. Service road off William Floyd Parkway south. Closed Sunday.

Moriches Hospital For Animals, 214 Main Street, (across from St. John's Church), Center Moriches, ☎ 631-878-1600. Primarily dogs and cats. Boarding. Closed Sunday.

Center Moriches Veterinary Hospital, 654 Main Street, Center Moriches, ☎ 631-878-0050. Dogs and cats only, by appointment. Boarding. Closed Sunday.

Banks

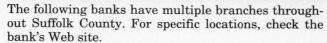

The following banks have multiple branches through-out Suffolk County. For specific locations, check the bank's Web site.

Astoria Federal Savings Bank . . . . www.astoriafederal.com

Bank of New York . . . . . . www.bankofnewyork.com

Chase Manhattan Bank . . . . www.chase.com

Citibank . . . . www.citibank.com

Dime Savings Bank of NY . . . . www.dime.com

First National Bank of LI . . . . www.fnbli.com

HSBC . . . . www.us.hsbc.com

North Fork Bank . . . . www.northforkbank.com

Roslyn Savings Bank . . . . www.roslyn.com

State Bank of LI . . . . www.statebankofli.com

Suffolk County National Bank . . . . . www.scnb.com

Houses of Worship

Baptist

First Baptist Church, 39 East John Street, Lindenhurst, ☎ 631-226-2177; 85 Parkway Boulevard, Wyandanch, ☎ 631-643-8777; 295 Half Mile Road, Central Islip, ☎ 631-234-5986; 324 Lakeland Avenue, Sayville, ☎ 631-589-7842, www.fbc.sayville.com; 482 North Ocean Avenue, Patchogue, ☎ 631-289-0230.

Heritage Baptist Church, 1380 5th Avenue, Bay Shore, ☎ 631-968-5358.

Catholic

St. Patrick's Church, 9 West Clinton Avenue, Bayshore, ☎ 631-665-4911.

Our Lady of Mount Carmel, 495 New North Ocean Avenue, Patchogue, ☎ 631-475-4739.

Suffolk County's South Shore

St. Jude's Roman Catholic Church, 89 Overlook Drive, Mastic Beach, ☎ 631-281-5743.

Episcopal

St. Peter's Episcopal Church, 500 South Country Road, Bay Shore, ☎ 631-665-0051.

St. John's Episcopal Church, 1 Berard Boulevard, Oakdale, ☎ 631-244-3971.

St. Ann's Episcopal Church, 257 Middle Road, Sayville, ☎ 631-589-6522, www.saint-anns.org.

St. Paul's Episcopal Church, 31 Rider Avenue, Patchogue, ☎ 631-475-3078.

St. Mark's Episcopal Church, 754 Montauk Highway, Islip, ☎ 631-581-4950.

Emmanuel Episcopal Church, 320 Great River Road, Great River, ☎ 631-581-3964.

Jewish – Orthodox

Young Israel of Patchogue, 28 Mowbray Street, Patchogue, ☎ 631-654-0882, www.ou.org/network/shuls/yipatch.html.

Jewish – Conservative

Congregation Beth Sholom, PO Box 64, Babylon, ☎ 631-587-5650.

Temple Beth-el of Patchogue, 45 Oak Street, Patchogue, ☎ 631-475-1882.

Jewish Center of the Moriches, 227 Main Street, Center Moriches, ☎ 631-878-0388.

Jewish – Reform

Sinai Reform Temple, 39 Brentwood Road, Bay Shore, ☎ 631-665-5755.

B'nai Israel Reform Temple, 67 Oakdale Bohemia Road, Oakdale, ☎ 631-563-1660.

B'nai Shalom, Neighborhood Road, corner Hemlock Drive, Mastic Beach, ☎ 631-281-8282.

Lutheran

St. John's Evangelical Lutheran Church, 36 East John Street, Lindenhurst, ☎ 631-226-1274.

Cross of Christ Lutheran Church, 576 Deer Park Avenue, Babylon, ☎ 631-661-7245.

St. John's Lutheran Church, 48 Greene Avenue, Sayville, ☎ 631-589-3202. www.stjohnsayville.org.

Lutheran Church of our Savior, 231 Jayne Avenue, Patchogue, ☎ 631-475-5725.

Methodist

United Methodist Church of Bay Shore, East Main Street at Second Avenue, Bayshore, ☎ 631-666-7194, www.gbgm-umc.org/bayshore.

United Methodist Church of Sayville, 164 Greene Avenue, Sayville, ☎ 631-589-7673.

United Methodist Church, 10 Church Street, Patchogue, ☎ 631-475-0381, www.ghgm-umc.org/patchogue.

East Moriches Methodist Church, 370 Montauk Highway, East Moriches, ☎ 631-878-0887.

Presbyterian

Presbyterian Church, 263 Main Street, Center Moriches, ☎ 631-878-1993.

Information Sources

Chambers of Commerce

Town of Brookhaven Chamber of Commerce, ☎ 631-451-6668, www.brookhaven.org.

Amityville Chamber of Commerce, ☎ 631-598-0695, www.amityville.com/chamber.htm.

Copiague Chamber of Commerce, ☎ 631-226-2956.

Lindenhurst Chamber of Commerce, ☎ 631-226-5453.

Babylon Village Chamber of Commerce, ☎ 631-661-2229, www.babylonvillage.com.

West Islip Chamber of Commerce, ☎ 631-661-3838, www.westislip.com.

Bayshore-Brightwaters Chamber of Commerce, ☎ 631-665-7003.

Brentwood Chamber of Commerce, ☎ 631-273-4443.

Islip Chamber of Commerce, ☎ 631-581-2720, www.islipchamberofcommerce.org.

East Islip Chamber of Commerce, ☎ 631-859-5000.

Central Islip/Islandia Chamber of Commerce, ☎ 631-581-0510.

Oakdale Chamber of Commerce, ☎ 631-567-5941, mylongisland.com/biz2biz.htm.

Greater Sayville Chamber of Commerce, ☎ 631-567-5257, www.sayville.com/chamber.html.

Holbrook Chamber of Commerce, ☎ 631-471-2725.

Bayport/Blue Point Chamber of Commerce, ☎ 631-472-5555, www.bayportbluepoint.com.

Greater Patchogue Chamber of Commerce, ☎ 631-475-0121, www.patchoguechamber.com.

Medford Chamber of Commerce, ☎ 631-576-0166, www.mylongisland.com/biz2biz.htm.

Bellport Chamber of Commerce, ☎ 631-758-6766.

Chamber of Commerce of Mastic & Shirley, ☎ 631-399-2228, www.communitylibrary.org/chambercommerce.html.

Center Moriches Chamber of Commerce, ☎ 631-878-0003.

Community Web Sites

Amityville . . . . www.amityville.com
Babylon . . . . www.babylonvillage.com
Bayport/Blue Point . . . . . . www.bayportbluepoint.com
Bellport Country Club . . . . . . www.bellportvillage.com
Blue Point . . . . www.bluepoint.org
Islip . . . . www.islip.org
Lindenhurst . . . . www.lindenhurst.com
Patchogue . . . . www.patchoguechamber.com
Sayville . . . . www.sayville.com
Town of Islip . . . . www.isliptown.org
West Islip . . . . www.westislip.com

Liquor Stores

Ferraro's Wine and Liquor Store, 66 West Main Street, Babylon Village, ☎ 631-669-0039, www.babylonvillage.com/ferraros.htm.

Bright Shores Wines & Liquors, 273 West Main Street, Bay Shore, ☎ 631-665-4985. Bright Shores and Sun Shore Wines & Liquors (below) make deliveries to Fire Island ferries.

Sun Shore Wines & Liquors, 1241 Sunrise Highway, (in Bally's Shopping Center), Bay Shore, ☎ 631-665-1466.

Bellport Liquors, 129 Main Street, Bellport, ☎ 631-286-0316.

Medical Facilities

Brunswick Hospital Center, 366 Broadway, Amityville, ☎ 631-789-7000.

South Oaks Hospital, 400 Sunrise Highway, Amityville, ☎ 631-264-4000.

Good Samaritan Hospital Medical Center, 1000 Montauk Highway, West Islip, ☎ 631-376-3000.

Southside Hospital, 301 East Main Street, Bay Shore, ☎ 631-968-3000 (Southside is part of the North Shore-LI Jewish Health System).

Brookhaven Memorial Hospital Medical Center, 101 Hospital Road, Patchogue, ☎ 631-654-7100, www.BrookhavenHospital.org or www.bmhmc.org.

Movies

Farmingdale Multiplex (14), 1001 Broad Hollow Road, Farmingdale, ☎ 631-777-8080 (recording), 631-777-1122 (office).

UA Farmingdale Stadium (12), 20 Michael Avenue, Farmingdale, ☎ 631-755-0940 (recording), ☎ 631-755-0944 (office).

Lindenhurst Theater (1), 20 Montauk Highway, Lindenhurst, ☎ 631-957-5400 (recording), ☎ 631-957-5401 (office).

South Bay Cinema (4), Montauk Highway in Pathmark shopping center, West Babylon, ☎ 631-587-7676 (recording), ☎ 631-587-7808 (office).

Babylon Triplex Theatre, 34 West Main Street, Babylon, ☎ 631-669-0200 (recording), ☎ 631-669-3399 (office).

Islip Triplex, 410 West Main Street, Islip, ☎ 631-581-5200 (recording), ☎ 631-581-5203 (office).

Sayville Theaters (4), 103 Railroad Avenue, Sayville, ☎ 631-589-0232 (recording), ☎ 631-589-0040 (office).

UA Movies of Patchogue (13), Sunrise Highway, Patchogue, ☎ 631-363-2100 (recording), ☎ 631-363-2238 (office).

Brookhaven Multiplex Cinemas (14), 400 Express Dr South, Medford, ☎ 631-289-8900 (recording), ☎ 631-289-8912 (office). Off Exit 64 LIE.

Movieland Cinemas (10), 1708 Montauk Highway, Mastic, ☎ 631-281-8586 (recording), ☎ 631-281-8571 (office).

Newspapers & Magazines

Amityville Record serves Amityville, North Amityville, Copiague, and East Massapequa; ☎ 631-264-0077, www.amityvillerecord.com.

Babylon Beacon serves Babylon village, West Babylon, North Babylon, Deer Park, Lindenhurst and West Islip; ☎ 631-587-5612, www.babylonbeacon.com.

The *Islip Bulletin* and *Suffolk County News* are published by Johnlor Publishing, Sayville, ☎ 631-589-6200.

The *Long Island Advance*; *Suffolk County News* and *Islip Bulletin* all cover Patchogue.

Half Hollow Hills Newspaper is published by Long Islander Newspapers, founded by Walt Whitman; ☎ 631-425-7680, www.longislandernews.com.

Suffolk Life is published by Suffolk Life Newspapers for communities in southern Suffolk County (Selden/Farmingdale; Amityville; Lindenhurst; West Babylon; Deer Park; West Islip, Bay Shore, Brentwood, East Islip; Central Islip/Hauppauge; Sayville/Oakdale; Holbrook/Bohemia; Patchogue; Bellport/East Patchogue; Medford/Holtsville; Mastic/Shirley; Moriches); ☎ 631-369-0800, www.suffolklife.com.

South Bay's Newspaper, Lindenhurst, ☎ 631-226-2636. www.southbaynews.com.

South Shore Monthly, ☎ 631-969-3969, is a complimentary regional magazine covering the bay community.

The Amityville Record *and the* Babylon Beacon *are family-run newspapers.*

Pharmacies

The Medicine Shoppe Pharmacy has locations at 178 East Montauk Highway, Lindenhurst, ☎ 631-957-9723; 64 Carlton Avenue, #B, Central Islip, ☎ 631-277-9515; and 747 Montauk Parkway, East Patchogue, ☎ 631-654-2444.

Suffolk County's South Shore

Zip Codes

Amityville	11507
Babylon	11702
Bayport	11705
Bay Shore	11706
Bellport	11713
Blue Point	11715
Bohemia	11716
Brentwood	11717
Brightwaters	11718
Brookhaven	11719
Center Moriches	11934
Central Islip	11722
Copiague	11726
Deer Park	11729
East Islip	11730
East Moriches	11940
Great River	11739
Holbrook	11741
Holtsville	11742
Islandia	11722
Islip	11751
Islip Terrace	11752
Lindenhurst	11757
Mastic	11950
Mastic Beach	11951
Medford	11763
Moriches	11955
North Babylon	11703
Oakdale	11769
Patchogue	11772
Ronkonkoma	11779
Sayville	11782
Shirley	11967
West Babylon	11704
West Islip	11795
Wyandanch	11798
Yaphank	11980

Fire Island

Nature, to be commanded, must be obeyed.

– Francis Bacon

Fire Island is a haven for everyone and a special place for me – I met my husband here 35 years ago. A pencil-thin barrier beach 32 miles long, Fire Island extends from **Robert Moses State Park** in the west to **Moriches Inlet** in the east. The island runs parallel to the South Shore of Long Island and protects it from the forces of nature. Fire Island is no more than a half-mile wide from ocean to bay, so its 17 communities are side by side. The island is home to roughly 200 families year-round; most live in Ocean Beach or Kismet, where there is a year-round water supply. In the summer, thousands of sun-worshipers descend upon Fire Island; where they land depends on proclivity. Families, singles and gays (in Cherry Grove and the Pines) each have their own patch of heaven.

Fire Island has no roads and therefore no cars (with the exception of those in Robert Moses State Park and Smith Point County Park). Years ago, we would crowd onto the ferry on Friday nights, leaving our cars and cares behind. Our friends would be waiting at the dock with wagons to haul the weekend's worth of groceries we'd brought from the mainland. Thankfully, little has changed since we had our summer shares in Ocean Bay Park. We revisited the area a few years ago and the only noticeable change was the overgrown vegetation. Flynn's restaurant – then the only hangout in Ocean Bay Park – was still there!

Once you step off the ferry, the modern world melts away. You are in a beachfront community with no traffic or tall buildings, where the only mode of transport is bicycles or water taxis.

Interested in an evening cruise leaving Captree Boat Basin and lobster buffet at Flynn's? See page 332.

Fire Island

Fire Island

1. Robert Moses State Park
2. Captree State Park & Boat Basin
3. Fire Island Lighthouse
4. Bay Shore–Fire Island Ferries
5. Heckscher State Park
6. Sunken Forest
7. Sayville–Fire Island Ferries
8. Islip-MacArthur Airport
9. Patchogue–Fire Island Ferries
10. Watch Hill
11. Otis Pike Wilderness Area
12. Smith Point County Park

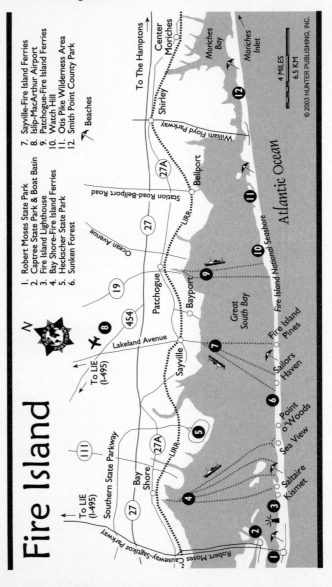

© 2003 HUNTER PUBLISHING, INC.

SUMMER SHARES

Many Fire Island homeowners advertise for summer renters to offset their expenses; houses are rented out for the entire summer. Generally, several people take full shares in a "group house," entitling them to occupy the house every weekend. Those with half shares naturally pay less and can use the house every other weekend. A harmonious group will often share food expenses, cooking and cleaning.

Getting Here

By Ferry

Fire Island Ferries, ☎ 631-666-3600 or ☎ 631-665-3600, www.fireislandferries.com, serves the communities of Atlantique, Dunewood, Fair Harbor, Kismet, Ocean Bay Park, Ocean Beach, Seaview, and Saltaire, all from its dock in Bay Shore. The round-trip fare is $12.50 for adults; $10 for seniors; $6 for children ages two-12. Parking at the dock is $15 on weekends. The ride takes 30 minutes. The peak season is May-September; limited service is available year-round, weather permitting. The ferry terminal is about 41 miles from the Throgs Neck Bridge. Head east on the Southern State Parkway to Exit 42S; turn right at the light onto Fifth Avenue and proceed to the Bayshore business district. Turn left at Main Street and follow signs to the dock.

Sayville Ferry Service, ☎ 631-589-0810, www.sayvilleferry.com, runs ferries to Cherry Grove, Fire Island Pines, and Water Island, a private community (round-trip fare is $11); and to Sailor's Haven and Sunken Forest (round-trip fare is $9). These ferries operate from mid-May through mid-October; the ride takes 20 minutes. In September and October, the schedule can change to weekends only. Heading east,

The board-walk at the Sunken Forest is wheelchair-accessible. Call the Sayville ferry in advance to arrange a ramp.

from Main Street in Sayville, turn right on Foster Avenue and follow signs to the terminal. Parking is across the street in private lots; the daily rate is $6 on weekdays and $8 on weekends.

Davis Park Ferry Co., ☎ 631-475-1665, leaves Patchogue for Davis Park and Watch Hill, from March to September. The trip takes 20 minutes; one-way fare is $5.50.

> ★ Famous Faces
>
> Tony Randall, John Turturro and Ally Sheedy all have homes on Fire Island.

Getting Around

By Ferry

South Bay Water Taxi, ☎ 631-665-8885, makes stops at all communities and provides 24-hour cross bay service by reservation; guided lighthouse tours.

Fire Island Ferries, ☎ 631-666-3600 or ☎ 631-665-3600, www.fireislandferries.com, operates a ferry service that runs between Kismet and Ocean Bay Park, from July Fourth through August, every day except Friday and Sunday. The fare for adults is $5 one-way; $9 round-trip; and the fare for children under 12 is $3 one-way.

Sea Taxi, ☎ 866-732-8294, is awaiting its license at press time but expects to be in business by the 2003 season, offering lower rates and newer boats than its competition.

By Bicycle

Fire Island Watersports, Ocean Bay Park (on the bay side), ☎ 631-583-8937, sells and rents bikes; they also rent surfboards, kayaks, canoes and sailboats. Open daily, from Memorial Day to mid-September.

Sunup to Sundown

Historical Societies & Sites

The Fire Island National Seashore encompasses the **William Floyd Estate** in Mastic Beach (on the South Shore; see page 267); the Fire Island Lighthouse (see below); **Watch Hill**, which has a 188-slip marina, camping and visitor center; and **Sailor's Haven**, which includes the Sunken Forest (see page 322).

The **Ocean Beach Historical Society**, ☎ 631-583-8972, www.obvillage.com, sponsors three or four exhibits each summer relevant to Ocean Beach history; exhibits are held at the society's headquarters in the Community House building on Bay Walk. In mid- to late July, the space is given over to the works of local artists, some of which are for sale. The calendar of events, usually ready by March, can be viewed on the village Web site. Admission is free. The society office is open daily except Tuesday and Wednesday, 10am-2pm and 7-10pm.

Another attraction here is the **Fire Island Lighthouse**, just east of Robert Moses State Park. To get there from Robert Moses, park in Field 5 (there's a parking fee), and walk along the boardwalk; it's .7 mile to the lighthouse. From the eastern part of the island, take the ferry from Bay Shore to Kismet and walk one mile west. The keeper's quarters house a museum and gift shop, and tours to the top of the 192-step tower are available. Open Wednesday-Sunday, July through Labor Day; and weekends, April through June. Tour fees are $4 for adults; $3 for seniors and children under 12; reservations are required. For more information, call the Fire Island Lighthouse Preservation Society at ☎ 631-321-7028, or the Visitor Center at ☎ 631-661-4876.

Fire Island

Parks & Preserves

The **Sunken Forest** is a wonderful place to visit in the summer and in early autumn when it's cool; in winter and spring it's too windy and cold. A maritime forest, 250 to 300 years old, its three predominant trees are **American holly**, an evergreen with thick, waxy, spine-tipped leaves; **sassafras**, which has three different leaf types (oval, mitten-shaped and three-lobed); and **shad-blow**, also called shadbush, juneberry and service-bush. Other varieties of trees found here include **tu-pelo**, **red oak** and **pitch pine**. Stay on the boardwalk to steer clear of deer ticks (we saw a doe and her fawn on the beach) and poison ivy. In the fall, poison ivy turns bright red and is easily spotted.

No one knows how Fire Island got its name, but one theory is that the blaze of red ivy made it look like the island was afire.

Trees rarely grow tall on Fire Island because they are subjected to wind and salt spray off the ocean. The continuous spray provides nutrients to the trees, while retarding their growth and pruning them like a tree trimmer. The result is a canopy of almost uniform height.

★ TIP

If you can't visit the Sunken Forest, log on to www.nps.gov/fiis/exploring.htm for a virtual tour.

The path runs through the forest and the swale, which is the space between the primary and secondary dunes. The primary dune – the one closest to the ocean – provides some protection to the secondary dune, which shelters the trees and enables the forest to develop. When you stand in the swale the forest seems to disappear, hence its name. As you walk through the forest, notice the tree trunk with hundreds of holes. It's the work of yellow-bellied sapsuckers. You'll also observe trees that are gnarled and bent into intriguing shapes. In contrast, the oldest trees in the main rest area stand straight and seem to be growing out of the wood planks.

These 250- to 300-year-old trees are foolers, though. They are neither tall for their age nor wide in the trunk.

☞ DID YOU KNOW?

Dunes are not manmade. Beach grass captures windblown sand and forms hills. Behind these barricades, shrubs take hold and build soil. The vegetation that holds dunes together is fragile and can be easily destroyed by human traffic. Without the anchoring roots of beach grasses there would be no dunes and without sheltering dunes there'd be no forests. As a weathered inscription on a rock in the Sunken Forest reminds us, this primeval forest is "here to enjoy, but not to injure or destroy."

There is no sound in the forest but the rustling of trees. The ocean seems far away until you reach the overlook. The community of **Point O'Woods** can be seen off to the west, but otherwise the ocean view reveals another magnificent natural wonderland.

Bring your bathing suit and spend the day; a lifeguard is on duty in season. **Sailor's Haven**, a half-mile west of Cherry Grove and one mile east of Point O'Woods, is where you enter Sunken Forest, which runs between Point O'Woods and Sailors Haven, and from dunes to bay. The Sailors Haven facilities (visitor center, snack bar, 42-slip marina, picnic areas, restrooms, showers and gift shop) are open mid-May through mid-October. The National Park Service administers the area and offers guided tours in season. If you go solo, remember to pick up a trail guide in the Visitor's Center located in Sailor's Haven Marina near the ferry; ☎ 631-597-6183.

Fire Island

Smith Point Beach and **Robert Moses State Park**
are the only sections of Fire Island accessible by car.
Smith Point Beach is more secluded, but when 3,000 to
5,000 people descend on Robert Moses in the summer,
the two- to three-mile-long beach can handle the crowd.

TRIBUTE

A 12-foot black granite memorial and botanical garden set on a two-acre site were dedicated in July, 2002 at Smith Point Park, as a
tribute to the 230 victims of TWA Flight 800,
their families, and the agencies and organizations who aided in search and recovery. The
plane exploded south of Moriches Inlet on July
17, 1996, and is one of the worst aviation disas-
ters in American history. The memorial was
unveiled around the sixth anniversary of the
crash.

According to Ranger Steve Henderson of the National
Park Service, the **Otis Pike Wilderness Area**, just
west of Smith Point Beach, is the only federally recognized wilderness in New York State, home to deer, foxes
and 350 bird species (that's a lot of birds, when you consider that there are 1,200 different species of birds in
the US). Bathers and campers are welcome. Between
the beach and the park is the Fire Island Wilderness
Center, accessible from William Floyd Parkway. The
parking fee is $8. Contact the park service at ☎ 631-
281-3010 for information on free twilight and nature
walks.

Recreation

Boating

Seaview Marina, ☎ 631-583-9380, has 54 slips that
can accommodate boats up to 60 feet, both seasonal
and transient. Open from May 15 to September 15, the

marina has ice, water, barbecue grills, picnic tables and portable toilets. This is the only solid-fill marina on the island; it's enclosed on three sides so, regardless of the turbulence on the water, boats do not bounce.

Biking

Fire Island Watersports, Ocean Bay Park, located on the bay side, ☎ 631-583-9561, sells and rents bikes at $15 per day; they also rent surfboards, kayaks, canoes and sailboats. Open daily, Memorial Day through mid-September.

Tennis

Ocean Beach has two outdoor tennis courts, open mid-May through mid-October. Contact the village office at Cottage Road & Bay Walk, ☎ 631-583-5940, about reserving court time.

Shop Till You Drop

Ocean Beach

ICE CASTLE SWEET SHOPPE
319 Bay Walk
☎ 631-583-0225 (Ice Castle)
☎ 631-583-9286 (Internet Café)

In the hot summer, there's nothing like cold, sweet refreshments. Ice Castle sells fruit smoothies, sorbets and gelati, along with fresh fudge. In 2002, the owners opened the **Internet Café** next door; key pads and screen savers read "Wire Island." The fee is 30¢ a minute. Kids comprise most of the users during the day; adults have their turn at night. Open daily, June through September; and weekends, May and October.

Fire Island

☞ DID YOU KNOW?

You can get that homemade fudge on the mainland at **Just Barged Inn**, ☎ 631-665-2427, a convenience store at the ferry terminal in Bay Shore. It's under the same ownership as Ice Castle.

KENNY GOODMAN'S FIRE ISLAND GALLERY
325 Denhoff Walk, next to Rachel's restaurant
☎ 631-583-8207 or 888-898-6789
www.kennygoodman.com

Kenny Goodman is an artist who has lived and worked on Fire Island since 1968. His large wood carvings of bearded patriarchs are both quirky and touching. Kenny explains his obsession with father figures. "I have respect for fathers," he says. "Fathers are very, very important." His sterling silver jewelry embossed with surfboards can be worn as a pendant, and surfers and beachcombers like to wear them.

Kenny does much of his sculpting on the front porch of his studio, and from May to October he welcomes people to come and watch (his winter shop is in Nyack, at 92 Main Street, ☎ 845-727-6950). Everything you could possibly want to know about the artist and his work is on his Web site.

KLINE'S
Ocean Beach
☎ 631-583-5333

This is an all-purpose shop – it sells cards, T-shirts, beach toys, candy, backpacks, sunglasses, beachwear, and beach umbrellas. Kline's is open daily, May-October.

Best Places to Stay

In terms of accommodations, there have been some changes since we had our summer shares. This is especially true in Ocean Beach, which now has many more guesthouses, along with shops and restaurants; and in Ocean Bay Park, which now has a resort. On most of the island, only a few lodgings are desirable, which is why there are few non-homeowners or non-renters there. Day-trippers, of course, are numerous, but for many the island is simply too far and too expensive for a day-trip.

ACCOMMODATIONS PRICE SCALE
Price scale is based on the cost of a double room, two people per room on a weekend, and does not include the 9.25% hotel tax.
Inexpensive . . . . under $130
Moderate . . . . $130-$200
Expensive . . . . $201-$300
Deluxe . . . . more than $300

Ocean Beach

Ocean Beach is the island's largest and busiest community. The unofficial capital of Fire Island, it has the island's only movie house (showing current films), a year-round post office, several guesthouses, art galleries, and an elementary school. Like East Hampton, it has a reputation of being a "land of no." Dogs are not allowed on the beach during the summer, and eating is never permitted. Some restrictions have been lifted, however; bicycling is now permitted on weekends, as is barbecuing (with a permit).

Fire Island

SEASONS B&B
468 Denhoff Road
☎ 631-583-8295
www.fivacations.com
Moderate

Fire Island's only bed and breakfast has celebrated more than 10 seasons. Close to the bay, it has 10 units, all with TV and air conditioning (no children or pets are allowed). Buffet breakfast and afternoon tea are served daily. Guests are provided with beach umbrellas, chairs and towels, and bikes. In addition, the owner rents six one- to three-bedroom apartments in nearby Bayhouse by the week or season, at rates starting at $1,600 per week for a one-bedroom. Pets are allowed in the apartments at no extra charge, barring any damage. Owner Harvey Levine and innkeeper Jane are welcoming hosts. Open from the end of April through October.

CLEGG'S HOTEL
478 Bayberry Walk
☎ 631-583-5399
Deluxe

Directly across from the Ocean Beach ferry terminal, Clegg's has 14 units and three studio apartments. The guest rooms have shared baths; rates are high, but drop to nearly one-third during the week – even in prime season. Also, inquire about three-night packages in May and June. Children are welcome. *The New York Times* reviewed Clegg's as "clean, if not immaculate." Open May through September.

Ocean Bay Park

FIRE ISLAND HOTEL & RESORT
25 Cayuga Walk
☎ 631-583-8000
www.fireislandhotel.com
Moderate to Expensive

One hundred yards from the ocean, this resort has a pool, tiki bar, gift shop and fitness facility. Its poolside grill, **Hurricanes**, is open daily for lunch and dinner until 10pm. There are 46 rooms, all with private baths, plus time share units. Resort and restaurant open on Memorial Day and close in early October.

Inquire about mid-week promotions at Fire Island Hotel & Resort.

Cherry Grove

Cherry Grove and the Pines are the gay communities, with reference to both sexual preference and the availability of entertainment on the island. Local papers are filled with reviews of full-scale theatrical productions, fundraisers, concerts, and parties in the Grove.

The community developed 120 years ago when a Patchogue couple, Mr. and Mrs. Archer Perkinson, built a two-story hotel. After World War II, the Grove began to assume its identity as a gay resort.

CHERRY GROVE BEACH HOTEL
☎ 631-597-6600
ww.grovehotel.com
Inexpensive to Expensive

This hotel has 64 units, all with private baths. Daily rates range from $40 for an economy room to $300 for a deluxe. The property has a 30- x 60-foot swimming pool.

Fire Island

Best Places to Eat

Kismet

KISMET INN & MARINA
Oak Walk
☎ 631-583-5592
Moderate

Within walking distance of the lighthouse, the Kismet Inn specializes in fresh seafood, steaks and pasta, and has daily blackboard specials. It is open from the first weekend in April through November. The marina has 52 slips, and boaters pay $30 per day or $60 for an overnight stay. Vouchers are given toward dinner at the restaurant.

Ocean Beach

MAGUIRE'S BAY FRONT RESTAURANT
Bay Walk
☎ 631-583-8800
Moderate to Expensive

Maguire's has a large dining room in addition to seating on its deck. Lunches start at $9 for a salad or burger. Granted, the baby arugula salad with candied pecans, roasted red onion, mango and sherry-honey vinaigrette is well worth $9; but it, like the burger, is reduced to $6 at dinner, which is à la carte. A further turn-off is the $2 for bread. A kids' menu is available. Open daily, for lunch and dinner, June through September; and weekends only, in May and October.

MATTHEW'S SEAFOOD HOUSE
935 Bay Walk
☎ 631-583-8016
www.matthewsseafood.com
Moderate

Matthew's is a restaurant, seafood market and a 22-slip marina on the bay. Family owned for 28 years, it has mostly outdoor seating. For boaters, four hours of free docking, with a minimum purchase of $40, is offered from 6pm Sunday through 6pm Friday; look for Buoy 15. Fresh fish and pasta dominate the menu, and most of the pasta entrées are served with seafood. A kids' menu is available. Matthew's is open daily, for lunch and dinner, from Mother's Day to mid-September. Dinner reservations are highly recommended; entertainment is featured nightly.

Matthew's Margarita Madness – margaritas served in fishbowls – is the rage on Thursday nights.

ISLAND MERMAID
☎ 631-583-8088
www.islandmermaid.com
Moderate

This bar/restaurant/nightclub on the bay has a dance club and docking space. Serves New American cuisine. Primarily outdoor seating. Lunch features burgers and wraps. Reservations are recommended for dinner on Friday and Saturday. On Monday night entrées are half-price. Open April through mid-October. Days vary in off-season; open daily, Memorial Day through Labor Day.

Fire Island

Ocean Bay Park

FLYNN'S
One Cayuga Street
☎ 631-583-5000
www.flynnsfireisland.com
Moderate

The Flynn family has been serving food in Ocean Bay Park since 1937. The restaurant can seat 250 people and has a 50-boat marina (free docking for restaurant patrons). A special Friday night menu includes a glass of wine, salad, full entrée and coffee and dessert for $19.95. Every Tuesday through Thursday in July and August, and on selected nights in June and September, the *Moonchaser* leaves Captree Boat Basin at 7pm for Flynn's, returning at 10:45pm. The boat ride is $11.00 round-trip. The hot-and-cold buffet is $28.95, plus tax, and includes appetizers; entrées such as sliced sirloin steak, hot steamed lobsters, chicken Marsala, and stuffed sole or seafood Newburg; and homemade muffins and coffee. You'll dine on the water and dance to live music. For reservations, call Flynn's between 10am and 5pm. To reach Captree Boat Basin, take the Robert Moses Causeway (via Sunrise Highway Exit 41 South, or Southern State Parkway Exit 40 South). Follow the causeway for four to five miles, and take the second right turn after the drawbridge to Captree State Park and Boat Basin (do not turn at Captree Island). Flynn's is open daily in summer (from late June through Labor Day); and weekends only in spring and fall (mid-May to mid-June, and Labor Day through mid-September).

Fire Island A to Z

Information Sources

Tourism

Fire Island Tourist Bureau, ☎ 631-563-8448, www.
fireisland.com.

Chamber of Commerce of the Moriches, ☎ 631-
874-3849, www.moricheschamber.org.

Community Web Sites

Ocean Beach . . . . www.obvillage.com
Fair Harbor . . . . www.fairharbor.com
Saltaire . . . . www.saltaire.org
Fire Island Pines . . . . www.fipines.com

Newspapers

Fire Island Tide, ☎ 631-567-7470, published biweek-
ly.

Fire Island News, ☎ 516-583-5345, published weekly
from Memorial Day to Labor Day.

Houses of Worship

Catholic

Our Lady of the Magnificat Church, Ocean Beach,
☎ 631-583-5868.

Episcopal

St. Andrews by the Sea, Marine Walk, Saltaire, ☎ 631-
583-8382.

Fire Island

Jewish – Conservative

Fire Island Synagogue, Beachwold Avenue and Central Walk, Seaview, ☎ 631-583-4189. Also 212-644-8100 (weekdays), or 631-583-7844 (weekends).

Liquor Stores

Fire Island Liquor Store, Ocean Beach, ☎ 631-583-5994.

Seaview Liquor, Seaview, ☎ 631-583-8482. Open from April through October (Seaview Liquor and the market next door are the only vendors in Seaview).

Pines Liquor Shop, on the harbor, Pines, ☎ 631-597-6442.

Zip Codes

Cherry Grove 11782
Davis Park 11772
Fair Harbor 11706
Fire Island Pines 11782
Ocean Beach 11770
Point O' Woods 11706
Saltaire 11706

Suffolk County's North Fork

A Brief History

In 1640 a small band of Puritans who escaped from England because of religious intolerance became dissatisfied with conditions in New England. Led by the Reverend John Youngs, they crossed the Sound and came ashore at Founder's Landing in what is today the village of **Southold**. In 1682 their descendants secured 30 to 40 acres of woodland and settled at the north edge of what is now Greenport, but was then called Stirling.

Some 25 years after the pioneers stepped foot in Southold, second-generation immigrants settled Cutchogue, one of the newly cleared lands outside Southold that were tax-exempt. Farmers planted potatoes, Brussels sprouts and cauliflower. In the 1960s and 1970s rows of grapevines were planted, heralding a new industry.

Today, nearly all of Long Island's farms are located within the **Town of Riverhead**, which has been the county seat since 1727; the Town is also home to a mega mall. Riverhead marks the point where the North and South forks separate, with the Great and Little Peconic and Gardiner's Bays between them like the space between two fingers. Nestled in these bays are islands, namely Shelter Island and privately-owned Gardiner's Island.

Spanning almost 70 square miles from Wading River to Jamesport, the Town of Riverhead borders Long Island Sound on the north and the Towns of Brookhaven, Southampton and Southold on three sides. The town is home to 27,680 people and includes the hamlets of Aquebogue, Baiting Hollow, Jamesport, Northville, Riverhead, Wading River and part of Calverton. Because the Town of Riverhead extends from West Suffolk County into the North Fork, it's considered part of both

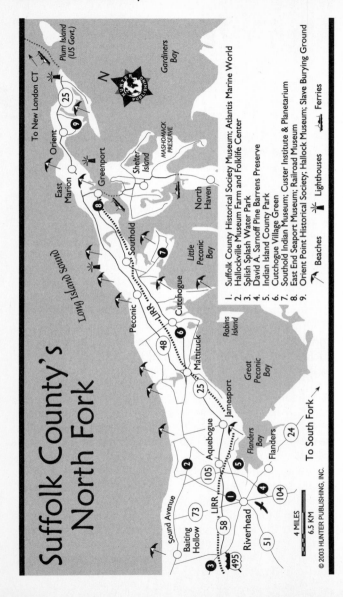

Suffolk County's North Fork

1. Suffolk County Historical Society Museum; Atlantis Marine World
2. Hallockville Museum Farm and Folklife Center
3. Splish Splash Water Park
4. David A. Sarnoff Pine Barrens Preserve
5. Indian Island County Park
6. Cutchogue Village Green
7. Southold Indian Museum; Custer Institute & Planetarium
8. East End Seaport Museum; Railroad Museum
9. Orient Point Historical Society; Hallock Museum; Slave Burying Ground

Beaches   Lighthouses   Ferries

© 2003 HUNTER PUBLISHING, INC.

regions. Since it reaches the knuckle of the North Fork, Riverhead is listed in the *North Fork* section of this book.

Getting Here & Getting Around

By Car

The North Fork begins at **Riverhead** and ends at **Orient Point**, 28 miles to the east. From Exit 73 (LIE's last exit), go east on Route 58, which will take you through Riverhead's commercial district of car dealerships and fast food restaurants. Once 58 merges into Route 25 the vista turns rural.

Rental Cars

All American Auto Sales & Rentals has locations in Riverhead, 245 West Main Street, ☎ 631-208-4000; and Mattituck, 7655 Main Road, ☎ 631-298-1039.

By Taxi

Moonlight Classic Taxi, Riverhead, ☎ 631-727-5800.

Maria's Taxi offers local and long distance service with pickups on the North Fork and in NYC. Locations are in Southold, ☎ 631-765-2020; Greenport, ☎ 631-477-0700; Mattituck, ☎ 800-698-2944; and Riverhead, ☎ 631-369-TAXI. Out of area, call ☎ 800-MY-TAXI-4.

McRide's, Riverhead, ☎ 631-727-0707. Taxi and van service. Local, airport and service to NYC. Accepts all major credit cards.

Southold Taxi serves Southold and Greenport, ☎ 631-765-2020; 765-CAB-1 (2221).

By Ferry

The **Cross Sound Ferry** (www.longislandferry.com) carries passengers and cars daily, year-round, between Orient Point (☎ 631-323-2525) and New London CT (☎ 860-443-5281). Passenger reservations are not necessary but vehicle reservations are strongly suggested. Sailing time is approximately one hour and 20 minutes. Departures are from the end of Route 25 at Orient Point; the ferry also goes to Rhode Island and Block Island. Call for fare and schedule information.

North Ferry Company, Route 114, Shelter Island, ☎ 631-749-0139, carries passengers and cars year-round between the north side of Shelter Island and Greenport. The trip takes seven minutes each way; call for fare and schedule information.

By Bus

Sunrise Coach Lines, West Front Street, Greenport, ☎ 631-477-1200 or 800-527-7709, www.sunrisecoach. com, provides daily service to/from NYC, organized tours and individualized charters.

By Limousine

Sea-Aire Limousine, ☎ 631-298-4082. This company, based in Mattituck, serves the North Fork from Orient to Riverhead. Hourly rate to airports, NYC; 24-hours-a-day, year-round.

Islander Limousine, Southold, ☎ 631-765-5834, offers pickups "from Manhattan streets to North & South Fork Retreats," airports, parties.

Sunup to Sundown

Museums & Historic Sites

Riverhead

**SUFFOLK COUNTY HISTORICAL
SOCIETY MUSEUM**
300 West Main Street
Riverhead
☎ 631-727-2881
www.riverheadli.com
Free admission

Since the museum's founding in 1886, its mission has
been to collect, preserve and interpret the ongoing history of Suffolk County through permanent and tempo-
rary exhibits that change two or three times a year.
Although the huge red-brick structure resembles a college administration building, it has housed the museum since it was built in 1930. Wings were added in
subsequent years; in 1994 the Georgian Revival-style
building was placed on the National Register of Historic Places.

*The Suffolk
County Histor-
ical Society
Museum is not
handicapped-
accessible.*

Indian history, farming, transportation and whaling
(the newest exhibit) comprise the bulk of the permanent collection. There is also a collection of ceramics;
Huntington and Greenport were important pottery
centers in the 1800s, although pottery was never a big
industry in Suffolk County. Most earthenware and por-
celain was imported from England, France and China.
The best example of the melding of European artistry
with American patriotism is in the large collection of
blue Staffordshire plates, popular in the 1830s. This
was pearlware, transfer-printed with important American scenes, events and inventions.

The museum's lower level houses larger exhibits of
early Suffolk County transport, including carriages,
wagons, sleighs and bicycles. It was the popular use of
bicycles, in fact, that fostered the growth and improve-

ment of roadways on the Island as early as 1704. There are also dioramas of important local events during the Colonial era. One diorama depicts the arrival of the first English settlers from Lynn, Massachusetts at Conscience Point in Southampton in 1640. Among the families are some familiar names: Howell, Farrington, Welbee, Walton, Stanborough, J. Sayre, Needham, and T. Sayre.

HOOKED ON TAXES

One name, "Fishhook" Samuel Mulford, is especially prominent in the East End. Legend has it that Mulford was so angered by a tax on whale oil and bone marketed by Long Island whalers that he sailed to England in 1716 to present his grievance to the king. He wouldn't have succeeded as a mere Colonial without his ingenuity. After being pickpocketed in London, Mulford sewed fishhooks in his pockets; the next pickpocket had a painful surprise. The story circulated widely, and "Fishhook" Mulford got his audience with the king. The tax lapsed after 1720, largely due to these protests.

The museum is open Tuesday-Saturday, 12:30-4:30pm, year-round. To get here, take the LIE to Exit 71; continue east on Route 24 for four miles to Riverhead. Turn left onto Peconic into the business district and bear right. The museum is straight ahead.

Be sure to stop in the bookstore and gift shop. It boasts the largest collection of history and genealogy books on Long Island. The museum also has a research library, currently open Wednesday, Thursday and Saturday, 12:30-4:30pm; $2 admission.

HALLOCKVILLE MUSEUM FARM AND FOLKLIFE CENTER

6038 Sound Avenue
Riverhead
☎ 631-298-5292
www.riverheadli.com/hallock.html
Admission $4

The main house of the Hallock Homestead dates to 1765, with additions dating as late as 1907. Until the 1930s, the 50-acre property was a working farm that grew corn, wheat and potatoes. Members of the Hallock family continued to live there until 1979, when the last survivor was in her late 90s. (During a recent summer, Hallocks came from all around the country for a family reunion.)

The focus of the museum is the period from 1880 to 1910; farm animals and costumed interpreters help bring that era alive. There are seven outbuildings that are pretty much intact. The Corn Crib, for instance, is more than a century old and has never been restored. Kids enjoy trying out the old corn shucker. A four-seater outhouse indicates that the family was well off (wealthier owners had four to six seats), even though Sears catalogues and corncobs served as their toilet paper.

In the main house we find other indications of the family's financial status – there is a separate room for laundry, a cigar and brandy room, and a dining room only used on Sunday. In the parlor is a fainting couch where young girls would place arsenic under their tongues to look as pale as possible and then faint – if they didn't die first (it was considered feminine).

Animals include a cow, calf and chickens; the gift shop sells eggs from the chickens. There are picnic tables under shade trees. If not for the cars racing by on Sound Avenue, you'd swear you were back in the 1890s.

The farm is open year-round for one-hour tours, 11am-4pm, Wednesday-Saturday (no costumed guides from November to May). To reach the center, follow Route 58

Suffolk County's North Fork

East from the LIE's Exit 73 and turn left onto Northville Turnpike (by Kmart); continue to the end, then
turn right onto Sound Avenue. Hallockville is on the
left, 1.1 miles east of Palmer Vineyards. Look for a
white picket fence and historic markers. The museum
is handicapped-accessible.

Southold

SOUTHOLD INDIAN MUSEUM
Bayview Road
Southold
☎ 631-765-5577
Admission $2 donation; 50¢ for children

*Visit
Newsday's
Web site to
take a virtual
tour of
Southold's
popular spots
and explore
the town's rich
history;
www.newsday.
com / features /
features.htm.*

The Native American artifacts displayed in other Long
Island museums take on much more meaning once you
visit the Indian Museum. Because it's devoted to the
history of Long Island Algonquins (and a few other
American tribes), the museum can show many more aspects of their lives, such as food, fishing, tools, weapons
and pottery. Displays cover four major time frames:
Paleo (10,000-7,000 BC); Archaic (8,000-4,000 BC);
Transitional (4,000-3,000 BC); and Woodland (3,000-
300 BC).

During the Paleo epoch the land was home to several
big game animal species. The Paleo-Indians hunted
mastodon, mammoth and caribou on grassland that is
now under water; scallop fishermen are still finding
the bones and teeth of these animals, though all were
extinct by the Archaic period. Before the bow and arrow were used in Woodland times, and before guns
were introduced by the European colonists, the Indians
used spears with projectile points. The museum has
two specimens of Paleolithic fluted points used by these
early big-game hunters; fewer than two dozen of these
have been found on Long Island.

The museum has the largest collection of clay pots on
Long Island, some dating back 1,500 years. Some were
found in pieces and restored, while others were found
pretty much intact.

Children are especially fascinated by the similarities between ancient and modern tools, demonstrating how form follows function. Collections of projectile points arranged solely for their aesthetic value contrast with collections of modern archeologists, whose focus is on the people behind the objects, rather than their appearance.

The changing summer exhibits complement the permanent collection and give voice to the artifacts. "We want to show there's more to this than just stone," explains Ellen Barcel, the museum's vice president. Recent exhibits have featured Indian medicine, baskets, music and dance.

The museum, which is operated by the New York State Archaeological Association, opened in 1962. It is not wheelchair-accessible. Tours are self-guided but guides are always available to answer questions. The museum also hosts lectures from September through June, generally on the third Sunday of every month. Their library has books on Native Americans and is open to the public. From Route 25 in Southold make a sharp right at the Gulf station onto Bayview Road. The museum is .2 mile down, on the right (100 miles from the Triboro Bridge); it is open year-round, 1:30-4:30pm, Saturday and Sunday in summer; Sunday only in the off-season; and by appointment.

HORTON POINT LIGHTHOUSE
NAUTICAL MUSEUM
End of Lighthouse Road
Southold
☎ 631-765-2101
Admission $2

The lighthouse is in a park with picnic tables and sweeping views of Long Island Sound. Some 7,000 people visit the nautical museum annually and are welcome to climb to the tower (it has only about 45 steps). In the park is an anchor from a 19th-century sidewheeler, the *Commodore*, which met an untimely end. Fishermen recovered the anchor in 1995; it is displayed

Hungry after sightseeing? Drive back into town. The Country Corner Café, a luncheonette on Main Street next to the IGA supermarket in Southold, is open daily, year-round.

in the same orientation as it was when the *Commodore* was wrecked.

Hallockville Homestead and Horton Point Lighthouse are on the National Register of Historic Places.

At the entrance to the parking lot are steps leading down to a stretch of beach popular with divers (there are signs here about requiring a permit to park; these refer to street parking).

The lighthouse museum is maintained by the Southold Historical Society; it is open Saturday and Sunday, 11:30am-4pm, Memorial Day to Columbus Day; it is handicapped-accessible.

☞ DID YOU KNOW?

The Town of Southold is called the "Lighthouse Capital of the US" because it has the greatest number of lighthouses in the country. Furthermore, seven of the eight lighthouses in Southold are operational. To learn about them, visit www.eastendlighthouses.org.

Greenport

EAST END SEAPORT & MARITIME MUSEUM
North Ferry Dock, Third Street
Greenport
☎ 631-477-2100
www.eastendseaport.org
www.greenport.com/maritime/welcome.htm
Free admission

Founded in 1990, the museum is located in the former railroad station house near the Shelter Island ferry terminal. It is dedicated to preserving the maritime heritage of Eastern Long Island through exhibits and educational activities. The two-level museum houses rare and valuable Fresnel lenses from the Plum Island Lighthouse (which rotates) and from the original Long

Beach Bar lighthouse on Gardiners Bay, some two to three miles east of Greenport.

SEEING THE LIGHT

The Long Beach Bar lighthouse was built in 1871 to mark the entrance to Greenport and Orient Harbors and to steer sailors away from the shoals of Long Beach. The Victorian structure was commonly known as The Bug Light because it was supported by spindly pilings that from afar looked like a huge bug upon the water. On July 4, 1963, the lighthouse was burned to the ground by arsonists, who were never identified. It was a sad day, and for many years the spot was marked on charts as "Lighthouse Ruins." The East End Seaport Museum and Marine Foundation raised $140,000 to rebuild the lighthouse; in 1990 its flashing light resumed guiding mariners. The Bug Light can be rented for special occasions but is otherwise closed to visitors.

The USS *Holland* was the US Navy's first submarine, and it was built in New Suffolk. A mock-up of the crew compartment gives visitors a taste of the tight living space aboard a submarine. A sign at the New Suffolk dock near Legends Restaurant marks the spot where the USS *Holland* and six other submarines built by the Holland Submarine Torpedo Boat Company were based between 1899 and 1905.

This Long Beach is not to be confused with the city of the same name in Nassau County.

In the museum's collection are some of the private yachts that were used as coastal picket patrols during World War II to search for German submarines within a 15-mile radius of shore. The government did not have enough ships and these yachts were loaned to the Navy; Greenport was a large base for picket patrols. A model of the *Wandering Jew*, the largest sailing vessel ever built in Greenport, is also on display. Through World War II, Greenport was a center for wooden boat building, whereas today the boatyards mostly do maintenance and repair. However, boatbuilding demonstrations are a popular activity at the museum every Saturday and Sunday in season, from 10am-5pm. The museum also has a small aquarium featuring local fish.

Special annual events in Greenport include **Lighthouse and Maritime History Cruises** in early June, and a **Maritime Festival** in late September (see page 389). A lecture series on nautical history is held throughout the year, and there are special exhibits and monthly lectures in the summer. The first floor of the museum is handicapped-accessible; a small park with benches and picnic tables is in the back. The museum is open from June through October; hours are 11am-5pm, daily except Tuesday.

RAILROAD MUSEUM
Fourth Street
☎ 631-477-0439
www.rmli.org

In 1844, the railroad was extended to Greenport, which then became the main rail-steamboat link between New York and Boston. Greenport remains the last stop on the North Fork (Ronkonkoma) branch of the LIRR. The Railroad Museum, at the foot of Fourth Street near the Maritime Museum, is housed in the Rail Road's former freight house; it's open weekends, noon-5pm, from Memorial Day to Columbus Day. The $2 admission includes a visit to the caboose.

To reach these attractions, take the LIE to its end at Exit 73. Follow Route 58 east; continue when it becomes Route 25. In Greenport, turn right onto Third Street at the traffic light and continue one block to the museum.

TIP

The North Ferry Passenger Terminal in Greenport has a public restroom (just in case).

Historical Societies & Tours

THE MATTITUCK HISTORICAL SOCIETY
☎ 631-298-5248

The society, on Main Road at the corner of Cardinal Drive, maintains a historical museum, an 1846 schoolhouse, and a milk-house, all open year-round, by appointment.

THE CUTCHOGUE-NEW SUFFOLK HISTORICAL COUNCIL
☎ 631-734-7122

The council conducts tours of a half-dozen buildings from three different eras; the buildings are all situated on the Cutchogue Village Green, right off Route 25. One is **The Old House**, built in Southold in 1640 for Benjamin Horton and moved to Cutchogue 20 years later; it is constructed of wooden slats and nails, and is a National Historic Landmark. Locals claim it's the oldest English-type frame house in New York State, pre-dating the old Halsey House in Southampton. The **Wickham Farmhouse**, c. 1704, is a typical Long Island farm home of the early 18th century, and **The Old Schoolhouse**, built in the 1840s, was the area's first district school. A 19th-century **Carriage House** displays local memorabilia, a carriage and tools; and the 1862 **Congregational Church** now houses the local library. Admission to all of these buildings is free but donations to the council are welcome. Tours are given 1-4pm, Saturday-Monday, from the last weekend in June through the first weekend in September; visitors are assigned to a tour upon arrival.

There are picnic tables on the Cutchogue Village Green.

SOUTHOLD HISTORICAL SOCIETY
54325 Main Road
☎ 631-765-5500
Suggested donation $2

The Town of Southold comprises Cutchogue, Mattituck, Peconic, Greenport, Southold and Orient.

The Southold Historical Society maintains a museum complex of about 14 historic structures (including the **Ann Currie-Bell House** (ca. 1900), which was built for Joseph & Ella Hallock, parents of Ann Currie-Bell, founder of the society); these buildings are open Wednesday, Saturday and Sunday, 1pm-4pm, from July through September. The society also maintains the **Horton Point Lighthouse & Museum** (see page 343). The society office is open 9:30am-2:30pm, Monday-Friday, year-round. A gift shop is located in the Prince Building next to the office; it is open Monday to Saturday, 10am-4pm, from Memorial Day through December 31.

OYSTERPONDS HISTORICAL SOCIETY
Village Lane
Orient
☎ 631-323-2480

The Orient Historic District encompasses about 120 late 18th- and early 19th-century residences.

Founded in 1944 to honor local participants in World War II, the Society maintains the **Orient Historic District**, a complex of four buildings: **Village House**, whose original owner, Augustus Griffin, kept a comprehensive journal published in 1856 that provided much of the history of Oysterponds. Until 1836, Oysterponds included Orient and East Marion; the **Hallock Building**, a 19th century dormitory for farm workers, now headquarters of the society; a **19th century Schoolhouse**; and the **Webb House**, an elegant example of Federal architecture. The buildings are open to the public for tours from June through September, Saturdays and Sundays, 1-5pm, or by appointment. The schoolhouse and museum office are open year-round, Tuesday-Saturday. Admission is $3 for adults; 50¢ for children under 12.

Another site worth visiting in the Oysterponds area is the **Slave Burying Ground**, on Narrow River Road. The sign tells you that slavery persisted in Oysterponds until about 1830 and that Dr. Seth H. Tuthill, proprietor of Hog Pond Farm (who died in 1840), and his wife, Maria (who died in 1850), wanted their 20 former servants buried with them. It's no surprise that the Tuthills' inscribed tombstones overshadow the small bare stones with no identifying marks.

SHELTER ISLAND HISTORICAL SOCIETY
☎ 631-749-0025

The society runs summer programs with events such as walking tours of Shelter Heights, Revolutionary War encampments at Havens House Barn, and a variety of lectures and readings.

Wineries

Wine is bottled poetry.
– Robert Louis Stevenson

Visiting the Vineyards

With 25 wineries on the North Fork, it's hard to decide which ones to visit. Even if you've checked all the Web sites you may still be overwhelmed. A day tour with Jo-Ann Perry of **Vintage Tours** (see page 351 for details) will solve your dilemma. Amiable and outgoing, Jo-Ann drives a 15-passenger van and will pick you up at your lodging, marina or railroad station. Now in her fifth season, she knows that visiting three or four wineries in 5½ hours is sufficient.

My husband and I visited on a beautiful Saturday in mid-October. At 11:30am, Jo-Ann and four others – a couple from New Jersey with parents from New Hampshire – picked us up at our motel in Mattituck. Another young couple from Brooklyn Heights had taken the train so we drove to the station before heading out.

Many of the wineries were holding harvest festivals and U-pick pumpkins were everywhere. By afternoon, the line of cars was a turnoff. "We call them the pumpkin people," Jo-Ann noted. Had we been alone, we never would have fought the traffic, but Jo-Ann grew up on the North Fork and knows all the shortcuts.

Palmer's wines are served to first-class passengers on American Airlines.

Our first stop was **Palmer Vineyards**, one of the most award-winning of the North Fork wineries. Standing by the vines, Jo-Ann explained why the wires are constantly raised to keep the expanding leaves away from the grapes. "The North Fork is considered the sunniest spot on the northeastern seaboard," she said, and "lots of sun increases the sugar content, making for a better wine." Expanding on the role of weather in winemaking, she said, "When a hurricane is forecast, the winemaker must decide whether to leave the grapes alone or pick them early." Likewise, while we're all savoring the spring, winemakers are agonizing over the cold, the heat, and the rain. "... everyone is focused on the weather," a viticulturist wrote. "It would not be uncommon to see a vineyard manager watching the Weather Channel at 5am prior to jumping on the tractor for a day's work."

Our group moved on to the de-stemming machine that separates the leaves from the berries, and the pressing machine "that replaces the *I Love Lucy* method of crushing grapes." The barrel cellar is where the winemaker demonstrates his style and preference in blending the grapes. This is why a wine such as a Merlot varies from one winery to another. Jo-Ann explained that only 75% of a "Merlot" must be made from Merlot grapes; the remaining 25% is left to the winemaker's discretion. The same is true of most other varietals.

After the tour, we joined the festivities on the back porch where a bluegrass band was playing. To my delight, our picnic lunch was prepared by **Coeur des Vignes** (see page 394), accompanied by a glass of "hand-picked" Pinot Blanc.

Next we stopped at **Martha Clara**, owned by Robert Entenmann, grandson of the bakery king (see page

354). After selling the company, he bought a former potato farm in Mattituck and raised thoroughbred racehorses. After turning his attention to wine, he opened the winery in 1996, naming it after his mother, whose wedding picture adorns the wine label. The old farm stand was converted into the tasting room.

Our group went for a ride in a carriage pulled by two Clydesdales, passing sleek racehorses and Entenmann's mansion. Robert made a brief appearance before turning over our private tasting to David, a young Frenchman with a thick accent and a hilarious presentation.

Our last visit was to **Corey Creek**. In 2000, Michael Lynne, president of New Line Cinema, became the new owner of both **Bedell** and Corey Creek Vineyards. The former owner of Bedell, Kip Bedell, has stayed on as winemaker. It was so jammed that Jo-Ann took us on a brief tour of the North Fork instead.

Between winery visits we stopped at farm stands to sample the sweet corn. **Harbes Family Farm** has a corn maze ($3.50) and a corn festival every weekend in October. Its fresh-picked rotisserie-roasted corn is so sweet you can eat it as dessert: see *Farm Markets*, page 565.

Vintage Tours, ☎ 631-765-4689, www.northfork.com/tours, operates year-round. Advance booking is advised, as the gourmet kitchen that prepares lunches needs 24 hours advance notice. The cost is $45 per person from November through May 24th; and $52 per person from May 25th through October 31. Ask about group discounts.

Winery Tours

Long Island Wine Tours, ☎ 631-924-3475, specializes in educational group tours (minimum 30 people) aboard a luxury motor coach. Three to five wineries are visited during a full-day tour (9am-6pm); side trips to local farm stands or produce markets can also be included. The $75 per person fee includes pick-up and drop-off at your home, wine tasting fees, buffet lunch, a

video presentation, behind-the-scenes winery tours
and raffles. An added bonus is tasting wine right out of
the barrel as it ages. Tours operate year-round.

Islander Limousine, ☎ 631-765-5834, offers winery
tours of the North and South Forks to groups of six to
10 passengers; tours last a minimum of three hours
and visit an average of five wineries. Trips are from
Manhattan and run year-round; the cost ranges from
$35 to $65 depending on the vehicle and size of the
group.

The Vineyards

Most of the wineries on the North Fork were once potato farms; many host special events, have an inviting
deck overlooking the vineyards, are available for private functions, have received rave reviews and hold
several gold medals. All are open year-round unless
otherwise specified.

SCHNEIDER VINEYARDS
2248 Roanoke Avenue
Riverhead
☎ 631-727-3334
www.schneidervineyards.com

22 acres. Opened in 2001; tasting room is in the planning stages.

PALMER VINEYARDS
Sound Avenue
Aquebogue
☎ 631-722-WINE
www.palmervineyards.com

125 acres. Open daily at 11am. Free wine tastings.

PAUMANOK VINEYARDS
Main Road
Aquebogue
☎ 631-722-8800
www.paumanok.com

77 acres. Open daily at 11am. No fee for tasting five selected wines; fee for vintage ones.

JAMESPORT VINEYARDS
Main Road
Jamesport
☎ 631-722-5256
www.jamesport.vineyards.com

60 acres. Open 11am-5pm; occasionally closed on Tuesdays. Tasting room opens at noon. $1-$8 tasting fee.

LAUREL LAKE VINEYARDS
Main Road
Laurel
☎ 631-298-1420

17 acres. The tasting room has an antique landmark
bar and gift shop. Open daily, 11am-6pm in season.
Closes at 5pm in winter. No tasting fee.

LIEB CELLARS
35 Cox Neck Road
Mattituck
☎ 631-734-1100
www.liebcellars.com

50 acres. The modern tasting room opened Memorial
Day weekend, 2001 and is open daily, 11am-6pm. No
tasting fee.

MACARI VINEYARDS & WINERY
150 Bergen Avenue
Mattituck
☎ 631-298-0100
www.macariwines.com

370 acres. Tastings daily, 11am-5pm. No tasting fee.

MARTHA CLARA
2595 Sound Avenue
Mattituck
☎ 631-298-0075
www.marthaclaravineyards.com

112 acres. Open daily, 10am-6pm. No tasting fee.

SHERWOOD HOUSE
2600 Oregon Road
Mattituck
☎ 631-298-2157, or 212-759-3540
www.sherwoodhousevineyards.com

38 acres. This is strictly a vineyard and there is no tasting room, but its Chardonnays and Merlots are available at restaurants and liquor stores.

BEDELL CELLARS
Main Road
Cutchogue
☎ 631-734-7537
www.bedellcellars.com

57 acres. Open daily, 11am-5pm. No tasting fee.

BIDWELL VINEYARDS
Route 48
Cutchogue
☎ 631-734-5200
www.northfork.net/bidwell

37 acres. Owned by three Bidwell brothers. Tasting room opens daily, 11am-6pm, in season; closes at 5pm in winter. $1 tasting fee, refundable with purchase.

CASTELLO DI BORGHESE HARGRAVE VINEYARD
Route 48 and Alvah's Lane
Cutchogue
☎ 631-734-5111, 800-734-5158
www.castellodiborghese.com

85 acres. Open daily at 11am for tastings. Calls itself the "Founding Vineyard" since its first vines were first planted in 1973. No tasting fee.

GRISTINA GALLUCCIO ESTATE VINEYARDS
Main Road
Cutchogue
☎ 631-734-7089
www.gristinawines.com

100 acres. Open daily at 11am for tastings. Fee for tastings of estate ($2) and reserve ($3) wines only.

PECONIC BAY WINERY
Main Road
Cutchogue
☎ 631-734-7361
www.peconicbaywinery.com

200 acres. Open at 11am daily. A new 14,000-square-foot tasting facility is replacing the barn that served the winery for 15 years. Minimal or no charge for tastings, depending on the wine.

PELLEGRINI VINEYARDS
Main Road
Cutchogue
☎ 631-734-4111
www.pellegrinivineyards.com

70 acres. Tasting room open daily, 11am-5pm. $2-$6 tasting fee.

PUGLIESE VINEYARDS
Main Road
Cutchogue
☎ 631-734-4057
www.pugliesevineyards.com

50 acres. Open daily, 10am-5pm. No fee for tastings.

LENZ WINERY
Main Road
Peconic
☎ 800-974-9899
www.lenzwine.com

60 acres. Open daily at 10am. Complimentary tastings; minimal fee for some wines.

OSPREY'S DOMINION VINEYARDS
Main Road
Peconic
☎ 631-765-6188, 888-295-6188
www.ospreysdominion.com

90 acres. Tasting room opens at 11am, Monday-Saturday, and noon on Sunday. No tasting fee for most wines, $1 for some, applied toward purchase.

PINDAR VINEYARDS
Main Road
Peconic
☎ 631-734-6200
www.pindar.net

667 acres. Open daily, 11am-6pm, for tours and tastings; call for tour schedule. Pindar, named for the Greek poet who lived around 500 BC, is the largest local vineyard and produces the most wine. Complimentary tastings; tasting fee for some wines is refundable with purchase.

RAPHAEL
Main Road
Peconic
☎ 631-765-1100
www.raphaelwine.com

60 acres. Opened in summer 2001. Specializes in Merlot and harvests entire crop by hand. Tasting room opens daily at noon. $8 fee for tasting.

COREY CREEK VINEYARDS
Main Road
Southold
☎ 631-765-4168
www.coreycreek.com

30 acres. Open daily, 11am-5pm. There is a tasting room and vineyard but no winery here; its wines are produced at various East End wineries. No tasting fee.

TERNHAVEN CELLARS
331 Front Street
Greenport
☎ 631-477-8737

Ternhaven calls itself the "Last winery before France." They are a boutique winery, dedicated to producing handcrafted Bordeaux-style red wines. They are open for tastings 11am-6pm. In early April, Friday-Sunday; beginning the last weekend in April, Thursday-Monday. $2 fee for three tastings, applied toward purchase. Closed January-March.

Information Sources

LONG ISLAND WINE COUNCIL
☎ 631-369-5887
info@liwines.com
www.liwines.com

The council and Times/Review Newspapers of Mattituck jointly publish *The Wine Press*, a seasonal guide to the Long Island wine country, distributed free at wineries, restaurants, liquor stores and other locations throughout the North and South Forks. Call or e-mail the council for a free copy.

Family Fun

The family is the nucleus of civilization.
— Will and Ariel Durant

ATLANTIS MARINE WORLD
431 East Main Street
Riverhead
☎ 631-208-9200
www.atlantismarineworld.com
Admission for adults, $11.50; children three-11, $9

See Atlantis Explorer *under* Cruises *for a tour boat adventure.*

Plato described Atlantis as the fairest of islands facing the sea. The designer of this $8 million creation probably compared the mythical lost city's beauty and relationship to water to Long Island. Here you'll see sharks swimming in a 120,000-gallon tank amidst the crumbling walls of an ancient civilization.

The mission of Marine World, opened in June 2000, is to teach children about the environment through a hands-on experience. There are three touch tanks among the 80 exhibits, and fish food is provided to encourage interaction with marine animals. What's more, prior to the sea lions' feeding time, children can talk with the divers.

There are plenty of visual wonders as well. A replica of a 23-foot great white shark near the stingray pool demonstrates how large they can be. (A 17-footer was caught off Montauk Point in 1985.) Some sharks and rays lay eggs, and visitors can see a moving shark fetus in the lighted egg case. Atlantis also boasts the largest (enclosed) live coral reef display in North America. A new exhibit is an 80-foot tower with rotating gondolas offering aerial views of Peconic Bay. The sea lion show in the outdoor coliseum is as good as any I've seen in Florida or California. Marine World has a café and picnic grounds; it is open year-round.

The **Riverhead Foundation for Marine Research and Preservation** (☎ 631-369-9840; www.riverhead-foundation.org) is housed in the same facility. Its mission is to save marine mammals (dolphins, whales and harbor seals) and sea turtles that are stranded anywhere in New York State. During my visit, there were 22 seals and six sea turtles in the "hospital." Once they are rehabilitated, they will be tagged and released. The Foundation maintains a 24-hour hot-line – ☎ 631-369-9829 – and spotters are asked to call even if the animal is dead so it can be tested for disease.

To reach the aquarium, take the LIE to Exit 71. Make a right onto Route 24 and follow for approximately 3½ miles. Turn left after you go around the traffic circle, then right at the light onto East Main Street. There is no on-site parking. If you can't find a spot on the street, look for signs directing drivers to several parking lots. The museum is handicapped-accessible.

SPLISH SPLASH
2549 Splish Splash Drive
Riverhead
☎ 631-727-3600
www.splishsplashlongisland.com
Admission for adults, $25.95; children under 48" and seniors, $17.95

Imagine a pine forest where the sun shines on the water and the trees provide shade wherever needed. Picture beach chairs on sand around the pools, a family of contented tubers on a lazy river and a smiling dad holding his son on a roller coaster water slide. Listen to squeals of delight when a waterfall erupts like a geyser over the wave pool at 10-minute intervals.

Now in its 11th season, Splish Splash doesn't disappoint. Everything is water related, even items in the gift shop. Rides are geared to all ages, from an 80-foot speed slide and mammoth river rapids to wading pools and kiddie rides. (Six rides have height restrictions and yardsticks for measurement.) Five baby-pool playgrounds are tucked away in a separate area. The tropical bird revue, one of two daily shows, is immensely popular.

WATER PARK WISDOM

Chip Cleary designed and built Splish Splash, Long Island's largest water park, and serves as its president. Formerly with Adventureland in Farmingdale, his vision was to meld the natural landscape with the spirit of Huck Finn. The 50-ish Irishman cherishes his childhood memories of Nunley's, the defunct Baldwin amusement park. (My husband and I took our daughter and her Long Island cousins there when they were tots; we love replaying our 35-millimeter film of the three little girls spinning around together on the tilt-a-whirl.) As an adult, Cleary is a Mel Brooks fan and has placed (mostly corny) signs with double meanings around the park. With it all, he has a serious side and hopes to get his message across to parents who plan to visit his 64-acre attraction. These are some of his tips.

- To avoid crowds, choose an overcast day. Splish Splash averages 8,000 people on a bright sunny day as opposed to 1,500-2,000 in inclement weather. The real water park aficionado knows the day to come is a gray day.

- Avoid peak times of the year when kids are home from camp and blasting their parents for not taking them places. Try not to go to any park in the northeast the last week of the season.

- Arrive a half-hour before the park opens. Most water parks are arranged in a circle. Ask for a park map and head left – opposite the others.

- Do your research beforehand to plan strategy. What are the most popular rides, and when are lines likely to be lightest?

- Don't eat at noon during the stampede. Eat lunch at 11:00am, and see the shows when everyone else is eating.

- Parents should determine if a ride is appropriate for their children; you should look at a ride before your child boards it.

- Mega rule – Choose a meeting place in case you get separated. It amazes me that some parents have no game plan at all. Always educate your children. Show them the uniforms the staff is wearing. Tell them if they get lost to look for people in that type of clothing. Have them practice saying, "My name is Johnny. I am lost."

- What to bring: Bathing suit (without metal buckles), water shoes or old sneakers, ratty towel, water wallet and swim diapers for infants. (All these items are sold at the park.) Rental lockers can be accessed all day. Keys can be rented for $7, $3 of which will be returned after use.

In 2001, Splish Splash was ranked fifth in the "Top 10 USA Waterparks" by the Travel Channel. In a *Newsday* survey of 77 children from third through fifth grades, 43 voted Splish Splash as their favorite Long Island summer attraction – ahead of Jones Beach, Adventureland, Riverhead Aquarium and Bayville Beach & Arcade.

The water park is open on weekends from Memorial Day through mid-June; and daily, from mid-June to Labor Day. The park will also open on the second weekend in September, weather permitting. Admission includes unlimited use of all rides and shows, but there is an additional $6 parking fee. Take the LIE to Exit 72 West.

Turn left at the first traffic light onto Splish Splash
Drive. Plan to buy lunch and snacks at the food court or
bring your own to the picnic pavilion near the main entrance; no food is allowed in the park.

CUSTER INSTITUTE
Bayview Road
Southold
☎ 631-765-2626
www.custerobservatory.org

Starry-eyed? The Custer Institute invites you to observe the night sky (weather permitting) through various telescopes every Saturday at dusk, year-round.
You're asked to walk in and yell since lights are out for
better viewing! See the Institute's Web site for more information about this non-profit facility and it's history,
for special events, or for directions.

Parks & Preserves

Poison Ivy
Leaves of three – Let them be!
                    – Sign in Indian Island County Park

WILDWOOD STATE PARK
Hulse Landing Road
Wading River
☎ 631-929-4314 or 929-4262

Right off Sound Avenue, this rustic 769-acre park is a
perfect stop whether you're shopping for pumpkins or
heading home after a weekend farther out on the North
Fork. It has a large picnic area where you'll find trails
to hike. Before you do that, head down the path to the
beach on Long Island Sound (this is a bathing beach
and a lifeguard is on duty in season). The dunes are
huge and the view is breathtaking. You might decide to
hike the beach instead.

With 242 tent and 80 trailer campsites, this park is a
camper's paradise. Fishermen love it for the saltwater

fishing. (A fishing chart is posted along the beach pathway.) The park also has a playground, snack bar, softball field, and basketball court. Open daily, year-round.

DAVID A. SARNOFF
PINE BARRENS PRESERVE
Route 4
Riverhead
☎ 631-444-0273
www.dec.state.ny.us

The Radio Corporation of America purchased these 2,183 acres of undeveloped land in the early 1900s to conduct pioneering experiments in radio communications and electronics. By the 1920s, this facility, along with the company's facility in Rocky Point, formed the hub of RCA's research in worldwide radio communications. In the mid-1970s, satellite communication technology largely replaced land base stations, and RCA closed the facilities. In 1978, RCA offered the land to the New York State Department of Environmental Conservation. There are 7½ miles of marked trails for hiking, biking and horseback riding. To reach the preserve, take the LIE to Exit 52; go a mile south on Route 4 (Commack Road). Access is by (free) permit only; information is available on their Web site.

Be aware that hunters may be in the Pine Barrens Preserve from October through February.

INDIAN ISLAND COUNTY PARK
Cross River Drive off Route 105
Riverhead
☎ 631-852-3232
Parking fee weekends and holidays, $4; $2 with green key; other fees as listed below

A beautiful woodsy park on the water, next to Indian Island Country Club, this 275-acre county park has 150 tent and trailer campsites, playground, picnic area, field with benches, three swimming pools, tennis, handball, volleyball and basketball courts, ball fields, pond, and ice rink (non-resident fee for two hours: adults, $10; children, $6).

LAUREL LAKE PARK
Main Road
Laurel
☎ 631-765-5182 (Southold Town recreation office)

Laurel Lake Park has a visitor information booth, two baseball fields and a playground. Parking is available for those who wish to use the adjacent state land for fishing (a New York State Fishing License is required and can be obtained at the Town Clerk's Office in Laurel).

MITCHELL PARK
Front Street, between First and Third Streets
Greenport

This park recently opened and features a rehabilitated 1920s glass-enclosed carousel; $1 per ride.

GREENPORT SKATE PARK
Moore Lane
☎ 631-477-1133
www.greenportskatepark.com
Summer: full day, $10; half day, $6
Winter: weekends, $10; weekdays, free

A new skate park has opened in Greenport. There is a fee at all times during the year except weekdays in winter. To reach the park, drive about 50 feet past the 7-11 on Main Road and turn left onto Moore Lane. The skate park is open daily, year-round.

Health & Beauty

Fitness Centers

Advanced Health & Racquet Club, 320 Depot Road, Cutchogue, ☎ 631-734-2897. Full-service health club, two racquetball courts. Day fee, $10 for health club; court fee, $25 per hour. Free childcare. Open daily, year-round.

Sports Rehab Network at **Gladys Brooks Fitness Center**, 46520 North Road, Southold, ☎ 631-765-9389. Small fitness facility and separate physical therapy center. Open Monday-Saturday with evening hours.

Day Spas

New Beginnings Salon Day Spa, 46950 Route 48, Southold, ☎ 631-765-5035. Full-service salon. Open Tuesday-Saturday.

Suki's Spa, 18 Sterlington Commons, Greenport, ☎ 631-477-1864. Full-service hair and spa. Appointments essential. Closed Sunday.

Recreation

Boating

Cruises

ATLANTIS EXPLORER
East Main Road
Riverhead
☎ 631-208-9200
www.atlantismarineworld.com

Take the family aboard Atlantis Marine World's environmental "Tour Boat Adventure," with certified naturalists from the Cornell Cooperative Extension Marine Program. The 2½-hour ecological tour operates April through October along the Peconic River and Flanders Bay.

PECONIC RIVER CRUISES
Riverhead
☎ 631-369-3700
www.peconicrivercruises.com

Step aboard the riverboat *Peconic River Queen* for some sightseeing along the East End. Choose among a three-hour weekday lunch, early-bird dinner, grand buffet dining, Saturday dinner dance, Dixieland Sunday brunch or a full-day excursion. Sails from the Riverhead Village Pier. Recommends two-week advance reservations.

GLORY
Greenport
☎ 631-477-2515
www.greenportlaunch.com

Glory is Long Island's only electric-powered passenger vessel, which means no noise and no fumes. The 45-minute cruise on Peconic Bay, in the words of Captain David Berson, is a transforming experience. Originally designed in the 1890s, the 30-foot fantail launch "goes slow like a sailboat," he says. Passengers bring their own food, but the captain hands out Tootsie Roll Pops as a nostalgic token. Children get bubbles and other goodies and a chance to steer. *Glory* begins sailing on Memorial Day, with five daily cruises, Friday-Monday, until July 4th. Cruises are then run daily until Labor Day, then weekends only through Halloween. Leaves from Preston's Dock (see page 373) at the foot of Main Street.

MARY E
Greenport
☎ 631-477-8966, 516-381-1825
http://themarye.netfirms.com

The *Mary E*, a historic 1906 schooner, sails daily from Preston's Dock with Captain Ted Charles, owner of "Greenport's Official Tallship" for 27 years. Full-day and half-day tours. Season starts June 25.

MALABAR

Greenport

☎ 631-477-3698 (summer); ☎ 207-546-2927 (winter)

www.downeastwindjammer.com

Malabar is a 105-foot schooner departing three times daily from Mitchell Park in Greenport for 1½- to two-hour windjammer sails with Captain Steven F. Pagels. The sunset sail is the most popular and often includes live music. Season begins in May.

PECONIC STAR II

Greenport

☎ 631-289-6899

www.peconicstar.com

This is a 150-passenger cruiser captained by Dave Brennan; from mid-May through November he sails daily from the Greenport Railroad Dock at the end of Third Street, adjacent to the LIRR station and the Shelter Island ferry dock. Moonlight sails are also available.

Charters & Fishing Boats

CELTIC HORIZON II

☎ 631-734-4295

www.celtichorizon.com

Fishing in- or off-shore with Captain Dave Lawrence. Sailing out of Orient Point for full- or half-day sportfishing trips. Family charters are very popular. Operates from May to November.

ISLAND STAR

Mitchell Park, in front of A.P. White Bait Shop

Greenport

☎ 631-696-0936

Captain Dennis' *Island Star* fishing boat, boasts "best in family fishing." Operates from March to Thanksgiving.

Marinas & Boat Rentals

*I am the captain of this ship and I have my wife's
permission to say so.*

— Sign in marine supply store

PECONIC PADDLER
89 Peconic Avenue
Riverhead
☎ 631-369-9500, 727-9895
www.peconicpaddler.com

Kayaks and canoes in stock for rental and sales. Open
year-round. Closed Tuesday.

TREASURE COVE RESORT MARINA
469 East Main Street
Riverhead (On Peconic Bay near Atlantis Marine
World Aquarium)
☎ 631-727-8386
www.treasurecoveresortmarina.com

Transient dockage, canoe/kayak rentals, marine store,
fuel, electric, bait, laundry, restrooms, pool, picnic area,
restaurant (Jerry & the Mermaid; see *Best Places to
Eat*, page 408). Open daily, year-round.

WEST MARINE
☎ 631-369-2628, 800-BOATING
www.westmarine.com

In Suffolk County, West Marine has locations in Riverhead, West Islip, Port Jefferson, Huntington Station,
Babylon, and Patchogue. Everything for the boater:
fishing supplies, electronics, apparel, footwear, books,
videos, charts. Open year-round.

LARRY'S LIGHTHOUSE MARINA
Meetinghouse Creek Road
Aquebogue
☎ 631-722-3400
www.lighthousemarina.com

Sales, dockage, storage, hauling, restrooms, showers, laundry, fuel, deli, marine store, picnic area, pool, restaurant (Meeting House Creek Inn, open year-round; closed Tuesday in off-season; ☎ 631-722-4220). The marina is open daily, year-round.

EAST CREEK MARINA
Town Beach Road
South Jamesport
☎ 631-722-4842

Dockage, fuel, picnic area, bait and tackle, tennis, showers, snack bar, electric, restrooms, beach. Open year-round.

GREAT PECONIC BAY MARINA
Washington Avenue
South Jamesport
☎ 631-722-3565
www.greatpeconicbaymarina.com

Sales, dockage, electric, fuel, hauling, storage, showers, picnic area, beach. Open year-round; closed Monday.

MATT-A-MAR MARINA
Wickham Avenue
Mattituck
☎ 631-298-4739
www.mattamar.com

Dockage, sales, storage, hauling, fuel, picnic area, showers, tours, canoe/kayak sales and rentals, instruction, pool, volleyball, restrooms, electric, snack bar, restaurant (A Touch of Venice, ☎ 631-298-5851; open Tuesday-Sunday, year-round, for lunch and dinner).

MATTITUCK INLET MARINA & SHIPYARD
5780 West Mill Road
Mattituck
☎ 631-298-4480
www./vikingboatsales.com

Sales, storage, fuel, electric, dockage, hauling, showers, pool (open three days a week). Next to Old Mill Inn restaurant (see page 410). Open daily, year-round.

STRONG'S MARINE
Camp Mineola Road
Mattituck
☎ 631-298-4770
www.strongsmarine.com

Boat rentals, repairs, sales, dockage, bait and tackle, electric, hauling, fuel, showers, clubhouse, picnic area, playground, beach. Open daily, year-round. Strong's also has a location in Southampton.

VILLAGE MARINE
175 Bay Avenue (right off Main Road on James Creek)
Mattituck
☎ 631-298-5800

Dockage, sales, storage. Open daily, year-round.

NEW SUFFOLK SHIPYARD
6775 New Suffolk Road
New Suffolk
☎ 631-734-6311

Storage, fuel, electric, hauling, showers, restrooms, marine store. Open daily, year-round.

CAPTAIN MARTY'S
First Avenue & King Street
New Suffolk
☎ 631-734-6852

Boat rentals, complete tackle shop, outboard motor sales and repairs. Open daily from April to October; closed Sunday and Monday in winter.

EAGLE'S NECK PADDLING COMPANY
49295 Main Road
Southold
☎ 631-765-3502
www.eaglesneck.com
www.northfork.com/eaglesneck

Eagle's Neck sells and rents kayaks and canoes and runs guided kayak tours. The company manufactures their own paddles and gives paddling instruction. Offers nightly wildlife/sunset tours at $25 per person; these are especially good for beginning paddlers, says owner Doug Murphy.

PORT OF EGYPT
Main Road
Southold
☎ 631-765-2445, 800-244-8765
www.poemarine.com

Bait and tackle, electric, storage, dockage, fuel, pool, playground, marine store, showers, laundry, boat sales, motel and restaurant (Seafood Barge, see page 413). Open daily, year-round.

ALBERTSON MARINE
Main Road (next to Port of Egypt)
Southold
☎ 631-765-3232
www.albertsonmarine.com

Sales, marine store, docking, storage, electric, hauling, restrooms. Bait and tackle next door. Open daily, March

through November; closed Sunday, December through
February.

GOLDSMITH'S BOAT SHOP
Main Road
Southold
☎ 631-765-1600
www.goldsmithboatshop.com

Storage, dockage, sales, hauling, fuel, restrooms. Open
daily, year-round.

SOUNDVIEW SCUBA
46455 Route 48
Southold
☎ 631-765-9515
www.webmarket.com/soundview

Soundview offers kayaking tours, in addition to sales
and rentals of kayaks, scuba diving equipment, skis
and wake board equipment, wetsuits and dry suits.
Also teaches water skiing, spearfishing and scuba diving. Open daily, year-round.

SOUTHOLD MARINE CENTER
49900 Main Road
Southold
☎ 631-765-3131

Storage, dockage, marine store, hauling, restrooms.
Open daily, year-round.

BREWER YACHT YARD
Manhanset Avenue
(mailing address: 500 Beach Road)
Greenport
☎ 631-477-9594
www.byy.com

Storage, dockage, sales, hauling, showers, electric, restrooms, pool, laundry. Open daily, year-round. Seasonal
restaurant (Antares Café, ☎ 631-477-8839) open for

Boating 373

Suffolk County's North Fork

lunch and dinner daily, late March through November; Thursday-Monday, December through mid-March.

CLAUDIO'S MARINA
Main Street
Greenport
☎ 631-477-0355
www.claudios.com

Dockage, fuel, showers, snack bar, clam bar, electric, restroom. Open May-October. The Claudio family has been in Greenport since 1870 and **Claudio's Restaurant**, ☎ 631-477-0627, is advertised as the "Oldest Same-Family Owned Restaurant in the United States." Open mid-April through December; closed Tuesday. Other dining options are the **Wharf Clam Bar**, ☎ 631-477-1889, open May-October, closed Wednesday; **Crabby Jerry's**, a self-serve family eatery, ☎ 631-477-8252; and **Sweet Temptations**, closed Wednesday. All are seasonal.

PRESTON'S
Main Street Wharf
Greenport
☎ 631-477-1990
www.prestons.com

Dockage, tackle, electric, marine store, dinghy dock. A replica of a great blue heron guards the dock. Open daily, year-round. S.T. Preston & Son has been at Main Street Wharf for 122 years and has two gift shops and a showroom; see *Shop Till You Drop*, page 385.

STIRLING HARBOR SHIPYARD & MARINA
1410 Manhanset Avenue
Greenport
☎ 631-477-0828

Fuel, electric, pool, cabana, tennis, spa, mini-resort, restrooms. Open year-round.

NARROW RIVER MARINA
Narrow River Road
Orient
☎ 631-323-2660

Canoe and kayak rentals, dockage, storage, hauling,
electric, restrooms. Open mid-April through October.

ORIENT BY THE SEA MARINA
Main Road
Orient
☎ 631-323-2424

Dockage, summer storage, electric, fuel, showers and
restaurant, Orient by the Sea. Open daily, May through
November.

COECLES HARBOR MARINA & BOATYARD
Hudson Avenue
Shelter Island
☎ 631-749-0700

Dockage, storage, hauling, pool, picnic area, marine
store, laundry, showers, restrooms, fuel, electric. Open
from May 15 to October 15.

DERING HARBOR MARINA
Bridge Street, at J.W. Piccozzi service station
Shelter Island
☎ 631-749-0045

Showers, restrooms, laundry, transient dockage, bike
shop (see page 378). Open May 15-October 15.

SHELTER ISLAND KAYAK TOURS
Route 114 & Duvall Street
Shelter Island
☎ 631-749-1990
www.kayaksi.com

Guided kayak trips twice a day, with complimentary
water and snacks. Rentals and sales of kayaks. Open

April-October, but phone appointments are welcome year-round.

Ferry Service

Cross Sound Ferry, ☎ 631-323-2525 (from Long Island) or 860-443-5281 (from Connecticut), www.long-islandferry.com, has been providing year-round vehicle and passenger service between Orient Point and New London, Connecticut for 20 years. Call for fare and schedule information.

The *Sea Jet Express* is Cross Sound Ferry's high-speed, passenger-only ferry; it makes daily trips to New London from April through November, with hourly service during the summer. Shuttle buses at the dock in New London take you to Foxwoods or Mohegan Sun casinos.

Beaches

On The Sound

The beaches on **Long Island Sound** tend to be pebbly, and sneakers are advised for walking on the sand. Parking at town beaches when an attendant is present requires a permit. Non-resident parking permits for Riverhead Town beaches are $10 per day and available at all beaches and the recreation department office, ☎ 631-727-5744. Southold Town charges $12 per day for beach parking; daily passes are available at beaches with attendants and at Town Hall, ☎ 631-765-1801.

Wading River Beach at Wildwood State Park, Wading River, ☎ 631-929-4262 or 631-929-4314, is at Hulse Landing Road off Sound Avenue; it has a bathhouse, lifeguard, boardwalk, and snack bar. Saltwater fishing is permitted year-round. Open daily, year-round. The fee for parking in this state park is $7; for more information on the park, see *Parks & Preserves*, page 362.

Reeves Park Beach is a Riverhead Town beach at the end of Park Road, off Sound Avenue. Lifeguards, restrooms.

Iron Pier Beach, at the end of Pier Avenue off Sound Avenue in Jamesport, has restrooms, boat ramp, lifeguards.

Breakwater Park, on the sound, with parking area and restrooms, located on the west side of Mattituck Inlet, and **Bailie's Beach Park**, on the east side of the inlet, are Mattituck Park District beaches.

Goldsmith Inlet County Park, Peconic, is a 60-acre park with a half-mile hiking trail leading to the sound. Goldsmith Inlet is at the end of Mill Road on the sound. There is a restroom but no lifeguard. Limited off-road parking is available on Soundview Avenue.

McCabe's Beach, North Sea Road, is at the end of Horton Lane on the sound. Lifeguards, restrooms.

Southold Town Beach is a sound beach on North Road. Lifeguards, restrooms, playground, picnic area.

Kenneys Beach, Kenneys Road, Southold is on the sound. Restrooms, lifeguards.

Truman Beach off Route 25 on the sound is an Orient-East Marion Park District beach with no services.

On The Bays

Peconic Bay beaches tend to be warmer and shallower, and the sand less pebbly, which makes them ideal for children. Guests at lodgings should ask the innkeeper for a beach pass. Some have passes for both town and park district beaches.

South Jamesport Beach, Jamesport Avenue, off Peconic Bay Boulevard on Peconic Bay, has lifeguards, playground, bathhouse, showers, food stand, tennis courts, picnic area, and basketball court.

New Suffolk Beach, Jackson Street, is at the end of New Suffolk Avenue on the bay. Lifeguards, boat launch, restroom and ample parking facilities.

Goose Creek Beach is off North Bayview Road on the bay in Southold. Lifeguards, playground, restrooms.

Norman E. Klipp Marine Park (a/k/a Gull Pond Beach) is a Southold Town beach at the end of Manhanset Avenue, Greenport, featuring lifeguards, playground on sand, boat launch and large parking lot. To reach the park from Route 48 heading east, drive a few blocks past the turnoff for Greenport to Manhanset Avenue. From Main Street, take Champlain Place to the end (at cemetery) and turn right.

Two Southold Park District bay beaches are free to residents and their guests. **Emerson Park**, located at the end of South Harbor Road, is a sandy beach with no lifeguards on duty. **Founders Landing**, at the end of Hobart Road, has picnic tables, swings, restrooms, roped-off swimming area, and lifeguards.

Nassau Point Beach on Little Peconic Bay, and **Pequash Avenue Beach** (a/k/a Fleets Neck Beach), are Cutchogue-New Suffolk Park District bay beaches. Both have playgrounds, picnic tables and grills, basketball court, handicapped-accessible ramp, roped-off swimming areas, restrooms and lifeguards.

Orient Beach State Park, ☎ 631-323-2440, an Orient-East Marion Park District beach, is on Main Road, Orient Point; it's a 48-acre park with a mile-long bay beach and half-mile hiking trail. Amenities include snack bar, picnic area, bathhouse, playground, restrooms, dressing rooms, playing field, fishing. Located at the end of Route 25; Parking, $7.

Biking

Sales & Rentals

Country Time Cycle, 6695 Main Road, Mattituck, ☎ 631-298-8700, www.ctcycle.com. Open year-round; daily in season, closed Sunday and Monday in off-season.

Thistlebees, a new country and antiques shop on Main Road, Cutchogue, ☎ 631-734-5362. Rents bikes in summer. Reserve ahead to guarantee availability. Call for store hours.

Bike Stop, 200 Front Street, Greenport, ☎ 631-477-2432. Rents mountain, hybrid, and tandem bikes. Open year-round; closed Tuesday.

Piccozzi's Bicycle Shop, Bridge Street, Shelter Island (in Piccozzi's gas station, at Dering Harbor Marina), ☎ 631-749-0045. Bike sales and rentals include mountain and English bikes. Open daily, May-November.

Horseback Riding

Hillcrest Sport Horses, 1219 Middle Road, Riverhead, ☎ 631-369-1176. Hillcrest has 40 horses, an indoor arena, hunt course, dressage, jump ring. Private and semi-private lessons. Minimum age five. Also boards, trains and sells horses. Open daily, year-round.

Hidden Lake Farm Riding School, Route 48, Southold, ☎ 631-765-9896. Hidden Lake Farm has an indoor arena, cross-country course, three rings, pony camp, "fox hunting" in winter, shows in summer, beach and woodland trails. Offers horseback riding and private and group lessons in English style, hunt and equitation in indoor arena and outdoor course. Open daily, year-round.

Golf

Great Rock Golf Club, Fairway Drive off Sound Avenue, Wading River, ☎ 631-929-1200. A quote from a golfer in one of its ads reads: "This is a monstrous, uphill, 444-yard, par 4." Readers of *Dan's Papers* voted Great Rock as having the Best 10th Hole on any public or semi-private golf course on the East End. Features include pro shop, lessons, rentals, driving range. A restaurant, Blackwells, is open for lunch and dinner, year-round; closed Monday night; ☎ 631-929-1800.

Who was voted the Best 11th Hole? **Long Island National Golf Club**, 1793 Northville Turnpike, Riverhead, ☎ 631-727-4653. This semi-private 18-hole, par 71 course features a pro shop, lessons, rentals, practice area, and a restaurant. Both course and restaurant are open April-November.

Cherry Creek Golf Links, 900 Reeves Avenue, Riverhead, ☎ 631-369-6500, www.cherrycreeklinks.com. A few miles off the LIE, this privately owned par 73 course has a clubhouse, pro shop, driving range, practice bunker and an extra-large practice putting green. It also boasts the Metropolitan area's only par 6 hole (on the 18th green). Elevated tees. Soft spikes are mandatory. Carts are required from Friday to Sunday. A friend who has played the course characterizes it as relatively easy. Open year-round; call a week ahead for tee times. The 19th Hole Restaurant, ☎ 631-369-7294, is open weather permitting.

Indian Island Golf Course, Indian Island Country Club, Riverside Drive, Riverhead, ☎ 631-244-7776, is on the site of a former duck farm, offering scenic views of the Peconic River. Among its newest features are a computerized irrigation system and the planting of 150 trees throughout the 18-hole, par 72 course.

Island's End Golf & Country Club, Route 25, Greenport, ☎ 631-477-0777. A semi-private 18-hole, par 72 course open to the public for a daily fee. Tee times available a week in advance. Open daily, year-round.

Suffolk County's North Fork

Shop Till You Drop

Malls & Shopping Streets

TANGER OUTLET CENTER
LIE, Exit 72
Riverhead
☎ 631-369-2732; ☎ 1-800-407-4894 for Customer Service; ☎ 1-800-4-TANGER
www.tangeroutlet.com

All of these establishments are open year-round unless otherwise noted.

This outdoor mall has almost 200 stores, including 170 brand-name outlets such as Gap, Banana Republic and Lenox. Open Monday through Saturday, 9am-9pm; Sunday, 10am-7pm.

SWEZEY'S
111 East Main Street
Riverhead
☎ 631-477-8737
www.swezeys.com

You'll find more thrift shops than high-end stores in the village of Riverhead, although several independent stores have thankfully survived. Swezey's, owned by the same family for its 106 years in business, is an institution on Long Island. What is the secret of its lasting success? Customer service and a liberal return policy. In Riverhead, plans are afoot to centralize the department store, furniture store and gift shop into a single space across Main Street from the current location. The new quarters will include an escalator and elevator.

Swezey's has other branches in **Patchogue** (225 West Main Street, ☎ 631-475-0280); **East Setauket** (Three Village Plaza Shopping Center, ☎ 631-689-9800); **Glen Cove** (24 School Street, ☎ 516-609-2700); and **West Babylon** (Great South Bay Shopping Center, Open daily; ☎ 631-661-2900).

Specialty Shops

HEIRLOOM COUNTRY COLLECTIBLES
31 McDermott Avenue
Riverhead
☎ 631-727-5909
www.heirloomcountry.com

Located on the bank of the Peconic River in downtown
Riverhead, this shop specializes in 100% cotton fabrics
for quilters in a full spectrum of solids, prints and
plaids. Quilting lessons are provided daytime, evening
and weekend. The shop also sells candles, Boyds Bears,
handcrafted dolls and other gift items. Open daily in
fall and winter; closed Sunday in July and August.

BRIERMERE FARMS
4414 Sound Avenue
Riverhead
☎ 631-722-3931

Don't leave the North Fork without stopping at Brier-
mere Farms; its fruit pies are renowned for good reason. One fall day I counted 25 varieties! Located at the
junction of Sound Avenue and Route 105. Open daily.

> ★ TIP
>
> Continue eastward on Sound Ave-
> nue for fruit and vegetable stands.
> If you're hungry, only a short dis-
> tance from Briermere Farms on
> Sound Avenue is **Wegert's Gro-
> cery**, open all the time.

WILL MILOSKI'S POULTRY FARM
Route 25
Calverton
☎ 631-727-0239

Bring your kids to see the turkeys in the field, who are
oblivious to their fate. Turkeys, ducks, geese and phea-

sants are the name of the game here, sold fresh or cooked. Closed Tuesday.

ARLINES
1116 Main Road
Aquebogue
☎ 631-722-8045
www.arlines.com

This is the place to go for your summer or winter needs be it clothing, skateboards, or backpacks.

JAMESPORT COUNTRY STORE
Main Road
Jamesport
☎ 631-722-8048

Stop in and visit this wonderful old-fashioned country emporium run by three generations of the Waldman family since 1973. Out front is a Sinclair gas pump from 1951 (not for sale) that registers 25¢ a gallon! The store carries the popular Yankee Candle products along with bent willow and wicker furniture. In the fall, Howard Waldman roasts peanuts on his 1915 peanut machine. The store is housed in a red brick building that was once the home of the telephone company. The newspaper announcement of the phone company's move into the building in 1931 noted that Jamesport was now disconnected from the Riverhead central office and hooked up to the new central office, and subscribers were now able to dial all of Jamesport directly. Open daily, 10am-5:30pm.

TIP

Antiques addict? One block of antiques stores awaits you on Route 25 in Jamesport across from the cemetery. The exception is **Cozy Corner Collectibles**, which sells doll houses and miniatures and posts a sign reading "No Antiques." The **North Fork Antique Dealers Association** maintains a Web site at www.northforkantiques.com.

TOM HEALTY'S FRUITWOOD SMOKED FISH & FOWL
3543 Sound Avenue
Riverhead
☎ 631-727-5877

Next stop is for some local tuna, bluefish, Atlantic salmon, Long Island duck legs or eels (after October 10). All smoking is done on the premises. Open Wednesday-Sunday.

LOVE LANE
Mattituck

Love Lane, a pretty tree-lined block in Mattituck, was once used as a canoe path for Indians moving from the Sound to the Peconic Bay. It later became a lover's lane. So it's surprising that most of its shops are utilitarian – post office, barber, pharmacy, launderette, bank, nail salon, bank, market and deli. As explained by Lauretta Bauer, proprietor of Bauer's, a gift shop on the street, "This is our village." Visitors who stroll down Love Lane will enjoy the exceptions.

♦ **Bauer's**, 100 Love Lane, ☎ 631-298-0204. This is primarily a gift shop with a wonderful scent from Greenleaf sachets. The store also carries Vera Bradley bags, small antique items and unusual lamps.

♦ **Love Lane Sweet Shoppe**, 124 Love Lane, ☎ 631-298-2276, or 800-371-0086, www.lovelanesweets.com. This shop specializes in chocolates, gift boxes, greeting cards, reproduction ceramic carousel horses, wine totes and picnic baskets.

♦ **Rudy's Gourmet Coffee & Ice Cream Bar**, 10 Love Lane, ☎ 631-298-7407. Like Rudy's Bookworm Café in the Riverhead library, the décor here encourages coziness. This one has old upholstered chairs and couches to sink into with a good book and a cup of café; it also has a pool table.

THE DOWN HOME STORE
Main Road and Skunk Lane
Cutchogue
☎ 631-734-6565

Bears are its trademark but the Down Home Store is not a country store. It carries everything from one-of-a-kind gift items to books, linens, greeting cards and hand-painted furniture. The work of local artists is featured and an alcove is devoted to children's clothing. Deliveries are made daily so the merchandise is always changing. Open March-December; closed Tuesday.

GREENPORT
As someone wrote in one of the complimentary publications, "It would take a whole book to write about the wacky and wonderful shops in the harborside Village of Greenport." Below is a mere sampling of the dozens of stores concentrated mainly on Front and Main Streets in Greenport, all open daily, year-round.

More information on North Fork shopping can be found on-line at www.northfork.org/shopping.html.

♦ **Coastal Candleworks**, 110 Front Street (across from the carousel), ☎ 631-477-3515, www.coastalcandleworks.com. Hand-carved, custom-colored refillable candles that glow from within are one of the many products sold here. The store also carries crystal oil lamps and oil-burning ceramic lighthouses. Customers are welcome to watch owner/carver Jeffrey Colton or an apprentice demonstrate candlemaking.

♦ **Nature's Wild Side**, 8 Front Street, ☎ 631-477-0402. This shop is jam-packed with windsocks, kites, Woodstock chimes, flags, weather instruments and other free-flowing items.

♦ **Burton's Bookstore**, 43 Front Street, ☎ 631-477-1161. Burton's is a family-run business that specializes in books on nautical themes, local interest and children's books. The store also has a nice selection of cookbooks.

♦ **S.T. Preston & Son**, on the Main Wharf, ☎ 631-477-1990. Preston's has two gift shops. One is a catalogue showroom store (their mail-order catalogue of ship models, marine clocks, etc. is sent to six million homes). The other shop is a maritime gallery where most of the merchandise is for sale. A section is set aside for Christmas items, beginning in September.

♦ **Claudio's Little Wheel Gift Shop**, 111 Main Street, ☎ 631-477-0627. Claudio's gift shop is next to its restaurant (see page 373) and carries sports apparel and mementos.

♦ **Curran's Irish Shop**, 119 Main Street, ☎ 631-477-3503. Farther up the street is this shop featuring Waterford crystal, Nicholas Mosse pottery, jewelry and Irish knits. From January through March, Curran's is open only on weekends.

♦ **Goldsmith's**, 138 Main Street, ☎ 631-477-0466. Across the road from Curran's is Goldsmith's, which carries specialized, made-in-USA toys such as Thomas Trains, along with small electronics.

♦ **Just Kid'n**, 44 Front Street, ☎ 631-477-1100, is a childrens' store carrying clothing in sizes 0-16, toys, books, gifts and accessories.

♦ **Just Diva**, behind Just Kid'n, is geared to womens' junior sizes 1-13. Just Diva and Just Kid'n are open daily in summer, 9:30am-9pm; call for winter openings (as of this writing, Just Diva does not have a phone).

♦ **Zeller's Pastry Shop**, 37 Front Street at Bootleg Alley, ☎ 631-477-1306. Bootleg Alley was no doubt the path of the rumrunners who conducted a thriving business on the Greenport waterfront during Prohibition. Today, instead of the smell of whiskey, it's the aroma of homemade bread, cakes, cookies, scones and cinnamon rolls wafting along. The bakery also makes sugar-free cookies. Call for winter hours.

♦ **Special Effects**, 455 Main Street, ☎ 631-477-2265, www.special-effects.com. Now it's time to relax. This full-service salon and retreat is housed in a funky old house. Treatments run from a $7 lip waxing to a $228 retreat package. The premises include a small boutique and beauty parlor. Open Tuesday-Saturday in season, and Thursday-Saturday in winter.

THE CANDYMAN
Main Road
Orient
☎ 631-323-2675

If you love homemade chocolate, this family-owned shop – started in the 1930s in Glen Cove – still makes it the old-fashioned way. The store has gift baskets, chocolate covered strawberries (dipped in the morning), truffles – you name it. They will ship orders to customers, except in summer. Open daily, except in January.

 # After Dark

The Arts

EAST END ARTS COUNCIL
133 East Main Street
Riverhead
☎ 631-727-0900
www.riverheadli.com/eeac.html

Founded in 1972, the council is located in two historic residences: the **Benjamin** and **Corwin** homes. It sponsors a variety of events, such as year-round rotating gallery exhibitions, dance performances, children's theater, the Wine Press concert series at North Fork vineyards, and an annual Harvest Gospel concert at three churches. The Council also runs a school for theater and art, and a summer camp.

Bars & Clubs

THE FLATTED FIFTH
70 West Main Street
Riverhead
☎ 631-369-5323

Riverhead's only blues and jazz club; serves Southern style food.

RUDY'S COFFEE BAR
Love Lane
Mattituck
☎ 631-298-7407

Rudy's features live entertainment (folk singers, acoustic acts) Friday and Saturday. Now serves beer and wine in addition to coffees, desserts and cheese platters. Also sells cigars. Mixed crowd. Open daily, year-round

THE ½ SHELL RESTAURANT
10300 Main Road
☎ 631-298-4180
Mattituck

This restaurant (see *Lite Bites*, page 415) features weekend entertainment.

BAY & MAIN
300 Main Street
Greenport
☎ 631-477-1442

Bay & Main has live light jazz on weekends (see *Best Places to Eat*, page 414).

Festivals & Events

June

The three-day **Strawberry Festival** in Mattituck includes an array of strawberry delights to savor along with entertainment and craft vendors. Mid-June; ☎ 631-298-2222.

Greenport's **Lighthouse and Maritime History Cruises** in early June take passengers to numerous historic Long Island lighthouses. The cruises cost $85 and include continental breakfast, lunch, entertainment, historical narration and raffles. Call the LI chapter of the United States Light House Society (USLHS) at ☎ 631-477-2121.

July

The three-day **Riverhead Blues Festival** is held the third weekend in July at the Peconic Riverfront in downtown Riverhead. Musicians jam to various styles of music. For a complete list of performers, visit the festival's Web site at www.riverheadblues.com, or call ☎ 631-727-0048.

August

Riverhead has a large Polish community, centered on Pulaski Street. You'll know you're there when you see the old-style street lamps, decorative shutters, and a sign that reads: Krakow: 3,786 miles. The **Riverhead Polish Town Fair & Polka Festival** in mid-August features more than 200 vendors showcasing food, art, crafts; also polka music and corn-husking contest. Free. Two miles east of LIE Exit 73. ☎ 631-369-1616, www.polishtownusa.com.

:

September

The **Maritime Festival** in Greenport features a parade, clam shucking contests, whale boat races, air-sea rescue operations, roving pirates, street fair and music. Usually held near the end of the month; ☎ 631-477-2100.

October

The **Riverhead Country Fair** celebrates its agricultural heritage with best-of-show produce (including pumpkins weighing hundreds of pounds), homemade goodies, carnival rides, tractor pulls, folk music and 500 craft, antique and food vendors along Main Street and the Peconic waterfront. The fair is usually held on a weekend early in the month; call for this year's dates. Free admission. ☎ 631-727-1215 or 727-7600.

Best Places to Stay

All accommodations on the North Fork are close enough to the wineries to include them in your agenda.

Room rates generally fall between $150 and $180. The B&Bs usually have only queen beds so it's advisable to inquire if you want otherwise.

ACCOMMODATIONS PRICE SCALE	
Price scale is based on the cost of a standard double room, two people per room on a weekend, and does not include the 9¼% hotel tax.	
Inexpensive	under $130
Moderate	$130-$200
Expensive	$201-$300
Deluxe	more than $300

Hotels & Inns

Jamesport

RED BARN B&B
733 Herricks Lane
Jamesport
☎ 631-722-3695
www.northfork.com/redbarn
Moderate

Pets are sometimes welcome at Red Barn; ask in advance.

Would you like to stay in a 19th-century farmhouse with weathered red barns surrounded by fields as far as the eye can see? Perhaps the grueling life of a farmer and smell of manure doesn't appeal to you. Well, in this case the two-story house was lovingly restored and the guest rooms are spacious and airy. In place of cows to milk or chickens to feed you're treated to terrific gourmet breakfasts made from local produce.

Red Barn opened as a B&B in September 2001. Former Glen Cove residents Linda and Jim Slezak spent three years restoring the 1877 farmhouse once owned by Lemuel Beecher Hallock, grandson of one of the founding families on the North Fork. The main floor retains the original doorframes and wood floor.

The house is on two acres, surrounded by vineyards and tree farms. The one suite and two guest rooms all have private baths. The décor is country and the wide pine plank floors absolutely glisten. There is a common sitting room for guests and a TV downstairs.

Linda loves to bake, and her mushroom tarts and coconut bars are superb. In warm weather, breakfast and afternoon tea are served on the porch. Jim is an amateur astronomer with professional-quality telescopes who'll happily show you the stars (some New York City residents have never seen them!).

Guests can relax in the hammock, borrow a bicycle or head for the beach on either Peconic Bay (1½ miles) or Long Island Sound (one mile). Beach passes are available. Red Barn is across from Martha Clara Vineyards, a 66-mile drive from the Throg's Neck bridge. Take the LIE to Exit 71. Make a left onto Edwards Avenue and continue north for about four miles to Sound Avenue. From there, go east about nine miles to Herrick's Lane (about a half-mile past the sign for Hallockville Farms and Museum) and make a right. Open April-October and winter weekends on request.

Mattituck

MATTITUCK MOTEL
2150 Bay Avenue
Mattituck
☎ 631-298-4131
www.mattituckmotel.com
Inexpensive to Moderate

The Mattituck Motel is more like an inn than a typical motel, so I've placed it in this section. All 19 units are nicely decorated, comfortable and have wood-paneled walls, TV, telephone and refrigerator. The rooms range in size from standard to spacious and include a two-bedroom apartment and three one-bedroom apartments.

The new owner, a general contractor by trade and an experienced innkeeper, has plans to upgrade the two-acre property, installing new beds, sundeck and handicapped-accessible rooms.

Inquire at the Mattituck Motel about monthly promotions tied in with local attractions.

With a wealth of information on the North Fork, he seems to have infinite patience in helping guests with their travel plans. Guests have access to the tennis courts across the street. Two passes are available for guests, one for all beaches in the Town of Southold and one for those under the jurisdiction of the Southold Park District (the bay beach and park within walking distance of the motel fall in the latter category). For those who prefer to stay put, there are grills on the property and picnic tables under the shade of old oak trees. Forget to bring something? The motel is less than a half-mile from Route 25 and a Waldbaum's supermarket and Genovese drugstore.

Mattituck is about 83 miles from the Throgs Neck bridge. To reach the motel, take Route 25 into Mattituck; continue past Waldbaum's, and turn right at the Hess Station onto Bay Avenue. You'll see a big sign for the motel.

Cutchogue

VINTAGE BED AND BREAKFAST
580 Skunk Lane
Cutchogue
☎ 631-734-2053
www.northfork.com/vintagebnb
Moderate

The Vintage is unique in that it was designed and built as a B&B, with one-third of the house for guests' use. Opened in August 2001, the Georgian-style Colonial is on 2.65 acres and is tastefully decorated in a vineyard theme with gleaming wood floors. The three guest rooms are the color of Chardonnay, Merlot or Zinfandel and the main entrance is in grape. Each room has a private bath, whirlpool tub and super-thick featherbed. Guests have their own entrance, a common room with TV, and tasting room for complimentary samples of local wines. "We want people to feel they are in their own home," says Jeanne Genovese, who lives with husband, Lou, their two young children and two dogs on the other side of the house.

Jeanne likes to pamper guests by having a pot of coffee ready in the morning, preparing a sensational gourmet breakfast on Saturday and a champagne breakfast on Sunday. "We want people to leave as friends," she says.

While living in Sayville, the Genovese family often visited the North Fork. They moved east with the idea of building a B&B. "Build it and they will come," winemakers told them. Lou makes his own wine as a hobby and when the basement is finished a portion will be used as a wine cellar. The couple also plan to add an in-ground pool and exercise room.

The Vintage is 16 miles from the LIE; continue east on Route 25 and turn right on Skunk Lane (the Down Home Store is on the corner). It's the seventh house on the right. Look for sign in driveway.

WHAT'S IN A NAME?

Cabbage farms were once abundant in this area, and when cabbages are cooked we all know the smell – like skunk. Legend has it that this is how Skunk Lane got its name.

Southold

SHORECREST B&B
54300 North Road
Southold
☎ 631-765-1570
www.northfork.com/shorecrest
Moderate to Expensive

If Susan and John Barnes were not as quick to anticipate a guest's every need and operate their two-year-old B&B like veterans, the formal furnishings and exquisite antiques might be a bit intimidating. But what can ordinary folk expect?

Simply this: down-to-earth people sensitive to their guests' frenetic lives. The couple once lived by the clock, too – he was a school superintendent in Sag Harbor, she a school psychologist. This is a place to relax as you wish – an elderly German gentleman found this out when he discovered weathered German books on the shelves. "We try to create an atmosphere to let people disappear for a day or two," says Susan.

Disappear to the town beach across the road (Shorecrest overlooks Long Island Sound) or take a kayak out on Hashamomuck Pond behind the house (see *Boat Rentals*, pages 368-374). At night, you may want to take advantage of the bath salts left out for your enjoyment and then disappear under the copious covers.

One room can convert to a bridal suite and has a feather-bed to sink into – via a stepladder.

Shorecrest is a pre-Victorian mansion with four guest rooms, two with en-suite full baths and two with semi-private baths. The back porch overlooks the pond, replete with osprey, egrets and cormorants. Candlelit gourmet breakfasts are served in the elegant dining room – all adding up to a fairy-tale escape.

Follow Route 25 to Southold. In Southold, turn left on Young's Avenue (at stoplight) and go .6 mile to Route 48 (North Road). Turn right and continue 1.5 miles to the Town Beach (on your left). Proceed 300 feet to Ruch Lane (on your right). Shorecrest is the first house on the left. The B&B is open year-round.

COEUR DES VIGNES
57225 Main Road
Southold
☎ 631-765-2656
www.coeurdesvignes.com
Moderate

Coeur des Vignes means heart of the vines.

Now housing a B&B and a restaurant (See *Best Places to Eat*, page 412), the building dates back to 1760, when it was a carriage stop. The burgundy-and-white color scheme of the restaurant carries through to the four lovely guest rooms. Each fairly large room has a queen-size sleigh bed, private bath, multiple windows and fresh flowers. Two rooms have chimney walls. TV is available on demand. Guests may enjoy complimentary continental breakfast and Sunday Champagne Brunch. Coeur des Vignes is open year-round.

Greenport

THE GREENPORTER HOTEL AND SPA
326 Front Street
Greenport
☎ 631-477-0066
www.thegreenporter.com
Moderate to Expensive

Like the Atlantic, Bentley and Capri in Southampton (see page 509), The Greenporter is a boutique hotel that has been transformed from a rundown motel. The Greenporter was designed inside and out by New York City architect Wendy Evans Joseph, who grew up in Woodmere and once worked with noted architect I.M. Pei. All rooms open to the custom-designed heated swimming pool and are surrounded by a translucent rippled fence that lets in light and assures privacy. The ultra-modern interiors have light wood floors and aluminum desktops that cascade wave-like over the wall-to-wall unit. A strip of photos of Greenport by a local photographer is the sole decoration and there's an in-room safe and minibar. According to owner Deborah Rivera, The Greenporter is the first American hotel to provide the Annick Goutal line of soaps and lotions from Paris in its rooms. The bed, with a fluffy 6" mattress resting on a steel frame, gives its occupant a night's sleep of sheer heaven.

At this writing, there are 15 units; an additional 13 are being built. Spa services are in-room until the spa facility is completed, and must be booked in advance. A wine bar and retractable canopy for the outdoor deck are also under construction.

The inn is conveniently located in town near the wharf and stores. It's directly across from Ternhaven Cellars, which bills itself as the last winery before Paris (see page 357). The Greenporter is open year-round. Children under 12 stay free in parents' room. Pet-friendly; any size pet is $50, plus a $100 refundable deposit.

Greenport is a one-square-mile village with 2,100 residents.

HARBOR KNOLL

424 Fourth Street
Greenport
☎ 631-477-2352
www.northfork.com/harborknoll
Expensive

Inquire about family packages at Harbor Knoll.

If you prefer a Victorian-era Dutch Colonial with a fabulous view and a private beach, within walking distance of town, this B&B is for you. Opened in July 2001, Harbor Knoll has four homey guest rooms piled high with books and magazines. There are in-room TVs and private baths down the hall. The house has the delightful nooks and crannies that lend charm to old houses and traditional furnishings with a nautical theme. All rooms but one have panoramic views of Greenport Harbor, which is especially striking at dusk when ships return and light the darkening skies. During the summer, the harbor is busy with yacht races and tall ship flotillas.

Leueen and Gordon Miller purchased the waterfront property as a vacation home 29 years ago when their children were young. Greenport was then a shabby hick town and friends inquired with astonishment, "You bought a house *where*?"

The Marine Foundation oversees the Seaport Museum, the Bug Light, the Maritime Festival and offers boating safety programs.

Not one to sit still, Leueen serves as president and chair of the East End Seaport Museum & Marine Foundation (see pages 344-345) and is an ambassador for the Cornell Extension Program for oyster farmers. Prior to taking up innkeeping, she was UN Ambassador to Romania and Cyprus. Both roles require diplomacy, she says.

To reach Harbor Knoll, take Main Street to Front Street and turn right. Make a left at Fourth Street and turn into the first gravel driveway on the left. Follow the driveway toward the water and turn right at the last entrance. Open year-round.

East Marion

TREASURE ISLAND B&B
14909 Main Road
East Marion
☎ 631-477-2788
Expensive

You couldn't ask for nicer views than from this waterfront estate. Set off from the road by a winding driveway, the B&B is sandwiched between Truman Beach and Long Island Sound on the north and Orient Harbor and Gardiners Bay on the south. Buffet breakfast, of course, is enjoyed al fresco whenever possible.

Lovingly restored, the 1895 Dutch Colonial-style house has three suites, all with water views. Each has a customized antique bed, fireplace and sitting room. One suite has a private bath; two share a bath-and-a-half in a private area that would be ideal accommodations for close friends or relatives. Owners Marjorie and Norman Whitehead hail from Rhode Island and have been operating the B&B for six years. The house has been in her family since 1922. It originally had no bathrooms so all of them are newly installed.

Marjorie prides herself on a meticulous and quiet atmosphere and abhors high tech in such a setting. Thus, there are no rate sheets, brochures or Web site. "This is more for people who like nature," she says – glorious sunsets, bird watching, canoeing, fishing, hiking, swimming or biking. Complimentary refreshments are always available and beach towels and parking permits are provided.

Located three miles east of Greenport on Route 25, the B&B is five miles west of the Orient Point ferry docks. Heading east, the driveway is the first left on the causeway and from the west it's the last right before crossing the causeway. Open year-round.

QUINTESSENTIALS BED & BREAKFAST SPA
8985 Main Road
East Marion
☎ 631-477-9400
www.quintessentialsinc.com
Moderate (spa services extra)

Inquire about Quintessentials' overnight spa package, which includes breakfast, afternoon tea, two massages and a $25 credit toward wine and dessert at a local restaurant.

Why not combine a relaxing weekend with an on-premises facial or European massage? Proprietor Sylvia Daley is a licensed massage therapist who caters to the rejuvenation of mind, body and spirit with such spa services as Reiki energy balancing, makeup lessons and paraffin wraps. "Quintessential" in this case means not only the "purest, most perfect" but also plays on her five-star logo representing the five heavenly bodies.

Sylvia knows about stress. As a high-powered business executive who speaks four languages, she lived and worked in countries all over the world. In 1995 she opened the B&B following a massive restoration. Built in 1840, the house originally belonged to a captain and retains the widow's walk, a small space at the top of the house where wives would pace while awaiting return of their seafaring spouses.

Simply furnished, the 15-room house is enormously comfortable. Each of five large guest rooms has a private bath, TV and cheerful florals. Children are welcome, as evidenced by coloring books and toys. In Jamaica, where she was born, "children are part of the fabric," shares Sylvia, a spunky woman who wants her guests to have a "complete experience," i.e., massage and full "brunch" breakfast – even if it's for only two days. Sylvia prepares a fresh breakfast each morning and guests love eating on the rear sundeck overlooking the woods. When she bought the house, one thing she had to have was a huge garden typical of those in Jamaica. Guests are often sent off with freshly picked veggies.

Sylvia's brother-in-law, Wilfred, who owns Arbor View House (an elegant Victorian B&B across the street) with his wife, Vita, initially "hated Long Island" but found the North Fork "so peaceful." Contrasting the two forks, he says, "We come out here to do nothing. We watch sunsets, eat sweet corn, go to the beach in the winter. It is so different on the North and South Forks, you won't believe they are both on the east end of Long Island."

Quintessentials issues permits and beach towels, and both the B&B and the Spa are handicapped-accessible. To reach Quintessentials, follow Route 25 to East Marion. Slow down at the blinking yellow light and the sign for the Fire House. The B&B is four houses past the light on the left.

North Fork Bed & Breakfast Association

Shorecrest, Red Barn, Harbor Knoll, Quintessentials (see above) and Arbor View House (Main Road, East Marion, ☎ 631-477-8696, www.arborviewhouse.com) are members of the North Fork Bed & Breakfast Association, www.northfork.com/nfbba. To qualify for membership, B&Bs must maintain the highest standards of cleanliness, hospitality and guest comfort, have private or semi-private bathrooms, and operate year-round. There are nine other members (listed below). Room rates range from $125 to $200.

BARTLETT HOUSE
503 Front Street
Greenport
☎ 631-477-0371
www.greenport.com/bartlett
Inexpensive to Moderate

Bartlett House is a 10-room manor dating from 1908. Each room has a private bath. Buffet breakfasts. In walking distance of village. Children over 12 welcome. Proprietors are Michael and Patricia O'Donoghue.

MORNING GLORY
912 Main Street
Greenport
☎ 631-477-3324
www.themorningglory.com
Inexpensive to Moderate

This charming 1822 home has three rooms, all with private baths. Full breakfast.

FREDDY'S HOUSE B&B
1535 New Suffolk Road
Cutchogue
☎ 631-734-4180
www.wickhamsfruitfarm.com, www.northfork.com
Inexpensive to Moderate

Wickham's Fruit Farm is a 300-acre working fruit farm one block from the village (see page 566). The 1700s house is meticulously restored; it has two guest rooms, each with a private bath. Full breakfasts. Short walk to beach. No credit cards. Your hosts are Dan & Prudence Heston.

KUDOS FOR CUTCHOGUE
In 2000, Cutchogue was named one of America's 77 most charming, off-the-beaten-track burgs in National Geographic Society's *Guide to Small Town Escapes*. It's the only village on Long Island to receive this designation.

THE RHINELANDER
26405 Main Road
Cutchogue
☎ 631-734-4156
www.northfork.com/rhinelander
Inexpensive

The Rhinelander offers European ambience and homemade breakfasts. Three guest rooms. Children over 12 welcome. No credit cards. Gisela Morchel is the proprietor.

TOP O' THE MORNIN'

26350 Main Road
Cutchogue
☎ 631-734-5143
www.northfork.com/topomornin
Moderate

Irish hospitality and full country breakfasts characterize this B&B in the heart of wine country. Three guest rooms, each with private bath. No credit cards; two-night minimum in season (summer and fall). Proprietors are Pat and Tom Monihan.

THE BELVEDERE

3070 Peconic Lane
Peconic
☎ 631-765-1799
www.northfork.com/belvedere
Moderate

The Belvedere is in a Victorian manor. Two rooms, each with private bath. European style breakfast. Children over 14 welcome.

HOMEPORT

2500 Peconic Lane
Peconic
☎ 631-765-1435
www.northfork.com/homeport
Moderate

Pat and Jack Combs created Homeport in an 1876 Victorian farmhouse. Beautifully furnished and relaxing. Full breakfast. Short walk to beach. No credit cards.

ALWAYS IN'
14580 Soundview Avenue
Southold
☎ 631-765-5344
www.northfork.com/alwaysin
Inexpensive

This elegant woodland Colonial has two guest rooms with featherbeds. Semi-private baths. Full breakfast. No credit cards. Jay and Marguerite Schondebare are the proprietors.

The B&B runs a program called Always Hope for families with a sick child being treated at an area hospital; the program offers one- or two-night stays to the parents and child, free of charge. Always Hope works with Long Island Jewish, Memorial Sloan-Kettering, Columbia Presbyterian, and University Hospital.

SEAHOUSE
12910 Main Road
East Marion
☎ 631-477-0472
www.northfork.com/seahouse
Inexpensive

SeaHouse is a beach cottage with panoramic views of Orient Point lighthouse. Two rooms, each with double beds.

Motels

MOTEL PRICE SCALE

Price scale is based on the cost of a double room, two people per room, in season, and does not include the 9.25% hotel tax.

Inexpensive	under $100
Moderate	$100-$150
Expensive	over $150

WADING RIVER MOTEL
5890 Middle County Road
Wading River
☎ 631-727-8000
32 units. Inexpensive to Moderate.

Open year-round.

BUDGET HOST INN
30 East Moriches Road
Riverhead
☎ 631-727-6200
www.budgethosteastend.com
68 units. Inexpensive to Moderate.

Near the Riverhead traffic circle. Open year-round.

GREENVIEW INN
1433 West Main Street
Riverhead
☎ 631-369-0093
56 units. Inexpensive to Moderate.

Open year-round.

BEST WESTERN EAST END
1830 Route 25
Riverhead
☎ 631-369-2200
www.rieastend.com
100 units. Moderate to Expensive.

One handicapped-accessible room. Pet-friendly; well-behaved pets welcome. Open year-round. Inquire about promotions.

DREAMER'S COVE MOTEL
Peconic Bay Boulevard
Aquebogue
☎ 631-722-3212
www.northforkmotels.com
18 units. Inexpensive to Moderate.

Free dockage. Open year-round.

J&S REEVE SUMMER COTTAGES
28 White's Road
Aquebogue
☎ 631-722-4096
www.liny-cottages.com
Inexpensive to Expensive.

One, two and three-bedroom cottages. Pet-friendly; well-behaved pets welcome. Open year-round.

VINEYARD MOTOR INN
Main Road
Jamesport
☎ 631-722-4024
21 units. Inexpensive.

Open year-round.

MOTEL ON THE BAY
Front Street
South Jamesport
☎ 631-722-3458
www.northforkmotels.com
17 units. Inexpensive to Moderate.

Open year-round.

NORTH FORK MOTEL
52325 County Road 48
Southold
☎ 631-765-2080
25 units. Moderate.

Closed in January and February.

SOUTHOLD BEACH MOTEL
County Road 48
Southold
☎ 631-765-2233
12 units. Inexpensive.

Across from Southold Town Beach; open from May through October. Pet-friendly; small pets welcome, but in the fall only.

DROSSOS MOTEL
Route 25
Greenport
☎ 631-477-1334
15 units. Inexpensive.

18-hole miniature golf course and family game room. Open from April through November.

SILVER SANDS MOTEL
Silvermere Road
Greenport
☎ 631-477-0011
www.silversands-motel.com
40 units. Inexpensive to Expensive.

Motel, apartments and cottages. Open year-round. One
handicapped-accessible cottage. In season only weekly
reservations are accepted.

SOUND VIEW INN
North Road (Route 48)
Greenport
☎ 631-477-1910
www.greenport.com/soundinn
49 units. Inexpensive to Moderate.

Both the inn and the adjacent restaurant (Sound View
Restaurant, ☎ 631-477-0666, www.greenport.com/soun-
drest) are open from mid-March through December.

SUNSET MOTEL
Route 48, between Southold & Greenport
☎ 631-477-1776
20 units. Inexpensive.

Open from April through November. Two wheelchair-
accessible units.

TOWNSEND MANOR INN
714 Main Street
Greenport
☎ 631-477-2000
www.greenport.com
23 units. Inexpensive to Moderate.

Marina and restaurant are open for lunch and dinner
in season; they close after Thanksgiving and reopen
around Easter. Motel is open year-round.

BLUE DOLPHIN MOTEL
Main Road
East Marion
☎ 631-477-0907
www.bluedolphinmotel.net
20 efficiencies. Moderate to Expensive.

At this writing, the Blue Dolphin is open only in summer, but it is under new management, so that may change.

STAR CABINS
Main Road & Stars Road
East Marion
☎ 631-477-0492
10 units. Moderate.

Open from Memorial Day weekend through Labor Day weekend.

Best Places to Eat

DINING PRICE SCALE	
Price scale includes one entrée, with glass of wine and coffee. There is an 8.5% tax on food in both Nassau and Suffolk Counties.	
Inexpensive	under $25
Moderate	$25-$40
Expensive	over $40

Riverhead

JERRY & THE MERMAID
469 East Main Street
Riverhead
☎ 631-727-8489
Inexpensive

*Karaoke, key-
board players
and other mu-
sicians enter-
tain in the
evening at
Jerry & The
Mermaid. Call
for schedule.*

This bar/restaurant near Atlantis Marine World (see
page 358) is a fun place, with larger-than-life mer-
maids and fish mobiles overhead. The menu is the
same for lunch or dinner, and daily specials are offered.
Cold and hot appetizers such as steamers and Jerry's
Famous Buffalo Wings compete with a host of clam offerings: Manhattan clam chowder, clams casino, clams
on the half shell, linguine with clams, baked stuffed
clams and fried clams. Still, I was as happy as a clam
with my fresh crab cake on a bun, crisp waffle fries, and
cole slaw – all for $5.95. Open daily, for lunch and din-
ner; closed Monday in the off-season

COOPERAGE INN
2218 Sound Avenue
Baiting Hollow
☎ 631-727-8994
Inexpensive to Moderate

On the road to the wine country, the Cooperage Inn was
named for the village coopers who for centuries skill-
fully stored and aged wines in handmade barrels. Surrounded by farms in the Baiting Hollow section of
Riverhead, the restaurant/bar serves fresh and "down-
home" American cooking like chicken pot pie and rack
of lamb. A large selection of regular and light entrées,

*Dishes can be
prepared with
low fat and
low salt at the
Cooperage
Inn.*

pastas and daily specials are offered. The Cooperage
salad ($5.50) is a winner – filled with chicken breast,
Mandarin oranges, toasted almonds, raisins and apples. Entrées are served with a garden salad and potatoes or rice.

In summer, expect homemade zucchini bread that
tastes like spice cake. In the fall, look for delicious

homemade pumpkin bread. It's safe to assume that anything in the breadbasket – prepared by CIA-trained chef Thomas Laimo - can easily double as dessert – *if* you can hold out.

The smoke-free restaurant holds a fall festival celebration every weekend in September and October and is expanding to include outdoor dining and a tiki bar. The Inn is open daily, year-round, for lunch and dinner. Reservations are recommended.

Jamesport

JAMESPORT COUNTRY KITCHEN
Main Road
Jamesport
☎ 631-722-3537
www.northfork.com/catering
Inexpensive to Moderate

As its name suggests, this restaurant is made to look like home and hearth with shirred curtains and wallpaper above wainscoting. Some rooms are papered in flowers and other in stripes. Light jazz is piped in.

Service is speedy – maybe too much so. The food is prepared fresh from local produce and the bread is homemade. The wedges of focaccia served before the meal are gone before one can say "salmon cakes," and those are also delicious – and I don't usually eat salmon. Entrées come with a salad, and there is a children's menu. Open for lunch and dinner year-round. Closed Tuesdays. Reservations recommended summertime and on weekends.

Mattituck

OLD MILL INN
West Mill Road
Mattituck
☎ 631-298-8080
www.theoldmillinn.net
Moderate

The Old Mill Inn features live music on weekends in season.

The Old Mill Inn may be the best-kept secret on the North Fork. Because it's way off the beaten path, this casual, handicapped-accessible restaurant is hard to find the first time, especially at night, but it's well worth the effort. Follow Cox Neck Road from Route 48 and bear right at West Mill Road; take it to the end (it's only about 1½ miles from Route 48, though it seems longer).

The restaurant's slogan is Fine Food & Friendly Spirits, and the word "spirits" could easily refer to the spirited and welcoming staff. Dishes run the gamut but fish is the mainstay here, and the Irish chef can turn a simple piece of flounder into a gourmet treat. Menu items and specials are made to order and dinners come with salad and side dishes. A children's menu suggests that families are more than welcome.

The restaurant is modern, with low ceilings and windows on all sides. It is close to the water and the outdoor dining area overlooks Mattituck Inlet. The dining room is adjacent to the bar, which was originally the mill. Descendants of Samuel Cox, who owned much of Southold prior to 1659, built the gristmill in the early 1800s and it operated day and night. Customers would bring their grist to the mill and hoist it up to the second floor where it was fed into a hopper. The ground grist would drop into a chute to be weighed. Payment for the grinding was a percentage of the grist. Names and dates carved into the beams above the bar date back more than a century – the owner at the time encouraged his clientele to carve their names; he also had a collection of animals, including a beer-drinking monkey, to keep them amused. The Library of Congress later recognized the mill as an engineering marvel.

Whether you eat in the air-conditioned dining room or on the outdoor deck, you're invited to "Come by car, boat or wagon." Closed from January to St. Patrick's Day; the rest of the year they are open for lunch and dinner daily, except Wednesday. Hours vary in spring and fall.

New Suffolk

LEGENDS
835 First Street
New Suffolk
☎ 631-734-5123
www.northfork.com/legends
Inexpensive to Moderate

The catchword at this popular sports-themed bar and restaurant should be "share." Portion sizes would please a football player! Decorated with photos of sports legends and athletic equipment, Legends has a New American menu and a wonderful chef from the Culinary Institute. The restaurant menu consists of local seafood dishes, steaks and chops (the hefty grilled boneless pork chops marinated in the chef's special sauce is outstanding). A salad, vegetables and starch accompany all entrées. The bar has a pub menu and attracts a mixed crowd. Legends boasts 200 beers from around the world (15 on tap), and local wines available by the glass. The restaurant has only 11 tables and does not take reservations. There are a few tables in the bar.

New Suffolk is on a point about two miles south of Cutchogue, and Legends is on the waterfront. To get here, turn right at the intersection of Route 25 and New Suffolk Road; at the blinking light in New Suffolk, turn onto New Suffolk Avenue, then turn onto First Street. Legends is open daily, year-round, for lunch and dinner.

Southhold

COEUR DES VIGNES

57225 Main Road
Southold
☎ 631-765-2656
www.coeurdesvignes.com
www.greatrestaurantsmag.com
Moderate

Coeur des Vignes has received the Wine Spectator *Award of Excellence for the past four years and was rated excellent in a Zagat survey.*

Coeur des Vignes is the place to go for a romantic dinner – or to have a small wedding. Three small mirrored rooms for intimate parties augment the main dining room, where a wood-beamed ceiling, piped-in French music, lace curtains, fireplace, and candlelit tables transport you to France.

This is a family affair, and Donna and George Pavlou will make you feel right at home. Their eldest son, Aristodemos (Arie), is the chef. A graduate of Le Cordon Bleu, he worked at Michelin two-star restaurants and briefly at Le Cirque and René Pujol before his parents opened this restaurant three years ago.

The restaurant has "a library of specials" that vary seasonally. Everything is cooked to order, whether you choose game, meat, poultry or fish. "We fish," boasts Donna, pointing to a photograph near the bar of the couple and their catch – a 30-pound bass. A prix-fixe lunch and dinner are also available.

Every restaurant on the North Fork features some local wines, of course, but local vintages dominate Coeur des Vignes' 10-page wine list. Some of them are sulfite-free.

On a special diet? Coeur des Vignes can accommodate you; just call ahead.

My satisfying meal began with hot herbed garlic rolls, followed by a flavorful bowl of lentil soup. Potatoes Daphne and string beans almondine made a nice complement to my coq au vin, sweetened with spicy honey sauce and candied carrots. Save room for dessert. The crème brûlée is to die for, lighter than air, with a barely-there crust.

CANINE CUISINE

Do you have a dog? The restaurant makes its own natural pooch biscuits that are fit for human consumption (the ingredients include whole-wheat rye, semolina and peanut butter and do not contain sugar, leavening, yeast or baking soda; the restaurant will ship the biscuits to you).

Open year-round, for lunch, Friday-Sunday; and dinner, daily, except Tuesdays (closed Monday and Tuesday in winter). See page 394 for information about accommodations at Coeur des Vignes.

SEAFOOD BARGE
62980 Main Road (Route 25)
Southold
☎ 631-765-3010
Moderate

With executive chef Jim Slattery at the helm, diners are assured of a sensational meal. A graduate of the New York Restaurant School, he spent a year at the Inn at Quogue before sharing his skills at the Dodge City Steakhouse in Westhampton. The North Fork is lucky to have him. If the food is less exciting when Slattery is absent, that's testimony to his wizardry.

For take-out from the Barge, call ahead.

Slattery's specialty is game. When that's not in season, you can choose from pasta, meat and fish entrées, daily specials, and a host of seafood appetizers. The Caribbean-spiced swordfish steak topped with a criss-cross bonnet of white jicama matchsticks was superb. The apple-carrot flavor blended beautifully with the pineapple-and-mango salsa and fresh orange-and-carrot juice reduction. The dessert menu is large, but I'd recommend the plate of gelato or sorbet. The chocolate hazelnut gelato tastes like creamy rich ice cream. Long Island wines are well represented. Wines by the glass are all from neighboring vineyards, giving diners a chance to sample the local varietals.

The Barge, located at the Port of Egypt Marina (see page 371), has a harbor view; candles burn on each table; and mood music plays softly in the background. See for yourself why both *The New York Times* and *Dan's Papers* have called Seafood Barge the best restaurant on the North Fork. Open year-round for lunch and dinner; reservations are mandatory on weekends.

BAY & MAIN
300 Main Street
Greenport
☎ 631-477-1442
Inexpensive to Moderate

Bay & Main features live light jazz on weekends.

This is a funky-looking place with electric yellow walls, red-painted tree trunks used as columns, plush velvet sofas and a tiled bar. It has indoor and outdoor dining and a menu that ranges from specialty sandwiches for $8 to entrées under $25. Salads are extra.

The one negative is that restaurant and bar are in one room. Notwithstanding the law about no smoking, some folks continue to light up at the bar. Open year-round for lunch and dinner; daily in summer; closed Monday in the off-season. Reservations are suggested.

Lite Bites

Ever wish you could eat in the library? Both the East Northport-Northport (see page 247) and Riverhead libraries have cafés. In Riverhead, **Rudy's Bookworm Café**, ☎ 631-208-2965, is in a cozy corner of the library beside a fireplace, with classical music piped in. The café serves bagels, rolls, pastries, coffee, tea and soda. The hours for the café are Monday-Friday, 9am-9pm; Saturday, 9am-5pm; and Sunday, October through April, 1am-5pm. The library is on West Main Street next door to the Suffolk County Historical Society; ☎ 631-727-3228.

North Fork Bagel Café, ☎ 631-298-8521, is open daily, year-round, for breakfast and lunch. Sandwiches are named for Southold hamlets. It's located in Mattituck Plaza next to the movie theater.

The food at **Do Little's**, also in Mattituck Plaza, ☎ 631-298-4000, is a mixed bag, but they have a kids' menu; they are open for dinner daily until 11pm; and for lunch on Saturday and Sunday, year-round.

Directly across Route 25 from the plaza is the ½ **Shell Restaurant,** ☎ 631-298-4180, which serves seafood and steak; open for lunch and dinner year-round.

Greenport Tea Company, 119A Main Street, Greenport, ☎ 631-477-8744, is a charming Irish tea parlor open from 11am-5pm, from mid-March through Christmas. The lunch menu consists of quiches, wraps, sandwiches and daily specials. Dinner is offered Friday and Saturday evening in the summer. High tea is served the American way – all day. Of the large assortment of teas, the house specialty is Irish black tea. The house desserts are Irish scones and bread pudding served warm with strawberry sauce and whipped cream.

Hellenic Snack Bar & Restaurant, Main Road, East Marion, ☎ 631-477-0138. This family restaurant opened in 1976 as a six-stool shack that made "the best lemonade in the world." It's still a modest restaurant, more on the order of a coffee shop. Word is, though, that the $13-$20 dinner entrées (served with pita bread, soup or salad) are good. The menu features many Greek appetizers and entrées and a full page of homemade desserts. There is an outdoor patio for dining in season. Open daily, year-round (except for one month in winter), for breakfast, lunch and dinner.

> ★ TIP
>
> If you're lunching on your own at the Hellenic Snack Bar, a good choice is the baby-sized Greek salad ($3.50) and a glass of their famous lemonade ($2). Made with fresh lemons, it's more tart than sweet and is a real summer refresher.

North Fork A to Z

Animals Hospitals & Shelters

Town of Riverhead Animal Control, Osborne Avenue, Riverhead, ☎ 631-727-3200, extension 306. Strays are held for one week before they are put up for adoption. Open daily.

V.I. Pets, Wading River, ☎ 631-929-5000, 369-0286, is a mobile unit, from which Dr. David L. McCarthy makes house calls.

Riverhead Animal Hospital, 1182 West Main Street, Riverhead, ☎ 631-727-2009, www.riverheadpetcare.com. Small animals. Boarding. Open Sunday for boarding only, 9am-noon.

Aquebogue Veterinary Hospital, Route 25, Aquebogue, ☎ 631-722-4242. Cats and dogs; by appointment only. Boarding. Closed Sunday. Late hours Tuesday and Thursday, 6:30-8pm.

Mattituck-Laurel Veterinary Hospital, 940 Franklinville Road, Laurel, ☎ 631-298-1177. Large and small animals. Boarding. Open daily.

North Fork Animal Hospital, 58605 Main Road, Southold, ☎ 631-765-2400. Small animals, avian and exotic animals. Boarding. Open Monday-Saturday, year-round. Sunday, emergencies only.

Kent Animal Shelter, 2259 River Road, Calverton, ☎ 631-727-5736, www.kentanimalshelter.com. Spay and neuter clinic ☎ 631-727-7797. Open daily, year-round.

Southold Animal Shelter, Peconic Lane, Peconic, ☎ 631-765-1811, has stray dogs and cats available for adoption. Open daily, 10am-3pm, year-round.

Banks

Astoria Federal Savings Bank. . . . . www.astoriafederal.com

Bank of New York . . . . www.bankofnewyork.com

Dime Savings Bank of NY . . . . www.dime.com

Bridgehampton National Bank www.bridgenb.com

Fleet Bank . . . . www.fleet.com

Suffolk County National Bank. . . . . www.scnb.com

North Fork Bank . . . . www.northforkbank.com

A LITTLE BANKING HISTORY

North Fork Bancorp was chartered on April 26, 1905, under the name Mattituck Bank; in 1950 the name was changed to North Fork Bank and Trust; it was a commercial bank operating primarily on eastern Long Island. In the 1980s and 1990s, on Long Island, North Fork Bank acquired Southold Savings Bank and Bank of Great Neck. In May 2000, *US Banker*, a leading industry publication, accorded the bank a #1 ranking among the nation's top banks and thrifts. Surprisingly, branches on the North Fork are far fewer than those on the rest of Long Island and the Greater New York region.

Houses of Worship

Baptist

Calvary Baptist Church of Riverhead, 515 River-leigh Avenue, Riverhead, ☎ 631-727-4112.

Unity Baptist Church, Factory Lane, Mattituck, ☎ 631-298-8669.

First Baptist Church, 650 Main Street, Greenport, ☎ 631-477-0047.

Catholic

Our Lady of Good Counsel, 14300 Main Road, Mattituck, ☎ 631-734-6722.

Sacred Heart, 27700 Main Road, Cutchogue, ☎ 631-734-6722.

Our Lady of Ostrabrama, Depot Lane, Cutchogue, ☎ 631-734-6446.

St. Patrick Roman Catholic Church, Main Road, Southold, ☎ 631-765-3442.

St. Agnes Roman Catholic Church, Front Street, Greenport, ☎ 631-477-0048.

Episcopal

Grace Episcopal Church (c. 1873), Roanoke Avenue, Riverhead, ☎ 631-727-3900.

Church of the Redeemer, 13225 South Avenue, Mattituck, ☎ 631-298-4277.

Holy Trinity Church, 768 Main Street, Greenport, ☎ 631-477-0855.

The all-wooden Tifereth Israel synagogue marked its 100th birth-day in 2002.

St. Mary's Episcopal Church, 26 St. Mary's Road, Shelter Island, ☎ 631-749-0770, www.stmarys-si.org.

Jewish – Conservative

Congregation Tifereth Israel, 519 Fourth Street, Greenport, ☎ 631-477-0232, www.northfork.com (look under "Links"), or http://pweb.netcom.com/~pbirman/ tifereth/index.html.

Temple Israel, 490 Northville Turnpike, Riverhead, ☎ 631-727-3191, www.templeisraelriverhead.org.

Jewish – Reform

North Fork Reform Synagogue, 910 New Suffolk Avenue, Mattituck, ☎ 631-298-5229.

Lutheran

Our Redeemer Lutheran Church, 269 Main Road, Aquebogue, ☎ 631-722-4000.

Advent Lutheran Church, 200 Legion Avenue, Mattituck, ☎ 631-298-4918/4271.

St. Peter's Lutheran Church, Main Road, Greenport, ☎ 631-477-0662.

Methodist

Riverhead United Methodist Church, 204 East Main Street, Riverhead, ☎ 631-727-2327.

Cutchogue United Methodist Church, Main Road, Cutchogue, ☎ 631-734-6033.

Greenport United Methodist Church, 621 Main Street, Greenport, ☎ 631-477-0497.

Southold United Methodist Church, Main Road, Southold, ☎ 631-765-3449.

Orient United Methodist Church, Village Lane, Orient, ☎ 631-323-2555.

Presbyterian

Mattituck Presbyterian Church, 21605 Main Road, Mattituck, ☎ 631-298-4145.

Cutchogue Presbyterian Church, Main Road, Village Green, Cutchogue, ☎ 631-734-6418.

*First Presby-
terian in
Southold,
organized in
1640, is "the
nation's oldest
Presbyterian
church with a
continuous
ministry."*

First Presbyterian Church, Main Road, Southold
☎ 631-765-2597.

Shelter Island Presbyterian Church, 32 North
Ferry Road, Shelter Island, ☎ 631-749-0805.

Information Sources

Chambers of Commerce

Riverhead Chamber of Commerce, 542 East Main
Street, Riverhead, ☎ 631-727-7600, www.riverhead-
chamber.com.

Mattituck Chamber of Commerce, ☎ 631-298-
5757, www.mattituckchamber.org.

*There is a
tourist infor-
mation booth
on Main Road
(Route 25)
west of
Greenport
village, ☎ 631-
477-1383.*

Greenport-Southold Chamber of Commerce,
☎ 631-765-3161, www.greenportsouthold.org.

Shelter Island Chamber of Commerce, ☎ 800-9-
SHELTER, 631-749-0399, www.shelter-island.net, or
www.onisland.com/si/chamber.

North Fork Promotion Council, ☎ 631-298-5757,
www.northfork.org.

Laurel Tourist Information, ☎ 631-298-5757.

Community Web Sites

Town of Riverhead . . . . www.riverheadli.com
Riverhead, Babylon, Port Jefferson, Bellport
. . . . www.lieast.com
Aquebogue, Jamesport, Laurel . www.northforkajl.com
Cutchogue . . . . www.cutchogue.com
Town of Southold . . . . www.greenportsouthold.org
Southold Town Hall http://southoldtown.northfork.net
Greenport Business Improvement District
. . . . www.greenport.cc
Shelter Island . . . . www.shelter-island.org,
www.shelterislandinns.com
The East End . . . . www.eastendcommunity.com
Phone Directory & Weather . . . . . . www.northfork.net

Liquor Stores

Conlan's Wines & Liquors, 207 Railroad Avenue, Riverhead (opposite the LIRR station), ☎ 631-727-4297.

Michael's Wines & Liquors, 802 East Main Street, Riverhead, ☎ 631-727-7410.

Roanoke Plaza Liquors, 1096 Route 58, Riverhead (in T.J. Maxx Shopping Center), ☎ 631-727-4331.

Peconic Liquors, King Kullen Shopping Center, Main Road, Cutchogue, ☎ 631-734-5859.

Village Liquor Store, Main Road, Southold, ☎ 631-765-5434.

Harvey's Claudio Wines & Liquors, 219 Main Street, Greenport, ☎ 631-477-1035.

Showcase Wine & Liquor, Route 48, Southold, ☎ 631-765-2222.

Medical Facilities

Central Suffolk Hospital, 1300 Roanoke Avenue, Riverhead, ☎ 631-548-6000, www.centralsuffolkhospital.org. Physician referral service, ☎ 631-548-6085. This 214-bed acute care hospital is 50 years old.

Eastern Long Island Hospital, 201 Manor Lane, Greenport, ☎ 631-477-1000. Suffolk County's first hospital serves all the communities of the North Fork and Shelter Island.

Both of these North Fork hospitals are affiliates of North Shore-Long Island Jewish Health System.

Movies

Cineplex Odeon Theaters (8), Main Road in Mattituck Plaza, Mattituck, ☎ 631-298-4400.

Village Cinema (4), Front Street, Greenport, ☎ 631-477-8600.

Newspapers

The *Suffolk Times*, serving the North Fork since 1857, is the official paper of Southold Town and the Village of Greenport; ☎ 631-369-0800, www.suffolktimes.com. It is published by Times/Review Newspapers, Mattituck, ☎ 631-298-3200, www.timesreview.com. Other Times/Review publications are the *Riverhead News-Review, The Wine Press, North Fork Vacation Guide*, and *Shelter Island Reporter*.

North Fork Country is a free tabloid distributed at area shops on the North Fork, South Fork and Shelter Island.

Pharmacies

Barth's Drug Store, 32 East Main Street, Riverhead, ☎ 631-727-2125.

Barker's Pharmacy, 195 Love Lane, Mattituck, ☎ 631-298-8666.

Cutchogue Drug Store, 28195 Main Road, Cutchogue, ☎ 631-734-6796.

Southold Pharmacy, 6 Main Street, Southold, ☎ 631-765-3434.

Zip Codes

Aquebogue	11931
Cutchogue	11935
East Marion	11939
Greenport	11944
Jamesport	11947
Laurel	11948
Mattituck	11952
Orient	11957
Peconic	11958
Riverhead	11901
Southold	11971
Wading River	11792

Suffolk County's South Fork

The Hamptons

The southern peninsula, or South Fork, of Long Island, is 44 miles long; it begins in **Riverhead** and ends at **Montauk Point**. The Hamptons is the name given to the region between Westhampton and Montauk Point, although some would argue that its western border is where the Shinnecock Canal cuts through Hampton Bays. Whatever the borderline, from July 4th through Labor Day the South Fork is a constant traffic nightmare along Montauk Highway (Route 27), beginning around Hampton Bays. "It's so crowded that traffic is at a standstill," observes Michael Finney, manager of Suffolk Auto Parts on Hill Street in Southampton. So why would folks subject themselves to this? "It doesn't seem to bother people who live in the city – they're used to it," he theorizes. "They come out en masse."

Locals also complain about the year-round "trade parade" – workmen heading east between 7:15am and 9:30am and returning to their more affordable homes between 4pm and 6pm.

The best advice is to avoid traveling east on Friday if at all possible. We returned from the Hamptons one Friday around noon in June and eastbound traffic was already backed up on Sunrise Highway near Hampton Bays.

Why do they do it? Long Island has beaches closer to New York City and equally good restaurants in Nassau County. What's so special about the Hamptons?

Spotting Celebrities

The Hamptons are like nowhere else on the planet. Only in the Hamptons will a visitor glimpse Barbra Streisand waiting for takeout with Donna Karan; Christie Brinkley exercising her favorite horse; Martha Stewart grocery shopping; Calvin Klein taking a stroll; Kurt Vonnegut chatting with E.L. Doctorow; or Billy Joel cruising for a parking space, all within a few miles on a single balmy afternoon. Hamptons Babylon – life among the super-rich on America's Riviera.

★ FAMOUS FACES

Richard Gere and Mel Brooks have homes in Water Mill.

Award-winning Beaches

Westhampton Beach's village beach, **Rogers Pavilion**, and East Hampton Village's **Main Beach** were rated 11th in the country by Dr. Stephen P. Leatherman, director of the International Hurricane Center at FIU in Florida and a self-described "Dr. Beach" who visits, then ranks, the nation's shorelines every year. He bases his rankings on 50 criteria, including water quality, safety and easy access. Check his Web site at www.drbeach.org.

Rubbing Elbows with the Rich

Maybe it's our fascination with wealth. We meander through mansions in Newport and on Long Island's Gold Coast, salivating at the statuary while recoiling at the excess. *The New York Times* often reports on happenings in the Hamptons, especially regarding real estate – up to $50 million a pop at last count. Or perhaps it's simply that there's so much to do in the Hamptons; read on.

Getting Here & Getting Around

By Car

Several options are available to drivers. Take the **Long Island Expressway** to Exit 70 (Manorville) and follow Route 111S to 27E (Sunrise Highway); or stay on the LIE to Exit 71 and then take Route 24, which goes east and south through Riverhead, where it feeds into Route 27 at Hampton Bays. Yet another option is to take the **Southern State Parkway** from western Long Island to Exit 42; bear left off the exit and then turn right onto Fifth Avenue to 27 East.

Route 27 (Sunrise Highway) joins with Montauk Highway (27A) in Southampton Village; this highway is called 27/39 in Southampton, then continues as Montauk Highway/Route 27 all the way to Montauk.

Rental Cars

Daily rental rates for a mid-sized car range from around $25 up to $75, some with unlimited free mileage. All operate year-round unless otherwise specified.

A-Car Auto Rental, Montauk Highway, Blue Point, ☎ 877-296-CARS (2277). Service from New York City to Hamptons.

Avis Rent-A-Car, Southampton, ☎ 800-331-1212; customer service, ☎ 800-352-7900, www.avis.com. Open from April 15 to September 13.

Budget Rent-A-Car has several locations on Long Island; ☎ 800-527-0700 or 631-283-7042, www.budget.com.

Hertz, Montauk Highway, Bridgehampton, ☎ 631-537-8119; reservations, ☎ 800-654-3131.

Pam Rent-A-Car, 150 North Main Street, East Hampton, ☎ 631-329-1010, ☎ 800-894-6102, www.516-

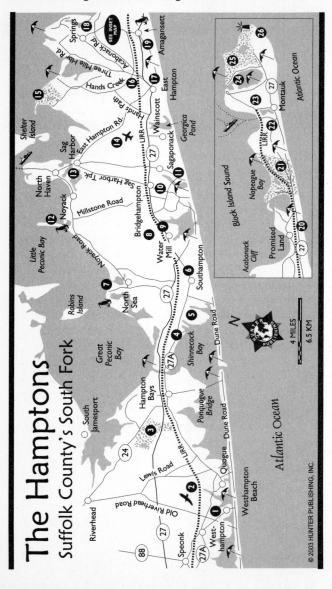

The Hamptons
Suffolk County's South Fork

The Hamptons Map Key

1. Westhampton Beach Walking Tour; Performing Arts Center
2. Quogue Wildlife Refuge & Nature Center
3. Sears Bellows County Park
4. Long Island University's Avram Theater
5. Shinnecock Indian Reservation
6. Parrish Art Museum & Arboretum; Old Halsey House; Southampton Historical Museum
7. Conscience Point National Wildlife Refuge
8. Channing Daughters Winery
9. Corwith Windmill; Duck Walk Vineyards
10. Dan Flavin Art Institute; Beebe's Windmill; Corwith House; Bridge Gardens Trust
11. Wolffer Estate Winery; Madoo Conservancy Gardens
12. Elizabeth A. Morton National Wildlife Refuge
13. Sag Harbor Whaling & Historical Museum; Old Whaler's Presbyterian Church; Custom House; Annie Cooper Boyd House; Sag Harbor Windmill; Bay Street Theatre
14. East Hampton Airport

15. Cedar Point County Park
16. LongHouse Reserve
17. Home Sweet Home Museum; Old Hook, Gardiner and Pantigo Windmills; Osborn-Jackson House; Mulford Farm;Clinton Academy; Town House; Guild Hall & John Drew Theater
18. Pollock-Krasner House & Study Center; Green River Cemetery
19. Miss Amelia Cottage; East Hampton Town Marine Museum; Amagansett National Wildlife Refuge
20. Napeague State Park
21. Hither Hills State Park
22. Second House Museum
23. Montauk Downs Golf Course; Signal Hill
24. Montauk Harbor; Montauk Airport
25. Montauk (Theodore Roosevelt) County Park; Third House Museum
26. Montauk State Park; Lighthouse & Museum

➤ Beaches   ⚓ Ferries to Shelter Island, New London, Block Island and Martha's Vineyard

Suffolk County's South Fork

web.com/pam, has 12 locations between Montauk and Westbury.

Hampton Car Rental, 18A Ponquogue Avenue (across from the train station), Hampton Bays, ☎ 631-723-2277 (CARS), www.hamptoncarrental.com.

 TIP

Ask auto rental establishments for hours of operation. Some close at noon on Saturday and reopen on Monday.

By Taxi

McRide's offers taxi and van service. Local, airport and service to NYC. Accepts all major credit cards. Local numbers are:

Hampton Bays . . . . ☎ 631-728-0070
Southampton . . . . ☎ 631-283-1900
Riverhead . . . . ☎ 631-727-0707
Westhampton . . . . ☎ 631-288-3252
Shirley/Mastic . . . . ☎ 631-281-8581
Patchogue . . . . ☎ 631-475-6213
East Northport . . . . ☎ 631-261-0235
Rocky Point (main office) . . . . ☎ 631-744-0005

Hampton Coach serves passengers from Speonk to Montauk. Local numbers are:

Southampton . . . . ☎ 631-283-0242
Sag Harbor . . . . ☎ 631-725-8900
Hampton Bays . . . . ☎ 631-728-0050
Wainscott . . . . ☎ 631-324-0777

East Hampton Taxi serves East Hampton and Amagansett, ☎ 631-267-2006.

East Hampton and Amagansett Taxi, ☎ 631-324-9696, or 324-2006.

Sag Harbor Car Service, Sag Harbor, ☎ 631-725-9000. Local and long distance.

Pink Tuna Car Service, Montauk, ☎ 631-668-3838. Local and long distance.

By Limousine

The South Fork and Brookhaven phone books each contain more than five pages of listings of limousine companies. This is a mere sampling.

Beach Limousines, ☎ 631-288-7777, provides transportation to and from NYC and throughout the tri-state area in its new luxury sedans, stretch limousines or mini-buses (from out of NY state, ☎ 888-288-0644).

Southampton Limousine, ☎ 631-287-0001, serves the tri-state area.

Friends Limousine Service, Yaphank, ☎ 800-660-9668, offers pick-up service throughout Long Island for destinations near and far.

Hampton Hills Beach Limousines, ☎ 800-287-5757. Transportation to and from Long Island, NYC and throughout tri-state area. Local numbers are:

Westhampton . . . . ☎ 631-288-7777
East Quogue . . . . ☎ 631-653-7820
Southampton . . . . ☎ 631-283-7820
East Hampton. . . . . ☎ 631-324-0108

Hampton International Limousine, Westhampton, ☎ 631-288-4737; and East Hampton, ☎ 631-324-6751, serving all of Long Island and Manhattan.

Islander Limousine, Southold, ☎ 631-765-5834, offers pickups "from Manhattan streets to North & South Fork Retreats," including airports.

By Bus

The **Hampton Jitney**, ☎ 631-283-4600, or 800-936-0440, www.hamptonjitney.com, operates daily, year-round, between New York City and the South Fork.

Eastbound trips depart from several locations: 86th Street between Lexington & Third avenues; 69th & Lexington; 59th & Lexington; and 40th between Lexington and Third. On westbound trips there are several stops along Third Avenue between 39th and 86th streets. Rates are around $25 each way. Reservations recommended.

The Hampton Jitney also runs a **Hampton Petney** shuttle service to the Hamptons (☎ 631-283-4600 or 866-PETNEY1, www.petney.com). Your pet will have its own private cabin with complimentary water and gourmet dog biscuits. Reservations are required.

Hampton Luxury Liner, ☎ 631-537-5800, www.hamptonluxuryliner.com, is not a ship, but a luxury 21-passenger coach that has several pick-up and drop-off points in Manhattan, Southampton and Amagansett. Rates are around $37 each way in summer. Reservations are required.

By Ferry

Viking Lines Ferry, West Lake Drive, Montauk, ☎ 631-668-5700, carries passengers (no cars) between Montauk and Block Island and Montauk and New London CT, from mid-May through Labor Day. The trip to Block Island takes 1¾ hours and costs $40 round-trip, $20 one-way. Parking in New London is $8. On both ferries, bikes and surfboards are an extra $10 round-triop or $7 one-way.

South Ferry, Route 114, Shelter Island, ☎ 631-749-1200, www.webscope.com/li/ferries.html, carries cars and passengers, year-round, between the south side of Shelter Island and North Haven (near Sag Harbor). The trip takes five minutes each way. Fare is $7 for passenger and car one-way; $8 for passenger and car round-trip; $1 for each additional passenger each way.

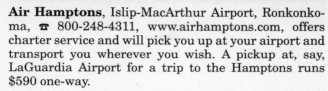

By Air

Air Hamptons, Islip-MacArthur Airport, Ronkonkoma, ☎ 800-248-4311, www.airhamptons.com, offers charter service and will pick you up at your airport and transport you wherever you wish. A pickup at, say, LaGuardia Airport for a trip to the Hamptons runs $590 one-way.

HSI (Helicopter Services & Instruction), ☎ 866-U-FLY-HIS, www.helicopterservicesinc.com, offers summer packages of 14 round trips, Manhattan-Hamptons, at $8,500 (a single one-way trip is roughly $900). Depart and arrive from NYC heliports. Operates year-round.

East Hampton Airlines, ☎ 631-537-3737, or 800-359-8654, is based at East Hampton Airport. Its corporate jets, helicopters, turboprops and single-engine planes are available for charter every day, year-round.

New York Helicopter, ☎ 631-777-3733, www.nyhelicopters.com, provides executive charter service (with a minimum of three confirmed reservations) from Manhattan's East 34th Street Heliport to three Hamptons airfields: Westhampton Airport; Dune Road Heliport in Southampton; and East Hampton Airport. Operates daily, round-the-clock, year-round.

New England Airlines, ☎ 800-243-2460, www.BlockIsland.com/NEA, flies between Montauk and Block Island in about 15 minutes. Travelers to Foxwoods Casino in Connecticut fly to Westerly, Rhode Island and take a cab to the casino. Cost varies according to the number of passengers, so bring family and friends.

Peconic Air, ☎ 631-765-2954, based at Suffolk County Airport in Westhampton Beach, provides charter flights throughout the Northeast.

Sound Aircraft (☎ 800-443-0031) runs commuter flights between East Hampton Airport (☎ 631-537-2202) and to Manhattan via seaplane or helicopter, April-October. Charters available year-round.

Suffolk County's South Fork

Sunup to Sundown

Sightseeing

Walking Tour

Westhampton took the worst battering of any Long Island community during the 1938 hurricane.

Main Street in Westhampton Beach is beautiful. In the summer, window boxes and baskets of flowers bursting with color hang from old-fashioned street lamps. The hamlet was once wild in the summer, but no more. A longtime resident and shopkeeper described Westhampton Beach today as a year-round community of families, with the sidewalks on weekends "lined with strollers." Like other residents, she likes the proximity to the city (roughly 85 miles) and the area's heterogeneous population. Located on the western end of the town of Southampton, Westhampton Beach is known as the "first" Hampton because it's the closest to New York City. With a few exceptions, Westhampton village closes down after Labor Day. Westhampton and Westhampton Beach are both off Sunrise Highway Exit 63S (Old Riverhead Road).

SELF-GUIDED TOUR

What does it take for a town to become a Tree City? Call the village office at ☎ 631-288-1654, or visit www.whb-cc.org/tree-news.htm.

The Village of Westhampton Beach has been named a **Tree City USA** by the National Arbor Day Foundation for the past 13 years for helping to keep some 803 trees healthy and attractive. A *Tree Walk* map pinpoints 31 noteworthy trees of various species within a two-mile radius. Since few trees stand alone, each special tree is labeled for easy identification. A map is also posted outside the Bank of New York on Main Street. For your own copy, visit Lynn's Cards & Gifts, 137 Main Street; the Westhampton Free Library, 7 Library Avenue; or the Westhampton Chamber of Commerce at its new headquarters on Glovers Lane.

Museums & Historic Sites

A page of history is worth a volume of logic.
                              – Oliver Wendell Holmes Jr.

Southampton

PARRISH ART MUSEUM
25 Jobs Lane
☎ 631-283-2118
http://thehamptons.com
$2 suggested donation

Samuel Longsteth Parrish was a 19th-century New York lawyer who summered in Southampton. He financed the construction of the wooden building that currently houses the museum. The exterior of the Parrish is a museum in itself. In the arboretum are 1903 marble copies of the 18 Imperial Caesars, and on the walls of the building are terra cotta reproductions of Luca della Robbia's religious and mythological scenes.

The museum, whose emphasis was originally on European art, is devoted to 19th- and 20th-century American work, and its collection is considered among the finest anywhere. However, until the Parrish moves its permanent collection – permanently – into the building next door (vacated by the Rogers Memorial Library), visitors will not see its internationally recognized holdings of the works of William Merritt Chase and Fairfield Porter; there is simply not enough space for the museum to display all of its 2,000 pieces, though the exhibits in the two large rooms change frequently.

The Parrish is handicapped-accessible and has a gift shop and a children's bookstore. It also sponsors events, trips, workshops, films, educational programs, concerts and lectures. Open year-round except January; hours are Monday, Thursday, Friday and Saturday, 11-5; Sunday, 1-5; closed Tuesday and Wednesday.

SOUTHAMPTON HISTORICAL MUSEUM
17 Meeting House Lane
☎ 631-283-2494
Admission: adults, $3; seniors, $2; students, $1

Parking is available across the street from the Historical Museum.

The museum's main campus was a whaling captain's mansion built in 1843. Samuel Parrish, the "Santa Claus of Southampton," who founded the Parrish Art Museum and served as village mayor, purchased and enlarged the house when he retired. He was a gardener and liked lots of windows so he could look out at his flowers. He even installed a skylight.

Yet the furnishings and exhibits do not represent the owner, but the history of Southampton – in photographs, antique quilts, furniture and Indian artifacts. The former servants' quarters are now filled with antique toys. A library is on the premises. Special exhibits are featured four times a year. The museum is open daily, 11-5, in season; closed Sunday and Monday in the off season.

Eight outbuildings, including two that are off-site, are open from June through September. Buildings on the museum grounds include a one-room schoolhouse, barn, blacksmith's shop, carpentry shop, drugstore and paint store. On Southampton's Main Street are a silversmith shop and the Halsey House, ☎ 631-283-3527, believed to be the oldest wood frame house (c. 1648) in New York State. Now a museum, Halsey House is open mid-June-September.

Springs

The Pollack-Krasner house and studio and Home Sweet Home are on the National Register of Historic Places.

POLLOCK-KRASNER HOUSE AND STUDY CENTER
830 Springs-Fireplace Road
☎ 631-324-4929
www.pkhouse.org
Admission: $5

Visitors are asked to remove their shoes when they enter the converted barn to protect the paint-splattered floor. The 1879 farmhouse where Jackson Pollock and his wife, Lee Krasner, lived is a National Historic Landmark. The paint cans and brushes are just as they were the day he died. Yet in his lifetime, Jackson Pollock never earned more than $8,000 for his work.

On the floor I am more at ease. I feel nearer, more a part of the painting, since this way I can walk around it, work from the four sides and literally be in the painting.

– Jackson Pollock

The guided tour through the house and studios of two of America's foremost Abstract Expressionist painters tells the story behind their struggles and the acceptance of Pollock's groundbreaking paintings after his death. Consider this: Pollock was so poor at times that he tried bartering his paintings for food. Few wanted his work, except for the owner of Springs General Store, who accepted a small painting to pay off Pollock's $60 bill. After Pollack died in a fiery car crash on Springs Fireplace Road, the grocer sold that painting for $56,000.

In contrast to Pollock, an alcoholic with few social skills, artist Lee Krasner was an educated, brilliant, well-connected art dealer. After her husband died, she dedicated herself to nurturing his legend. Krasner amassed a fortune by manipulating the market and left everything to the Pollock-Krasner Foundation. "She wanted it to be his legacy," our guide said. "The Foundation gives more (grants to struggling artists) than any other organization in the world."

Guided tours are by appointment, 11am to 4pm, Thursday-Saturday, from May to October. A ramp makes the ground floor of the house handicapped-accessible, but the studio and inside the barn can be reached only by stairs.

Jackson Pollock (1912-1965) is buried in **Green River Cemetery** off Accabonac Road. Should you want to visit, ask for a map. Pollock's monument is a 50-ton boulder with a modest plaque located at the head of the horseshoe-shaped driveway on the right. Lee Krasner (1908-1984) is buried beside him. The map gives directions to the cemetery and pinpoints where 38 notables are entombed, including Elaine de Kooning (wife of Willem, and an accomplished painter herself), Stuart Davis and Abraham Rattner.

Bridgehampton

DAN FLAVIN ART INSTITUTE
Corwith Avenue, off Main Street
☎ 631-537-1476 (in season)
☎ 212-989-5566 (off-season)
www.diacenter.org
$3 suggested donation

Dan Flavin, who died in 1996, was an established artist born in New York City. His last 20 years were largely spent in Bridgehampton and Wainscott. The **DIA Center for the Arts**, one of the largest charitable organizations in the United States dedicated to contemporary art and culture, maintains the Art Institute, which is housed in the former First Baptist Church of Bridgehampton. It was originally built as a firehouse in 1908; in 1979, DIA purchased and renovated the structure for use as a gallery for Flavin.

The permanent installation, "Dan Flavin: Nine Works," traces his practice of using standard fluorescent fixtures and tubes as his primary medium. Special exhibits examine different aspects or periods in his life. The gallery is open Thursday-Saturday, noon-6pm, from Memorial Day to mid-September.

In addition to the Dan Flavin Institute, DIA supports the commission of site-specific installations in Grand Central Station and elsewhere. Headquartered at 548 West 22nd Street in Manhattan, DIA is opening a new museum in Beacon, New York, in 2003 that will feature more than 40 additional works by Flavin.

East Hampton

Mid pleasures and palaces though we may roam,
Be it ever so humble, there's no place like home.

— John Howard Payne

HOME SWEET HOME MUSEUM
14 James Lane
☎ 631-324-0713
Admission for adults, $4; for children under 12, $2

It's a common misconception that John Howard Payne was born on Long Island and that this c. 1680 saltbox and its contents belonged to him. In fact, the house was owned by Payne's maternal grandfather, Aaron Isaacs, the first Jewish person to settle in East Hampton. Payne was a sickly child who often visited his grandfather, as well as aunts and uncles in the area.

Gustav and Hannah Buek bought the house in 1908 and filled it with 18th-century antiques, china and pewter, and a huge collection of 19th-century lusterware, which is displayed in a corner cabinet. They also made the house a shrine to Payne. When Mr. Buek died in 1927, the village of East Hampton bought the house and opened the museum a year later. The name comes from Payne's popular 1822 song, *Home Sweet Home*, from an operetta. When Payne wrote the words to the song he was living a peripatetic life as an actor and playwright abroad and was probably dreaming about his only real home. He served as American Consul to Tunis, Africa in the last years of his life and died there in 1852.

Driving east into East Hampton, look for the flagpole before the village center; make a U-turn into James Lane. The house is only partially wheelchair-accessible, but the tour is on video and can be shown in the front office. Open daily, from May through September; weekends, in October and November; and by appointment, from December through April.

John Howard Payne never received a nickel for the 100,000 copies of the song that were sold; he subsequently became a champion of copyright laws.

Suffolk County's South Fork

☞ DID YOU KNOW?

Both Home Sweet Home and neighboring Mulford Farm (see page 448), are called saltbox houses because their shape resembles containers that were used for storing salt during the Colonial era. This shape was popular because it allowed one side of the house to take advantage of sunlight while the other remained sheltered from severe weather.

Sag Harbor

So be cheery, my lads, let your hearts never fail,
While the bold harpooneer is striking the whale!
                                    – Nantucket song

SAG HARBOR WHALING AND HISTORICAL MUSEUM

200 Main Street
☎ 631-725-0770
www.sagharborwhalingmuseum.org
Admission: adults, $3; children, $1

The Whaling Museum, Old Whaler's Presbyterian Church, Miss Amelia Cottage and Montauk Lighthouse are all on the National Register of Historic Places.

There was a time when most domestic activities ceased after sundown. It was too dark to read or sew; and candles burned out quickly and caused fires. Along came the whalers, returning from the sea with barrels of lamp oil rendered from whale blubber. What heroes they must have been in the early 1800s!

When you think of whalers, what comes to mind? *Moby Dick*? New Bedford? Sag Harbor also has a proud whaling heritage, memorialized in its museums, monuments, cemeteries and large Victorian homes once belonging to these salts of the sea.

The best place to begin your educational voyage is at the whaling museum, housed in a Greek revival mansion once owned by the Huntting family. It later belonged to Mrs. Russell Sage, widow of one of America's original robber barons, who left her $80 million. Her family was from Sag Harbor, and Margaret Olivia Slocum Sage used the building as a summerhouse from 1907 to 1918. She was Sag Harbor's biggest benefactor, having financed construction of the John Jermain Memorial Library across the street (it's named for her grandfather), Pierson High School and Mashashimuet Park. After she died, the Society of Masons bought the building and became life tenants. The name above the Corinthian columns still reads "Masonic Temple," and the Masons continue to meet on the top floor. The museum occupies several rooms on the main floor.

Before stepping through the jawbones at the entrance, look to the left and observe the replica of a six-man whaleboat and its heavy oars. To the right of the museum are three giant pots once used for rendering whale fat. A successful voyage would yield about 2,000 barrels of oil.

Note the magnificent spiral staircase and Italian Carrara marble fireplace in the parlor room, where a large collection of scrimshaw, featuring finely decorated whale teeth, tusks and bones, testifies to lengthy voyages. More intricate pieces, such as swifts for spinning yarn, were designed for the ladies.

Another room houses the tools used to capture whales. As whales became depleted near shore, the boats went farther afield and a trip could last three years. Even on longer voyages, captains avoided island hopping – for good reason. "The young hands received shares of profits but no wages," according to museum board director David Cory, "so they never went to civilized places for fear the hands would escape."

The museum is open daily, from mid-May through September; exhibit areas are handicapped-accessible (although access to bathrooms is limited). Call the museum for a list of special events. Those interested in visiting the **Old Whaler's Presbyterian Church** (c. 1844) may call David Cory, ☎ 631-725-4118, to arrange a tour.

Suffolk County's South Fork

⭐ FAMOUS FACES

Monologist Spalding Gray recently purchased a new house in Sag Harbor.

THE CUSTOM HOUSE
Garden Street
☎ 631-692-4664 (Preservation Society)
Admission: adults, $3; children and seniors, $1.50

The Custom House, next door to the Whaling Museum, was the home of Sag Harbor's first US Custom Master, Henry Packer Dering. Appointed by George Washington, Dering maintained an office in the house that served as a post office (Long Island's first, opened in 1794) and the repository of tax collections. The Dering family lived there from 1790 to 1830 and was considered Sag Harbor's first family. On display are the original furnishings, including those fashioned by East End craftsmen. The Custom House is open for guided tours daily during July and August, and weekends only from Memorial Day through June and from Labor Day through Columbus Day.

The Dering family, along with the Hunttings, Hands, Hunts, and Hildreths as well as George Fahys III (1941-53), are buried in **Oakland Cemetery**. Take Main Street past the museum and turn left on Brick Kiln Road. The cemetery is a few blocks down on the right.

WHERE'S THE STEEPLE?
Sag Harbor's First Presbyterian Church is listed on the National Register of Historic Places. Built between c. 1844, the Egyptian/Greek Revival-style building lost its steeple in the 1938 hurricane.

☞ **DID YOU KNOW?**

James Fenimore Cooper was among those lured by the whaling fever. He came to Sag Harbor, invested in a ship, and spent a good part of three years sailing the Sound and exploring Eastern Long Island.

Amagansett

MISS AMELIA COTTAGE
129 Main Street at Windmill Lane
☎ 631-267-3020
Small donation requested

Mary Amelia Schellinger (1841-1930) was the last member of her family to live in this 1725 house built by Jacob Schellinger. Miss Amelia was a descendant of Jacob, the Dutch founder of Amagansett. In 1794 the cottage was moved from its original location to higher ground. Two teams of oxen hauled the house 300 yards along Main Street (which was then a dirt path) to its present spot.

Miss Amelia never married and lived without electricity or running water until five years before her death. The Amagansett Historical Association bought the property in 1964, saving it from a future as an IGA supermarket and parking lot. The Association was also instrumental in getting Main Street established as an official Historic District in 2000.

★ TIP

A booklet called *Main Street Treasures* showcases 59 historic buildings in Amagansett. It is available from the Amagansett Historical Association, PO Box 7077, Amagansett, NY 11930.

Suffolk County's South Fork

Miss Amelia's cottage has not been altered and retains all the original Colonial furnishings. The carriage museums on the grounds are unrelated to the cottage, but contain photographs of old Main Street. "You can see how wide Main Street was without sidewalks and paved streets," observes Peter Garnham, president of the Association. The historic houses are privately owned, he says, so residents are surprised to see them in vintage photographs. "Locals are so used to these houses, they don't see them any more." The cottage is open Friday-Sunday, 10am-2pm, from May through September.

Montauk

Unlike the claims of so many historic sites that "George Washington Slept Here," we know that Theodore Roosevelt was at the Montauk Lighthouse because he signed the register.

MONTAUK LIGHTHOUSE
Montauk Point
☎ 631-668-2544
Admission: adults, $4; seniors, $3.50; children, $2.50 (children must be at least 41" tall to climb)
www.montauklighthouse.com

This is a must-see museum even if you're unable to climb the 137 steps to the top (it's an open spiral staircase and very narrow, especially near the top). On a clear day, you can see Block Island. However, the view from the base is almost as spectacular, given that there's a raging ocean all around. It almost feels like the end of the world.

Montauk Lighthouse was commissioned by George Washington; completed in 1796, it is the oldest lighthouse in New York State. Its purpose was to provide safe passage for international and domestic trade by directing ships into Long Island Sound and away from the rough waters of the Atlantic. Its beacon still rotates and can be seen for 19 nautical miles. From 1860 to 1961, the light had to be hand-cranked every three hours. You can see the original kerosene lens in the oil room. Everything comes later to Montauk so it's no surprise that the lighthouse was not fully automated by the Coast Guard until 1987. That year the property was deeded to the Montauk Historical Society, which continues to preserve its past.

> ☞ DID YOU KNOW?
>
> The layered cliffs and large boulders at Montauk Point are two of the most visible legacies of the glaciers that left Long Island about 20,000 years ago.

Events are held at the lighthouse on holiday weekends year-round, beginning with Martin Luther King Weekend and culminating in Christmas at the Lighthouse.

Lighthouse keepers were so important that US presidents commissioned them. The museum has on display the original proclamations signed by Thomas Jefferson (Washington's Secretary of State) and Andrew Jackson (who commissioned Patrick Gould, keeper of the light from 1832 to 1849). The museum is located in the 1860 keeper's house. Don't get scared when you see uniformed James Scott sitting there. The replica of the 15th lighthouse keeper (1885-1910) looks very real. He sits near the desk dated 1812 that belonged to the second keeper, Jared Hand. The United States Coast Guard took over the lighthouse in 1939 and the last keeper retired in 1943. The Keeper's Room was recently restored with help from designer Ralph Lauren, a Montauk resident who, in 1999, donated $10,000 toward its completion.

There are several memorials on the grounds. The largest and most impressive is the 16-foot-tall **Lost at Sea Memorial** behind the lighthouse, which depicts a fisherman hauling in a line. It's dedicated to the more than 120 Long Island commercial fishermen lost at sea.

The lighthouse and museum open at 10:30am daily, from mid-May through October; they are open weekends only in winter, except daily during spring break. Take the LIE to Exit 70 (Manorville Road). Go south on Route 111 to Route 27E, and continue to Montauk Point. For more information about Long Island lighthouses, log on to www.longislandlighthouses.com.

Suffolk County's South Fork

Especially popular with kids is the lighthouse's button-operated diorama of 28 light stations.

According to Weather Bureau records, Montauk Point is the windiest spot on the North Atlantic coast. No surprise then that Montauk is referred to as "The Land of Many Winds."

THIRD HOUSE MUSEUM
Theodore Roosevelt County Park
Montauk Highway
☎ 631-852-7878
www.suffolk.ny.us/exec/parks

The Third House was built in 1747 to house cattlemen from the Hamptons who drove their herds here every summer, according to our guide. These annual cattle drives ended in 1926. Third House was one of three houses built in Montauk to accommodate the cattlemen. First House, built in 1744, was destroyed years ago. The Montauk Historical Society operates Second House (see *Historical Societies*, page 449).

Third House gained fame in 1898 when it served as one of the headquarters of Camp Wikoff. Following the brief Spanish-American War, which ended in Cuba, Colonel Theodore Roosevelt brought his volunteer Army regiment of 600 men (his beloved Rough Riders) along with 23,000 other soldiers to be quarantined in the camp, which remained open from mid-August through October (what better place than the tip of Long Island to recuperate?). In early September of that year, Edith Roosevelt and her daughters, Alice and Ethel, stayed at Third House while visiting with Colonel Roosevelt. The Spanish-American War Exhibit at Third House commemorates this historic event in photographs and books. Our guide said the house became county property in 1974, after being used as part of a dude ranch after 1948. Plans are being made to restore the house to its 1898 condition.

The house is located three miles east of the village, in Theodore Roosevelt County Park, on 1,200 acres that include Montauk Downs golf course. The name was changed from Montauk County Park during the Spanish-American War Centennial in 1998. Open Wednesday through Sunday, 10-5, from late May to early October.

☞ DID YOU KNOW?

You probably never learned this in school, but cattle ranching began in the east, specifically in Montauk. It was the treeless peninsula's major industry for nearly 300 years, before the country expanded out west and refrigeration came into use.

Windmills

One of the more difficult concepts for people new to this area to understand is that things, particularly historic things, were not always where they are now.

– Dan Rattiner, Publisher, Editor-in-Chief, *Dan's Papers*

Long Island has more surviving 18th-century windmills than any other section of the country, all in Suffolk County. The Dominy family, one of the founding families of East Hampton, were furniture makers, clock makers and windmill builders; their creations are found in several museums on the East End. The family built one of East Hampton's windmills, the **Old Hook Mill** on North Main Street (built by Nathaniel Dominy V in 1806); it's now the only one in operating condition. The Old Hook Mill is open daily in June, July and August, 10am-4pm (Sunday hours are 2-4pm).

The other East Hampton windmills are both on James Lane. The **Gardiner Windmill**, across from the Lion Gardiner tomb in the coffin-shaped South End Burying

Ground, is open by appointment; ☎ 631-324-0713. Also in the cemetery is a stone effigy of Gardiner resting under a Gothic arch designed by James Renwick, the architect of both Saint Patrick's Cathedral and Grace Church in NYC. The Buek family (see *Home Sweet Home Museum*, page 437) moved the **Pantigo Windmill** (1771), from Pantigo Road to its present location behind Home Sweet Home, and both are open at the same time. Admission to all three of the windmills above is $2 for adults; $1 for children; ☎ 631-324-0713 for information.

All three East Hampton windmills are patterned after English, and not Dutch, designs.

📖 HISTORICAL INTEREST

In 1639, Lion Gardiner, standing over six feet tall and red-bearded, bought Gardiners Island from the Montaukett Indians and it remains in the Gardiner family. With 3,000 acres and 27 miles of coastline, Gardiners Island is said to be the nation's largest privately owned island and oldest family estate.

The Wainscott, Corwith and Beebe windmills are on the National Register of Historic Places.

Beebe Windmill, built in 1820 by Samuel Schellinger and originally in Sag Harbor, was moved in 1837 to Ocean Road in Bridgehampton, where it operated until 1911. This windmill, built later than the others, had machinery made of iron rather than wood.

The **Sag Harbor Windmill** on the wharf stands roughly on the spot where the first windmill in Sag Harbor stood; it is a scaled-down version of the original.

The **Wainscott Windmill** was built in Southampton in 1813, moved to Wainscott in 1852, and then transferred to Montauk in 1922. During WW II, it was acquired by the Georgica Association, which built many of the elegant homes on Georgica Pond in Wainscott in the 1890s. The windmill is now located on Main Street in Wainscott; it is not open to the public.

The **Corwith Windmill** on the commons at Water Mill is open for tours, year-round, by appointment. Built in Sag Harbor in 1800 and moved to Water Mill in 1813, it operated until 1887. The mill is named for the Corwith family, its original owners. Donations are appreciated. ☎ 631-726-5984.

Ironically, Windmill Lane, named for a windmill that once stood slightly north of the Main Street intersection in Southampton, is sans windmill. Relocated to a spot east of the flagpole and later moved back again to Windmill Lane, the windmill burned down in 1924.

Historical Societies

EAST HAMPTON HISTORICAL SOCIETY
101 Main Street
East Hampton
☎ 631-324-6850
www.hamptonsweb.com/ehhs/#sites
Admission: adults, $4; children and seniors, $2, for all five following sites combined.

The East Hampton Historical Society operates the following sites.

The **Osborn-Jackson House**, c. 1740, is the home of the society's headquarters at 101 Main Street. Open year-round, Monday-Friday, 9am-5pm, the museum interprets the lives of families who lived there and displays changing exhibits of decorative arts and textiles from its permanent collection.

The **Marine Museum**, Bluff Road, Amagansett, ☎ 631-267-6544, is dedicated to eastern Long Island's maritime history. Discovery rooms and indoor and outdoor exhibits illustrate the history of whaling and fishing on the East End. Open daily, 10am-5pm, July and August; spring and fall weekends; and by appointment.

The following three properties, also operated by the Historical Society, are open 1-5pm, July and August; spring and fall weekends; and by appointment.

Mulford Farm, 10 James Lane, East Hampton, ☎ 631-324-6869, is a National Register property built c. 1680 for Josiah Hobart, High Sheriff of Suffolk County. Comprising four acres, Mulford Farm is considered one of America's most significant and intact 17th-century farmsteads. A barn built in 1721 and an award-winning garden are on the property. Costumed interpreters present living history programs. The farm is next to Home Sweet Home (see *Historic Sites*, page 437).

Clinton Academy, 151 Main Street, East Hampton, ☎ 631-324-1850, was built in 1784 as the first chartered coeducational academy in New York State; it was named for Governor George Clinton. Distinguished by brick ends, gambrel roof and bell tower, the Academy houses an extensive collection of eastern Long Island artifacts dating from the 17th century. Evening lantern tours and living history programs are offered year-round.

Adjacent to the Academy is the **Town House** at 149 Main Street, ☎ 631-324-6850, which was built c. 1731 as the town trustees' meeting hall, and which housed a one-room schoolhouse. Visitors may experience a living history "class" set in the early 1700s, presented by a costumed interpreter. The Town House is open year-round.

BRIDGEHAMPTON HISTORICAL SOCIETY
2368 Montauk Highway
Bridgehampton
☎ 631-537-1088
www.hamptons.com/historicalsociety

The **Corwith House**, across from the Candy Kitchen and Community House, is society headquarters and a museum. Open year-round; from March through May and from September 15 through December, hours are Monday-Friday, 11am-4pm; from June to September 15, hours are Tuesday-Saturday, 11am-4pm; or by appointment.

SAG HARBOR HISTORICAL SOCIETY
Main Street
Sag Harbor
☎ 631-725-5092
www.hamptons.com/shhs

The society's home is in the **Annie Cooper Boyd House**, which was built in the 1790s. The house is under renovation, but the society's reference library is open by appointment.

MONTAUK HISTORICAL SOCIETY
☎ 631-668-5340

The society offers tours of **Second House**, on Second House Road off Montauk Highway, a half-mile west of the village. The late-1700s farmhouse was used by cattle drovers and is the oldest and most historic building in Montauk. The property has an herb and rose garden. The society also operates the lighthouse museum (see page 442). Second House is open on weekends, from Memorial Day through June; and daily except Wednesday, from July to Columbus Day.

Cultural Tours

Hamptons Art and Culture Tour, a new initiative that includes lodging, meals, shopping and visits to ten cultural organizations, including the Pollack-Krasner House and Study Center (see *Historic Sites*, page 434), takes the hassle out of planning your own itinerary. Accommodations are provided at the Southampton Inn (see *Best Places to Stay*, page 469). The cost is $179 per person, per night. Contact Long Island Holidays at ☎ 631-734-4226, or 800-905-0590; www.longislandholidays.com.

The **Pollock-Krasner House and Study Center** runs an annual autumn art excursion that includes first-class accommodations, two meals a day, admission to all attractions, round-trip coach transportation from East Hampton, and a full-time guide. In 2002 the group visited the Berkshires.

Garden Tours

The Hamptons have three public gardens with limited viewing hours. Admission to each is $10. Bridge and LongHouse offer gardening workshops during the summer.

Bridge Gardens Trust, 36 Mitchell Lane, Bridge-hampton, ☎ 631-537-7440, www.bridgegardens.org, is open Wednesdays and Saturdays, 2-5pm, from the end of April through September.

LongHouse Reserve, 133 Hand's Creek Road, East Hampton, ☎ 631-329-3568, www.longhouse.org, is noted for its 16 acres of gardens and is open 2-5pm on Wednesdays and on the first and third Saturdays of the month from the end of April through mid-September.

Madoo Conservancy, 618 Main Street, Sagaponack, ☎ 631-537-8200, www.madoo.org, is open Wednesdays and Saturdays, 1-5pm, from May through September. Madoo, Scottish for "my dove," was the two-acre house/studio/garden of artist/plantsman Robert Dash.

Wineries

No poems can live long or please that are written by water-drinkers.

– Horace

The South Fork has three wineries, all of which produce reds and whites. The local soil, called Bridge-hampton loam, together with cool breezes from the Atlantic, makes the South Fork a perfect host for grapevines. **Wolffer Estate** and **Duck Walk**, both award-winning wineries, have soaring ceilings and verandas out back overlooking their vineyard. Each hosts concerts in season.

DUCK WALK VINEYARDS
Montauk Highway
Water Mill
☎ 631-726-7555
www.duckwalk.com

The red brick Norman-style château built in 1986 has a modern wooden interior with a high steeple ceiling. The 11,000-square-foot tasting room sells wines, preserves, books and T-shirts. Walk toward the patio overlooking the vineyard and peer through the glass in the door leading to the fermenting room; you'll see gleaming stainless steel tanks holding more than 75,000 gallons of wine.

Duck Walk produces 25,000 cases a year.

The owner, Dr. Herodotus "Dan" Damianos, a Stony Brook internist, also owns Pindar Vineyards on the North Fork (see page 356). In 1994, he purchased Southampton Winery, Duck Walk's predecessor, which went bankrupt. Son Jason Damianos is now the winemaker at Duck Walk. One of its popular wines is Blueberry Port ($12.95), made from Maine's wild mountain blueberries and aged for a year in French oak barrels. It won a medal in a national competition. Tasters are offered a piece of dark chocolate with the Blueberry Port. The winery is open daily, year-round, at 11am. In the off-season, tours of the vineyard are given on weekends, at noon, 2pm and 4pm; in the warmer months they are given daily. There is a $4 charge for tasting any of the reserves, which is applied toward a purchase.

CHANNING DAUGHTERS WINERY
1927 Scuttlehole Road
Bridgehampton
☎ 631-537-7224
www.channingdaughters.com

Channing Daughters is a smaller and less imposing winery than its South Fork sisters. It doesn't enter its wines in competitions because of the owners' belief that the tasting of wine is very personal. They have 30 acres devoted to grapes and plan to remain small to retain

Walter and Molly Channing named the winery for their four daughters.

Suffolk County's South Fork

the hands-on philosophy. The converted potato farm is
the oldest vineyard on the South Fork, having begun
planting 19 years ago. Yet it's the newest winery, having opened to the public only four years ago.

Larry Perrine, who teaches at the International Wine
Center in Manhattan and conducts monthly wine tasting classes here, is the manager. Lisa Michel, the
knowledgeable sales manager and wine tasting hostess, explains that their wines are very dry and close to
the fruit, with no oak taste.

*The primary
reason there
are only three
wineries on
the South
Fork, as com-
pared to the
dozens on the
North Fork, is
that land is so
expensive here.*

To reach the winery, take Montauk Highway east to
Bridgehampton. Just past the Hess station, you'll see a
sign for the winery. Turn left onto Scuttle Hole Road
and continue for 3.6 miles. The winery is on the right; it
is open daily, 11am-5pm, year-round. In addition to
wine tastings, Channing Daughters hosts special
events year-round, such as wine tasting classes, wine
festivals and dance parties.

WINE & WOOD

Walter Channing is also a sculptor; his free-
form pieces are displayed at the winery (they
sell for $2,500 and up). An old-fashioned
wooden sled is quite remarkable, as are many
of his sculptures, which are made with found
wood from piers and trees.

WOLFFER ESTATE
Formerly known as Sagpond Vineyards
139 Sagg Road
Sagaponack
☎ 631-537-5106
www.wolffer.com

*Wine mavens
have consis-
tently praised
Wolffer's rosé
table wine.*

Resembling a Tuscan estate, complete with a coin-filled
fountain out front, the visitors center building is
equally magnificent inside. Once a simple potato farm,
the 55-acre vineyard opened in 1987; it is owned by
Christian Wolffer and managed by Roman Roth, both

German-born. The winery produces 13,000 cases annually.

In addition to musical presentations, Wolffer hosts a busy calendar of events between May and August, including the James Beard Foundation's annual Chefs and Champagne fund-raiser, and the Al Fresco Chef Series. Check the winery's Web site for information about special events. The tasting room is open daily, year-round, 11am-5pm.

To find wine stores throughout the US that sell Long Island wines, go to www.winesearcher.com and type in the name of a winery.

Wildlife Refuges

QUOGUE WILDLIFE REFUGE AND NATURE CENTER
Old Country Road
Quogue
☎ 631-653-4771
www.dec.state.ny.us/website/education/edquog.html

Injured birds and other wild creatures will find a home here. Adults and children who love animals and the outdoors will find this an ideal place to visit. It's free, and has 305 ecologically varied acres to explore on foot or on skis any day of the year.

 TIP

Pick up the trail guide booklet at Quogue Wildlife Refuge – it's quite educational.

Duck hunters, disturbed by the decline of the local black duck population, founded the refuge in 1934. They were given the use of an ice house belonging to the Quogue Ice Company, which had been idle since about 1925 (prior to the advent of refrigeration, ice was packed in sawdust and stored in an icehouse, and could stay frozen for three years). The ice house still stands and has a display of ice-cutting tools.

No biking, fishing or dogs are allowed in the Quogue Nature Center.

Suffolk County's South Fork

Year-round programs for all ages are held in the large exhibit room that has a borrowing library of books on nature, meteorology and evolution; most are free. Members receive a monthly newsletter. Plans are being made to start a Saturday afternoon program for children that will cost $2 to $3. The most popular program, now in its 34th year, is a hands-on field ecology program for kids from Monday to Friday, every week from July Fourth through the second week in August. The fee is $70 to $100.

Visitors may feed the ducks and geese on the pond (but are asked to use seeds and grains instead of bread, which simply fills the stomach and offers no nutrition). The **Distressed Wildlife Complex** houses animals that were hit by cars, shot, or otherwise incapacitated; residents include a red-tailed hawk, a turkey and a bald eagle.

Trails are open year-round; the building is open Tuesday, Thursday, Saturday and Sunday, 1-4pm. To reach the refuge, which is partially wheelchair-accessible, take Sunrise Highway to Exit 64S and follow County Route 104 south for two miles to the right fork. Proceed to Old Country Road and turn right. The refuge is less than a mile on the right.

ELIZABETH A. MORTON NATIONAL WILDLIFE REFUGE

Noyac Road, west of Sag Harbor
☎ 631-286-0485
Parking and entrance fee, $4 ($2 for bike/pedestrian)

This 187-acre refuge on a point of land extending into Little Peconic Bay has exceptionally diverse habitats. Bay and sea birds are common during the winter, and wading birds and shorebirds visit in warmer months. The nature trail passes through upland areas and onto the 1¾-mile beach, a portion of which is closed from April through August. The Montauketts and Shinnecocks once occupied what is now the refuge. From Southampton, take North Sea Road to Noyac Road; turn right and go five miles to the refuge entrance on the left. Open daily, year-round, from a half-hour before sunrise to a half-hour after sunset. No permit required.

CONSCIENCE POINT NATIONAL WILDLIFE REFUGE

North Sea Road
Southampton
☎ 631-286-0485

This 60-acre refuge was established in 1971; it is one of the few maritime grassland communities on Long Island. Wading birds and osprey are commonly observed in spring and summer, and waterfowl in winter. Entrance is by special use permit only.

CONSCIENCE POINT

Conscience Point is a restful spot overlooking North Sea Harbor. It's said that the name originated when settlers from Massachusetts landed here and a woman said: "For conscience sake, we're on dry land." Off to the left of the parking lot is a short walk leading to a large boulder bearing this inscription: "Near this spot in June, 1640, landed the colonists from Lynn, Mass. who founded Southampton, the first English settlement in the State of New York." Conscience Point is 4.2 miles from Jobs Lane in Southampton. Follow Main Street, which feeds into North Sea Road, and take it to the end. At the roadside plaque, follow the dirt road to the parking lot.

☞ DID YOU KNOW?

The first National Wildlife Refuge, Florida's **Pelican Island**, was established in 1903 by President Theodore Roosevelt, Long Island's most famous resident.

Suffolk County's South Fork

Health & Beauty

Fitness Centers

SPORTIME
2571 Old Riverhead Road (Route 104)
Quogue
☎ 631-653-6767, or 888-NY-TENNIS
www.sportimetfm.com

All facilities are open daily, year-round, unless otherwise noted.

Pool, gym, aerobics, multi-sport court, snack bar. Non-members pay fee for use of facilities (no rates quoted over phone). Sportime has 23 outdoor and six indoor tennis courts, all Har-Tru. Lessons, tournaments, snack bar.

OMNI HEALTH & RACQUET CLUB
395 County Road 39A
Southampton
☎ 631-283-4770
www.omnihealthclub.com

A full-service fitness facility for all ages, Omni has a weight room on two levels, a warm and cold pool, whirlpools, saunas, steam rooms and a dressing room for handicapped members. Classes include swimming for infants and children, yoga, high and low impact aerobics, step, spinning, aquatic and private swimming lessons. In addition, every month there are special classes, such as boxing. An ongoing program of rigorous physical training, patterned after the regimen used by the US Navy Seals, is offered one night a week for beginner, intermediate and advanced students. Day care (for members only) is available every day except Sunday, at $1 per child. The day rate for non-members is $20. Open Monday-Friday, 6am-10pm; Saturday-Sunday, 7am-8pm.

TIP

Omni is in the same complex as the Hampton Jitney office, should you want to exercise before buying your bus ticket home.

AMERICAN FITNESS FACTORY
15 Hill Street
Southampton
☎ 631-283-0707

This facility has Cybex equipment. Open Monday-Friday, 6am-9pm; Saturday, 7am-9pm; and Sunday, 8am-8pm. The day fee is $20. Child care, $2 per child. They also have a location in Sag Harbor, on Bay Street; ☎ 631-725-0707.

EAST HAMPTON GYM
2 Fithian Lane
East Hampton
☎ 631-324-4499

East Hampton Gym has Cybex equipment; they are open Monday-Friday, 6am-9:30pm; Saturday, 7am-8pm; Sunday, 7:30am-7pm. Day fee is $20. Entrance is in back of Plaza Surf & Sports.

YMCA EAST HAMPTON RECenter
2 Gingerbread Lane
East Hampton
☎ 631-329-6884
www.ymcali.org

Opened January 1, 2001, this is the eighth branch of the YMCA on Long Island and, according to its Web site, has the largest indoor pool complex on the East End. The Y offers daily exercise classes and personal trainers. The day fee is $10; babysitting is available.

Suffolk County's South Fork

BODY TECH (a/k/a Amagansett Fitness Center)
249 Main Street
Amagansett
☎ 631-267-8222

Body Tech is a three-floor facility. They offer daily, monthly and yearly rates. Open Monday-Friday, 6:15am-9pm; Saturday, 7:30am-7pm; Sunday 7:30am-5pm. Day fee, $16.

BUSY BODIES FITNESS CENTER
South Elmwood Avenue
Montauk
☎ 631-668-4858

Full-service facility featuring coed, beginner, advanced and children's classes; day and evening. Personal trainers are available. The day fee is $13; no childcare. Open daily between Memorial Day and Labor Day; Tuesday-Friday in winter.

Day Spas

English Garden Day Spa, 193 Montauk Highway, Speonk (just west of Westhampton), ☎ 631-325-5952. Full-service salon, but no tanning. Open Tuesday-Saturday.

Westhampton Day Spa, 64 Old Riverhead Road, Westhampton Beach, ☎ 631-288-4900, www.westhamptondayspa.com. Full-service salon. Open daily in season, closed Tuesday in off-season.

Ileana Skin Care, Jobs Lane, Southampton, ☎ 631-287-1977. See *Shop Till You Drop*, page 491.

La Carezza, 43-45 Windmill Lane, Southampton, ☎ 631-283-7683, www.lacarezza.com. A hair salon and day spa offering a full range of skin treatments, including microdermabrasion and massages. Open Monday-Saturday, year-round.

Fay Teller Salon, Corwith Avenue, Bridgehampton (across from Candy Kitchen), ☎ 631-537-3393. Full-service hair salon and spa. Closed Sunday. Appointments recommended in summer; walk-ins welcome in winter.

Scott J. Aveda Salon and Spa, 2415 Main Street, Bridgehampton, ☎ 631-537-6696, www.scottj.com. Complete spa and hair salon. Appointments necessary. Open daily.

Gemayel Salon & Spa, 2044 Montauk Highway, Bridgehampton Commons, Bridgehampton, ☎ 631-725-8500, www.gemayelspa.com. Full-service, including hair salon and treatments such as microdermabrasion. Packages for men and women. No tanning. Extensive retail shop carries some of Gemayel's own products. Open Tuesday-Saturday. Their Manhattan salon at 70th and Broadway has been open for more than 20 years; ☎ 212-787-5555.

Naturopathica, 74 Montauk Highway (Red Horse Plaza), East Hampton, ☎ 631-329-2525. Holistic health spa with its own line of products. No hair or nails. Open daily, from Memorial Day to Labor Day; closed Tuesday and Wednesday in off-season.

Susan Ciminelli Day Spa, 34 Pantigo Road, East Hampton, ☎ 631-267-6300, www.susanciminelli.com. All body treatments, no hair salon. Open daily Memorial Day-Labor Day, otherwise Friday-Sunday by appointment.

Style Bar, One Bay Street, Sag Harbor, ☎ 631-725-6730, www.stylebarspa.com, is a day-spa with myriad treatments, including non-surgical cellulite reduction and facial sculpting. Closed Tuesday in winter.

Sage Hampton Spa, 382 Montauk Highway, Wainscott, ☎ 631-537-7300. Holistic spa offering massages, facials and acupuncture. Walk-ins welcome. Open daily.

Oasis Massage Center, On the Plaza, (above the Book Shoppe), Montauk, ☎ 631-668-4815, www.oasis-massage.com. Massages and body treatments for men and women. Open daily Memorial Day-Labor Day and off-season by appointment.

Suffolk County's South Fork

Recreation

Boating

Fishing Charters

Viking Fishing Fleet, West Lake Drive, Southampton, ☎ 631-668-5700, www.vikingfleet.com, operates from mid-January through early November, with local and off-shore fishing trips, half-day fishing trips with free lessons, and night fishing between May and October. They also offer casino cruises, whale watching and special cruises, as well as operating ferries to Block Island (daily); see page 430.

Double Haul Charters, 85 Osbourne Lane, East Hampton, ☎ 631-907-9004, www.allmontaukflyfishing.com. Captain Jim Levison's fly-fishing and light tackle charter service offers half- and full-day trips. The boat leaves from Three Mile Harbor on Gardiners Bay in spring and summer, and from Montauk in the fall. Fishermen and non-fishermen alike are invited on his summer sunset cruises.

Select "Boating & Fishing" on www.hamptonsweb.com for more information.

SOMETHING'S FISHY HERE

Montauk bills itself as the "Fishing Capital of the World" because it boasts the largest commercial harbor in New York and has some of the best sportfishing and captains around. Indeed, Montauk Harbor is quite impressive – year-round. In summer, it's busy, busy and in winter the huge vessels are docked for all to admire.

Marlin V, Salivar's Dock, Montauk Harbor, ☎ 631-668-2818, or 668-5852. Two trips daily in July and August on the 65-foot boat. All-day trips for fluke run from May through September, and for local cod in March and April. Reservations are essential for night bass-fishing with live eels; this is offered Wednesday-Sunday, 7pm-

1am, from May to December 15. $30 for half-day trips; $55 for a full day. Make the first right after the Viking Fleet pier.

Flying Cloud of Montauk, on Viking Fleet's dock (behind Dave's Grill on Montauk Harbor), ☎ 631-668-2026, is available for half-day fishing trips for fluke, sea bass, cod, flounder, porgies and other local fish in season, with Captain Fred E. Bird. Two trips daily, from May to Labor Day; all-day trips ($48) from Labor Day through mid-November.

Sailing & Cruises

***Aliento* Charters**, 948 Fireplace Road, East Hampton, ☎ 631-267-6817, www.hamptons.com/aliento. Captain George Wilson's 50-foot sailing ketch is available for charter for full- or half-day sails or for a sunset cruise. The 12-passenger boat is $600 for a half-day; $1,000 for a full day, plus 15% gratuity. Three-hour sunset cruises are $450 plus tip. Trips leave from East Hampton Point Marina.

Sag Harbor Sailing School, Sag Harbor Yacht Yard, Bay Street, Sag Harbor, ☎ 631-725-5100 or 877-725-5200, www.sagharborsailing.com, rents a 23-foot sloop for half- or full-day trips, and larger craft (such as Islanders and Catalinas) for bareboat or captained charters (these are typically one- to seven-day trips but may be longer). The 23-foot, six-passenger sloop is rented at $225 for a half-day and $275 for a full day (weekday rates slightly lower); if you need a captain, add $75 for a half-day and $125 full day. The school also offers beginner and advanced sailing instruction for adults and teenagers. Open from May through October for sailing; open all year for their weekend Coastal Navigation course.

Suffolk County's South Fork

Marinas

Eastport, Westhampton & Quogue

The Town of Southampton no longer provides transient marina space in Hampton Bays, East Quogue or Eastport because of the overwhelming demand.

Eastport Marina, 50 South Bay Avenue, Eastport, ☎ 631-325-8900. Storage, dockage, sales, fuel, electric, restroom, showers. Open year-round. Restaurant next door (Trumpets On the Bay, ☎ 631-325-2900).

Surfside 3 at South Shore Boats, 33 Library Avenue, Westhampton, ☎ 631-288-2400. Sales, fuel. Open year-round.

Village Marina, Library Avenue, Westhampton, ☎ 631-288-9496. Dockage, electric, restrooms, showers. One block to Main Street and a half-mile to beach. Open from April 15 to October 15.

Aldrich Boat Yard, 33 Weeseck Avenue, Quogue, ☎ 631-653-5300. Dockage, electric, hauling, storage. Open daily in season. Call for winter hours.

Hampton Bays

Hampton Watercraft & Marine, 44 Newtown Road, Hampton Bays on Great Peconic Bay, ☎ 631-728-8200. Dockage, sales, service, showers, electric, restrooms, waterski pro shop, and a restaurant in the works. Open daily, year-round.

Indian Cove Marine, Old Montauk Highway, Hampton Bays, ☎ 631-728-5366. The marina, with dockage, showers, electric and restrooms, is private; the marina's restaurant is open to the public. Marina and restaurant are both open from May through October; the restaurant then continues to serve dinner on weekends through December.

Jean Marie Dive Charters is located at Jackson's Marina; ☎ 631-728-5168.

Jackson's Marina, 6 Teepee Street (on Shinnecock Canal), ☎ 631-728-4220, www.jacksonsmarina.com. Storage, dockage, fuel, picnic area, sales, showers, electric, groceries, restrooms, showers. Open daily, year-round.

Mariner's Cove Marine, 9 Canoe Place Road (on Shinnecock Canal), Hampton Bays, ☎ 631-728-0286, www.marinerscovemarine.com. Storage, dockage, sales, hauling, picnic area, bait and tackle, showers, restaurant, snack bar, electric, restrooms and private beach. In the summer, says owner Robert Arcate, "it's like Times Square on the water." Open year-round; closed Sundays in winter.

Modern Yachts Marina, 36 Newtown Road, Hampton Bays, ☎ 631-728-2266. Storage, dockage, hauling, fuel, electric, pool, marine store. Open daily in season; closed weekends from November through April.

Molnar's Landing, 31 Alanson Lane, Hampton Bays, ☎ 631-728-1860. Storage, dockage, hauling, picnic area, bait and tackle, snack bar, mechanic on duty. Open mid-April through October. The tavern and lounge on the property are open year-round.

Ponquogue Marine Basin, 86 Foster Avenue, Hampton Bays, ☎ 631-728-2264. Storage, dockage, picnic area, electric, showers, restrooms, beach, mechanic on duty. Adjacent to Tully's Restaurant. Open daily from mid-March through November, and by appointment the rest of the year.

Shinnecock Bay Fishing Station, 22 Shinnecock Road, Hampton Bays, ☎ 631-728-6116. Dockage, fuel, picnic area, bait and tackle, groceries, snack bar, electric, restrooms, boat rentals. Open daily, year-round. The restaurant is open for lunch and dinner.

Shinnecock Marina, at the northeast end of Shinnecock Canal, Hampton Bays, ☎ 631-852-8291. Storage, dockage, showers, electric, restrooms. This facility is run by the Suffolk County Department of Parks, Recreation & Conservation. For a slip reservation, call the department at ☎ 631-854-4952.

Spellman's Marine, 262 East Montauk Highway, Hampton Bays (the turn is just before the Shinnecock Canal Bridge), ☎ 631-728-8662, www.spellmansmarine.com. Storage, dockage, sales, hauling, towing, picnic area, showers, snack bar, electric, restrooms and large indoor showroom. Open daily, year-round. Spellman's other location at 23 Rampasture Road (on Smith Creek), Hampton Bays, ☎ 631-728-1341, provides the same services but has no showers or snack bar. Open Monday-Saturday, year-round.

Frank's Landing, 3 Rampasture Road, Hampton Bays, ☎ 631-728-0619. Storage, dockage, sales, hauling, fuel. Open Tuesday-Saturday, year-round.

Southampton

Conscience Point Marina, 1976 North Sea Road, Southampton, ☎ 631-283-8295. Dockage, fuel, showers, electric, restrooms. Open from April through October.

Strong's Marine, 1810 North Sea Road, Southampton, ☎ 631-283-4841, www.strongsmarine.com. Dockage, storage, hauling, restrooms, electric. (Strong's main office is in Mattituck; see page 370.)

East Hampton

Three Mile Harbor Boatyard, Three Mile Harbor Road, East Hampton, ☎ 631-324-1320. Storage, dockage, sales, marine store, bait, hauling, picnic area, bait and tackle, showers, electric,restrooms. Open year-round.

East Hampton Point Marina, 295 Three Mile Harbor Road, East Hampton, ☎ 631-324-8400, www.easthamptonpoint.com. Storage, dockage, sales, hauling, fuel, picnic area, tennis, showers, snack bar, electric, laundry, pool, beach, mechanics on duty; 13 cottages (daily, $275-$475). Open year-round (the East Hampton Point Restaurant is seasonal; ☎ 631-329-2800).

Halsey's Marina, Three Mile Harbor Road, East Hampton, ☎ 631-324-9847. Dockage, picnic area, showers, electric, restrooms. Open from May through September.

Harbor Marina, 423 Three Mile Harbor, Hog Creek Road, East Hampton, ☎ 631-324-5666, www.harbor-marina.com. Storage, dockage, sales, marine store, electric, fuel, groceries, restrooms, showers, snack bar, mechanics on duty, restaurant (Bostwick's Seafood Grill & Oyster Bar). Open year-round.

> ★ BOATING TIP
>
> The Town of East Hampton does not provide transient docking spaces. Six moorings are available at Three Mile Harbor on a first-come, first-served basis at $25 per night. Contact the Town of East Hampton Trustees, ☎ 631-267-8688.

Sag Harbor

Mill Creek Marina, 3253 Noyac Road, Sag Harbor, ☎ 631-725-1351. Dockage, electric, showers, fuel, storage, hauling, restaurant. Open from March through December. There is a restaurant, Jessups on the Bay; it is currently open year-round but may be changing hands, so call ahead; ☎ 631-725-1116.

Ship Ashore Marina, 30 Redwood Road, Sag Harbor, ☎ 631-725-3755. Electric, fuel, hauling, storage. Seasonal.

Montauk

Diamond Cove Marina, 364 West Lake Drive, Montauk, ☎ 631-668-6592. Sales, storage, dockage, fuel, hauling, picnic area, showers, electric, restrooms. Open daily, from March through November.

Gone Fishing Marina, 467 East Lake Drive, Montauk, ☎ 631-668-3232, www.screamingreel.com/marina/gonefishing.html. Dockage, electric, hauling, fuel, marine store, groceries, bait, showers, laundry. Open year-round; closed weekends in January and February. There is a restaurant, the After Fishing Bar and Grill, open seasonally; ☎ 631-668-6535.

Suffolk County's South Fork

Montauk Marine, 426 West Lake Drive, Montauk, ☎ 631-668-5900, www.montaukmarine.com. This marina recently completed a major bulkhead replacement and upgraded their electrical wiring, water lines and cable connections for TV hook-ups and on-line computer access for those who'd like to surf the Web. Their full-service boatyard offers sales, service, fuel, hauling, picnic area, showers, restrooms, laundry, phone, dockage, certified mechanics, indoor and outdoor storage, bait and tackle, groceries. Special rates for charter boats. They are in walking distance to Montauk Harbor. Open daily, year-round.

Offshore Sports Marina, West Lake Drive, Montauk, ☎ 631-668-2406. Storage, dockage, sales, service, hauling, towing, fuel, picnic area, bait and tackle, showers, electric, restrooms, laundry, bar. Open daily, year-round.

Star Island Yacht Club & Marina, Star Island Road (next to the Coast Guard Station), Montauk, ☎ 631-668-5052, www.starislandyc.com. The East End's "Largest Charter Boat Fleet" carries tackle, bait, rods & reels, footwear, clothing. Services include storage, dockage, sales, service, hauling, fuel, picnic area, groceries, bait and tackle, restaurant, snack bar, pool, laundry and cable TV. Open year-round at 5am; closing time varies seasonally.

"Swim, ski, cruise or fish, When you rent at Uihlein's it's whatever U wish," reads Uihlein's brochure.

Uihlein's, 444 West Lake Drive, Montauk, ☎ 631-668-3799, www.hamptonsweb.com/uihleins. This is a full-service marina with a year-round motel on premises (see West Lake Drive Motel, page 531), summer dockage for boats up to 40 feet, sales, storage, fuel, hauling, repairs, boat rentals (hourly, daily or weekly). Uihlein's offers lessons in waterskiing, kayaking, parasailing and personal watercraft in the calm waters of Lake Montauk and Long Island Sound. Also rents and sells rods and reels. Open daily, year-round.

Westlake Fishing Marina, West Lake Drive, Montauk, ☎ 631-668-5600. Charters, transient docking, bait, tackle, showers. Open April-December. A restau-

rant, the Clam & Chowder House, has indoor and outdoor seating and is open May-November.

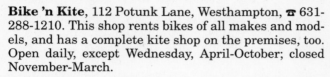

Biking

Sales & Rentals

Bike 'n Kite, 112 Potunk Lane, Westhampton, ☎ 631-
288-1210. This shop rents bikes of all makes and models, and has a complete kite shop on the premises, too.
Open daily, except Wednesday, April-October; closed
November-March.

Bermuda Bikes Plus, 36 Gingerbread Lane, East
Hampton, ☎ 631-324-6688, www.bermudabikes.com.
Bermuda Bikes has sales, service, rentals and lessons.
Open from April through January, daily in season; call
for off-season hours. Closed in February and March.

Espos Surf & Sport, The Old Barn, Main Street, East
Hampton, ☎ 631-329-9100. Bike rentals are available
here; repairs are made at their Amagansett shop,
which is open in season only.

Khanh's Sports, 60 Park Place, East Hampton,
☎ 631-324-0703, sells and rents bikes and surfboards.
Sells skateboards and boogie boards. Open daily, year-
round.

Plaza Surf & Sports, 2 Pantiago Road, East Hampton, ☎ 631-329-6300, sells a full line of sporting goods
and apparel, and rents 15-speed mountain bikes ($25 a
day), wetsuits and surfboards. Open daily, year-round.
They also have a location at 716 Main Street, Montauk;
☎ 631-668-9300; see page 468.

Bike Hampton, 36 Main Street, Sag Harbor, ☎ 631-
725-7329, sells and rents bikes. Open daily in season;
closed Wednesday in winter.

Rotations Bicycle Club, 32 Windmill Lane, Southampton, ☎ 631-283-2890, www.rotationsbicyclecen-
ter.com. This store – the South Fork's only cycling club
– has been in business for more than 20 years. Owner
Rick Laspesa builds custom bikes, and sells these

*Red Creek
Park in
Hampton Bays
is open to
inline-skaters.*

Suffolk County's South Fork

Laspesa Cycles as well as those of other manufacturers – predominantly road and kids' bikes. The store also has bicycles for rent. Closed Wednesday.

Cycle Path Bikes, 330 Montauk Highway, Wainscott, ☎ 631-537-1144, www.pinchflat.com, has sales and rentals of mountain and hybrid bikes. Open daily in summer; closed Tuesday and Wednesday in winter.

Amagansett Beach & Bicycle Company, Montauk and Cross Highway, at Abrahams Path, Amagansett, ☎ 631-267-6325, www.amagansettbeachco.com, rents and sells bicycles. Also rents kayaks (and gives lessons), surfboards, body boards, skates, wetsuits, windsurfers. Open daily; closed January and February.

Plaza Surf & Sports, 716 Main Street, Montauk, ☎ 631-668-9300, sells a full line of sporting goods and apparel, and rents 15-speed mountain bikes ($25 a day), wetsuits, surfboards and mopeds. Open daily, year-round.

Montauk Bike Shop, 725 Montauk Highway, Montauk, ☎ 631-668-8975, www.montaukbikeshop.com. Chris Pfund sells and rents "anything that pedals." He also gives biking instruction, and 40% of his students are adults. Chris guarantees success in one hour or your money back (and he claims a 100% success rate in four years of operation). He also conducts bike tours for groups and evening BBQ tours. Open year-round, daily in season; call for winter hours.

Cycling Club

The **Five Borough Bicycle Club**, ☎ 212-932-2300 Ext. 115; www.5bbc.org, is based in New York City, but its annual "Montauk Century" involves cycling the 100 miles from the city to the Hamptons in one day in May. The ride is geared to all levels, and riders can go at their own pace. The club offers free training rides at various locations in New York and New Jersey. This popular event has expanded from 100 riders and one departure place to 1,000 people departing from four separate locations. The club also sponsors day and weekend trips.

Walking & Hiking

How does a full moon hike in the walking dunes or an early riser's paddle on Three Mile Harbor strike you? **Group for the South Fork**, ☎ 631-537-1400, www.thehamptons.com/group, an education and advocacy organization, runs a full range of guided biking, hiking and boating "explorations." Non-members pay $5.

The **East Hampton Nature Trail** begins at a duck pond and is for walking only – no bikes or dogs are allowed. It's an easy, short trail with benches, ideal for families with small children. Turn onto David's Lane at the white Presbyterian Church and follow the road for less than a mile.

Swimming

BATH & TENNIS HOTEL
231 Dune Road
Westhampton
☎ 631-288-2500
www.bathandtennis.com

Heated saltwater pool. Deck memberships available; call for details. The hotel also has a fitness club, tennis courts, and a restaurant, Tierra Mar (see page 533).

SOUTHAMPTON INN
91 Hill Street
Southampton
☎ 800-832-6500

Southampton Inn Pool and Tennis offers monthly and individual memberships that provide access to the hotel's heated swimming pool, tennis court, game room, fitness room, and Cooper's Beach (one mile from the inn); a parking spot is also included. A summer membership runs $1,200 for a family of four.

Parks & Beaches

Westhampton

Rogers Pavilion, Dune Road, ☎ 631-283-6306, is a village beach at the end of Beach Lane. It has lifeguards, food pavilion, restrooms, outdoor and indoor showers, picnic tables. This beach, as well as its extension, **Lashley**, farther west, is a members-only beach. Westhampton Beach residents and summer residents purchase season passes. Some lodgings provide passes, but guests must park their cars across the Beach Lane Bridge.

Hampton Bays

The beach season in Hampton Bays is July 1 to September 1.

Two town beaches are **Ponquogue Beach**, which is frequented by families, and **Tiana Beach**, a singles hangout with a huge parking lot. They are a few miles apart on Dune Road. Both are to the right when exiting the Ponquogue Bridge, and have full facilities and lifeguards.

Shinnecock Inlet

There's a small beach at Shinnecock Inlet County Park on Dune Road. It has a nice view of the jetties and Southampton on the other side, but no lifeguard.

To reach Dune Road, head south on Ponquoque Avenue at the light in the village of Hampton Bays (Mulligan's is on the corner) and take Ponquogue Avenue to the end. Turn left onto Shinnecock Road and make a right onto Foster Avenue. Go over the Ponquogue Bridge and turn right. Ponquogue Beach is the closest.

THE SHINNECOCK INLET

The Shinnecock Inlet didn't exist before 1938; it was formed by the hurricane of that year, in which Westhampton Beach took the worst battering of any Long Island community. Twenty-eight people from the area were killed and the damage was estimated at around $2 million. Before the storm created a new passage from the ocean, the barrier island extended from Moriches Inlet to Southampton.

Southampton

A parking permit is required for most beaches. Non-residents pay $10 for a daily parking pass at town beaches and $25 for a weekend parking pass at village beaches. Check with your hotel or guesthouse first; some lodgings provide passes to their guests. For more information, call the Southampton Town Hall, ☎ 631-283-6011.

For **Cooper's Beach** (a village beach), follow Main Street to the end and turn right onto Gin Lane. Follow the road past Main Beach and the exotic red St. Andrew's Dune Church. At the stop sign, turn left and follow the road to the beach.

ST. ANDREW'S DUNE CHURCH

Built by the US government in 1851 as a life-saving station and converted into a church in 1879, St. Andrew's holds Sunday services with prayer and meditation for all until 4pm , June through September. Inside are beautiful windows, some by Tiffany, and walls with biblical texts.

Emma Rose Elliston Park, Millstone Road, in the village of North Sea, ☎ 631-283-9426, has lifeguards, restrooms, showers, picnic tables.

Water Mill

Beach passes are like gold, so when summer rentals are down some landlords actually throw in an old car with a beach sticker as an incentive to rent.

Flying Point Beach, Flying Point Road, ☎ 631-726-2604, has lifeguards, showers, restrooms, food stand, but there is no daily access. It is open only to seasonal holders (resident or non-resident) of Town of Southampton permits.

East Hampton

East Hampton Nature Trail begins at a duck pond and is for walking only – no bikes or dogs. It's a short, easy trail with benches, ideal for toddlers. Turn onto David's Lane at the white Presbyterian Church and follow the road for less than a mile.

> ★ TIP
>
> A parking permit is required for most beaches. Non-residents pay $15 for a parking pass at both town and village beaches. Check with your hotel or guesthouse first. Several lodgings provide passes to their guests.

Main Beach. This ocean beach at the end of Ocean Avenue is a family beach and the most crowded. Lifeguards.

Georgica Beach is an ocean beach at the end of Apaquogue Road and Lily Pond Lane, East Hampton.

Two Mile Hollow is an ocean beach at the end of Two Mile Hollow Road, East Hampton. No lifeguards or facilities.

Amagansett

Maidstone Park, at the end of Flaggy Hole Road off Three Mile Harbor Road and Hog Creek Highway, extends for 400 feet on Gardiner's Bay. Lifeguards, restrooms, picnic area.

Atlantic Avenue Beach is an ocean beach near the firehouse in Amagansett. Lifeguards, restrooms. No daily parking permits allowed on weekends or holidays.

Indian Wells Beach is an ocean beach at the end of Indian Wells Highway in Amagansett. Lifeguards, restrooms. Open to East Hampton Town residents only.

Part of Hither Hills State Park (see page 475) is the **Walking Dunes** area, where there's a bayside beach. The 80- to 100-foot dunes, formed over time by strong winds, are moving southeast about 3½ feet per year, burying the trees in their path. Pick up a map in the box at the park entrance and follow the sand path. It's a ¾-mile loop and you won't see the dunes until point #3 on the map. The dunes, which seem to appear out of nowhere, might give you an eerie feeling, as if you landed on the moon.

To reach the Walking Dunes, follow Napeague Harbor Road (across from the Sea Crest in Amagansett) to the end, where you'll see the sign about the piping plover, a federally designated threatened species.

Montauk Town Beaches

Kirk Park Beach, ☎ 631-324-2417, an ocean beach. Parking is available (non-residents pay $10). Lifeguards, picnic areas, restrooms.

Gin Beach, at the end of East Lake Drive on Block Island Sound, Montauk. Lifeguards, restrooms.

Ditch Plains (an ocean beach popular with surfers), off Ditch Plains Road, Montauk. Lifeguards, restrooms.

If you wish to assist in the Suffolk County Parks Plover Protection Program, call the Parks & Recreation office at ☎ 631-854-4949 to volunteer.

Suffolk County's South Fork

> ☞ DID YOU KNOW?
>
> In his 2002 survey, Dr. Beach (a/k/a Stephen P. Leatherman), www.dr-beach.org, rated East Hampton's Main Beach as one of America's top 10 beaches, and Montauk's Ditch Plains as among the best surfing beaches.

South Lake Beach, a Bay beach on southern end of Lake Montauk. Lifeguards.

Fresh Pond Beach. Bay beach at end of Fresh Pond Road at Napeague Bay. Lifeguards.

Albert's Landing Beach, a Bay beach at the end of Albert's Landing Road, off Old Stone Highway on Napeague Bay. Lifeguards, restrooms, picnic area.

You may park here. Don't mistake the sign, as we did, that reads "Permit required for beach vehicles." It refers to driving cars on the beach, not to parking.

> ☞ DID YOU KNOW?
>
> The 4½-mile stretch of dunes between Amagansett and Montauk, created by sand moved west by the tides, is called **Napeague**. This area gained fame in the 1920s when, thanks to its resemblance to an Arabian desert, it was the location for the famous silent film, *The Sheik*, starring Rudolph Valentino. Later, on June 13, 1942, four Nazi saboteurs in a submarine came ashore at Napeague beach with a plan to destroy bridges, plants and railroads. After a 15-day manhunt, they were captured, tried and convicted. Two of the four were executed in 1942; the others cooperated with the FBI and were given long prison sentences.

HITHER HILLS STATE PARK
Old Country Road, off Old Montauk Hwy.
Montauk
☎ 631-668-2554

The sign at the Old Montauk Highway entrance reads, "Family camping at its best." With 165 campsites (available from mid-April through mid-November), this 1,755-acre park is indeed geared to campers. The park provides weekly activities for the family in season, and children's movies are shown every night.

Non-campers will also find plenty to do. In season, lifeguards are on duty along the 2.5-mile ocean beach. Facilities include a bathhouse, ball field, bridle and hiking paths, general store, playground, picnic tables, and salt- and freshwater fishing (a permit is required for the latter).

Hither Hills is open year-round. Take Montauk Highway until you get to a fork; then go right on Old Montauk Highway. The road cuts through the park, which stretches from Napeague Bay to the Atlantic Ocean. This entrance is four miles west of Montauk village and 1.3 miles before Gurney's Inn & Spa. The fee for camping is $16 per night or $119 per week; to reserve a site, call ☎ 800-456-CAMP, www.ReserveAmerica.com. The fee for day use is $7 for parking, from the end of May through mid-September.

SEAL WATCHING
Visiting Montauk on a winter weekend between January and March 31? Sign up for a two- to three-hour guided beach walk with a naturalist to observe seals. The best time to see them is at low tide. $5. Call Montauk State Park for details, ☎ 631-668-3781.

Suffolk County's South Fork

Kayaking, Surfing & Skating

JETTIES SURF, SKATE AND SNOW
109 Main Street
Westhampton
☎ 631-288-0488

Daily and seasonal openings vary; call ahead.

Open daily in the summer, the store is open weekends in winter with ski merchandise. Manager Dan professes to be "the only shop in town open all winter — consistently." The store also rents kayaks and surfboards.

FLYING POINT SURF & SPORT
69 Main Street
Southampton
☎ 631-287-0075

Flying Point sells and rents boogie boards and surfboards, and sells women's and children's clothing.

MAIN BEACH SURF & SPORT
Montauk Highway
Wainscott
☎ 800-564-4386, or 631-537-2716

This shop rents surfboards, kayaks, canoes, and trimarans. Weekend kayak tours and lessons are available (surfing, kayaking, kite- and wakeboarding).

ESPOS SURF & SPORT
The Old Barn
Main Street
East Hampton
☎ 631-329-9100

Espos sells and rents surfboards. Also sells water-skis, wake boards and boogie boards.

KHANH'S SPORTS
60 Park Place
East Hampton
☎ 631-324-0703

Sells and rents surfboards. Sells skateboards and boogie boards.

EAST COAST ADVENTURE TOUR CO.
253 Noyack Road at Mill Creek Marina
East Hampton
☎ 631-267-2303
www.startkayaking.com

Sells and rents kayaks and bikes, gives kayak lessons and offers guided wildlife and ecology tours, children's treasure hunts and adventure tours. Also runs kayaking and birding trips to Florida, South America and even Cuba. Local paddle areas are in Amagansett, Southampton, East Hampton, Sag Harbor/Noyac, Bridgehampton and Water Mill, and Montauk.

AMAGANSETT BEACH & BICYCLE COMPANY
Montauk and Cross Highway, at Abrahams Path
Amagansett
☎ 631-267-6325
www.amagansettbeachco.com

Rents and sells kayaks (and gives lessons), surfboards, body boards, skates, wetsuits, windsurfers. Closed January and February.

ISLAND SURF
34 Main Street
Sag Harbor
☎ 631-725-0705
www.islandsurf.net

Island Surf sells everything for the surfer – surfboards, apparel, body boards, sunglasses, beach attire – plus skateboards and kayaks (only surfboards are for rent). They also have a store in Westhampton, at 121 C&D Main Street, ☎ 631-288-4144.

Suffolk County's South Fork

PLAZA SURF & SPORTS
716 Main Street
Montauk
☎ 631-668-9300

Sells and rents a variety of sporting goods and apparel, including wetsuits and surfboards.

Tennis

EASTSIDE TENNIS & FITNESS CLUB
142 Montauk Highway
Grassmere Inn
Westhampton
☎ 631-288-1540 (operator)
☎ 631-288-6288 (tennis shop)
www.whtenniscamp.com

Peter Kaplan, proprietor of the Grassmere Inn in Westhampton (see page 503), also offers overnight and day tennis camps for adults, juniors and famillies here in July and August. Participants who stay at the Grassmere Inn get a package rate. When the courts are available, the club rents time to non-campers. They also rent court time to non-campers. The club is open from May through October.

WESTHAMPTON BEACH TENNIS & SPORT CLUB
86 Depot Road
Westhampton
☎ 631-288-6060

This club has 25 Har-Tru outdoor courts, one hard court, and four indoor courts. Clinics (their small gym is being expanded), pro shop, concession stand. Open to members only in-season. Occasionally, weekday afternoons are available to non-members at $25 per hour, per court. Inquire about early-bird specials. Open daily, year-round. Heading east on Montauk Highway, turn left at the Gulf Station.

SOUTHAMPTON RACQUET CLUB
655 Majors Path
Southampton
☎ 631-288-5444

The racquet club has 10 Har-Tru courts, and offers lessons; they also have a junior tennis club. Day fee, $40/day (games can be arranged). Open May-October.

SANDY HOLLOW TENNIS CLUB
125 Sandy Hollow Road
Southampton
☎ 631-283-3422
www.sandyhollow.com

This club has 14 Har-Tru courts. Court fee, $20/hr. Sandy Hollow also runs a day camp. Open May-October.

BRIDGEHAMPTON TENNIS & SURF CLUB
231 Mid Ocean Drive
Bridgehampton
☎ 631-537-1180

Fourteen Har-Tru courts, plus two freshwater pools and a private beach. Guests must be accompanied by a member; the day fee is $50. Memberships are now being offered for the tennis club only. Open Memorial Day-Labor Day.

PAUL ANNACONE TENNIS ACADEMY
175 Daniels Hole Road
East Hampton
☎ 631-537-8012

The tennis academy has 20 Har-Tru courts, one hard court, and six indoor courts. Lessons and clinics are offered for adults and juniors, both on- and off-site. Nonmembers may play in the afternoon for $25 per hour, per person. Open daily, year-round.

Suffolk County's South Fork

BUCKSKILL TENNIS CLUB
Buckskill Road
East Hampton
☎ 631-324-2243
www.buckskilltennisclub.com

Buckskill has seven Har-Tru courts, three grass courts, pro shop and clubhouse, private lessons and racquet restringing. Café on premises. $25 per hour, per person. Open from the end of April to Labor Day.

EAST HAMPTON INDOOR TENNIS
Daniels Hole Road
East Hampton
☎ 631-537-8012

This club has eight Har-Tru indoor courts, 21 Har-Tru outdoor courts and one asphalt court. In summer, court time is on a first-come, first-served basis; the rest of year, call ahead. Court fees are $35 per person, per hour, before noon and $25 in the afternoon. Open year-round.

GREEN HOLLOW TENNIS CLUB
Green Hollow Road
East Hampton
☎ 631-324-0297

Green Hollow has 13 Har-Tru outdoor courts. Lessons, snack bar, pro shop, lockers, tournaments, clubhouse, lounge, social events. Open from Memorial Day through October. Court fee is $25 per hour.

RACQUET CLUB OF EAST HAMPTON
191 Buckskill Road
East Hampton
☎ 631-324-5155

The Racquet Club has 19 Har-Tru outdoor courts, pro shop, ball machines, clubhouse, showers, snack bar, lessons and clinics, junior program. Open May-October. Court fee is $25 per hour.

SAG HARBOR TENNIS
Mashashimuet Park
Sag Harbor
☎ 631-725-4018

Sag Harbor Tennis has eight Har-Tru courts at $25 per hour, and two hard courts at $20 per hour. Open from Memorial Day to Labor Day. Managed by Hamptons Tennis Company.

ABRAHAM'S PATH PARK
Amagansett
☎ 631-324-2417

This park has four public courts behind the ball field. Reserve on day of play. $8 per court per hour in summer; the rest of the year they're free.

DUNES RACQUET CLUB
Town Lane
Amagansett
☎ 631-267-8508

Dunes has 12 Har-Tru courts. Advance reservations are required. Court fee is $20 per person for the day. Open May-November.

HITHER HILLS RACQUET CLUB
Montauk Highway
Montauk
☎ 631-267-8525
www.hhracquetclub.com

Hither Hills is open to all ages and abilities, members and non-members. There are seasonal memberships, special rates for locals, and monthly, weekly, and weekend deals. The club offers advance court booking, five Har-Tru clay courts, lessons with the pros, and a new snack bar. Located six miles west of Montauk Village. $25 per hour weekdays; $40 per hour weekends. Open May-October.

Suffolk County's South Fork

LIONS PARK
Essex Street
Montauk
☎ 631-324-2417

This park has three courts. The court fee is $8 per hour.
Reservation requested on day of play.

MONTAUK RACQUET CLUB
West Lake Drive
Montauk
☎ 631-668-5252

The club has eight Har-Tru outdoor courts; the fee is
$20 per hour. Advance reservations preferred. Open
from the end of May through October.

MONTAUK DOWNS STATE PARK
South Fairview Avenue, off West Lake Drive
Montauk
☎ 631-668-6264 (in season only)

Montauk Downs has six Har-Tru courts, open mid-May
to October 15. Fees are $12 per court, per hour, on a
first-come, first-served basis.

Golf

Southampton Golf Range, North Highway, Southampton, ☎ 631-283-2158. Open at 8am daily, May-October. Golf range and lessons, plus an 18-hole old-
fashioned miniature golf course. Located just east of
Southampton College on Route 39.

Poxabogue Golf Center, 3556 Montauk Highway,
Bridgehampton, ☎ 631-537-0025, is two miles east of
town; it has a 9-hole course, driving range, instruction,
pro shop. Open daily, March-December. Closed January and February. The Fairway Restaurant, ☎ 631-
537-7195, is open year-round.

Montauk Downs State Park Golf Course, Fairview
Avenue off West Lake Drive, Montauk, ☎ 631-668-1100
(main number); tee times can be made a week in ad-

vance, ☎ 631-668-1234. The Robert Trent Jones-designed 18-hole, par 72 course has pro shop, lessons, tennis courts, café (open seasonally), swimming pools, lockers. Readers of *Dan's Papers* voted its first hole the Best First Hole on any public golf course on the East End. Open year-round.

Miniature Golf

Slo Jacks, 212 West Montauk Highway, Hampton Bays, ☎ 631-728-9601. This is an old-fashioned links in a pretty setting, built in 1961; owner Jack believes it's the oldest miniature golf course in America. Jack's concession stand sells shakes, smoothies, hot dogs, burgers, sandwiches and the "meanest chili," according to a regular customer, and there are picnic tables out front. Open daily, from mid-March through mid-November. Slo Jacks is west of the Hampton Bays Diner on Montauk Highway.

Lynch Links, 375 David Whites Lane, Southampton, ☎ 631-283-0049, has 18 holes with "rough" rocks and water hazards. $7 adults; $5 children under 12. Call for hours.

> ★ TIP
>
> You might want to make Lynch Links your last stop before heading home since it is right off Route 39, which feeds into Sunrise Highway.

Puff 'N Putt, a family fun center at 659 Main Street, Montauk (across from IGA), ☎ 631-668-4473, has an 18-hole mini-course and a video game room. The center rents sailboats, pedal boats, rowboats, canoes and kayaks to be used from its dock. Open daily, from Memorial Day to Labor Day, then weekends only through Columbus Day.

Suffolk County's South Fork

Horseback Riding

Stables

SEARS BELLOWS STABLES
Sears Bellows County Park
Route 24
Hampton Bays
☎ 631-723-3554 or 631-668-5453

This stable gives lessons and pony rides and operates a summer pony day-camp. Take Sunrise Highway to Exit 65N, and go north on Route 24 (Riverhead-Hampton Bays Road) to the entrance of the park. Open year-round; closed Wednesday. The stable is behind the Big Duck (see *Shop Till You Drop*, page 489).

One resident of the Quogue farm, seen grazing in the field, is a retired carriage horse, whose résumé includes a decade or more of pulling a hansom cab outside Manhattan's Plaza Hotel.

QUOGUE HORSE & PONY FARM
48 Lewis Road, off Route 104
Quogue
☎ 631-653-5987
www.ponyfarm.net

Situated on 30 green acres, this farm breeds ponies and is involved in training, boarding, leasing and sales. During my visit, the spotless stalls were boarding horses that were to compete in the North Fork and Hampton Classics. Private lessons are provided in English, hunter, equitation, cross-country, fox hunting and carriage driving. In addition to two lighted rings and a hunt course, the farm is across from 600 or 700 trails, often used by the local hunt club. They also run a summer camp. Open daily, year-round.

CLEARVIEW STABLES
449 North Main Street
Southampton
☎ 631-283-0073

Clearview gives lessons in dressage, hunting and jumping. The stable also has a boarding facility. Open daily, year-round.

ROSEWOOD FARM
344 Majors Path
Southampton
☎ 631-287-4775

Rosewood offers lessons for adults and children in hunting and jumping. The farm runs the Red Pony camp in summer, offering riding lessons to children ages four and up. Open daily, year-round.

TWO TREE STABLES
849 Hayground Road, off Scuttle Hole Road
Bridgehampton
☎ 631-537-3881

Two Tree gives lessons in dressage (summer), huntseat and jumping. Boarding. Open year-round; closed Wednesday.

SAGPOND FARMS
Narrow Lane East
Sagaponack
☎ 631-537-2879

Sagapond offers lessons in jumping and huntseat. Year-round boarding. Open year-round; closed Monday.

EAST END STABLES
171 Oakview Highway
East Hampton
☎ 631-324-9568 (stable); ☎ 631-329-7580 (home). Ask for André or Chris DeLeyer.

Year-round boarding and lessons (English saddle) for all levels and ages; no trail rides.

Suffolk County's South Fork

STONY HILL STABLES
Town Lane
Amagansett
☎ 631-267-3203

Stony Hill gives lessons in dressage and huntseat. Boarding. Summer programs for children. Open year-round; closed Wednesday in winter.

DEEP HOLLOW RANCH
Ranch Road
Montauk
☎ 631-668-2744
www.deephollowranch.com

Deep Hollow claims to be the oldest cattle ranch in the USA, and the birthplace of the American cowboy. Guided rides are available through the ranch's 3,000 acres of pasture, forest and beach. This working ranch, home to 100 head of cattle, boards, sells and leases horses and trains American quarter horses. Chuck wagon rides, Texas-style BBQ, and petting farm are some of the attractions. Near Third House (see page 444); open year-round, weather permitting.

RITA'S STABLES
West Lake Drive
Montauk
☎ 631-668-5453

Rita's, a family-owned business for 27 years, offers trail, beach and pony rides (for children ages five and up), and a summer Pony Camp. Rita Foster also maintains a petting farm ($5 per child). Lessons for all levels. Guaranteed to see turtles, ducks and deer on one-hour rides, especially in spring. To reach the stable, heading east on Montauk Highway, turn left onto West Lake Drive, 1½ miles east of the town center; make the first right onto a dirt road. Open year-round.

County Parks

Riders with their own horses may use the facilities in these two parks; permits are required, and are available at the Suffolk County Parks & Recreation administration office in West Sayville, Monday-Friday; ☎ 631-854-4949.

Sears Bellows County Park, Hampton Bays; park office, ☎ 631-852-8290; stable, ☎ 631-723-3554.

Theodore Roosevelt County Park, Montauk (see Third House Museum, page 444); park office, ☎ 631-852-7878; stable, ☎ 631-668-2744.

Shop Till You Drop

Whoever said money can't buy happiness didn't know where to shop.

– Unknown

Westhampton Beach

Westhampton Beach is basically a 16-week town and seems to have dibs on beachwear. All of these shops are on Main Street and are open daily in season.

Coolwear, #123-3, ☎ 631-288-8887, makes and sells clothing and bathing suits in junior sizes.

Summer Salt, #96, ☎ 631-288-8807, sells swimwear, sportswear and accessories.

Wetter or Not, #132, ☎ 631-288-0682, sells swimwear and clothing, along with footwear, bags and workout gear (closed January-March).

Shock, #133, ☎ 631-288-1772, features fashions for all ages ("I guess that's kind of shocking," the salesgirl surmised, although the naked lady on the bicycle on their business card is even more so).

Baby Shock, which carries specialty clothing for infants through girls' size 14 and boys' size 7, is located at #99, ☎ 631-288-2522. In back of the store is Baby

Shock's old-fashioned ice cream parlor, Maxwell's Famous, featuring homemade ice cream and desserts. Open daily, April-December.

Fahrenheit 451, #119, ☎ 631-288-5724, is a small shop packed to the rafters with clothing, bags and bathing suits. "It's hard to browse so we outfit you," the salesgirl explained. Personal service has attracted a cadre of regular customers. Open weekends in winter.

Now that you have something to wear, you'll need a gift for the next party. **O'Suzanna**, #108, ☎ 631-288-2202, 800-O-Susanna, specializes in Italian ceramics and tabletop figurines, linens, silk flowers. The shop also carries paper goods and Crabtree and Evelyn products. Open daily, April-December; closed Tuesday and Wednesday, January-March.

A store specializing in plants and gardens, **Beach Greenery**, #83A, ☎ 631-288-0648, carries gardening accessories such as birdhouses and chimes, as well as indoor plants. Open daily, year-round.

Westhampton Sporting Goods, #77A, ☎ 631-288-9156. has lots of team apparatus, including apparel and sports equipment, plus sandals and sneakers. Open year-round, weekends only in winter; closed Wednesday in season.

Need something to read? The **Open Book**, #128A, ☎ 631-288-2120, is a small bookstore but it's the only one in town.

Hampton Bays

Oaktree Bookstore, 264 Montauk Highway, Hampton Bays, ☎ 631-723-3137, is small so expect lots of personal service. All books on *The New York Times* Best Seller List are discounted at 30% off for hardcover books and 20% off for softcover. Other branches of Oaktree are in Mastic, Selden, Baldwin, Franklin Square and Merrick.

Macy's in Hampton Bays Plaza is just off Route 24 before reaching the Hampton Bays Diner (if you're heading south).

Skidmore's Sports & Styles, 9 East Montauk Highway, Hampton Bays, ☎ 631-728-0066, has everything for the beach, as well as skateboards. Surfboards are in stock in the summer. Open daily, year-round.

Southampton

Montauk Highway

Attention smokers: it's ironic, given Suffolk County's strict non-smoking laws, but on Montauk Highway between East Quogue and Southampton Village is the **Shinnecock Trading Post**, ☎ 631-283-8047 or 888-543-CIGS, www.shinnecocktradingpost.com, which sells tax-free cigarettes (all major brands), along with Native American crafts, clothing, sand paintings and glassware. Directly across from the Southampton Fire Department, the post opens at 6:30am, year-round. In addition to the shop is a café and 24-hour ATM machine.

Before reaching the village of Southampton, be sure to stop at the **Big Duck** on Route 24 in Flanders, just south of Riverhead (☎ 631-852-8292). You can't miss it. The 70-year-old white concrete duck, listed on the National Register of Historic Places, is 20 feet high and 30 feet wide. Inside is a tiny museum/gift shop that's all kitsch. The "duck-a-bilia" merchandise on exhibit includes photographs, an Art Deco kitchen clock, and a huge circular road sign imploring viewers to "Enjoy Long Island Duckling – famous for its succulent flavor." Among the souvenirs for sale are duck-embossed ties, caps, T-shirts, toys, golf shirts, boxer shorts and beach towels. There's also a birdhouse in the shape of – you guessed it. Open daily, May-September, 10am-5pm, and on weekends through November. Bring your camera!

Suffolk County's South Fork

DUCK TRIVIA

Ducks have been part of life on Long Island for more than 130 years. According to legend, in 1870 a Long Island sailor traveled to China and returned with nine of the snowy-white, orange-beaked Pekin ducks. Soon duck farms sprang up all over Suffolk County, producing 60% of the nation's ducks by 1969 – now it's below 15%. At one time there were 130 duck farms on Long Island. Today there are four.

Main Street

Hildreth's Clearance Center is at 22 West Main Street, ☎ 631-283-8388.

When **E.A. & H. Hildreth's Department Store**, 51-55 Main Street, ☎ 631-283-2300, www.hildreths.com, opened in 1842, it was the only store on Main Street. It is still managed by the same family. The stairway to the second floor is lined with clippings and proclamations attesting to its longevity and success. "America's oldest department store" specializes in everything for the home: furniture (including nursery), fabrics, linens and housewares. Hildreth's has a third store, Hildreth's House & Garden, in Bridgehampton; see page 494.

A branch of East Hampton's Book Hampton, **Book Hampton South**, is at 91 Main Street, ☎ 631-283-0270. Open daily, year-round.

The Southampton branch of **Complements**, at 89 Main Street, ☎ 631-287-4788, is open daily, May through October; closed Tuesday and Wednesday, November-April.

Jobs Lane

Jobs Lane (opened in 1664) and neighboring Hill Street are quiet in the winter. Either the stores are only open on weekends or the owners have closed their shops until spring. There are a few that are open in winter.

Southampton Coins & Cards, #91, ☎ 631-283-7577, specializes in buying and selling coins and sports memorabilia. Items range from 75¢ to $5,000 for a one-of-a-kind poster mock-up of a TV ad for Ehlers Grade "A" Coffee (the sponsor of a New York Giants post-game show in 1950). The poster has 200 autographs of National League players, including Gil Hodges and Jackie Robinson. Older folks love the poster and fathers with their children are frequent customers, says owner Charlie Webb. With all the ladies' shops on the street, "There are very few stores that guys can come in and hang out." Open daily in season, 10am-5:30pm; closed Tuesday and Wednesday in the winter.

Harry Lillywhite & Son, #68, ☎ 631-281-2111, opened in 1895 and moved to its present location in 1910. This venerable shop carries specialty toys from such manufacturers as Brio and Creativity for Kids – not the toys you'll see on TV. Free gift-wrapping. Open daily, year-round.

Collette, #89, ☎ 631-204-9511, seeks designer or vintage clothing in good condition for resale. Bring in apparel, jewelry, shoes or bags that meet these criteria for consignment and receive half the selling price. Open daily in season; closed Tuesday and Wednesday in winter.

As if it were reflecting the mood of winter visitors, there's a store called **Going Nuts** at #47B, ☎ 631-283-3901. Open year-round, it carries a variety of nuts, candies, cards, party favors and stuffed animals.

Need a facial? Ileana Popeanos of **Ileana Skin Care**, #47C (Day's Court), ☎ 631-287-1977, was trained in her native Romania and specializes in European therapeutic facial treatments, body massages and face and leg waxing. She also has her own line of skin care products. Open Tuesday-Saturday, year-round.

Finally, if you've come to love Southampton by now, stop in at **Breezin'Up**, #54, ☎ 631-283-5680, where all the resort wear and some of the handmade jewelry is imprinted with "Southampton." (Same is true of the

Suffolk County's South Fork

East Hampton store where everything, of course, says "East Hampton.") Open daily. Closed in mid-winter.

Windmill Lane

Shops selling sporting goods abound in Southampton. The following are on Windmill Lane and all are open daily, year-round.

Sunrise to Sunset, #21, ☎ 631-283-2929, has everything for the surfer, along with bathing suits and family gear.

Gubbins Running Ahead, #7, ☎ 631-287-4945, sells sports apparel; sneakers; swim gear; baseball, football and tennis equipment; and weights.

Gym Source, #23, ☎ 631-287-1223, www.gymsource.com, is not a fitness club but a retailer of gym equipment for commercial and home use. (The flagship store is in Manhattan.) It also carries free weights, skipping ropes and boxing equipment.

☛ DID YOU KNOW?

The Dutch were among Southampton's early settlers; this area reminded them of Flanders in Holland.

Specialty Stores

Saks Fifth Avenue, ☎ 631-283-3500, has three stores in Southampton; the main store is at 1 Hampton Road; its shoe store is at 48 Main Street; and the men's store is at 50 Main Street.

Mecox Gardens, 257 County Road 39A, ☎ 631-287-5015, www.mecoxgardens.com, could be mistaken for a private estate. The big difference is that the exotic plants, fine antiques, handmade pottery and stone lions are for sale. This is not a gardening center but a homeowner's dream. "Looking for something special?" the savvy saleswoman asked a couple who were admiring some freeze-dried moss. "We would like it all," the man responded. Mecox Gardens is open daily in season, and four days a week in winter. The store also has locations in East Hampton; in Manhattan at 70th Street and Lexington Avenue; and on Worth Avenue in Palm Beach, Florida.

> ★ TIP
>
> A free brochure listing 77 antiques dealers in and around the Hamptons, with a map pinpointing their locations, is available by e-mailing jtcarlson@hamptons.com or online at www.znap.to/antiques. A free copy can also be obtained by mailing a stamped, self-addressed envelope to Antique Tour, PO Box 310, Sag Harbor, NY 11963.

Looking for a plain sweatshirt? **Sweatshirt Expresse** at 44 Jagger Lane, (across from Waldbaum's and next to Hampton Bagels), ☎ 631-287-1413, has them in various colors, along with those imprinted with typical tourist logos. The store runs an ongoing sale, with $35 sweatshirts sold for $15. Plain sweatshirts can be ordered on-line at www.sweatshirtexpresse.com. Open daily, year-round.

Bridgehampton

Bridgehampton Commons, a plaza on Montauk Highway, is home to national chains such as Speedo, Victoria's Secret, Williams Sonoma, The Body Shop, Lechters, Eddie Bauer and Banana Republic.

Women who love European lingerie with high-end labels like Joelle, Pluto, Only Hearts and Hanro will find them at **Complements**, 2486 Main Street, ☎ 631-537-7770. Their collection of La Perla bras with clear latex straps have been very popular. Open daily, year-round.

Suffolk County's South Fork

Waves, One Main Street, ☎ 631-537-7767, carries ultra-feminine garments as well as accessories; they also have a location in East Hampton (see below). Open daily from April through Christmas; closed Tuesday and Wednesday the rest of the year.

A branch of Hildreth's Department Store, called **Hildreth's House & Garden**, is at 2099 Montauk Highway, ☎ 631-537-2300; open daily, year-round.

East Hampton

Nostalgic about Naples? Fancying Firenza? Richard Feleppa, owner of **Florence & Son**, 16R Newtown Lane, ☎ 631-329-4444, caters to the mood by playing "schmaltzy Italian operas" to help his customers relive their trips to Italy. The merchandise is all handcrafted there and ranges from jewelry and pillboxes to sculptures and fountains. Open daily in season, and on weekends in winter.

Also on Newtown Lane, at #38, is **Steph's Stuff**, ☎ 631-329-2943, specializing in stuffed animals and dolls. There are also vintage lunchboxes, signs and posters. Open daily, year-round.

Women who love feminine, free-flowing European silks, cottons and rayons will be at home at **Waves**, 26 Newtown Lane, ☎ 631-329-0033. The shop also carries jewelry and cashmere sweaters. Open daily, year-round.

Fishs Eddy has two locations in Manhattan, at 889 Broadway (19th Street) and 2176 Broadway (77th Street).

Fishs Eddy, named after a small trout-fishing town in the Catskills, has a store at 35 Newtown Lane, ☎ 631-907-8510, www.fishseddy.com. Featured items include surplus china from famous former restaurants such as Trader Vic's and Bickfords. Special items by Nicole Miller and other designers are produced exclusively for the store. Everything they carry is unused. Open daily in season.

For bookworms, **Book Hampton** has been at 20 Main Street, ☎ 631-324-4939, for a quarter-century. It has two floors of books; popular categories are sailing and fishing, architecture and gardening. Open daily, year-round.

Breezin'Up, 21 Main Street, ☎ 631-329-9370, specializes in resort wear and handmade jewelry imprinted with "East Hampton." Open daily. Closed in mid-winter.

Gubbins Running Ahead is at 86 Park Place, ☎ 631-329-7678. See the description under Southampton, page 492.

Sag Harbor

For collectors, **Gallery of Accents** on Main Street, ☎ 631-725-8020, carries a custom-made line of Cat's Meow and Sheila's wood collectibles. The Cat's Meow pieces feature well-known attractions in Sag Harbor and the Hamptons. Open daily, year-round.

Paradise Books at 126 Main Street, ☎ 631-725-1114, is three-quarters bookstore and one-quarter restaurant and bar (see *Best Places to Eat*, page 550). An elevator and steps lead to the second floor, where books fill the entire space. Open daily, year-round.

Amagansett

Outdoors, 171 Main Street, ☎ 631-267-3620, www.outdoors4u.cc, has a 2,500-square-foot main store with a basement twice that size. The store carries a full range of sportswear, shoes, underwear, jeans, beach toys and tennis balls at all price levels for men, women and children. According to owner John Pawlukojc, people who make day-trips to Montauk always end up in his store on their way in or back. Open daily, year-round.

For the horsey set, the **Tack Trunk**, 137 Main Street, ☎ 631-267-2013, has everything for both rider and horse. The store even carries clothes for non-riders, like Dansko shoes. Open daily, year-round.

Suffolk County's South Fork

Montauk

On the Plaza – Montauk's business center – is **Book Shoppe**, ☎ 631-668-4599. Excellent customer service is the motto of proprietor Jeff Kearns, a people person who was formerly a mountain/river guide and thera- pist. Although small, Book Shoppe is a full-service book store promising next-day delivery of any available ti- tles. He also does searches for out-of-print materials. Open year-round, closed Tuesday in winter.

Wave Wear, Plaza South, ☎ 631-668-3888, has fun clothing and beach accessories, jewelry, and men's and children's bathing suits. Open daily, May-October.

Need a surfboard in the summer, skates in the fall and skis in the winter? **Air & Speed**, #7 The Plaza, ☎ 631-668-0356, sells them all, plus surfwear, kid's clothes, women's bathing suits and water shoes. Open daily, year-round, except for a few days a week in winter.

Montauk may seem like the end of the world, but every- day needs – magazines, film, gifts, beachwear – are al- ways available at **White's Drug & Department Store**, on the Plaza, ☎ 631-668-2994. White's has been a fixture in town since 1927 when Carl Fisher devel- oped Montauk. The founder, William White, originally opened the store in East Hampton in the late 1890s. The department store is open daily, year-round, at 8am, but the pharmacy is closed on Sunday.

Indoor plants, as well as terrace plants and cut flowers, can be found at **Strawberry Fields**, 695 Montauk Highway, ☎ 631-668-6279. The store also carries ador- able gifts, such as wood clocks and trinket boxes. Open daily, year-round.

After Dark

Without music life would be a mistake.
— Friedrich Nietzsche

The Arts

Westhampton Beach

WESTHAMPTON BEACH PERFORMING ARTS CENTER
76 Main Street
☎ 631-288-1500 (box office)
☎ 631-288-2350 (theater office)
www.whbpac.org

Opened in 1998, the center was converted from a c. 1932 UA movie theater to a 430-seat year-round entertainment complex. It has helped change the image of Westhampton, known for decades as "the other Hampton," to a vital year-round community. The center presents musicals, puppet shows and independent films; the 2001 lineup included singer Smokey Robinson, cabaret singer Donna McKechnie, and comedian Sandra Bernhard. Summer box office hours are Wednesday-Monday, noon-6pm. The center also presents Theater Thursdays for kids during the summer; tickets are $10.

Southampton

AVRAM THEATER
Long Island University
Montauk Highway
☎ 631-287-8480

LIU students, along with community actors, perform four shows a year here – musicals, dramas, and one-act plays – some of which are original productions. Tickets are $12; $8 for students and seniors.

East Hampton

JOHN DREW THEATER
Guild Hall
158 Main Street
East Hampton
☎ 631-324-4050 (box office)
☎ 631-324-0806 (general information)
www.guildhall.org

Music, dance and drama performances are presented year-round in the John Drew Theater; tickets range from $10-$50. Guild Hall also houses a museum, which has a permanent collection of 1,600 works with changing exhibits at four main galleries. The museum is open year-round; from Memorial Day to Labor Day, hours are Monday-Saturday, 11am-5pm; and Sunday, noon to 5pm. From Labor Day to Memorial Day, hours are Thursday-Sunday, 11am-5pm. Classes and workshops for adults and children are held throughout the year; call for a brochure.

Sag Harbor

BAY STREET THEATRE
Long Wharf
Corner Bay and Main Streets
Sag Harbor
☎ 631-725-9500
www.baystreet.org

Founded in 1991, this regional theater presents comedies, dramas and musicals from May through September in its 299-seat **Mainstage**. Tickets are $28-$50. Cabaret, children's events, and stand-up comedy are presented from March through November. In *Newsday's* opinion, Bay Street is "in the same league with the best major regional and off-Broadway theaters." Box office opens in early March.

Music & Dancing

CANOE PLACE INN
239 East Montauk Highway
Hampton Bays
☎ 631-728-4121

"Long Island's biggest club," with a capacity of 2,200, is open Thursday-Saturday. Live national acts, DJs and dance party. Cover. The club closes September 30 and reopens during the second week in May.

BRIDGES
964 Sag Harbor Turnpike
Bridgehampton
☎ 631-329-9751

Sunday brunch features a Southern-style menu and live gospel music. Dinner is accompanied by live jazz, R&B, gospel music and dancing. Closed in January.

EAST HAMPTON POINT
295 Three Mile Harbor Road
East Hampton
☎ 631-329-2800
www.easthamptonpoint.com

This club features live music on Thursday (salsa) and Sunday, 6-9pm, during the summer. They are open for dinner daily, from April to Labor Day, and for lunch after June 20.

MARY JANE RESTAURANT
128 North Main Street
East Hampton
☎ 631-324-8008

Live jazz Saturday in season, 7-10pm; the Italian restaurant is open year-round.

Suffolk County's South Fork

THE STEPHEN TALKHOUSE
161 Main Street
Amagansett
☎ 631-267-3117
www.stephentalkhouse.com

Probably the best known night spot in the Hamptons,
this bar/club is open from 7pm to 4am daily, year-
round, with premier local and national bands playing
everything from blues and jazz to funk and folk. Local
celebrity musicians Paul Simon, Billy Joel and Jimmy
Buffett have performed here. Cover varies from $5-
$100. The age of the crowd starts at 25.

WHAT'S IN A NAME?

Stephen Pharoah, a/k/a Stephen Talkhouse,
was a Montaukett Indian who lived in a small
house on the high, rocky moraine at Montauk
Point. He had a commanding presence and
was a local celebrity who thought nothing of
walking to Brooklyn and back. When he was in
his 40s, he enlisted as a soldier in the Civil
War and is buried in his uniform in the Indian
Cemetery on East Lake Drive.

NICK'S
148 South Emerson
Montauk
☎ 631-668-4800

Nick's is an oceanfront restaurant with live music ev-
ery night in its **Caribbean Club** and all day at its
Beach Bar. Open Thursday through Sunday in spring
and fall (from early May until Memorial Day and from
Labor Day to Columbus Day); open daily in summer
(Memorial Day through Labor Day).

RICK'S CRABBY COWBOY CAFE

435 East Lake Drive
Montauk
☎ 631-668-3200
www.montauk-online.com/ricks

Rick's is a waterfront eatery and marina with nightly entertainment. Open daily in season, for lunch and dinner.

MEMORY MOTEL

692 Montauk Highway
Montauk
☎ 631-668-2702

Live music every Friday and Saturday all year, in the bar. The Rolling Stones recorded a song, *Memory Motel*, about the motel. According to a reviewer, the song is one of the highlights of the group's *Black and Blue* album.

SHARK SHACK

South Elmwood Avenue
Montauk
☎ 631-668-0100

Open daily. Karaoke on Friday, live entertainment on Saturday.

PORT-O-CALL BAR

Gurney's Inn
Montauk
☎ 631-668-2345

Open daily. Live music on weekends, year-round; daily, in season (see page 515 for Gurney's Inn).

Suffolk County's South Fork

Festivals & Events

August

The **Hampton Classic** Horse Show is held at 240 Snake Hollow Road, Bridgehampton, ☎ 631-537-3177, www.hamptonclassic.com. It is one of the country's largest hunter/jumper horse shows, drawing about 50,000 spectators annually. The week-long event takes place in late August, and also features exhibitions of miniature horses, ponies, llamas and alpacas. Dozens of shops and restaurants are on-site. You can purchase tickets at the gate ($5) or use an order form to get a pass for $25, good for the entire week.

The **Westhampton Beach Art Show** is held the first weekend in August on the Village Green, 10am-6pm; ☎ 631-288-3337; free.

September

The Shinnecock Indian Nation celebrates its annual **Labor Day Powwow** at the Shinnecock Reservation off Montauk Highway in Southampton, ☎ 631-283-6143, or 631-287-3165. The four-day event features crafts, American Indian art and jewelry, native foods, bands, and a dance and drum contest. Admission is $8 for adults; $5 for seniors and children five-12.

October

The **Hamptons International Film Festival**, held at several locations in Southampton and East Hampton, ☎ 631-324-4600, www.hamptonsfest.org, features more than 60 independent and foreign films, as well as speakers, interviews with a celebrity, programs for student filmmakers, competitions, cocktail parties and social events. Prizes are awarded in various film categories. Tickets are $10 for individual films, $15 for panel discussions, $25 for a conversation with an artist, and $75 for the opening night gala.

Best Places to Stay

ACCOMMODATIONS PRICE SCALE	
Price scale is based on the cost of a standard double room, two people per room on a weekend, and does not include the 9.25% hotel tax.	
Inexpensive.................under $130	
Moderate ....$130-$200	
Expensive...................$201-$300	
Deluxe ....more than $300	

Hotels & Inns

Westhampton Beach

THE GRASSMERE INN
7 Beach Lane
Westhampton Beach
☎ 631-288-4021
www.esbba.com/Inns/grassmereinn.htm
Inexpensive to Moderate

The Grassmere, in a three-story white Victorian (built in 1885), is right off Main Street. That's one reason why tennis players are not the only occupants of the 20 guest rooms. Other reasons are the friendly staff and cozy quarters. On the lawn are barbeque grills and picnic tables. From noon to 1pm on Saturdays, a Pros Barbeque is offered at no charge to guests of the inn. In the morning, expect a substantial continental breakfast.

Despite refurbishing, the inn, with its narrow staircase and Colonial-style décor still has a 19th-century atmosphere. Grassmere has received accolades for both lod-

Grassmere Inn B&B provides free shuttle service to and from the train station, bus stop, beach and tennis camp.

ging and its tennis program from *Dan's Papers,*
Newsday and *Metroguide.*

The inn is open year-round. The tennis camp operates
in July and August, and several tennis/lodging packages are available. Eastside Tennis, located on Montauk Highway, has 12 Har-Tru courts and 11 pros on
staff (see *Tennis*, page 478).

TENNIS ANYONE?

A 30-something couple from Westchester staying at this B&B for two days had been search-
ing for a tennis camp in the New York Metropolitan area. Most tennis camps are on college
campuses and were too isolated, they found.
They chose **Peter Kaplan's Eastside Tennis
Club** because participants stay at the Grassmere Inn; they were impressed by the pros;
and there is nightlife and a nearby beach
(beach passes are available for guests).

Hampton Bays

Hampton Bays suffers from an image problem. For
nine months of the year, it's a quiet community of modest houses with boats in the backyard and more pickup
trucks than SUVs on the road. Then the season hits
and the place gets rowdy. One beer distributor said that
he does a booming business in the 13 weekends he's
open.

Some residents east of the Shinnecock Canal have ex-
pressed distaste toward the western Hamponites – no
doubt influenced by this summer scene, real or imag-
ined. Some Hampton Bays residents claim it no longer
exists.

There are advantages to staying in Hampton Bays; the
town probably has the greatest number of beach parking spaces in the Hamptons. Here, innkeepers do not
need to provide guests with passes – the town beaches
are not off-limits to non-residents. Visitors simply pay

a higher fee, although when the beaches are crowded, non-resident parking spaces are limited.

Hampton Bays takes pride in its natural beachfront. All the guesthouses are on the bay side. No fancy homes – or for that matter any buildings – line Dune Road along the Atlantic Ocean, save some dance clubs on the western end and **Oakland's Restaurant** out at Shinnecock Inlet. "I would rather look at sand dunes than mansions," commented a Hampton Bays retiree beach-walking with his wife. If you agree, this unpretentious community might be to your liking.

BOWEN'S BY THE BAYS
177 West Montauk Highway
Hampton Bays
☎ 800-533-3139, or 631-728-1158
Inexpensive to Expensive

A hideaway in the woods, Bowen's is a peaceful reprieve from the hustle and bustle along Montauk Highway. With nine guest rooms, seven cottages, swimming pool, playground, putting green, and a lighted tennis court, it's ideal for families, couples, singles, and tennis lovers. Kevin Bowen, proprietor with wife, Eileen, is a tennis pro and gives lessons to both guests and non-guests. Guests, however, can play on their own for free, day or night, and Bowen's will happily lend you rackets.

All rooms have TV, telephone and refrigerator. The guest rooms are large and tastefully decorated with plush beds. The one- and two-bedroom country cottages have fully equipped kitchens and screened-in porches. With 3½ acres, there's ample space for meandering.

Take Sunrise Highway to Exit 65S (Route 24). Follow to the end and turn right onto Montauk Highway. Bowen's is .2 mile on the left; look for their sign. Open year-round.

Suffolk County's South Fork

Pets are welcome in the cottages at Bowen's.

COLONIAL SHORES

83 West Tiana Road
Hampton Bays
☎ 631-728-0011
www.webscope.com/hotels/colonial
Moderate to Deluxe

*Children un-
der 12 stay
free in room
with parents
at Colonial
Shores.*

The new owners have done a wonderful job of creating
a comfortable and pretty place for a family or couple.
The carpeted rooms are newly decorated in tan and
mauve, and the beds are as comfy as those found in
B&Bs. The 24 units include motel-style rooms, suites
with kitchens, and cottages. All have TV and telephone. The waterfront property features a free-form
swimming pool, boat slip, basketball net, picnic tables
and grills. I loved sitting on the Adirondack chair outside my room gazing out at an apple tree in the garden
and the expansive view of Tiana Bay.

Paddleboats, rowboats or Aqua-Cycles are there for the
asking. The resort will also arrange water-skiing or
fishing outings. Follow the same driving instructions
as for Bowen's; Colonial Shores is .6 mile on the left,
immediately after the underpass. Then it's another .6
mile from Montauk Highway to Colonial Shores. Open
year-round; two-night minimum.

HAMPTON MAID

259 East Montauk Highway
Hampton Bays
☎ 631-728-4166
www.hamptonmaid.com
Expensive

A family-owned retreat where guests become regulars,
Hampton Maid oozes with rustic charm. Its antiques
and collectibles shop in the lobby is a fun place to
browse. Opened in 1959, the five-acre property in the
Shinnecock Hills section of Hampton Bays (east of the
Shinnecock Canal) has a swimming pool, playground,
shuffleboard court and restaurant open for breakfast
(See *Lite Bites,* page 548). Open from late April to Columbus Day.

☞ DID YOU KNOW?

Hampton Bays was settled in 1740; it was called Good Ground because it was an oasis of rich topsoil within the sandy soil of the Pine Barrens.

Southampton

Some call Southampton the "Grand Dame of the East End villages" because of its old money. Southampton Town includes the villages and hamlets of Remsenberg, Speonk, Westhampton, Westhampton Beach, Hampton Bays, Quogue, East Quogue, Southampton Village, Bridgehampton, Water Mill, and part of Sag Harbor.

SOUTHAMPTON INN
91 Hill Street
Southampton
☎ 800-832-6500, or 631-283-6500
www.southamptoninn.com
Inexpensive to Deluxe

A guidebook author once described the Southampton Inn as "motel-like" in décor. The book was written a decade ago, before the inn had its $5 million facelift following a change in ownership in 1998. The only remaining motel-like aspect of the inn is its layout: the two-story brick building is sprawling, and cars are parked perpendicular to the 90 rooms.

The lobby is shaped like a keyhole; its circular portion is bright and book-lined with a fireplace, piano and comfy chairs and couches arranged for group seating. The inn is open year-round; dogs and cats are welcome at $29 per pet, per night; dogs even have their own run. What's more, their food bowls and toys are set beside the (light continental) breakfast table, where coffee and tea are available round-the-clock. March is pet month, meaning the owner pays and the pet stays free. In warm weather, breakfast and lunch are served on the outdoor patio.

Suffolk County's South Fork

The Southampton Inn has been awarded three stars by AAA.

Children are also welcome; there's a huge game room with activities for older kids and suitable toys for tots. There are also three exercise machines for parents. Guests have unlimited use of the outdoor pool, all-weather tennis court, volleyball, horseshoes, bocce and shuffleboard – all surrounded by shrubbery and flower gardens.

The guest rooms, be they the standard ones or the four rooms designed by Paloma Picasso, clothing designer Nicole Miller, and interior designer Chris Madden, are large and nicely furnished with natural wood, thick mattresses and spanking-new bathrooms. The inn has one handicapped-accessible guest room. All rooms have TV and telephone; other amenities are a TV and VCR in the game room, and 7,200 square feet of flexible space for meetings or parties. The 2,285 square-foot ballroom, the largest on the East End, can be divided.

The inn is in the heart of town. A shuttle bus transports guests to Cooper's Beach so a parking pass is unnecessary. The inn offers pool and tennis memberships; see Swimming for information. Inquire also about spa and fitness packages.

THE ATLANTIC
1655 County Road 39
Southampton
☎ 631-287-0908
www.HRHresorts.com
Inexpensive to Expensive

The Atlantic is not your typical motel!

The Atlantic was the first of three boutique properties in Southampton to be renovated by Utopia Lifestyle Inns, and is the only one open year-round. Hampton Resorts & Hospitality manages The Atlantic, which is roughly 90 miles from New York.

After a $5 million renovation, what was once the Sandpiper Motel is now a lovely five-acre property featuring a pool, two tennis courts, volleyball court and lots of greenery. The rooms are sleek and modern and all have comfy down comforters and lots of bathroom amenities. There are 57 oversized rooms and five suites, as well as some slightly smaller rooms with two double beds. Some rooms have walk-in closets; others have curtained alcoves with foldout sofas. All have TV/VCR, telephone, and a radio with CD player.

Complimentary Starbucks coffee is available all day. A continental breakfast is offered in season. Tennis rackets and videotapes are available for rent. Beach towels are available at the front desk. No smoking is allowed indoors.

HAMPTONS A-B-C

In addition to the Atlantic, Hampton Resorts has two nearby properties with similar features. The **Bentley** (previously called the Concorde) has 39 suites with private patios, swimming pool, sun deck, tennis court; $130 to $400 per night. The **Capri** (formerly known as the Bayberry Inn) has 27 rooms and four suites surrounding an interior courtyard swimming pool, and has a restaurant/lounge; rates are $130-$350 per night. All have meeting rooms.

MAINSTAY
579 Hill Street
Southampton
☎ 631-283-4375
www.hamptons.com/mainstay
Moderate to Deluxe

Elizabeth Main was dissatisfied with her career as a photography stylist in Manhattan and wanted to contribute something to others. A decade ago she looked for a house big enough to open a bed and breakfast, and found this shingled, three-story colonial with 10 guest rooms one mile from town. Both the house and her new lifestyle have answered her prayers. "People who live in New York need to get away," she said. "People need to relax, and that's healthy. They need a more intimate experience and to interact with other people."

Suffolk County's South Fork

Inquire about a mid-week discount in June and September at Mainstay.

The Mainstay is indeed an intimate setting yet without the pressure to socialize. The continental breakfasts are buffet-style, which Elizabeth believes is less awkward than a formal setting where guests wait to be served.

The rooms range from small to huge; six have private baths with clawfoot tubs. Some rooms have TVs. All rooms are beautifully decorated with country pine furniture and antique iron beds covered with plush down comforters and throw pillows.

The Mainstay is open year-round. There is a garden on the grounds where small weddings have been held and a 20x40-foot black-bottom pool.

ENCLAVE INN
2688 Montauk Highway
Bridgehampton
☎ 877-998-0800, 631-537-0197
www.enclaveinn.com
Inexpensive to Expensive

Inquire about spa treatments at the Enclave. Film and fashion people have discovered this lovely place but one needn't be a fashion plate to feel comfortable here. The Wudyka family has created a warm and friendly atmosphere and they are actively involved in community charities.

Alexis Stewart, daughter of Martha Stewart, designed the 10 spacious guest rooms. They have a Caribbean chic, with skylights, tiled floors and upholstered deck chairs. Modern amenities include TV and refrigerator. One surprise touch was a water bottle on my night table (I'd forgotten to bring one), and another was a light breakfast for guests outside the office door. There is a heated swimming pool, and beach passes are provided. The Enclave is open year-round.

East Hampton

East Hampton makes a statement. Montauk Highway is one lane in each direction through most of the Hamptons, but at East Hampton it widens. Route 27 turns left and suddenly you're on a four-lane boulevard with wide pristine sidewalks. It's the bane of some merchants when villages ban sidewalk displays or excess signage. The law is clearly enforced in East Hampton, tagged "the village of no." These strict regulations are needed to retain the village's colonial charm and keep East Hampton the "most beautiful village in America."

East Hampton Town, including Wainscott, East Hampton Village, Springs, Montauk, Amagansett and part of Sag Harbor, is known as "Hollywood East."

> ★ FAMOUS FACES
>
> Jackie Kennedy was born in the Hamptons while the Bouviers were summering in East Hampton.

MILL HOUSE INN
31 North Main Street
East Hampton
☎ 631-324-9766
www.millhouseinn.com
Deluxe

Some folks are born to be innkeepers; their warmth and welcoming manner make guests feel pampered and special. Meet Sylvia and Gary Muller, who bought this 1790 inn in 1999 and proceeded to completely redecorate. The three-story house with dormer windows and a gambrel roof has been lovingly restored to its original country elegance (the inn's previous owners had made all the structural changes, although the breakfast room retains its original ceiling beams). Each guest room has a high comfy bed (my queen bed had 10 puffy pillows!) and a different theme. The Dominy Mill room is masculine, with a leather recliner and wood bed frame; Hampton Holiday, the most luxurious, has a seaside theme, with white chests and wicker chairs.

The Mullers retain the exuberance of new owners. Guests are welcome to cookies around the clock, and afternoon refreshments are served. Even before you arrive, a detailed room description, along with rates, policies, directions, and myriad gourmet breakfast se-

Suffolk County's South Fork

Guests at the Mill House Inn receive a discount when visiting the Old Hook Mill.

lections is e-mailed to you. They also put together a guidebook to the area, which can be viewed on their Web site using Adobe Acrobat Reader. No Internet access? You are not forgotten. A six-page color brochure will be snail-mailed to you.

The inn has nine rooms; four feature jetted tubs and six have gas fireplaces; all have TV, voice mail and telephone. There is wheelchair access to the breakfast room and to one guest room. The property has a backyard patio and parking lot. The Mill House Inn is easy to find. It's directly across the road from the Old Hook Mill (built by the Dominy family; see page 445). Open year-round.

Sag Harbor

Sag Harbor is unique in that there are no chain stores. The town is lively year-round. Many of the shopkeepers live above their stores and in season every one is open late. Water traffic picks up in the summer and Marine Park, along the harbor, is a good place to observe the yachts and cruisers. Steven Spielberg has been known to dock there, so keep your eyes peeled. Although Sag Harbor is not a target of snobbism, it lacks the cachet of its southern compatriots. Consider *Dan's Papers'* gossip column called *South O' the Highway (and North, too)*.

Writer Betty Friedan, known as one of the founders of Women's Lib, had rented houses in Sagaponack, Wainscott and East Hampton before purchasing her home in Sag Harbor. In her memoir, *Life So Far* (Simon & Schuster 2000), she wrote that shortly after buying the house a *Newsday* reporter called asking how she knew Sag Harbor was going to be "in." Ms. Friedan replied, "In! The thought had not crossed my mind and frankly I didn't care... Sag Harbor had – and still has – a strong sense of community, which I've always thought is very important. Some of my first magazine articles were about houses and community and communal living, as was a portion of *The Second Stage* (1981), which I wrote in that house in Sag Harbor."

You may notice that, in the "Un-Hamptons Hampton," as Sag Harbor is sometimes called, drivers seem more respectful of pedestrians and fellow motorists. In other parts of the Hamptons, drivers honk impatiently at the car in front – just like in New York City. My bubble burst regarding Sag Harbor when a lifelong resident of East Hampton informed me that the town has a large police presence!

HALFMOON HIDEAWAY INN & SPA
2663 Deerfield Road (on Geris Lane)
Sag Harbor
☎ 631-725-0992
www.halfmoonhideaway.com
Moderate to Deluxe

Six miles from town, deep in the woods, this magnificent, post-modern inn could easily be mistaken for a private home. Inside are several skylights adding to its sense of spaciousness and charm. The four-story inn has only eight rooms, but each is large and comfortable, with a TV; some have refrigerators. A pool table is on the first floor and there's a complete fitness center on the next level, just below the lounge. A private golf course is visible from the deck and Gunite swimming pool, but only when the trees are bare.

"We try to keep it cozy and quaint," explains innkeeper Jacob Avid, who also owns several budget hotels and hostels in Manhattan. The do-it-yourself breakfast resembles what you eat at home, but there's more of it – cold cereal, cheese, fruit, bagels, muffins and coffee cake – and no dishes to wash. It all adds up to a happy hideaway.

Take Montauk Highway to Water Mill. When you see the Citarella Shopping Center on the left and Green Thumb Nursery on the right, look for a left turn onto Deerfield Road. Follow it for about five miles. On your right you'll see two black wooden pillars. Geris Lane is on the right directly after them. Make a right and go all the way up the hill. 2663 is through the brick pillars. Open year-round.

Suffolk County's South Fork

THE INN AT BARON'S COVE
31 West Water Street
Sag Harbor
☎ 631-725-2100
www.baronscove.com
Inexpensive to Moderate

This harborside inn has been hosting visitors for over 35 years. Its 66 guest rooms are equipped with kitchenette, TV, and telephone, and overlook either the pool, meadow, or tranquil harbor. A tennis court is on the property and a spacious sundeck offers a spectacular view of the harbor. Getaway specials are offered year-round.

FROM EASTERN EUROPE TO THE EAST END

When the whaling industry ended in Sag Harbor in 1871 and the block-long steam cotton mill – the village's largest employer – closed, Sag Harbor went into a decline. But then **Joseph Fahys** married a woman from Sag Harbor and moved his huge watch-case plant from Carstadt, New Jersey to a four-story factory building on Division Street. His business relied on expert engravers, so Fahys or his agents made monthly trips from Sag Harbor to Ellis Island soliciting immigrants, all of them Jewish. Over time, Fahys hired more than 100 Hungarian and Polish Jewish families, accounting for 15% of Sag Harbor's population. In 1925, the watch factory was largely destroyed by fire. The Bulova watch company later purchased the plant, operating it until right after World War II. The red brick building still stands but remains vacant.

Montauk

GURNEY'S INN RESORT & SPA
290 Old Montauk Highway
Montauk
☎ 631-668-2345, 668-3203 or 800-8-GURNEY (reservations)
℅ 631-668-2509 (spa)
www.gurneys-inn.com
Expensive to Deluxe

The Atlantic Ocean was the inspiration for the ambience at Gurney's Inn.

The ocean should feel flattered. Everything at Gurney's faces seaward – guest rooms, exercise machines, restaurant, even the indoor pool chaises. If you haven't been there lately, you may recall the resort as rundown (Gurney's Inn opened in 1926 when the Monte family bought the property from Maude Gurney for $200,000), but that's no longer the case. In 1999, Gurney's emerged from bankruptcy and a year later began an $8 million renovation. The cottages are now shipshape, the 125 staterooms mirrored and modernized. The fitness center has been upgraded and the 20-yard-long seawater pool is kept at a comfortable 83°.

The property is designed like a ship with wooden walkways and steps supported by pilings. It's perched high on a cliff so be prepared to climb stairs. Beachfront cottages are ideal for families; there's even a swing set on the sand.

Start your day with a walk on the beach, solo or with a leader. Classes will cost you extra, but use of the weight room and pool are included. Guests at Gurney's also have golf privileges at Montauk Downs, ranked among the top public courses in the country. Of course, you may prefer to laze on your terrace gazing at the graceful gulls gliding by.

Want service and pampering? Head for the spa. The health and beauty specialists have been there for years so we're not dealing with amateurs. While awaiting my mineral bath, I heard women raving about their treatments. These treatments do not come cheap but are

Gurney's Inn's Foredeck cottage has a ramp and one handicapped-accessible guest room.

Suffolk County's South Fork

Inquire about Gurney's "Day of Beauty" package, with 35 treatments to choose from, and special overnight stays.

well worth the price (it's only $35 for an herbal wrap, but an ultimate healing experience will cost you $200). Add a 15% service charge to each treatment. Reserve a week or two ahead; the full-service spa is sometimes booked solid.

Breakfast and lunch are served in the café, and the patisserie serves light fare all day (Gurney's does not serve spa cuisine unless it's requested). Guests on the modified American plan have their buffet breakfast and dinner in the large-windowed dining room. The inn has a new chef and appears to have its act together; the tasty Manhattan clam chowder had lots of clams but came to the table lukewarm (the waitstaff was inattentive). The meal picked up with the pork chop, wrapped in a coat of tomatoes and accompanied by crisp vegetables. Hats off to the pastry chef for a luscious carrot cake! Music vibrations from an event in the banquet room below were an annoyance one Saturday night (all eight conference rooms are equipped with sound systems and one of the rooms can accommodate 300 people).

Follow Montauk Highway heading east until you get to a fork in the road. Take the right fork, Old Montauk Highway, toward Montauk Beach. The resort is two miles along on right (and 104.3 miles from the Throgs Neck Bridge). Open year-round.

MONTAUK MANOR
Edgemere Street
Montauk
☎ 631-668-4400
www.montaukmanor.com
Inexpensive to Expensive

Montauk Manor is listed on the National Register of Historic Places.

The dimly lit lobby with its grand arches, white pillars, stone floors and stuccoed walls bespeaks a bygone elegance, whereas the guest rooms are comfortably contemporary. Of the 140 condominium units, 95 are available to guests, ranging from studio accommodations to three bedroom suites, all with fully equipped kitchens. The rooms are sizable; a couple could be comfortable in even the smallest studio with its queen-size bed and convertible sofa.

The 12-acre resort has indoor and outdoor pools, fitness facility, saunas, whirlpool, indoor squash court and outdoor tennis courts. Its on-site restaurant, **Manucci's** (☎ 631-668-4455), is open daily, in season, for breakfast buffet, lunch and dinner. Off-season, it's open for dinner on Friday and three meals a day on the weekend.

FISHER'S FOLLY

Carl G. Fisher, the man who developed Miami Beach and built the Indy 500, came to Montauk in the 1920s and bought 9,000 acres for $2.5 million. He constructed several Tudor-homes to resemble those on the English moors, and he created **Montauk Downs Golf Course**. His seven-story office tower is the tallest structure in town and the street named Flamingo Avenue conjures up visions of palm trees on a Miami boulevard. Fisher's dream of creating the "most fabulous summer resort ever imagined in the western world" resulted in the English Tudor-style luxury hotel, **Montauk Manor**, atop Signal Hill. Opened in 1927, this "Castle on the Hill" was just that, luring the well-heeled to its grand ballrooms and lawn croquet. The Depression destroyed Fisher's dream and he went bankrupt in 1932. If he were alive today, Fisher would find his office building converted to condominium apartments and his hotel to a resort. Recently renovated, Montauk Manor has been restored to its former splendor, yet it's highly affordable.

Montauk Manor is ideal for those who crave tranquility and refinement. To get there from Montauk village, turn left at the Bank of New York onto Edgemere

Street (Fort Pond will be on your left). Follow the road to the hotel sign and proceed up the hill. Open year-round.

PERI'S B&B AND SPA
206 Essex Street
Montauk
☎ 631-668-1394
www.perisbb.com
Moderate to Expensive

If you love the rugged aspects of Montauk yet long for luxury lodgings, this B&B is for you. Peri Aronian was designing men's coats in Manhattan when she decided to flee the rat race to purchase a 1924 Fisher Tudor in the South Fork's fingernail community. In 1997, she opened the B&B on a year-round basis. Although she was inexperienced at innkeeping, Peri had observed hotel operations while traveling as a fashion designer and "tried to make a place where I would come."

Now in her early 30s, Peri has attracted young urban professionals through her ads in *New York Magazine*. It's no wonder. This is not a place for families with children, but for adults who like hiking and/or pampering. Peri serves healthy gourmet breakfasts made with vegetables and herbs from the garden and arranges for guided hikes and spa services (with advance notice) on her enclosed patio. Facials are $75; massages are $85-$110. If you wish to go to the beach and don't have a parking permit, Peri will lend you a bicycle.

The house is stucco inside and out and retains the original oak floors. It was once owned by Henri Soulé, the famed proprietor of New York's Le Pavillon restaurant. Peri decorated it with an artist's touch, combining her grandparents' antiques and tapestries with yard sale and flea market finds and carefully selected new items. The result is beautiful and yet comfortable. The three large guest rooms all have private baths with luxuries like handmade soap. Two rooms represent Peri's favorite places: Paris (where she travels frequently) and Morocco (where she's yet to go). The third is Art Deco, complete with cow-skin rug and mirrored dressing table. The French-themed room has a private balcony.

Pets are not allowed as guests, but Peri has a sweet-tempered dog named Sirus. One guest, originally nervous around the dog, soon relaxed when the Rhodesian ridgeback sat quietly at her feet.

The B&B is now open seasonally (May-October) since Peri has opened another in the Bahamas. To get here, take Route 27 east into Montauk. Turn left at the Mobil station at Essex Street (the last cross street in town) and continue uphill for a half-mile. Peri's is on the right behind a high hedge.

Resort Living

Dune Resorts, ☎ 1-800-684-DUNE, www.duneresorts.com, is the management company for eight properties in Montauk, Amagansett and East Hampton. Three of them, **Driftwood on the Ocean** (see below), **Sea Crest** in Amagansett (☎ 631-267-3159, 800-732-3297), and **Hermitage** at Napeague, Amagansett (☎ 631-267-6151), are side by side between the villages of Amagansett and Montauk (Driftwood has blonde wood, Sea Crest is tan, and Hermitage is white). Each has a private beach, but the Hermitage is the only one with lifeguards (beginning July 4th). Guests at the Sea Crest and Driftwood who want the security of a lifeguard are entitled to use the adjoining Hermitage beachfront. Guest rooms in two buildings at the 74-room Sea Crest are open all year. The property is not wheelchair-accessible; the building does have a ramp but the bathrooms are not designed for the handicapped.

All three resorts have swimming pools and tennis courts. If you can get away during the week before the rates rise in late June, a deluxe bedroom (without an ocean view) is only $80-$85 per night. Bear in mind that these are all family resorts; once the kids are out of school you will never have the pool for yourself. Otherwise, it's a real bargain. All the rooms are a few steps to the ocean and an umbrella and towel are provided gratis to guests.

DRIFTWOOD ON THE OCEAN
Montauk Highway
Montauk
☎ 800-48-DRIFT, or 631-668-5744
Inexpensive to Expensive

Many of the units in Driftwood, Sea Crest and Hermitage are for sale.

The 32 rooms at the Driftwood all have private porches, air conditioning, refrigerator, TV and telephone. Our deluxe bedroom was a good-sized, comfortable room with two double beds, overlooking the dunes of Hither Hills State Park. Our friends, who stay at the Sea Crest every summer, spent a little more and had an apartment with a fully equipped kitchen. At the Driftwood, many of the rooms have barbeque grills outside their doors. During our stay, several families had brought their own food and cooked out. Their kids spent time in the pool or playground, on the shuffleboard court or playing Ping-Pong. A fitness facility is available for adults. Driftwood is open mid-May to Columbus Day; there are wheelchair-accessible rooms on the ground floor.

Motels & Cottages

MOTEL PRICE SCALE
Price scale is based on the cost of a double room, two people per room, in season, and does not include the 9.25% hotel tax.
Inexpensive . . . . under $100
Moderate . . . . $100-$150
Expensive $151-200
Very Expensive . . . . over $200

Westhampton

BAILEY'S MOTEL
42 Montauk Highway
Westhampton Beach
☎ 631-288-1400
15 units. Moderate to Expensive.

Open year-round.

HARBORSIDE HOTEL AND MARINA
538 Dune Road
Westhampton Beach
☎ 631-288-4450
28 units. Very Expensive.

Open April-October.

SEABREEZE MOTEL
a/k/a Westhampton Motel
19 Seabreeze Avenue
Westhampton Beach
☎ 631-288-6886
12 units. Inexpensive.

Open year-round.

Hampton Bays

BEL-AIRE COVE MOTEL
20 Shinnecock Road
Hampton Bays
☎ 631-728-0416
www.belairecove.com
20 units. Moderate to Expensive.

Open year-round. Pet-friendly; small dogs welcome.

HAMPTON BAYSIDE MOTEL
29 Gardiners Lane
Hampton Bays
☎ 631-728-4018
18 efficiency apartments. Inexpensive.

Open year-round; two-night minimum.

HAMPTON STAR MOTEL
293 East Montauk Highway
Hampton Bays
☎ 631-728-6051
www.hamptonstar.com
12 units. Very Expensive.

Across from Shinnecock Bay. Open year-round.

OCEAN VIEW TERRACE MOTEL
285 East Montauk Highway
Hampton Bays
☎ 631-728-4036, 888-43 OCEAN
www.oceanviewterrace.com
16 units. Very Expensive.

Across from Shinnecock Bay. Open year-round; two-night minimum.

P.J.'S
23 Alanson Lane
Hampton Bays
☎ 631-728-1545
11 units. Moderate.

Year-round rentals only.

FISHERMAN'S QUARTERS MOTEL
87 North Road
Hampton Bays
☎ 631-728-9511
Eight units. Moderate.

Eight units mostly rented monthly. Open year-round.

SUNSET BAY MOTEL
53 West Tiana Road
Hampton Bays
☎ 631-728-7273
www.sunsetbay.com
27 units. Inexpensive to Moderate.

Open May-October.

Southampton

OAK TREE INN
606 Major's Path
Southampton
☎ 631-287-2057
Three units. Moderate to Expensive.

Pet-friendly; dogs only, but all sizes welcome at no extra charge. Open year-round.

VILLAGE LATCH INN
101 Hill Street
Southampton
☎ 631-283-2160, or 800-54-LATCH
64 units. Expensive.

Pet-friendly; any size dog or cat welcome. Open year-round.

EASTERNER MOTEL
639 Montauk Highway
Southampton
☎ 631-283-9292
10 units. Moderate to Expensive.

Open from the week before Memorial Day through the week week after Labor Day.

LONG VUE MOTEL
62 Longview Road
Southampton
☎ 631-283-9712
Six units. Moderate.

Open from Memorial Day to Labor Day.

SOUTHAMPTON VILLAGE MOTEL
315 Hampton Road
Southampton
☎ 631-283-3034
10 units. Very Expensive.

Open from mid-March through November; two-night minimum on weekends.

SOUTHAMPTON MOTEL
450 County Road 39
Southampton
☎ 631-283-2548
www.southamptonmotel.com
11 units. Moderate to Expensive.

One unit is handicapped-accessible. Open year-round.

East Hampton

EAST HAMPTON HOUSE
226 Montauk Highway
East Hampton
☎ 631-324-4300
www.easthamptonhouseresort.com
52 units. Inexpensive to Expensive.

BASSETT HOUSE INN
128 Montauk Highway
East Hampton
☎ 631-324-6127
www.peconic.net/tourism/accommodations/Bassett.htm
12 units. Expensive.

Pet-friendly; all pets welcome at $20 per night. Closed in December and January.

A BEND IN THE ROAD
East Hampton
☎ 631-324-4592
www.bendintheroad.com
Two units. Expensive.

Call for off-season rates and street address. Homemade breakfast served. Pet-friendly; pets, other than cats, welcome (listed on www.petswelcome.com). Open year-round.

CENTENNIAL HOUSE
13 Woods Lane
East Hampton
☎ 631-324-9414
www.centhouse.com
Six units and one cottage. Very Expensive

Pet-friendly; small dogs only. Open year-round.

THE DUTCH MOTEL & COTTAGES
488 Montauk Highway
East Hampton
☎ 631-324-4550
www.thedutchmotel.com
28 units. Inexpensive to Expensive.

Pet-friendly; small pets accepted. Open year-round.

Wainscott

SHADY PINES MOTEL
Montauk Highway
Wainscott
☎ 631-537-9320
Under new ownership and currently in limbo. For further information, contact Meredith's cell: ☎ 631-680-2470.

Montauk Motels

ATLANTIC TERRACE MOTEL
21 Surfside Place
Montauk
☎ 631-668-2050
www.atlanticterrace.com
90 units. Inexpensive to Expensive.

Open May-October.

BEACHCOMBER RESORT
727 Old Montauk Highway
Montauk
☎ 631-668-2894
100 units. Inexpensive to Expensive.

Open April-October.

BEACH PLUM MOTEL
779 Old Montauk Highway
Montauk
☎ 631-668-4100
www.beachplumrentals.com
28 units. Moderate to Expensive.

Open from May through November 3.

BREAKERS MOTEL
Old Montauk Highway
Montauk
☎ 631-668-2525
www.breakersmontauk.com
24 units. Inexpensive to Moderate.

Open from early May to Columbus Day.

BLUE HAVEN MOTEL
533 West Lake Drive
Montauk
☎ 800-789-5943, or 631-668-5943
www.peconic.net/bluehavenmotel
26 rooms. Inexpensive to Moderate.

Open March-November.

DAUNT'S ALBATROSS MOTEL
South Elmwood Avenue
Montauk
☎ 631-668-2729, or 631-668-2867
43 units. Inexpensive to Moderate.

Open year-round.

EAST DECK RESORT MOTEL
40 Deforest Road, on Ditch Plains Beach
Montauk
☎ 631-668-2334
28 units. Inexpensive to Moderate.

Open from April to November 1.

GOSMAN'S CULLODEN HOUSE MOTEL
540 West Lake Drive
Montauk
☎ 631-668-9293
29 units. Inexpensive to Moderate.

Some handicapped-accessible rooms available. Open from May 15 to October 15.

HARBORSIDE RESORT MOTEL
371 West Lake Drive
Montauk
☎ 631-668-2511
www.montaukharborside.com
27 units. Inexpensive.

Some units are open year-round.

Suffolk County's South Fork

HARTMAN'S BRINEY BREEZES MOTEL
693 Old Montauk Highway
Montauk
☎ 631-668-2290
www.brineybreezes.com
44 units. Inexpensive to Expensive.

Open from mid-March through mid-November.

THE LIDO RESORT MOTEL
South Emery Street
Montauk
☎ 631-668-3233
20 rooms. Inexpensive to Moderate.

Open March-November.

MEMORY MOTEL
692 Montauk Highway
Montauk
☎ 631-668-2702
43 units. Inexpensive to Moderate.

Open year-round.

MONTAUK MOTEL
South Edison Street
Montauk
☎ 631-668-2704
www.montaukmotels.com
24 motel units. Inexpensive to Moderate.

Montauk Motel has two cottages in addition to the motel units; call for rates. No credit cards. Open year-round.

OCEAN END
South Emerson Street
Montauk
☎ 631-668-5051
Seasonal; call for rates.

OCEAN SURF MOTEL
84 South Emerson Avenue
Montauk
☎ 631-668-3332, or 800-OCEANSURF
www.montauklife.com
Inexpensive to Expensive

Open May-September.

RONJO RESORT MOTEL
South Elmwood Avenue
Montauk
☎ 631-668-2112
33 units. Inexpensive to Moderate.

Open April-November.

ROYAL ATLANTIC BEACH RESORTS
South Edgemere Street
Montauk
☎ 631-668-5103
www.royalatlantic.com
152 units. Inexpensive to Expensive.

Open year-round.

SANDS MOTEL
Corner South Emery Street & Route 27
Montauk
☎ 631-668-5100
42 units. Inexpensive to Moderate.

Open April-November.

Suffolk County's South Fork

SEAWIND MOTEL
411 West Lake Drive
Montauk
☎ 631-668-4949
16 units. Inexpensive to Moderate.

Eight units are efficiencies. Open year-round.

SEASCAPE MOTEL
793 Old Montauk Highway
Montauk
☎ 631-668-2788

This 10-room motel is being converted to year-round rentals; call for rates and availability.

SHEPHERDS BEACH MOTEL
107 Emerson Avenue
Montauk
☎ 631-668-6700
26 units. Moderate-Expensive.

Off-season rates highly variable. Open year-round.

SNUG HARBOR MOTEL & MARINA
3 Star Island Road
Montauk
☎ 631-668-2860
www.peconic.net/snugharbor
34 units. Inexpensive.

Seasonal and transient dockage. Open March-November.

SUN-N-SOUND WATERFRONT RESORT
22 Soundview Drive
Montauk
☎ 631-668-2212
35 units. Inexpensive to Moderate.

Open from mid-March through October.

WEST LAKE DRIVE MOTEL

10 Wells Avenue
Montauk
☎ 631-668-2545
Four apartments, call for rates.

Open year-round.

BRING THE KIDS!

Montauk is a child-friendly place; 99% of the
lodgings welcome children. There's even a tree
in town surrounded by child-sized chairs and a
sign summoning kids.

Montauk Cottages

The fees listed for your pet at these seven Montauk
properties do not cover any damage it may cause.

ANN BREYER'S COTTAGES

560 West Lake Drive
Montauk
☎ 631-668-2710
Ten units. Off-season rates Moderate.

Full-season rentals only in summer; call for rates. Pet
friendly; dogs only, welcome in spring and fall; $20 per
night, per dog. Open May-October.

BORN FREE MOTEL

115 South Emerson Avenue
Montauk
☎ 631-668-2896
22 one-bedroom apartments. Moderate.

Pet friendly; fee is $25 per day. Open year-round.

HITHER HOUSE COTTAGES
10 Lincoln Road
Montauk
☎ 631-668-2714
www.hitherhouse.com
Eight cottages. Moderate to Expensive.

The cottages are in various sizes. Pet-friendly; any size pet, $15 per day. Open year-round.

SEPP'S COTTAGES
43 Ditch Plains Road
Montauk
☎ 631-668-2753
Nine cottages. Moderate.

Rates are based on the number of people a in cottage. (the rate for two people and pet in two-bedroom cottage would be $135). Pet-friendly. Open from May 15 to October 15.

BURCLIFFE BY THE SEA
397 Old Montauk Highway
Montauk
☎ 631-668-2880
Seven units. Moderate.

Three of the units are cottages. Pet-friendly; pets permitted in the cottages, but off-season only. Open year-round.

GANSETT GREEN MANOR
273 Main Street
Montauk
☎ 631-267-3133
www.gansettgreenmanor.com
13 units. Expensive.

Pet-friendly; all size pets welcome, but call ahead. Open May-October.

RED DOOR
293 Main Street
Montauk
☎ 631-267-6694
Two units. Moderate to Expensive.

Pet-friendly; well-behaved pets welcome. Open year-round.

Best Places to Eat

There is no love sincerer than the love of food.
— George Bernard Shaw

DINING PRICE SCALE
Price scale includes one entrée, with glass of wine and coffee. There is an 8.5% tax on food in both Nassau and Suffolk Counties.
Inexpensive . . . . under $25
Moderate . . . . $25-$40
Expensive . . . . over $40

Westhampton

TIERRA MAR
Bath & Tennis Hotel
231 Dune Road
Westhampton
☎ 631-288-2700
www.OnTheAtlantic.com, www.TierraMar.com,
www.greatrestaurantmag.com
Moderate to Expensive

If location determines the success of a restaurant, Tierra Mar has it made. Go before sundown to take it all in. White décor with blue accents, classical music, and a sweeping ocean view stir the heart along with the ap-

Atlantica, the catering arm of Tierra Mar, operates year-round for weddings and private parties; ☎ 631-288-6577.

Suffolk County's South Fork

petite. If weather permits, dine under the tent – it's open to the ocean. If not, try the glass-enclosed dining room, which is more elaborate, with columns and a huge chandelier. At the very least, have a drink at the bar.

Dancing is featured at Tierra Mar every Thursday from 6 to 8pm during the summer and through September. The rest of the year the salsa and swing party is scheduled one Thursday a month.

But the atmosphere is only partly due to the setting. There's a definite tone at Tierra Mar (the name means land and sea) that emanates from the kitchen and the energetic, cheerful and competent young staff.

Chef-owner Todd Jacobs, a graduate of the French Culinary Institute in Manhattan, is, remarkably, a master at New American cooking – be it fish, chicken or steak. Try the pan-fried softshell crab, crisp on the outside and sweet and tender to the taste, served with a side of vegetables steamed to perfection. The meal begins with homemade organic Tuscan bread that is impossible to resist. You can order à la carte or from the tasting menu offered Sunday through Friday ($28 for three courses). Portions are large, but not as vast as the wine list – it fills 33 pages, and includes a nice selection of Long Island reds and whites.

Tierra Mar is open daily for lunch and dinner, year-round. It is also open for breakfast, daily through Labor Day; and on weekends through October. Take Beach Lane to Dune Road and turn right, then continue for .9 mile; or take Jessup Lane to Dune Road and turn left, then continue on Dune Road for a short distance. Tierra Mar makes its home in the lobby of the Bath & Tennis Hotel. A ramp for wheelchair access is at the side entrance.

MEXICAN HUT
136 Old Riverhead Road (Route 31)
Westhampton
☎ 631-288-5397

Despite its name and the sombrero on their sign, the Mexican Hut is neither a Mexican restaurant nor a Mexican boutique. It's a gift and flower shop, open Friday-Sunday, year-round, where proprietor Bob Morgan serves dinner once a week and sings to piano accompaniment among the gift items. A former mayor of West-hampton Beach and a gourmet cook, Bob serves a full-course dinner on Saturday nights starting at 8pm, from June through New Year's Eve. Diners bring their own wine or beer. The cost is $60 per person and reservations should be made a week or two in advance. If you are driving south, it's just past Gabreski Airport.

STONE CREEK INN
405 Montauk Highway
East Quogue
☎ 631-653-6770
Moderate

Paneled windows with bamboo shades and a room divider of palms in a planter lend a festive air to this restaurant. The French-accented cuisine is superb, if a bit stingy, and the menu is à la carte.

You can skip the rolls, although portion sizes are erratic. The calamari appetizer and single crab cake entrée are minuscule, while the strip steak calls for a doggie bag. These, like all dishes here, come artfully arranged.

Open from mid-March through December; closed Wednesday in the off-season. Reservations are highly recommended. The restaurant is handicapped-accessible. Take Sunrise Highway to Exit 64S (Quogue/Riverhead Road). The left fork at Oakville brings you to East Quogue.

PAPA D'S ITALIAN KITCHEN
5 West Main Street
Hampton Bays
☎ 631-723-3412
Inexpensive

A sign over the register reads "Welcome to Our Home." The minute I accidentally stumbled into this eatery, I was greeted with warm smiles and an attentive waitress. Then I tasted the homemade garlic bread – followed by a luscious lasagna – and knew I'd discovered gold, despite the plastic-tablecloth décor. The menu is based on grandma's old and time-tested recipes.

Papa D's has two restaurants in Manhattan Beach, California, called Mama D's, which garnered a rave review in the Los Angeles Times. It's only a matter of time before New York foodies discover this gem. When I visited, the family-owned restaurant had opened only the previous August and already lines were forming outside the door on weekends. It has no bar – deliberately – choosing to serve beer and wine only. All wines on the sizable wine list are available by the glass. Open for dinner year-round.

JT'S PLACE
26 Montauk Highway
Hampton Bays
☎ 631-723-2626
Inexpensive

Credit cards are not accepted at JT's.

JT's is a casual restaurant with excellent service and generous portions; the restaurant is a blend of formal (tablecloths) and casual (baskets of packaged bread sticks and commercial rolls). The food is tasty, and a light bite or entrée, including seafood and pasta specials, is less than $20. On Wednesday night there is a lobsterfest dinner at $12.95. In season, JT's is open daily for dinner, and is generally packed; in winter, lunch and dinner are served Friday-Sunday. There is a separate bar.

OAKLAND'S
42 Dune Road
Hampton Bays
☎ 631-728-6900
www.oaklandsrestaurant.com
Inexpensive to Moderate

This is *the* place for fresh fish. The restaurant overlooks the harbor at Shinnecock Bay, and the fish comes in daily. Regardless of what you order, you'll swear it was just caught.

In the summer, a Lobster Fest dinner is offered Monday and Tuesday; after Labor Day it's on Friday. The small lobster (1¼ pounds) comes with soup or salad, mussels and shrimp, and a beer. It's well worth the $25. If you're not a fish lover, other entrées include vegetable lasagna and chicken dishes for under $20.

The restaurant celebrated its 10th anniversary in 2001 and, from the looks of it, will be around for a long time. Oakland's does not take reservations for parties under six and gets crowded on weekends, despite a huge outdoor deck. It draws singles, couples and a big family crowd, so you might have to wait. Oakland's is open on weekends only in spring and fall (from the beginning of April through Memorial Day, and from Labor Day through October); they are open daily in summer.

Southampton

75 MAIN STREET
75 Main Street
Southampton
☎ 631-283-7575
www.75main.com
www.greatrestaurantsmag.com
Moderate to Expensive

With its courteous professional service and superb cuisine, this has to be one of Southampton's best restaurants. Pale yellow walls, diffuse lighting and tables arranged in a horseshoe around the bar lend a romantic touch to 75 Main Street. Since no smoking is permitted at the bar, any table is fine.

Chef David Girard can turn even a chicken dinner into a gourmet meal. A basket of slightly warmed homemade focaccia was a delightful surprise. The duck spring roll appetizer, pretty as it is delicious, is American-Asian fusion at its best. The menu changes seasonally but recommended entrées are salmon and grilled sliced ribeye steak. Dessert offerings include a Belgian waffle napoleon ($6) and crème brûlée ($6). The $21.95

Suffolk County's South Fork

75 Main Street has been in business for a decade and its wine list has received the Wine Spectator *Award of Excellence since 1996.*

prix fixe menu is a better deal than ordering à la carte. Open daily, year-round. Brunch is served from 9:30am to 4pm; dinner service begins at 5:30pm. Reservations are recommended in season; the restaurant is handicapped-accessible.

PLAZA CAFE
61 Hill Street
Southampton
☎ 631-283-9323
www.plazacafesouthampton.com
www.plazawinedinners.com
www.greatrestaurantsmag.com
Expensive

The Plaza Café has received raves from The New York Times, *the* New York Post, Newsday *and* Zagat.

Noisy and festive, casual yet sophisticated, the spare dining room is bathed in golden yellow; the comfortable décor includes lots of wicker and wrought iron. Top-notch servers cater to customers whose attire may range from business suits to resort-casual.

Fish is the catchword here. The chef/owner's signature dish is a superb seafood shepherd's pie that's well worth its $32 tab. A chive-potato crust blankets shrimp, lobster, carrots and shiitake mushrooms prepared in a light cream sauce, with a shrimp placed in the center to resemble a handle. My husband enjoyed his generously sized serving of sesame-crusted tuna steak served with Chinese vegetables. Desserts are homemade, but not the rolls – they were the only disappointment in an otherwise perfect dinner.

The wine list is extensive, featuring many California wines and a handful from Long Island wineries. Open daily for dinner most of the year; closed for the month of February and on Mondays and Tuesdays in winter. Plans are underway to add a patio. The Plaza Café is located directly opposite the Southampton Inn and behind the movie theater on Hill Street. Reservations are recommended.

JOHN DUCK JR.
North Main Street
Southampton
☎ 631-283-0311
Inexpensive to Moderate

John Duck Jr. is an old-fashioned restaurant with a solid staff and tried-and-true dishes. The self-billed "home of good food" is not trendy, although celebrity customers are not uncommon. Pretense is not in its vocabulary.

All dishes at John Duck Jr. are cooked to order, so allow ample time.

The Long Island duckling, which accounts for about 25% of the dinner orders, is prepared according to the recipe the founder followed a century ago. And why not? While messier to eat than sliced duck, it's crisp on the outside, tender on the inside and filled with apple-raisin stuffing, so who's complaining? Complete dinners come with soup (the Manhattan clam chowder is spicy and delicious), potato, vegetables, their celebrated red cabbage, coffee or tea, and dessert. It makes sense to order a complete dinner, although Sunday brunch is à la carte. Daily specials are offered at both lunch and dinner, and children's portions are available.

☞ DID YOU KNOW?

John Duck Jr. was first opened in Eastport by John Bernard Westerhoff, a German immigrant and ardent duck hunter; the restaurant drew travelers from near and far to sample the famous Long Island duck dinners and Westerhoff soon became known as "John Duck." John Jr. and his brother, Mark, are fourth generation owners.

John Duck Jr. is the oldest restaurant in the Hamptons; it has five dining rooms and an enclosed patio. It was a century old in 2000; one customer has been coming here for 40 years. The restaurant's nautical décor –

Suffolk County's South Fork

wood-paneled walls, captains' chairs, prints of ships and ships-wheel chandeliers – completes the picture. John Duck Jr. is open year-round, for lunch and dinner; closed Monday. Reservations are recommended in season.

GEORGE MARTIN
56 Nugent Street
Southampton
☎ 631-204-8700
www.greatrestaurantsmag.com
Moderate

Although this restaurant opened in Southampton only a few years ago, the George Martin Group under the leadership of restaurateur George Korten has been operating restaurants on Long Island for 14 years – including George Martin and Max's Grille & Tavern in Rockville Centre, and Nick DeAngelo in Merrick.

Sunday brunch at George Martin comes with a complimentary mimosa.

Each restaurant has managing partners who oversee operations. In Southampton, Bernadette Keenan, who has a culinary background from her native Ireland, greets each customer warmly and the staff follows suit. The three chefs combine experience working in restaurants throughout Suffolk County and Europe. The savory dishes reflect their training. Steaks dominate the regional American menu and the platters are oversized – even the coffee cups are huge. The menu also features fish, pasta and chicken. The oven crisp free-range chicken served with garlic mashed potatoes comes with a dark and delicious Merlot sauce with roasted shallots. A prix fixe dinner at $23.95 is also available. Save room for the outrageous brownie sundae that's big enough for four people.

George Martin is a comfortable clubby restaurant; the décor features mahogany booths and banquettes. Although the bar is prominent, the dining room is partitioned for privacy. Open year-round for dinner and weekend brunch, and in season for lunch. Closed Monday in off-season. Reservations are required on weekends.

BARRISTER'S RESTAURANT
36 Main Street
Southampton
☎ 631-283-6206
Inexpensive

Barrister's doesn't pretend to be fancy; it's a simple restaurant with a simple menu and simple décor. The chef has been here for 16 years and serves good home cooking that's pleasing to both palate and pocketbook. Moreover, service is courteous and attentive. These are all good reasons why Barrister's is a favorite with locals who long for a hamburger, chowder, or a grilled chicken and arugula salad – without spending a fortune. The lunch and dinner menus are interchangeable (except for dinner specials). Sunday brunch is à la carte. Open daily, year-round, for lunch and dinner. An enclosed patio is open in season.

SAVANNA'S
268 Elm Street
Southampton
☎ 631-283-0202
Moderate

Savanna's is a cheerful, cream-colored restaurant across from the railroad station. The cuisine is New American and features seafood, but the menu includes several pasta and steak dishes as well. Truth be told, the food is good but portion size may vary; my $17.50 lunch of warm lobster salad left me feeling hungry. Open daily for dinner and weekends for brunch, May-September. Reservations are suggested.

Suffolk County's South Fork

Bridgehampton

BOBBY VAN'S
Main Street
Bridgehampton
☎ 631-537-0590
Moderate to Expensive

Bobby Van's, which also has locations in Manhattan and in Washington DC, has an extensive martini menu. What do you say to a chocolate martini?

Although it is renowned for steak, the restaurant's menu offers numerous fish dishes. The menu descriptions are minimal, especially among the meat offerings. All that is written beside "sirloin", "filet mignon," "veal chop," etc. is the price: each more than $32. The décor is simple, too: paintings by local and non-local artists (for sale) alternate with wall sconces. Fans twirl above the shoebox-shaped room, divided into restaurant and bar. Even when half-full, it's noisy. I determined that it wasn't the patrons or even the TV or music, but the effect of being in a large room without a buffer to suppress the din. What's more, if it's true that celebrities dine here, they have no place to hide!

Service is superb and meals are beautifully presented. I wanted to order a steak but was afraid it would be too much food (Friday and Saturday there is a split-plate charge of $10, but if you eat here during the week, you can share without paying extra). There was enough red sauce on my fettuccine pescatore to flavor the pasta (and stain my blouse) without drowning the flavor of the clams, mussels, shrimps and calamari. Open daily, year-round, for lunch and dinner.

East Hampton

DELLA FEMINA
99 North Main Street
☎ 631-329-6666
Expensive

Garden dining is now available at Della Femina.

This casual restaurant, one of many properties owned by celebrity adman Jerry Della Femina, has been a hit since it opened in 1991. It is first-class. The big butter-yellow room is softened with a wood-beamed ceiling, fireplace, wall sconces and dim lighting. Caricatures of celebrities and friends – Billy Joel, Martha Stewart – adorn the bar, which is separated from the dining room by glass doors.

Dinner begins with warm rosemary-flavored rolls. The menu changes daily, but one winning staple seems to be caramelized vegetables and fruit. My Amish chicken with sherry-bacon vinaigrette was both visually stunning and tender, served with Satur Farms smashed fingerling potatoes and caramelized Brussels sprouts. The warmed Granny Smith apple torte came with ginger-poached blueberries sweetened with caramel sauce and cold ginger gelato. The wine list is extensive and features Long Island wines.

Ordering from the $29 prix fixe menu makes sense (even though the $3 coffee is not included), but it's only available off-season.

Della Femina is open daily in season and daily except Wednesday in winter, for dinner only. In season, reservations are required two weeks in advance. The restaurant is wheelchair-accessible.

THE FARMHOUSE RESTAURANT
341 Montauk Highway
East Hampton
☎ 631-324-8585
www.hamptonsfarmhouse.com
Moderate

With hutch, hearth and wicker chairs, the restaurant lives up to its name. Look for the shingled farmhouse with green trim east of East Hampton village. Although the menu changes occasionally, patrons return for their old favorites – mainly fish and steak. The restaurant's Web site says, "beef is dry aged, fish is fresh that day and vegetables are picked the same day whenever possible." My husband raved about his dish, saying that the rack of lamb was something special. I ordered Long Island duckling, but was disappointed; wish I'd visited the Web site beforehand. Not listed on

The Farmhouse has won Wine Spectator's *Award of Excellence several times.*

Suffolk County's South Fork

the menu but a pleasant surprise was the early spring-time asparagus. In fact, all the vegetables tasted like they were just picked. For dessert we pigged out on their French profiteroles ($8). These three fudge-covered mounds filled with homemade hazelnut, vanilla and chocolate ice cream resembled an old-fashioned hot fudge sundae. Stash your guilt and share it! The restaurant offers a $24 prix fixe menu after 7pm every day except Saturday. Open daily except Tuesday for dinner, year-round.

PALM RESTAURANT
94 Main Street in the Huntting Inn
East Hampton
☎ 631-324-0411
Expensive

This classic American steak house was born in New York City in the early 1920s and now has branches in every major city in the country. The Hamptons restaurant is lively with a New York ambience – including a pressed tin ceiling and walls covered with a Sardi's-style horizontal line of reviews, photos, sketches and caricatures. Columns divide the booths and tables, allowing for a modicum of privacy (private dining rooms are also available).

The simple menu of steaks, seafood and poultry probably hasn't changed in years; it needn't. Go with friends and order the house specialty, a 36-ounce New York strip steak for two ($65) and share it; it could even serve three people (no extra charge for sharing). Have a side dish of cottage fries and fried onions. You'll swear you died and went to heaven. Reservations are accepted for groups of four or more. Open year-round, although they close a few days a week in winter.

Sag Harbor

PETER MILLER'S
Restaurant/Lounge; formerly the All Seasons Café on
Bay Street
16 Main Street
Sag Harbor
☎ 631-725-9100
Inexpensive to Moderate

Sometimes having a hamburger served by a cheerful
waitress in an airy atmosphere is a kick. That was my
reaction when my husband and I had our sirloin burgers on grilled Tuscan garlic bread at a candlelit table,
surrounded by butter yellow walls and with windows
all around. The menu features fish, steak and pasta
dishes; specials are offered. Our only criticism was concerning the liberal use of salt on everything from the
salad to the fries. "This is one of the best burgers I've
ever had," my husband said. "They just have to use a
little less salt." The hostess admitted that the kitchen
sometimes gets a bit heavy handed and she promised to
convey our comment to the chef/owner. Peter Miller's is
open for dinner year-round; closed Monday. A prix fixe
menu is available Tuesday through Thursday and
Sunday.

Montauk

HARVEST ON FORT POND
11 South Emery Street
Montauk
☎ 631-668-5574
www.harvest2000.com
Moderate

If you've ever eaten at Harvest in Hastings, NY, you
know they serve excellent food. This restaurant is under the same ownership. It's an airy, modern space
with open partitions, white wood trim and lots of tables
overlooking the pond. The small menu features meat,

fish and poultry offerings with a Tuscan flair. If you don't want to spend $24 to $36 for an entrée (salads are extra), have the delicious grilled pizza. I'd guess that one is sufficient for a parent and child. Since I was alone, I ordered pizza with bacon, onion, jalapeño, tomato and mozzarella ($14) and had two slices left to take home. (Harvest specializes in oversize portions; bring your friends or family and leave with a doggie bag.) Other toppings are sausage, broccoli, mushrooms and artichokes. Open daily for dinner, from May to November; Thursday through Sunday in the off-season; closed in January and February.

DAVE'S GRILL
Flamingo Road
Montauk Harbor
☎ 631-668-9190
www.davesgrill.com
Moderate

If you are having dinner in Montauk, consider walking down the block from Dave's Grill to Ben & Jerry's for dessert, and enjoy a cone al fresco at an umbrella table on the grass.

Ask for a table in the open-air section of this dockside restaurant with its lovely view of the harbor. The setting, combined with the restaurant's nautical décor, makes you feel like you're on a ship. The menu has more appetizers than entrées, but you can order a double portion of any of them. We were delighted with the friendly and efficient service and fabulous French fries. Some in our party ordered stuffed lobsters; while they loved the lobsters, they found the stuffing too sweet. If you're a sweet freak, try the Belgian chocolate bag filled with scoops of vanilla ice cream, fresh whipped cream and a puddle of raspberry sauce; one of our friends adores it. All desserts are $7.95.

Dave's Grill is open for dinner only, from the first Thursday in May to the end of October; Thursday through Sunday in May and June; and daily thereafter, when reservations are essential. To reach Montauk Harbor from the highway, turn north onto Edgemere Street at the Bank of New York in Montauk. Edgemere becomes Flamingo Road; a parking lot at the end offers a beautiful view of Block Island Sound.

SHAGWONG RESTAURANT
Main Street
Montauk
☎ 631-668-3050
www.shagwong.com
Inexpensive to Moderate

This is a good choice for fresh fish at reasonable prices. Shagwong advertises that it has been "serving very fresh seafood at reasonable prices for over 30 years" and *Newsday* has called the restaurant the "best value in town." If the seafood fra diavolo over linguine is any example, these statements are true. Shagwong is a casual eatery with booths and tables; the bar is in a separate room. The menu (fish, poultry and meat) changes daily and dinners include soup or salad. Service is nicely paced so you don't feel rushed. *Montauk Life* terms this venerable institution "the most popular year-round restaurant in Montauk" – for all of the above reasons. Open for lunch, dinner and late night supper.

Shagwong has a daily early-bird special from 4:30-6pm, and a take-out menu.

Lite Bites

Westhampton

Classic Cuisine Bagels & More, 65 Main Street, Westhampton, ☎ 631-288-6967, www.classiccooking. com, is open daily, year-round, for breakfast and lunch, serving bagels, wraps, and salads. Stool seating.

Hampton Bays

Don't look for a sit-down breakfast in the village of Hampton Bays. The only game in town is Dunkin Donuts in the movie theater complex. If you don't mind leaving the village, **Danny's Dockside Café**, hidden away behind the boats in Spellman's Marine beside the Shinnecock Bridge (see page 463), ☎ 631-728-8662, is a paper-plate kind of place that gives good value for your money. Open daily at 6am, year-round, for breakfast and lunch.

Suffolk County's South Fork

Another option is to drive into the Macy's Shopping Plaza in Hampton Bays. **Pancake Cottage Family Restaurants**, 190 West Montauk Highway, ☎ 631-728-1980, is a cheerful place with a varied menu. Owned by three women for 13 years, the restaurant is open daily, year-round, for breakfast, lunch and dinner; no credit cards.

Be sure to visit the antiques and collectibles shop in the lobby at Hampton Maid. Like breakfast, it's a real treat.

For breakfast in a country-style eatery, try the restaurant at **Hampton Maid**, 259 East Montauk Highway, Hampton Bays (see *Best Places to Stay*, page 506), ☎ 631-728-4166, www.hamptonmaid.com. I thought I made the best French toast until I tasted theirs. The kitchen uses only fresh ingredients and the chicken must have just laid the eggs! Kids are special here, too. Along with a children's menu, crayons are supplied. Items from the grill range from $5.50-$11.50; cold cereal and fruit are offered as well. Breakfast is served daily, 7am-1pm, from late April through Columbus Day. The restaurant at Hampton Maid now accepts credit cards from non-guests.

Hampton Bagels Too, 252 West Montauk Highway, Hampton Bays, ☎ 631-728-7893, has four tables in addition to take-out service.

> ★ TIP
>
> Hungry in the middle of the night? **Hampton Bays Diner**, a landmark at the intersection of Route 27 (Exit 65S) & Montauk Highway, ☎ 631-243-3919, is open daily, 24 hour, in the summer; and 24 hours on weekends the rest of the year. The village of Hampton Bays is east of the diner on Montauk Highway.

Southampton

The **Blue Duck Bakery Café**, Hampton Road, Southampton, ☎ 631-204-1701, serves fabulous fresh breads and pastries. Try the Pain Aux Cereales with cream cheese for a real treat. Sandwiches and soups are offered at lunch. Open daily, year-round.

The **Golden Pear Café**, 99 Main Street, Southampton, ☎ 631-283-8900, http://Goldenpearcafe.com, has several tables for enjoying its specialty sandwiches, salads and burgers. Open daily, year-round, for breakfast and lunch. The Golden Pear also has locations at 34 Newtown Lane, East Hampton; at 2426 Montauk Highway, Bridgehampton; and at 103 Main Street, Westhampton.

The only branch of the Golden Pear outside of the Hamptons is located in Stony Brook.

Thyme & Again, 14 Windmill Lane, Southampton, ☎ 631-287-7354, www.thymeandagain.com, does off-premises catering and has a take-out menu. Thyme and other herbs and spices are added to creative soups, salads, sandwiches, wraps and homemade desserts. Open daily in summer; closed Wednesday and Sunday in winter.

Hampton Bagels, 42 Jagger Lane, Southampton, ☎ 631-287-6445, has take-out and tables. Its other locations are in East Hampton and Hampton Bays.

Bridgehampton

World Pie on Main Street, Bridgehampton, ☎ 631-537-7999, is a popular and noisy place serving entrées under $20, pastas and 20 kinds of pizzas. It's open daily, year-round for lunch and dinner, and features a jazz brunch on Sunday, from noon to 4pm. Take-out is always available and there are tables outside.

Wainscott

Twice Upon a Bagel, 358 Montauk Highway, Wainscott, ☎ 631-537-5553, prides itself on freshness. It should: everything is made from scratch. The spinach in the bagel is fresh, not frozen; the orange juice is freshly squeezed. The 1,800-square-foot bakery/retail department is above the spotlessly clean kitchen. Specialty sandwiches are named for fairy-tale characters. There are 25 bagel flavors (how does sourdough-pecan-raisin grab you?) and about 37 different spreads. For the diet-conscious, the peach tofu is low fat and delicious. The store also makes soup and chili, and orders whitefish salad, herring and Nova from the same distributor as Zabar's. Lunch comes with a cookie and pasta salad. Originally located in Port Washington and Huntington, the store has essentially been in business for 26 years. It's basically take-out, except when the weather is right for eating at the outside tables. Open daily for breakfast and lunch, year-round.

East Hampton

There are several wonderful take-out places in East Hampton.

Delicious aromas waft from **Barefoot Contessa**, 46 Newtown Lane, ☎ 631-324-0240, www.barefootcontessa.com; it's a grocery/bakery/caterer selling homemade breads and cakes daily, year-round.

On the road to or from the Pollock-Krasner House is a small plaza with a deli and sweet-smelling bakery, **Jessie's Bake Shop**, 297 Springs-Fireplace Road, ☎ 631-907-8735; it's open daily, year-round.

Unlike its Southampton store, **Hampton Bagels**, 74 North Main Street, ☎ 631-324-5411, offers take-out only.

Sag Harbor

Books and food make for a nice combination, as patrons of Barnes & Noble and Borders have found. **Paradise Books**, 126 Main Street, Sag Harbor, ☎ 631-725-1114, has an elegant restaurant inside a bookstore. Dinner is a bit pricey but lunch is reasonable. Egg dishes, sandwiches and salads range from $7 to $13.95. Open daily, year-round, for breakfast, lunch and dinner.

The Ice Cream Club also has a store in Montauk next to Mr. John's Pancake House; ☎ 631-668-3115.

When it's hot and you need a fix, head for **The Ice Cream Club** on Main Street near the wharf in Sag Harbor, ☎ 631-725-2598. The store serves Hershey's ice cream from, believe it or not, 10am to 1am, from the end of April through September. Enjoy it – a small cone costs $3!

WHAT'S IN A NAME?

Sag Harbor was originally called Sagaponack Harbor or the Harbor of Sagg because residents of Sagaponack often used the harbor. It was shortened to Sag Harbor in 1707.

Estia's Little Kitchen, 1615 Sag Harbor Turnpike, Sag Harbor, ☎ 631-725-1045. Everything is made fresh daily. Estia's has its own garden, and vegetables are cut to order. Their "two-hour salad" is harvested early in the day and served at dinner time. Pasta is homemade and daily specials always include a seafood dish. mexican food is infused with eggs and other dishes to create what one guidebook writer called "excellent breakfast fare." Open for breakfast, lunch and dinner, but days and times vary; call ahead.

Amagansett

Everyone who has visited the Hamptons is familiar with **The Lobster Roll Restaurant** (a/k/a **Lunch**), on Montauk Highway, ☎ 631-267-3740, www.Lobster-Roll.com, where table service is at lightning speed (its proprietors are all former restaurant management professors). This roadside seafood shanty has been praised by virtually every publication in the Northeast since it opened more than 30 years ago. Woody Allen, Rodney Dangerfield and former president Richard Nixon are listed among its celebrity diners. The namesake specialty is fresh and tasty but the price is steep: lobster is sold at market prices and my average-size sandwich was $12.95. Other items are less expensive, and kids are not forgotten; there's a children's menu and crayons on the tables. Beer and wine are available. Open for lunch and dinner, from May through mid-October.

Estia's, Main Street, ☎ 631-267-6320, is open for breakfast, lunch and dinner in season; and breakfast

Suffolk County's South Fork

The restaurant's other location is Lobster Roll Northside in Riverhead, ☎ 631-369-3039.

and lunch in the off-season. Decorated with local art.
See Estia's Little Kitchen, above, for more information.

Montauk

*Both
Anthony's and
Mr. John's
have counter
and waitress
service and are
open daily for
breakfast and
lunch, year-
round.*

Mr. John's Pancake and Steak House, 111 Main
Street, Montauk, ☎ 631-668-2383, makes 16 varieties
of pancakes; they serve breakfast all day at reasonable
prices.

Anthony's Circle Restaurant, across the street at
the corner of South Embassy and Main Street, ☎ 631-
668-9705, also serves pancakes and eggs all day, and
can seat up to 100 customers (Anthony's does not ac-
cept credit cards).

South Fork A to Z

Animal Hospitals & Shelters

Hampton Veterinary Hospital, 176 Montauk Highway, Speonk, ☎ 631-325-1611. All animals. Conven-
tional medicine, acupuncture and Chinese herbs. Next
to North Fork Bank. Open daily.

The **Town of Southampton Animal Control Shelter**, ☎ 631-728-PETS (7387), moved to a new $1.4-mil-
lion facility in spring 2002. The new facility, located in
Red Creek Park, on Jackson Avenue in Hampton Bays,
has double the amount of kennels and cages than before.

Shinnecock Animal Hospital, 212 East Montauk
Highway, Hampton Bays, ☎ 631-723-0500. All animals. Also provides grooming, boarding and pet health
foods. Open daily, with limited hours on Sunday for
emergencies.

Old Towne Animal Hospital, 380 County Road 39A,
Southampton, ☎ 631-283-0611. Small animals. Boarding. Across from Hampton Jitney office. Open daily.

Southampton Animal Hospital (a/k/a Blue Cross
Animal Hospital), 191 Bishops Lane, Southampton,

☎ 631-283-1094. Primarily dogs and cats. Boarding. Closed Sunday, except for emergencies. From Southampton movie theater on Hill Street, drive west one mile and turn right.

South Fork Animal Hospital, Montauk Highway, Wainscott, ☎ 631-537-0035. Small animals, but no reptiles or birds. Boarding. Closed Sunday. Next door is **Pet Hampton & Aquarium**, ☎ 631-537-7387, open daily, 10am-6pm, which offers grooming, pets and supplies.

Animal Rescue Fund (ARF) of the Hamptons, Daniel's Hole Road, Wainscott, ☎ 631-537-0400, www.arf-hamptons.petfinder.com, provides shelter, adoption services and medical care to animals brought in from local animal control centers and individuals, and is a lost and found pet clearinghouse.

Westhampton Beach Animal Hospital, 126 Montauk Highway, Westhampton Beach, ☎ 631-288-8535. No snakes or lizards please. Boarding. Open daily, year-round.

Bide-A-Wee Shelter, 118 Old Country Road, Westhampton, ☎ 631-325-0200 (shelter); ☎ 631-325-0280 (clinic). Open daily, 10am-4pm, for adoptions.

Suffolk County SPCA, ☎ 631-382-SPCA, operates a mobile unit that does spaying and neutering of cats and dogs free of charge. It also investigates cases of animal neglect.

Banks

Astoria Federal Savings Bank . . . . www.astoriafederal.com

Bank of New York . . . . www.bankofnewyork.com

Bridgehampton National Bank www.bridgenb.com

HSBC . . . . www.us.hsbc.com

North Fork Bank . . . . www.northforkbank.com

Suffolk County National Bank . . . . . www.scnb.com

Suffolk County's South Fork

BRIDGEHAMPTON NATIONAL BANK

Bridgehampton National Bank was founded in
1910 by local farmers and merchants to serve
the needs of the agriculture-based villages
comprising the area. The East End remains
the bank's primary market area.

Houses of Worship

Baptist

First Baptist Church, 57 Halsey Avenue, Southampton, ☎ 631-283-4651.

First Baptist Church of Bridgehampton, Suwassett Avenue, Bridgehampton, ☎ 631-537-3114.

Catholic

Immaculate Conception, 580 Main Street, Westhampton Beach, ☎ 631-288-1423.

Episcopal

St. Mary's Episcopal Church, 336 Ponquogue Avenue, Hampton Bays, ☎ 631-728-0776.

St. Marks Episcopal Church, Main Street and Potunk Lane, Westhampton Beach, ☎ 631-288-2111.

St. John's Episcopal Church, 100 South Main Street, Southampton, ☎ 631-283-0549.

Jewish – Orthodox

The Hampton Synagogue, 154 Sunset Avenue, Westhampton Beach, ☎ 631-288-0534.

Jewish – Conservative

Conservative Synagogue of the Hamptons, 82 Hampton Street, Sag Harbor, ☎ 631-725-8188, www.synagoguehamptons.org.

Jewish – Reformed

Temple Adas Israel, Elizabeth Street and Atlantic Avenue, Sag Harbor, ☎ 631-725-0904.

The Jewish Center of the Hamptons, 44 Woods Lane, East Hampton, ☎ 631-324-9858, www.jcoh.org.

Temple Adas Israel, Long Island's oldest synagogue, welcomes everyone to its events at no charge.

☞ DID YOU KNOW?

In 1898, European Jews built the first Jewish temple on Long Island, Adas Israel. Then an Orthodox temple, it did not serve the needs of the Conservative Jews so they now hold Saturday services in the Old Whaler's Presbyterian Church in Sag Harbor. David Cory, director of the Sag Harbor Whaling & Historical Museum, whose family was among the original settlers in 1640, says, "You can see how Sag Harbor is a pretty accommodating place."

Lutheran

Christ Our Saviour Lutheran Church, 9 Terrace Drive, Hampton Bays, ☎ 631-728-3288.

Incarnation Lutheran Church, on Montauk Highway between Bridgehampton and Water Mill, ☎ 631-537-1187, www.incarnationlutheranchurch.org.

St. Michael's Lutheran Church, Montauk Highway, Amagansett, ☎ 631-267-6351, www.stmichaelslutheran.net.

Suffolk County's South Fork

Methodist

Hampton Bays United Methodist Church, 158 West Montauk Highway, Hampton Bays, ☎ 631-728-1660.

East Quogue United Methodist Church, 568 Montauk Highway, East Quogue, ☎ 631-653-5351.

Beach United Methodist Church, 41 Mill Road, Westhampton Beach, ☎ 631-288-1158.

United Methodist Church, 160 Main Street, Southampton, ☎ 631-283-0951.

Bridgehampton United Methodist Church, Montauk Highway and Church Lane, Bridgehampton, ☎ 631-537-0753.

Presbyterian

Westhampton Presbyterian Church, 90 Meeting House Road, Westhampton Beach, ☎ 631-288-2576.

Presbyterian Church of Bridgehampton, 2429 Montauk Highway, Bridgehampton, ☎ 631-537-0863.

The First Presbyterian Church, 5 Davids Lane, East Hampton, ☎ 631-324-0711.

Presbyterian Church, Main Street and Meeting House Lane, Amagansett, ☎ 631-267-6404.

Montauk Community Church, 850 Montauk Highway, Montauk, ☎ 631-668-2022.

Information Sources

Chambers of Commerce

Greater Westhampton, ☎ 631-288-3337, www.wh-bcc.com, www.peconic.net/westhampton.

Hampton Bays, ☎ 631-728-8599, fax ☎ 631-728-2211, www.hamptonbayschamber.com.

East Quogue, ☎ 631-653-5143.

Southampton, ☎ 631-283-0402, www.southampton-chamber.com.

East Hampton, ☎ 631-324-0362, www.easthampton-chamber.com.

Sag Harbor, ☎ 631-725-0011, www.sagharborchamber.com.

Montauk (serves Montauk, East Hampton & Amagansett), ☎ 631-668-2428, www.montaukchamber.com.

Community Web Sites

All the villages . . . . . . www.hamptonstravelguide.com
Town of Southampton . www.town.southampton.ny.us
Montauk . . . . www.montauk-online.com
General Information . . . . www.hamptons.com, www.hamptonsdirectory.com, www.easthampton.com, www.hamptonsweb.com,   www.webhampton.com, www.hamptonlife.com

Liquor Stores

Six Corners Liquors, 166 Mill Road, Westhampton Beach, ☎ 631-288-1387.

Sag Harbor Liquor Store, 52 Main Street, Sag Harbor, ☎ 631-725-0054, or 800-BIG WHAL (244-9425).

Amagansett Wine & Spirits, Main Street, Amagansett, ☎ 631-267-3939.

Shop to the sound of jazz at **White's Liquor Store**, Montauk, ☎ 631-668-2426.

Medical Facility

Southampton Hospital, 240 Meeting House Lane, Southampton, ☎ 631-726-8200, www.southamptonhospital.org. This 168-bed hospital opened in 1909; it's now the largest employer on the South Fork with more than 600 full-time employees.

Suffolk County's South Fork

Movies

Cineplex Odeon Hampton Arts Twins, Brook Road, Westhampton, ☎ 631-288-2600.

UA Hampton Bays (5), 119 West Montauk Highway, Hampton Bays (in Hamlet Green shopping plaza), ☎ 631-728-8676.

UA Southampton (4), 43 Hill Street, Southampton, ☎ 631-287-2774 (recording); 631-287-6235 (box office) Open year-round.

UA East Hampton (6), 30 Main Street, East Hampton, ☎ 631-324-0448.

Sag Harbor Cinema (3), 90 Main Street, Sag Harbor, ☎ 631-725-0010. Open weekends in winter and daily in season.

The Movie (3), Edgemere Street, Montauk (seasonal), ☎ 631-668-2393.

Pharmacies

Barth's Pharmacy, 58 Sunset Avenue, Westhampton Beach, ☎ 631-288-4345.

Southrifty Drug, 54 Jagger Lane, Southampton, ☎ 631-283-1506.

Park Place Pharmacy, 58 Park Place, East Hampton, ☎ 631-324-6660.

Newspapers

The *Southampton Independent*, 33 Flying Point Road, Southampton, ☎ 631-287-2525; and The *East Hampton Independent*, 74 Montauk Highway, East Hampton, ☎ 631-324-2500; www.indyeastend.com, are weekly tabloids distributed on Wednesday.

The *Southampton Press*, ☎ 631-283-4100, www.southamptonpress.com.

PRESSING ON

The *Southampton Press* has been covering the
Town of Southampton for more than a century.
Its Eastern edition covers East Hampton,
Bridgehampton, Sagaponack, Sag Harbor,
North Sea, Noyac, Water Mill, Southampton
and Shinnecock Hills. Its Western edition cov-
ers Hampton Bays, East Quogue, Quogue,
Westhampton, Speonk, Eastport, and parts of
Flanders and Riverhead.

Dan's Papers, ☎ 631-537-0500, www.danspapers.com.
Dan Rattiner's popular weekly is ubiquitous in the
Hamptons. The editions for this week, last week and
the week before are all on the same shelf. The tabloid
also has Manhattan delivery at more than 100 locations.

The *Hamptons Catalogue*, ☎ 970-925-5109, www.the-
catalogues.com, is a glossy annual magazine focusing
on shopping, fine art, fashion, home furnishings and
happenings, available at fine stores and by subscription.

Star Struck? Pick up a copy of *The Hampton Sheet*.

The *Hampton Star* publishes current events and allows users to access its archives; www.easthampton-
star.com.

To The Point, Hamptons to Montauk by Ingrid Lemme
is a hardcover marketing tool for visitors and is found
is most guest accommodations on the East End. The
book is well written and researched and filled with
helpful information on where to stay, eat and play on
both forks, www.tothepoint.net.

These publications are all complimentary, and are distributed all over Montauk, in stores, restaurants and
museums:

The Montauk Sun, ☎ 631-668-1600, is a monthly tabloid distributed throughout the East End.

Suffolk County's South Fork

Montauk Life, ☎ 631-283-9727, is a monthly tabloid; it is printed on heavy paper stock.

Montauk Pioneer, ☎ 631-537-0500, is a weekly tabloid published by Dan's Papers.

Zip Codes

Amagansett. 11930
Bridgehampton. 11932
East Hampton/Springs. 11937
Eastport. 11941
East Quogue 11942
Flanders 11901
Hampton Bays 11946
Montauk 11954
Noyac. 11963
Quogue 11959
Sagaponack. 11962
Sag Harbor 11963
Southampton 11968
Speonk. 11972
Wainscott 11975
Water Mill. 11976
Westhampton 11977
Westhampton Beach. 11978

Farm Markets

Long Island is one of the most important agricultural regions in New York State, producing more than 100 different crops. The Island leads the state in agricultural wholesale values at $115.2 million of products sold, most of which come from the eastern two-thirds of the Island. Riverhead has over 20,000 acres devoted to agriculture out of 35,000 acres throughout Long Island. Suffolk County's high water-to-land ratio provides moderate temperatures, mild winters and ample rainfall for an extended growing season.

The proliferation of farm stands in Suffolk County, particularly on the North Fork, offers visitors and residents a wealth of fresh local produce: fruit, vegetables, potatoes, pumpkins, wine, grapes, poultry, seafood, and nursery products. Many farm stands are open year-round; those marked seasonal are generally open from late May or early June through Halloween, Thanksgiving or Christmas. In October, many farms stage fall festivals with live music, hayrides, and corn mazes.

Contact the **Long Island Farm Bureau**, ☎ 631-727-3777, www.lifb.com, for a free booklet, titled *Guide to Farm Stands and U-Pick Fields*, or see the listings online at www.northfork.org/farms.html, and www.riverheadli.com/stands.html. The **Cornell Extension of Suffolk County**, ☎ 631-727-7850, also puts out a guide.

North Shore

WHITE POST FARMS
250 Old Country Road
Melville
☎ 631-351-9373

White Post sells pies, soups, vegetables and fruit. Open daily, year-round. See page 204 for information on their animal farm.

YELLOW TOP COUNTRY MARKET
602 Smithtown Bypass
Smithtown
☎ 631-361-7600

This market sells vegetables, fruit, jams, and Italian specialties. Open daily, year-round.

ANN MARIE'S FARM AND GARDEN STAND
72 North Country Road
Setauket
☎ 631-246-6195

Ann Marie's specializes in herbs, corn, plants, flowers, organic dairy products and bread. Open year-round; closed Monday.

NORTH SHORE FARM & GARDEN
Ridgeway Avenue at Route 25A
East Setauket
☎ 631-941-3470

This is North Shore's original farm stand; it opened 25 years ago. Their other locations are in Mt. Sinai, at the southwest corner of Mt. Sinai-Coram Road and Route 25A; and in Port Jefferson Station, at the Elks Club on Route 112. They specialize in greenhouse flowers, plants and fresh produce. Open daily, from around Easter through Christmas Eve.

LEWIN FARMS
812 Sound Avenue
Calverton
☎ 631-929-4327
www.lewinfarms.com

This farm stand sells a variety of produce at different times of year, such as U-pick apples from late July through October; pumpkins in October; Christmas trees from the day after Thanksgiving to Christmas; and more. See their Web site for details.

WINDY ACRES FARM
3810 Route 25
Calverton
☎ 631-727-4554

Windy Acres sells fruit, vegetables, flowers, homemade jams and jellies and pies, and in the fall they have a corn maze. Open from May through Christmas.

ROTTKAMP'S
2287 Sound Avenue
Calverton
☎ 631-727-1786

Rottkamp's has U-pick pumpkins, fruits and vegetables; they also have a corn maze. Seasonal.

SUNBURST ACRES
Sound Avenue
Riverhead
☎ 631-722-3572

Sunburst Acres sells produce and mums, and has the only wood-roasted corn on Long Island. One mile east of Palmer Vineyards; open May–December.

Farm Markets

South Shore

BRIGHTWATERS FARMS
1624 Manatuck Boulevard
Bay Shore
☎ 631-665-5411

This farm on over 12 acres has apples, corn, mums, pies, apple cider and U-pick pumpkins. During their harvestfest in October, look for a corn maze, pony rides, hayrides and a playland. Open from the last weekend in September through Halloween.

HANK'S FARM STAND
Barnes Road
Moriches
☎ 631-878-0574

"Vegetables fresh from our fields" and "fresh flowers from our (eight) greenhouses." Open from Mother's Day through September, and again at Christmas with trees and handmade wreaths, centerpieces and other decorations.

North Fork

STAKEY'S PUMPKIN FARM
324 West Lane
Aquebogue
☎ 631-722-3467

Open only in the fall, Stakey's has U-pick pumpkins, family hayrides, and a corn maze on a 24-acre field. Open Saturday and Sunday, from late September to Columbus Day.

WELLS HOMESTEAD
460 Main Road
Aquebogue
☎ 631-722-3796 (stand); 631-722-8097 (farm)

Lyle and Susan Wells are members of a family that has
been farming here since 1661. Their farm stand sells
fruits and vegetables, Long Island duckling and eggs,
bread, flowers, herbs, plants and grocery items. Open
daily, May-November.

BIOPHILIA ORGANIC FARM
Manor Lane
Jamesport
☎ 631-722-2299

This is a new certified organic farm selling veggies,
herbs, flowers and plants. Open weekends, 10am-6pm,
June-October.

SCHMITT'S FARM COUNTRY FRESH
Main Road
Laurel
☎ 631-298-1991

Schmitt's has U-pick pumpkins, apples, mums, roasted
corn, and a haunted trail corn maze. Seasonal.

HARBES FAMILY FARM
247 Sound Avenue, Mattituck, ☎ 631-298-2054
Route 25, Jamesport, ☎ 631-722-8546
Route 25, Cutchogue, ☎ 631-734-7703
www.harbesfamilyfarm.com

At their three locations you will find U-pick pumpkins,
roasted corn, a Wild West maze, hayrides, homebaked
goods, vegetables and flowers. Open daily, 9am-6pm,
May-October.

Farm Markets

GREENLAND FAMILY FARMS
17155 County Road 48
Cutchogue
☎ 631-734-5791
www.greenlandfamilyfarms.com

Greenland's farm stand sells wholesale trees, shrubs, flowers, vegetables, and U-pick pumpkins, and in the fall they have a corn maze ($2). They also sell goldfish and koi. Open April-October.

WICKHAM'S FRUIT FARM
Route 25
Cutchogue
☎ 631-734-6441
www.wickhamsfruitfarm.com

This is the oldest one-family-owned farm in America. Fruit, flowers, baked goods and B&B lodging (see Freddy's House, page 400). Open 9am-6pm, May-January; closed Sunday.

KRUPSKI'S PUMPKIN AND VEGETABLE FARM
38030 Main Road (Route 25)
Peconic
☎ 631-734-6847

Krupski's has vegetables, fruit, U-pick pumpkins, Indian and white corn, gourds and tomatoes, plus hay rides and a spooky barn. Open 8am-6pm, from June to Thanksgiving.

PUNKINVILLE USA
26085 Route 48 (North Road)
Peconic
☎ 631-734-5530
Admission to petting zoo: $4 adults; $3 children

You can shop at the farm stand while your kids visit with some 400 birds and barnyard animals in the large petting zoo (rabbits are for sale). Among the hundreds of birds are 15 different species of pheasant. The farmstand is in the westbound lane between Mattituck &

Peconic. Look for a house with green shutters, with pumpkin-head scarecrows out front; it is open May-November. Closed Wednesday.

SANG LEE FARMS
25180 Country Road 48
Peconic
☎ 631-734-7001

Sang Lee has specialty produce, primarily Asian. Open 9am-5pm, daily in season; Thursday-Saturday in winter.

SEP'S GREENHOUSES
Main Road
East Marion
☎ 631-477-1583

This farm stand has plants, flowers, herbs and vegetables. Open May-November.

South Fork

FRUIT KING FARMS
166 Montauk Highway
Westhampton Beach
☎ 631-288-3852

Fruit King sells produce, cheeses, coffee beans, pies and breads. Open daily, April-Thanksgiving.

SCHMIDT'S
120 North Sea Road
Southampton
☎ 631-283-5777

Schmidt's is a gourmet market with produce, flowers, baked goods, hot food, a salad bar and a butcher. Open daily, year-round.

Farm Markets

THE MILK PAIL
Route 27
Between Water Mill and Bridgehampton
☎ 631-537-2565
www.milk-pail.com

The Halsey family has been farming here since the 1640s, and have operated a farm stand since 1969. Now run by the 11th and 12th generations of the family, the Milk Pail is open from mid-August to the end of April, with produce, baked goods, plants and more. They also operate a U-pick apple and pumpkin orchard, Amy's Flowers, and the Mini Milk Pail, all on Mecox Road (the first right east of the Milk Pail). Visit their Web site or call their number for more information.

Index

HUNTER TRAVEL GUIDES

www.hunterpublishing.com

Hunter's full range of travel guides to all corners of the globe is featured on our exciting Web site. You'll find guidebooks to suit every type of traveler, no matter what their budget, lifestyle, or idea of fun. Full descriptions are given for each book, along with reviewers' comments and a cover image. Books may be purchased on-line using a credit card via our secure transaction system. All on-line orders receive a 20% discount.

ALIVE! GUIDES

Alive! guides tell you what's hot, and what's not, with plenty of suggestions for daytime activity and nighttime fun. Hundreds of restaurant and hotel profiles in all price ranges, including the best places to stay and eat if you're looking for pampering, adventure, nights in the city or value. Beyond where to stay and eat, *Alive!* guides focus on the things that make each destination unique – from scenic fall drives on Long Island to spectacular rain forest lodges in Costa Rica. There are full details about local celebrations, along with contact numbers for help in trip-planning. "Sunup to Sundown" sections describe daytime activities from sightseeing and swimming to shopping and beachcombing. "After Dark" sections give the lowdown on nightlife from mild to wild. An "A-Z" section provides a comprehensive list of useful contacts, including ATM and bank locations, doctors and medical facilities, tourism offices, religious services and web sites. All have town and regional maps, in-margin icons, and are indexed.

Alive! guides featured include: *Antigua, Barbuda, St. Kitts & Nevis*; *Aruba, Bonaire & Curaçao*; *Atlanta*; *Baltimore & The Chesapeake Bay*; *Bermuda*; *Bucks County & The Delaware River Valley*; *Buenos Aires & The Best of Argentina*; *Cancún &*

*Cozumel; The Catskills; Dallas & Fort Worth; Dominica & St.
Lucia; Hollywood & The Best of Los Angeles; Jamaica; Long
Island; Martinique & Guadeloupe; Martinique, Guadeloupe,
Dominica & St. Lucia; Miami & The Florida Keys; Nassau &
The Best of the Bahamas; St. Martin & St. Barts*; and *Vene-
zuela.*

ADVENTURE GUIDES

Adventure Guides are aimed at the independent traveler who enjoys outdoor activities
(rafting, hiking, biking, skiing, canoeing, etc.).
All books in this signature series cover places
to stay and eat, sightseeing, in-town attractions, transportation and more!

With over 30 titles, the *Adventure Guide* series
is recognized as a top resource for active travelers, whether your idea of fun is rock climbing, beachcombing or cycling. Each book offers
the ideal mix of practical travel information
along with activities. And the fun is for everyone, no matter your age or ability level. Never
galloped along a beach on horseback before?
Check out the lists of recommended outfitters
and training stables and give it a go! Have you
always yearned to see the colorful marine life
below the water's surface? *Adventure Guides* list plenty of
diver certification courses to get you started, plus the best
sites once you're ready to take the plunge.

Comprehensive background information – history, culture,
geography and climate – gives you a solid knowledge of your
destination, its people and their roots. Regional chapters take
you on an introductory tour, with stops at museums, historic
sites and local attractions. Then come the adventures – fishing, canoeing, water skiing, rafting, llama trips, snowboard-
ing and more. There are sections detailing places to stay and
eat; transportation to, from and around your destination;
practical concerns; useful web sites; e-mail addresses; and
tourism contacts. Detailed regional and town maps feature

walking and driving tours, historic sites, attractions, and parks. All guides in the series are fully indexed. Photographs enhance the lively text.

ROMANTIC WEEKENDS

Hunter's *Romantic Weekends* series offers myriad things to do for couples of all ages and lifestyles. Quaint places to stay and restaurants where the ambiance will take your breath away are included, along with fun activities that you and your partner will remember forever.

The ultimate series for romancers of all ages and lifestyles, with ideas to suit every budget. These books offer much more than just a listing of intimate restaurants with candlelit tables – the focus is also on fun activities that you and your partner can enjoy together. Beautiful places to stay, charming spots to eat and unusual things to do allow you to plan a unique weekend getaway. Savor wines at a local vineyard, have a five-star dinner delivered to your room and stay in for the evening, visit museums and quaint coffeehouses, stroll arm-in-arm under the stars, or enjoy a secluded picnic with champagne. These inspiring guidebooks will help you decide where, why and how you want to treat yourselves. Hunter's *Romantic Weekends* books make fine gifts for weddings and anniversaries, too!

LANDMARK VISITORS GUIDES

Touring itineraries take you through towns and villages, into the countryside to some of the best beaches. You'll visit museums, historic buildings, beautiful churches and perhaps stop to join in local celebrations. Interesting tidbits are highlighted in colorful callout boxes, and might tell how the landscape has been shaped, which birds you can expect to see, or where the best

fishing spot is. Whether you're planning your first trip or are a veteran traveler, don't leave home without a Landmark Visitors Guide, renowned as the best choice for sightseers. Lavish color throughout, plus detailed maps.

NELLES GUIDES

These great-value guides cover destinations far and wide around the globe. Established in 1990, *Nelles Guides* sought to provide travelers with comprehensive destination coverage in a handy, take-along format. Today, the tradition continues. Nelles Guides are researched and written by local correspondents and are updated regularly. Each book has a well-rounded introduction that delves into the country's history and culture, tempting the reader to explore.

The "What to See & Do" section for each area can cover anything from sightseeing and driving tours to jungle treks and visits to the local museums. You'll find detailed entries for restaurants, shopping, entertainment, festivals and more. All accommodations are categorized by price level, making it easy for the reader to select a place to suit his/her budget. Practical travel issues – health concerns, climate and clothing, visa requirements, currency, transportation, etc. – are also addressed. Priced at just $15.95 and packed with over 160 color photos per book, the value is unbeatable!

THIS WAY GUIDES

A remarkable series of handy pocket-size guides to take with you as you explore Prague, Amsterdam, Alaska, Florence, Munich, Vienna and even Tahiti. With stunning color photos and high-quality fold-out maps in back, they offer unbeatable value at just $5.95. Their durable design and light weight means you can tote them along all day, referring to them as often as you need. *This Way* guides provide travelers with a maximum of cultural, historical and practical information in the smallest package possible, directing you on walking tours to attractions and sights that you simply can't afford to miss. Historic buildings, the best museums, delightful parks and plazas – all are described and come with comprehensive directions for easy access on foot or by local transport systems. The "Dining Out" sections offer a good selection of places to eat, covering all kinds of cuisines and ensuring a pleasant meal for everyone, even the kids. Each book features a "Hard Facts" section that shows basic travel information at a glance – post office hours, pharmacies, driving and car hire concerns, tipping policies, tourist information offices, travel options and a list of recommended guides and tour operators. Up-to-date, authoritative and easy to use, these are the guides to take with you!

TRAVEL NOTES

TRAVEL NOTES

TRAVEL NOTES

